In Memory of
Darl Heller
from
Allen J. Levine &
Norman L. Levine

717 - 242 - 2391

ADVANCE THE COLORS!

✩✩
VOLUME II

ADVANCE THE COLORS!

PENNSYLVANIA CIVIL WAR BATTLE FLAGS

Richard A. Sauers ★ Capitol Preservation Committee

Copyright © 1991 by the Capitol Preservation Committee, Commonwealth of Pennsylvania. All rights reserved including the right of production in whole or in part, by any means, or in any form.

ISBN: 0-8182-0155-X

This book has been typeset in 11 point ITC Garamond Light.

Typography: SpectraComp, Mechanicsburg, PA
Design: John P. Wattai, Wattai Design Associates, Lebanon and Palmyra, PA
Color separations: Colortech, Inc., Lebanon, PA
Printing: Sowers Printing Co., Lebanon, PA
Binding: The CHM Edition, Ltd., Andalusia, PA

Overleaf: *Charge of the 14th Pennsylvania Cavalry at Winchester by Thure de Thulstrup. The original painting is in Soldiers and Sailors Memorial Hall, Pittsburgh, PA.*

Photograph by Herbert K. Barnett © 1987 TIME-LIFE Books, Inc., from *The Civil War* Series.

Capitol Preservation Committee Members

Front Row
Dr. Brent D. Glass, Executive Director-Historical & Museum Commission; Senator Robert J. Mellow; Senator John J. Shumaker; Representative James L. Wright, Jr.; David L. Jannetta, Treasurer, Secretary-Department of General Services; Senator John E. Peterson

Back Row
Representative Peter C. Wambach, Secretary; Representative Joseph R. Pitts, Chairman; Senator Leonard J. Bodack, Vice Chairman

Absent from picture
Representative Fred Belardi; John M. Dickey, William A. Real, and Leslie M. Gallery, Governor's Appointees; Mrs. Renee Jones, Chief Justice Appointee

The Capitol Preservation Committee is an independent Commonwealth Committee established by the General Assembly in 1982 for the purpose of coordinating and overseeing programs to conserve, restore, preserve, and maintain the Pennsylvania State Capitol and its historic contents for all future time.

The Capitol Preservation Committee consists of fifteen members who are appointed by officials of the Legislature, Executive, and Judicial branches of Commonwealth government, or who hold membership by virtue of office. This Committee meets regularly in Harrisburg to make decisions concerning the ongoing restoration and preservation programs.

In creating the Committee, the Legislature provided for establishment of a "Capitol Restoration Trust Fund" which may receive both public funds and contributions from the private sector. This fund is independent of the Commonwealth General Fund and used for various preservation projects.

Capitol Preservation Committee Staff

Front Row
Susan A. Ellison, Controller; Karen L. Galle, Flag Project Coordinator; Dr. Richard A. Sauers, Military Historian

Back Row
Ruthann Hubbert-Kemper, Administrator; Andrea L. Lentz, Textile Conservation Technician; Elana C. Maynard, Secretary; Diane Kessler, Textile Conservator

Capitol Preservation Committee and Staff

Acknowledgements

In addition to all the people and institutions mentioned in volume one, the following also contributed to this book:

Ted Alexander, Antietam National Battlefield Park; Herbert K. Barnett, Allison Park, PA; Gene Boak, New Bloomfield, PA; Cliff C. Breidinger, Trout Run, PA; Timothy R. Brookes, East Liverpool, OH; Bucks County Historical Society, Doylestown, PA; Chris Calkins, Petersburg National Battlefield Park; Canton Area High School, Canton, PA; Karen Carlson, PA State Library, Harrisburg, PA; Chester County Historical Society, West Chester, PA; Noel Clemmer, Morgantown, WV; Raymond Collins, Medal of Honor Historical Society, Alexandria, VA; Henry Deeks, East Arlington, MA; Robert Diem, Coatesville, PA; David Evans, Athens, GA; Charles F. Faust, Shillington, PA; Stephen Ford, Omaha, NE; SFC Robert Fugate, Battery C, 1/229 FA, Oil City, PA; Joseph Fulginiti, Haddonfield, NJ; Andrew W. German, Mystic, CT; Nicholas M. Graver, Rochester, NY; A. Wilson Greene, Fredericksburg, VA: Baldwin Griffin, North Palm Beach, FL; Hollidaysburg Area High School, Hollidaysburg, PA; Roger Hunt, Rockville, MD; Dr. Wayne A. Huss, Lower Gwynedd, PA; Michael Kane, Pittsburgh, PA; Vincent Karolewics, Uniontown, PA; Dr. James A. Kehl, University of Pittsburgh, PA; Mary Ruth Kelly, Wyoming Historical & Geological Society, Wilkes-Barre, PA; Patrick Knierman, William & Mary College, Williamsburg, VA; Michael G. Kraus, Creston, OH; Wendell W. Lang, Jr., Tarrytown, NY; Stephanie A. Lewis, Time-Life Books, Alexandria, VA; Joseph Long, Ezra S. Griffin Camp #8, Sons of Union Veterans, Scranton, PA; Roger Long, Port Clinton, OH; Dr. Edward G. Longacre, Papillion, NE; Mitch McGlynn, Springfield, VA; Carolee Michener, Franklin News-Herald, Franklin, PA; William Michener, Harrisburg, PA; Warren Motts, Groveport, OH; Representative Fred Noye, New Bloomfield, PA; Dr. George M. Oldenbourg, Jr., Berkeley, CA; Terry O'Leary, Gladwyne, PA; George E. Reed, Harrisburg, PA; Gary Roche, Belle Mead, NJ; Steven Rogers, Ithaca, NY; George & Ethel Ruhl, Lewisburg, PA; Joseph C. Rzotkiewicz, Weatherly, PA; Mark Schafer, Harleysville, PA; Betty Smith, Susquehanna County Historical Society, Montrose, PA; Kenneth Thomson, Hollidaysburg, PA; Marlin Troutman, Watsontown, PA; Kenneth C. Turner, Ellwood City, PA; Ted Twardowski, Nokesville, VA; Mildred G. Van Dyke, Canton, PA; Veterans of Foreign Wars Post 255, Duncannon, PA; Dr. Anthony Waskie, Levittown, PA; Lucy Wolf, Altoona Mirror, Altoona, PA; Bill Wolford, Indiana, PA; Barbara Zolli, Venango Museum of Art, Science and Industry, Oil City, PA.

Representative Joseph R. Pitts and the members of the Capitol Preservation Committee have given their support throughout the program. The Book Publication Subcommittee again supervised production of this volume. Senator John J. Shumaker was Chairman, aided by Senator Robert J. Mellow, Representative Fred Belardi, Mrs. Renee Jones, and Ms. Leslie M. Gallery. Assisting the Subcommittee was Ruthann Kemper (Committee Administrator). Our Textile Conservators, Diane Kessler and Margaret Morris, worked with the flags. They were assisted by Andrea L. Myers (Textile Conservation Technician) and Karen L. Galle (Project Coordinator). Our Office Secretaries, Arlene Hawk, Renee Powell, and Elana Maynard, typed the manuscript. I also thank Dr. Edward G. Longacre and Mr. William C. Williams for reading over the manuscript and giving me both stylistic and factual comments to improve the text.

Finally, I thank all the people who heard about our program and donated either original or copies of Civil War documents. Dr. Richard J. Sommers, Archivist at the United States Army Military History Institute, established a "Save the Flags" Collection to house all donated material. To date, more than twenty donations can be found in this collection. These fine people unselfishly wanted to share their treasures with historians and Civil War buffs researching America's most popular armed conflict. Donors include the following: Mr. & Mrs. Lloyd P. Anderson, Oakton, VA; Thomas A. Corcoran, Brigantine, NJ; Mrs. Peggy C. Cramer, Lansdale, PA; Gerald P. Emmer, Bethesda, MD; Mrs. Elaine Fox, Earlville, PA; W. J. Gobrecht, Harrisburg, PA; Chuck Hart, Bethlehem, PA; Richard W. Hartwell, Hummelstown, PA; John D. Hassler, Jupiter, FL; Howard J. Lamade, Jr., Williamsport, PA; Fred A. Lamond, East Rockaway, NY; Malcolm Macht, Malone, NY; Charles D. Minnenmeyer, Bloomington, IN; David Neville, Export, PA; John S. Perry, Elyria, OH; David Runkle, Shiremanstown, PA; Edith E. Van Dyke, Lower Burrell, PA; David Vargo, Bethel Park, PA; John G. Waite, Albany, NY; Leo Ward, Pottsville, PA; Mrs. Betty Welch, Endicott, NY; and Mr. & Mrs. Ronald Wickard, Plainfield, PA.

Table of Contents

Capitol Preservation Committee & Staff Members	v	130th Infantry	408
Acknowledgements	vii	131st Infantry	410
Introduction	ix	132nd Infantry	411
		133rd Infantry	414
PART II (Continued from Volume One)		134th Infantry	415
88th Infantry	307	135th Infantry	416
8th Cavalry (89th Regiment)	309	136th Infantry	417
90th Infantry	311	137th Infantry	419
91st Infantry	313	138th Infantry	420
9th Cavalry (92nd Regiment)	316	139th Infantry	423
93rd Infantry	318	140th Infantry	426
95th Infantry	321	141st Infantry	429
96th Infantry	325	142nd Infantry	432
97th Infantry	328	143rd Infantry	434
98th Infantry	331	145th Infantry	439
99th Infantry	333	147th Infantry	441
100th Infantry	336	148th Infantry	443
101st Infantry	340	149th Infantry	446
102nd Infantry	342	150th Infantry	450
103rd Infantry	346	151st Infantry	453
104th Infantry	348	3rd Artillery (152nd Regiment)	454
105th Infantry	351	153rd Infantry	456
106th Infantry	354	155th Infantry	458
107th Infantry	357	157th Infantry	462
11th Cavalry (108th Regiment)	360	14th Cavalry (159th Regiment)	463
109th Infantry	363	15th Cavalry (160th Regiment)	465
110th Infantry	366	16th Cavalry (161st Regiment)	467
111th Infantry	369	17th Cavalry (162nd Regiment)	469
2nd Artillery (112th Regiment)	372	18th Cavalry (163rd Regiment)	471
12th Cavalry (113th Regiment)	375	1862-63 Drafted Militia	
114th Infantry	377	(158th, 165th-179th Infantry)	473
115th Infantry	379	19th, 20th, 21st Cavalry	
116th Infantry	381	(180th-182nd Regiments)	479
13th Cavalry (117th Regiment)	384	183rd Infantry	482
118th Infantry	386	184th Infantry	484
119th Infantry	390	22nd Cavalry (185th Regiment)	485
121st Infantry	392	186th Infantry	487
122nd Infantry	395	187th Infantry	488
123rd Infantry	396	188th Infantry	489
124th Infantry	398	190th & 191st Infantry	
125th Infantry	400	(1st & 2nd Veteran Reserves)	492
126th Infantry	402	1864 One Hundred Days Troops	
127th Infantry	404	(192nd-197th Infantry)	494
128th Infantry	405	198th Infantry	497
129th Infantry	406	199th Infantry	499

Table of Contents

200th Infantry	501
201st Infantry	502
202nd Infantry	503
203rd Infantry	505
5th Artillery (204th Regiment)	507
205th Infantry	508
206th Infantry	509
207th Infantry	510
208th Infantry	511
209th Infantry	513
210th Infantry	515
211th Infantry	517
6th Artillery (212th Regiment)	518
213th-215th Infantry	519
Independent Batteries	522
1863 Militia	524
Miscellaneous Flags	526

PART III

Chapter V: Corrections to Volume One	531
Chapter VI: Additions to Volume One	532
Chapter VII: Addenda to Volume One Appendix	539
Chapter VIII: Saving the Flags: The Conservation Procedure	543
Chapter IX: Conclusions	550
Chapter X: Epilogue	563
Chapter XI: The Flag Sponsorship Program	570
Appendix: Pennsylvania Civil War Color-Bearers	575
Index	585
Photograph Credits	611

Introduction

This volume concludes the documentary history of Pennsylvania's Civil War flags. The format is the same as the first volume, published in 1987. The reader will find brief regimental histories of the 88th through 215th Regiments, Independent Batteries, and 1863 Militia, with the histories based around the flags. Notes are confined to flag references. Again, comprehensive bibliographies are provided for those interested in more information about favorite units. A chapter on conservation provides an overview of this aspect of the program, while a concluding chapter analyzes the state and government flags and briefly examines some of the problems encountered during research. Additions and corrections to Volume One are also included, based primarily on further research over the past three years. The Epilogue describes what happened to some of the color-bearers after they again donned civilian attire. An index to both volumes concludes this book.

Unlike the first volume, measurements for all the flags are not provided. Most of the flags are within a couple of inches of regulation size. For those that are not, such as the Evans & Hassall cavalry and artillery standards, we have included measurements.

There is one additional abbreviation not found in Volume One. The bibliographies list many entries from "*NT.*" This is an abbreviation for the *National Tribune*, a Grand Army of the Republic monthly magazine that began publication in the late 1870s, then shifted to a weekly newspaper format in October 1881. The paper eventually merged with the *Stars and Stripes* in the 1940s. For much of its heyday, this paper, in addition to providing veterans with information on pensions and GAR post news, printed articles and letters from the soldiers about their wartime experiences. The paper is a veritable goldmine of unused source material. Sadly, there is no comprehensive index for the *Tribune.* The author is working on a guide-index, from which the Pennsylvania-related items are included with the proper units.

The Pennsylvania flag collection is a public collection and is open for research and tours. For more information, contact the Capitol Preservation Committee, House P.O. Box 231, Main Capitol Building, Harrisburg, PA 17120, or call 717-787-2743. Readers desiring photographs of flags owned by the Commonwealth can obtain 8x10 color or black and white photographs for personal use by contacting the Committee at the above address. There is a charge for either format. If publication is desired, the Committee will consider such rights upon request.

In October 1987, the Committee sponsored a two-day symposium to address cooperation and identify needs and issues relating to flag collections. The twenty speakers addressed topics such as historical documentation, different conservation practices, and funding. The Committee published a softbound book which includes all papers presented at this conference. This book can be ordered directly from the Committee at a cost of $18 postpaid.

Finally, a note on the bibliographies. Over the six years that I have spent researching the flags, I visited many of the county historical societies across the state, corresponded with others, and delved through every bibliography I could locate. Still, more and more Civil War items keep surfacing. I would draw the reader's attention to the ongoing collections at the United States Army Military History Institute in Carlisle. Both the Archives (with its three major Civil War collections) and Special Collections (photographs) are continually receiving additional materials not listed in this volume. Visiting the Institute is a vital step in any Civil War research project.

88th Infantry

State Color

Nicknamed the "Cameron Light Guards," the 88th Infantry was composed of men recruited in Philadelphia and Berks counties. After organization in September 1861, the regiment proceeded to Washington, then on to Alexandria. It remained here as part of the garrison until April 1862. On January 5, the 88th received a state color manufactured by Horstmann Brothers, who sent it to the State Agency for distribution. The presentation ceremony was highlighted by the speeches of Speaker of the House Galusha Grow and Philadelphia Representative William D. Kelley.[1]

When the spring 1862 campaign opened, the 88th was sent to northern Virginia and became a part of the new Army of Virginia. The regiment was present on the battlefield of Cedar Mountain (August 9, 1862) but was not seriously engaged. Its first major struggle with Confederate troops was on August 30, during the Second Battle of Manassas. The Union army was defeated and fell back to Washington. Now attached to the First Corps, Army of the Potomac, the 88th participated in the Maryland Campaign, which culminated in the bloody fighting at Antietam on September 17. The 88th suffered battle casualties of more than 225 soldiers in these battles. However, Sergeant John B. Donohoe of Company B bore the state color safely through the fighting, although eight color-guards fell by his side.[2]

The 88th then fought at Fredericksburg on December 13. After spending the winter in camp near Falmouth, the regiment was marginally engaged in the Chancellorsville Campaign of April-May 1863. Moving north into Pennsylvania with the army, the 88th next fought Lee's troops at Gettysburg on July 1. The 88th suffered over a hundred casualties in the battle as the First Corps was driven off Seminary Ridge. Corporal Lewis W. Bonnin of Company B, bearing the state color, was badly wounded in the hip as the regiment fell back through the town. Bonnin managed to pass the flag to a comrade who retreated with the other survivors to reassemble on Cemetery Hill. After saving the flag, the bleeding corporal crawled into a building to die, but doctors found him and saved his life.[3]

State Color
Maker: HB
1985.001

Returning to Virginia after the Gettysburg Campaign, the 88th took part in the Bristoe Station and Mine Run campaigns before going into winter quarters near Culpeper. The state color was retired from active service on December 18 when a new stand of colors was presented to the regiment. Colonel Louis Wagner took the flag home to Philadelphia where it was apparently displayed in the Union League headquarters for a time. Emblazoned with battle honors, the flag was officially returned to the state on July 4, 1866.[4]

Union League Colors

On December 18, 1863, Colonel Wagner presented his old regiment with two new flags, compliments of the Union League of Philadelphia. The gift included a national color, a blue regimental color, and two blue general guide markers.[5] Colonel Wagner presented the flags to the regiment in a brief ceremony at its winter camp. Sergeant Thomas Hartman (Company H) and Corporal Francis Charles (Company C) were appointed to carry these new colors.[6]

During the 1864 campaign, the 88th engaged the enemy briefly in the Wilderness, then suffered heav-

88th Infantry 307

Regimental Color
1985.147

National Color
1985.146

ier losses at Spotsylvania. Here, during the fighting on May 12, Corporal Charles McKnight of Company K, carrying one of the colors, was struck in the head by a grapeshot. Luckily, McKnight was merely stunned by the spent ball.[7] After fighting at the North Anna River and Cold Harbor, the 88th took part in the initial assaults on the Petersburg defenses (June 18). Sergeant John Ewing (Company D) was wounded at this time, but continued to carry his banner.[8]

Thereafter, the 88th settled down in the trench warfare at Petersburg. It fought in the engagements along the Weldon Railroad (August 18-21) and then at Hatcher's Run on February 6-7, 1865. In this latter engagement, Sergeant John Devine (Company K) was cited for bravery in leading the regiment forward with his flag.[9] After Lee's surrender at Appomattox, the 88th moved north and was mustered out of service on June 30, 1865. Both Union League colors were included in the 1866 Philadelphia parade and were given to the state at this time.

Company Flag

On October 6, 1861, the 88th received some type of company flag as the regiment paraded through Baltimore on its way to Washington. This small flag, which Colonel George P. McLean described as "so tattered as to excite the laughter of the Rebels who see it," was used as a regimental flag until the state color was presented in January 1862. The flag apparently has not survived.[10]

Notes

1 "Flag Presentations to Pennsylvania Troops," *Philadelphia Inquirer*, January 6, 1862.
2 "The Color Bearer of the Eighty-eighth Regiment, P.V.," *Philadelphia Inquirer*, December 17, 1862.
3 Vautier, pp. 108, 238.
4 Colonel Wagner to Adjutant-General A. L. Russell, November 7, 1863, RG 19, 88th Pennsylvania Regimental Papers.
5 Vautier Diary, December 18, 1863.
6 General Orders #69, December 29, 1863, Regimental Order, Consolidated Morning Report and Letter Book, RG 94.
7 Vautier, p. 226.
8 Vautier, pp. 191-92.
9 *O.R.* 46.1, p. 292.
10 Vautier Diary, October 6, 1861; Colonel McLean to Samuel B. Thomas, December 21, 1861, RG 19, 88th Pennsylvania Regimental Papers.

Bibliography

"An Unfortunate Name." *NT*, July 16, 1891.
Boone, Samuel G. Memoirs. USAMHI, CWTI Collection.
____. "Captured at Gettysburg." *NT*, May 9, 1912.
____. "Gen. Schimmelpfennig." *NT*, September 28, 1905.
Grant, George W. Papers. Duke University.
Hunterson, Harry. "Escaped Capture." *NT*, March 23, 1911. (Gettysburg)
____. "Fighting at Thoroughfare Gap." *NT*, May 26, 1910.
____. "Gen. McDowell." *NT*, November 12, 1891.
Mass, E. A. "Libby Tunnel Once More." *NT*, April 23, 1885.
Threapleton, William. "Globe Tavern." *NT*, November 21, 1901.

Vautier, John W. Diaries. USAMHI.
____. "At Gettysburg. The Eighty-eighth Pennsylvania Infantry in the Battle." *Philadelphia Weekly Press*, November 10, 1886.
____. "The Gallant Record of the Eighty-eighth Pennsylvania Volunteers." *Philadelphia Weekly Times*, July 31, 1886.
____. *History of the 88th Pennsylvania Volunteers in the War for the Union, 1861-1865*. Philadelphia: J. B. Lippincott Company, 1894.
____. "Second Bull Run. How the Battle was Fought." *NT*, April 30, May 7, 1903.

8th Cavalry (89th Regiment)

First State Standard
Maker: HB
1985.148

First State Standard

Recruited in Philadelphia, Chester, and Lycoming counties during the summer and fall of 1861, the 8th Pennsylvania Cavalry was organized in Philadelphia that September. The new unit was sent to Washington, remaining in the area until the Army of the Potomac moved to the Peninsula in March 1862. A Horstmann-made state standard was presented to the regiment by the State Agency sometime after early December.

The regiment moved with the Army of the Potomac to the Peninsula in March 1862. Assigned to the Fourth Corps, the 8th Cavalry frequently skirmished with the enemy as the army moved towards Richmond. The regiment was lightly engaged during the fighting at Seven Pines and the ensuing Seven Days' Battles. It moved north and was engaged at Antietam on September 17, suffering no losses. During the Fredericksburg Campaign the regiment again fought in several small clashes with enemy cavalry, but was not engaged during the battle on December 13.

On May 2, 1863, the unit suffered its heaviest loss of the war when the troopers, in columns of two, slammed into Rebel infantry in the wooded terrain as the regiment moved to intercept Stonewall Jackson's command. The regiment unexpectedly met the enemy as it trotted down a narrow dirt road through the trees. With no room to maneuver, the men galloped forward and lost more than a hundred of their number before retiring. The regiment's sacrifice enabled

Piece of State Standard

8th Cavalry

Union artillery to wheel into position to oppose a further enemy advance.

After engaging enemy horsemen during the opening stages of the Gettysburg Campaign, the 8th's brigade remained in the rear to guard the army's trains, then rejoined the Cavalry Corps in time to fight Lee's retreating troops near the Potomac River. The regiment then suffered some loss during the October Bristoe Station Campaign, as well as during the succeeding operations at Mine Run in November.

During the 1864 Virginia Campaign, the 8th Cavalry shared in all the actions of the Second Cavalry Division of the Cavalry Corps. After skirmishing in the Wilderness, the unit took part in Sheridan's Richmond Raid (May 9-24). The regiment then rode in the cavalry raid to Trevilian Station. On June 24, the unit suffered heavy casualties at Saint Mary's Church. At some unspecified time during this period of active cavalry forays, the first state standard, having become worn out in hard service, was retired from field use. It was officially returned in 1866.

Second State Standard

An Evans & Hassall standard was sent to the State Agency in late May 1864. No documentation exists to indicate when the 8th Cavalry received it. After crossing the James River on July 1, the regiment participated in many of the operations around Petersburg, including late July engagements near the old Malvern Hill battlefield, Reams's Station (August 25), Poplar Spring Church (September 30 - October 1), Boydton Plank Road (October 27-28), Hatcher's Run (February 5-7, 1865), and Five Forks (April 1). During the 1865 fighting, Sergeant George Stephens of Company H was color-bearer.[1] Following Lee's surrender at Appomattox, the regiment moved to Lynchburg for guard duty. Here, the survivors were consolidated with the 16th Cavalry, which was mustered out of service on August 11. The second standard was never returned to state care. A June 1866 letter indicates that the flag was then in possession of Williamsport veteran Alfred Page.[2]

Notes

1 Special Orders #7, January 18, 1865, in Regimental Order & Miscellaneous Book, RG 94.

2 W.A. Corrie to Adjutant-General A. L. Russell, June 7, 1866, RG 19.

Bibliography

Carpenter, James E. "Charge of the 8th Pennsylvania Cavalry." *Philadelphia Weekly Press*, October 13, 1886.

____. "Charge of the 8th Pennsylvania Cavalry." *Grand Army Scout and Soldiers Mail*, May 12, 1883.

____. *A List of the Battles, Engagements, Actions and Important Skirmishes in Which the Eighth Pennsylvania Cavalry Participated During the War of 1861-1865*. Philadelphia: Allen, Lane & Scott's Printing House, 1886.

Collins, John L. "A Prisoner's March from Gettysburg to Staunton." *Battles and Leaders* 3: 429-33

____. "When Stonewall Jackson Turned Our Right." *Battles and Leaders* 3: 183-86.

Cummings, Robert. Letters. Rutgers University Library.

Dollar, John. Diary, June 28, 1862-September 18, 1864. USAMHI, HbCWRT Collection.

Dykins, Daniel B. "A Case of Hunger Cure, and the Tragedy that Followed." *Now and Then* 3 (1890-92): 139-40.

Eisenbrey, J. Lehman. 1865 Journal. Bucks County Historical Society.

Flack, George W. Diary, 1861-1864. Rutgers University.

Giles, J. E. "The Famous Charge of the 8th Pennsylvania Cavalry Against Jackson's Corps." *Grand Army Scout and Soldiers Mail*, March 10, 1883.

____. "The First Troops Across the Chickahominy." *Grand Army Scout and Soldiers Mail*, March 7, 1885.

____. "Great Charge of the 8th Pennsylvania Cavalry." *Grand Army Scout and Soliders Mail*, April 14, 1883.

____. "Supplementary Article." *Grand Army Scout and Soldiers Mail*, April 21, 1883.

____. "That Charge at Chancellorsville." *Grand Army Scout and Soldiers Mail*, May 26, 1883.

Hodge, George W. "A Sermon Preached in the Church of the Ascension, Philadelphia, by the Reverend George Woolsey Hodge, on the Occasion of the Unveiling of a Mural Tablet in Memory of Major James Edward Carpenter . . . March 2, 1902." Lancaster: Press of the New Era Printing Company, 1902.

Huey, Pennock. *A True History of the Charge of the Eighth Pennsylvania Cavalry at Chancellorsville*. Philadelphia: Porter & Coates, 1883.

Kelsey, Charles C. *To the Knife, The Biography of Major Peter Keenan, 8th Pennsylvania Cavalry*. Ann Arbor, 1964?

Kerr, William. Letters. Rutgers University Library.

Lindsay, Robert H. "8th Pennsylvania Cavalry at Chancellorsville." *Grand Army Scout and Soldiers Mail*, March 17, 1883.

Payne, R. C. "The Cavalry at Farmville." *NT*, July 4, 1912.

____. "Ranking Officers, 8th Pa. Cav." *NT*, May 30, 1918.

Phelps, L. D. "Prisoner of War." *NT*, August 8, 1889.

Pleasonton, Alfred. "The Charge of the Eighth Pennsylvania Cavalry at Chancellorsville." *Philadelphia Weekly Press*, September 29, 1886.

Wickersham, Charles I. "The Cavalry at Chancellorsville." *NT*, October 13, 1904.

____. "Personal Recollections of the Cavalry at Chancellorsville." In Military Order of the Loyal Legion of the United States, Wisconsin Commandery, *War Papers* 3: 453-62. Milwaukee: Burdick, Amitage and Allen, 1903.

Woodward, Daniel H. (editor). "The Civil War of a Pennsylvania Trooper." *Pennsylvania Magazine of History and Biography* 87 (1963): 39-62.

90th Infantry

State Color

The 90th Infantry was comprised solely of members of a pre-war Philadelphia militia unit, and was known as the 19th Infantry while in the three-months service in 1861. The regiment re-enlisted for three years and spent the winter of 1861-62 in camp outside Philadelphia. Governor Curtin presented a state color to the unit on December 6, when he came to the city to present flags to several new commands.[1]

State Color
Maker: HB
1985.149

After three weeks of guard duty in Baltimore, the 90th moved to Washington in late April 1862. It then was forwarded to the supply base at Aquia Creek. The regiment spent time guarding the base and then moved on to Fredericksburg. As part of the new Army of Virginia, the 90th was shunted around northern Virginia, reaching the battlefield of Cedar Mountain after the fighting had ceased (August 9). The 90th then fought at Second Manassas (August 30), suffering more than two hundred casualties. After the retreat to Washington, the 90th, as a component of the First Corps, Army of the Potomac, moved to counter Lee's invasion of Maryland and fought at Antietam on September 17. Returning to Virginia, the 90th took part in the Battle of Fredericksburg (December 13), then went into winter quarters.

The First Corps was only marginally engaged in the Chancellorsville Campaign, but suffered heavy losses at Gettysburg, primarily on July 1, 1863. Following Lee's army back to Virginia, the 90th took part in the Bristoe Station and Mine Run campaigns (Autumn 1863) before going into winter quarters near Culpeper. In the 1864 campaign, the regiment fought in the Wilderness, at Spotsylvania, North Anna River, Cold Harbor, and in the initial attacks on Petersburg. After spending time in the trenches, the 90th engaged the enemy at Weldon Railroad (August 18-21, 1864). This was the unit's last major fighting, since the majority of the unit had opted not to re-enlist. The survivors returned to Philadelphia and were mustered out of service in November 1864. The battered state color was left with Major Lane. Colonel Peter Lyle borrowed the flag prior to the 1866 ceremony, when it was officially returned to the Commonwealth.

Philadelphia Colors

The soldiers of the 19th Infantry received flags from the students of the Girls' High and Normal School and the ladies of Philadelphia's Sixth Ward (see Volume One, page 12, for a description). These were apparently carried by the 90th for an unspecified period as well. Sergeant Johnson Roney of Company G was maimed for life while carrying the Sixth Ward flag at some point during the war.[2] Three bearers of the High School flag were shot down at Fredericksburg before Lieutenant William H. Hewlings (Company C) seized the fallen banner and carried it to the rear as the regiment fell back.[3] The original High School flag was replaced by another flag presented by the school on January 5, 1863.[4] Of these four presented colors, only one seems to have survived. The War Library and Museum in Philadelphia owns the remnant of a national color attributed to the 90th, but not enough survives to ascertain which flag it is.

Color-Bearers

Sergeant Thomas E. Berger of Company K carried one of the unit's flags and was wounded at some unspecified time during the war.[5] During the fighting at Antietam, Corporal Theodore Mason (Company E) was killed while bearing a flag.[6] When the flag fell, Confederate soldiers rushed forward to capture the banner. Sergeant William H. Paul saw the oncoming enemy, rallied several men about him, and rushed forward to save the flag. Paul recalled: "We clashed with a shock, and a sharp hand-to-hand fight ensued in which two of our men were killed and five so severely wounded that they were unable to be of any assistance. A rebel had already seized the colors, but I grasped them and with one supreme effort wrenched the precious banner from his hold. Waving it high above my head, I carried it throughout the remainder of the battle." Indeed, Paul was allowed to remain a color-bearer until crippled at Gettysburg. For his effort at Antietam, Paul was awarded a Medal of Honor in 1896.[7]

Sergeant William H. Paul, Company E

Notes

1 "Grand Military Review," *Philadelphia Inquirer*, December 7, 1861.
2 Sellers, p. 34. The muster rolls of the 90th Pennsylvania are very deficient and there is no indication of when Roney was wounded in action.
3 *O.R.* 21, p. 501.
4 Taylor, *Philadelphia*, p. 350.
5 Sellers, p. 34.
6 "Casualties in Col. Lyle's Regiment," *Philadelphia Inquirer*, September 25, 1862.
7 Beyer-Keydel, p. 90; "Case of William H. Paul, Late Sergeant, Company E, 90th Pennsylvania Volunteers," Paul's Medal of Honor File, RG 94.

Bibliography

Jennings, Frank. Reminiscences. USAMHI, CWTI Collection.
Moore, Samuel B. Diary, March 31-September 22, 1862. Antietam National Battlefield.
Northrop Rufus P. "Booze Made Tigers Reckless?" *NT*, December 30, 1909. (Gettysburg)
____. "Going into Gettysburg." *NT*, October 11, 1906.
____. "Good-by Hoecake." *NT*, March 23, 1911.
____. "Silenced by a Sailor." *NT*, July 4, 1912.
Quayle, William H. "Rescued from Prison." *NT*, September 24, 1891.
Sellers, Alfred J. *Souvenir Survivors' Association Gettysburg, 1888-9.* Philadelphia: John W. Clark's Sons, 1889.
Smedley, Charles. *Life in Southern Prisons, From the Diary of Corporal Charles Smedley, of Company G, 90th Regiment Penn's. Volunteers, Commencing a Few Days Before the "Battle of the Wilderness," in Which He was Taken Prisoner, in the Evening of the Fifth Month Fifth, 1864. Also, a Short Description of the March to and Battle of Gettysburg, Together with a Biographical Sketch of the Author.* Lancaster?: Ladies' and Gentlemen's Fulton Aid Society, 1865.
Stulen, John. "Brave Old Dick Coulter." *NT*, December 17, 1908.
____. "Opening the Battle. A Penna. Boy Runs into the Enemy's Picket Line in the Wilderness." *NT*, April 22, 1909

91st Infantry

First State Color

Recruited at Philadelphia during the fall of 1861, the 91st Infantry was organized as a regiment in early December 1861. In company with four other regiments, the 91st received its state color on December 6, when Governor Curtin and staff visited Philadelphia to present the new flags.[1] The 91st remained in Philadelphia until mid-January 1862, when it moved to Washington. Acting as guards at various military installations, the 91st was relieved from this duty in late April, when the unit was ordered to Alexandria. Here, the regiment was employed as provost guards until late August.

At this time, the 91st was finally relieved from this onerous duty and assigned to the Third Division, Fifth Corps, Army of the Potomac. This division arrived too late to take part in the fighting at Antietam. The regiment's first combat action occurred on December 13 when the division was part of the troops assaulting the sunken road on Marye's Heights during the Battle of Fredericksburg. After this defeat, the 91st went into winter camp opposite the city, then took part in Burnside's abortive "Mud March" in January 1863. Thereafter, the regiment participated in the Chancellorsville

Photograph of First State Color

First State Color
Maker: HB
1985.150

Campaign, fighting the Confederates on May 3. During the ensuing Gettysburg Campaign, the regiment arrived on the battlefield early on July 2, then moved to Little Round Top and helped defend that vital hill. After the autumn campaigns (Bristoe Station and Mine Run) in northern Virginia, the regiment went into winter camp. Most of the soldiers in the regiment re-enlisted as veterans and the men went home on furlough in January 1864. The state color was taken along home and left in Harrisburg. It was returned during the 1866 parade.

Second State Color

When the regiment returned to Virginia in March 1864, it apparently took along a replacement state color which had been supplied to the state in February. During the grueling marching and constant fighting of the 1864 campaign, the 91st was engaged in the Wilderness (May 5-7), at Spotsylvania (May 9-12), along the North Anna River (May 23), and in the initial series of attacks on Petersburg (June 18). Thereafter, the regiment fought at the Weldon Railroad (August 18-21), at Poplar Spring Church (September 30),

Second State Color
Maker: HB
1985.151

and at the Boydton Plank Road (October 27-28). It then fought at Hatcher's Run (February 5-7, 1865) and in the series of engagements at Five Forks (March 29-April 1). After Lee's surrender at Appomattox, the regiment moved to Washington and disbanded on July 10. The battered state color was initially taken home by Colonel Edgar M. Gregory, who turned it over to Major Lane in Philadelphia.[2] Like the first color, the second was returned officially in 1866.

Philadelphia Flags

The 91st received at least two colors from friends of the regiment. The first was presented on December 11, 1861. This national color featured the thirty-four stars arranged as a single, giant star.[3] This flag was apparently carried until the regiment returned home on furlough in early 1864. At this time, a committee of admirers pooled their funds to obtain another flag for the 91st. The presentation took place on February 3, when ex-governor James Pollock did the honors on behalf of the donors. The newspaper accounts of this presentation do not agree whether one or two colors were given to the regiment.[4] None of these flags seem to have survived to the present. In April 1985, Mr. Baldwin Griffin donated a set of gold cords and tassels from one of these local presentations. His wife is descended from Colonel Gregory's family. The War Library and Museum in Philadelphia has a flank marker, but there is no existing documentation to indicate when this flag was presented to the the unit.

Color-Bearers

Names of six of the regiment's color-bearers have been found. As the 91st moved through the Wilderness on the night of May 7, some horses frightened from nearby gunfire galloped through the moving ranks of men. Sergeant Robert Chism was so badly trampled in the stampede that one of his legs had to be amputated, causing the sergeant's death on June 1.[5] During the June 18, 1864, attack on Petersburg, Sergeant Archibald Nimmo of Company C and Corporal Edward Gamble of Company B both were wounded while carrying the 91st's flags. Sergeant Franklin C. Wolfong seized at least one of the fallen standards and waved them defiantly at the enemy as the regiment advanced.[6] Private James C. Sweeney of Company D grabbed the other flag. He was quickly shot and later died from his wounds.[7] Corporal Thomas C. Deveraux of Company C saved a flag at Hatcher's Run (February 6, 1865) by stripping it from the staff and running to the rear as the regiment was outflanked and in danger of capture.[8] Finally, the roster of soldiers contacted for the 1914 ceremony lists Sergeant William H. Geary of Company D as a previous color-bearer.

Notes

1 "Grand Military Review," *Philadelphia Inquirer*, December 7, 1861.
2 Eli S. Sellers to Adjutant-General Russell, June 15, 1866, RG 19.
3 "Flag Presentation," *Philadelphia North American*, December 12, 1861; "Flag Presentation," *Philadelphia Inquirer*, December 13, 1861.
4 "Flag Presentation," *Philadelphia Public Ledger*, February 4, 1864; "Presentation of a Suit of Flags," *Philadelphia Inquirer*, February 4, 1864;

"Flag Presentation," *Philadelphia Inquirer*, February 3, 1864.
5 Bates 3: 191.
6 Eli S. Sellers to Lieutenant L. C. Bartlett, December 25, 1864, Regimental Letter and Order Book, RG 94.
7 *Norristown Herald*, July 5, 1864. This article supplies only the soldier's last name. The roster in Bates (3: 209) has James C. Sweeney unaccounted for on the muster roll of Company D.
8 *Pennsylvania at Gettysburg* 1: 498.

Bibliography

Moore, Thomas. "What Might Have Been. The Significant Closing Days of the Great Rebellion." *NT*, February 21, 1895.

Raitt, C. "An Incident at Chancellorsville." *NT*, September 21, 1911.

Reiff, William S. "A Boy Hero." *NT*, August 3, 1905.

____. "Coffee on Little Round Top." *NT*, May 19, 1904.

____. "His Worst Scare. Ghastly Adventure of a 91st Penna. Boy on the Antietam Field." *NT*, August 22, 1895.

____. "The Soldier that was Not Buried." *NT*, August 17, 1905.

____. "A Straddle Bug." *NT*, September 14, 1911.

____. "Struggle for the Union. Trials of a Boy in the Gettysburg Campaign." *NT*, August 6, 1896.

____. "Tortured for Sleep." *NT*, May 25, 1905.

Walter, T. F. "On the Left at Gettysburg." *Grand Army Scout and Soldiers Mail*, October 11, 1884.

____. "Personal Recollections and Experience of an Obscure Soldier." *Grand Army Scout and Soldiers Mail*, issues of August 2-December 27, 1884.

9th Cavalry (92nd Regiment)

First State Standard

Containing troopers from more than ten counties (from Blair in the west, to Lancaster in the south, and Susquehanna in the north), the 9th Pennsylvania Cavalry was organized at Harrisburg in the fall of 1861. The new unit remained in camp until mid-November, when it was ordered to Louisville, Kentucky. Before leaving camp, the regiment marched to the Executive Mansion, where Governor Curtin presented a state standard to the 9th on November 25.[1] After arriving at Louisville, the regiment remained in camp near the city until January 1862, when it moved to the region south of Louisville to protect the area from enemy guerrilla activity.

Called south into Tennessee in March 1862, the three battalions of the 9th Cavalry patrolled the central part of the state. While engaged in this area, the regiment fought Confederate cavalry forces several times, including Lebanon (May 4), Livingston (May 14), and Tomkinsville, Kentucky (June 6 and July 9). Many of these skirmishes were against Colonel John Hunt Morgan's command. When Morgan moved north into Kentucky, the 9th followed. It covered the retreat of a defeated Union infantry force from Richmond (August 30) as a Confederate army invaded the Bluegrass State. The regiment participated in the opening stage of the Battle of Perryville (October 8), where the invaders were defeated and fell back into Tennessee. Weakened by continuous marching and fighting, the 9th then moved to Louisville to obtain fresh horses and equipment.

The regiment then took part in a cavalry raid that covered 470 miles through eastern Tennessee and southwestern Virginia (December 20, 1862-January 5, 1863). After returning from this raid, the regiment was stationed at Franklin, Tennessee, to help guard the right wing of the Army of the Cumberland. Here, the 9th fought in several engagements, most notably at Thompson's Station on March 5, where it helped hold the victorious Confederate troops at bay until the remnant of the Union force could retreat to Franklin. It then participated in the Tullahoma Campaign, fighting at Triune, Rover, Middleton, and Shelbyville. The 9th was present at Chickamauga (September 19-20), where it guarded the right flank of the army, then aided the rearguard as the defeated Rosecrans fell back to Chattanooga. After this campaign, the regiment moved to eastern Tennessee, fighting at Mossy Creek, Dandridge, and Fair Garden before going into winter camp.

When the 9th returned from its veteran furlough in May 1864, it was stationed at Louisville, then protected Frankfort when Morgan raided through the state. While at Louisville, a replacement state standard arrived and the original was sent to Harrisburg. It was officially returned during the 1866 ceremony.

Second State Standard

This standard was completed in early June 1864 and received by the regiment on July 15, while the 9th was in camp near Louisville.[2] Soon thereafter, the troopers moved to Chattanooga, then participated in a series of engagements against Dibrell's Confederate cavalry as General Joseph Wheeler's troopers attempted to interdict Sherman's supply lines. When Sherman left Atlanta to march to the sea in November, the 9th was one of the cavalry regiments accompanying the army

First State Standard
Maker: HB
1985.152

316

Advance the Colors!

Second State Standard
Maker: HB
1985.153

as it swept through Georgia. The 9th contended with enemy forces quite often, primarily at Griswold (November 22) and Waynesborough (December 4), suffering more than a hundred casualties.

When Sherman moved north through the Carolinas, the 9th again screened the advance. During this last campaign, Sergeant Jacob Wolfley of Company C was standard-bearer.[3] After fighting at Averasborough, North Carolina, on March 16, 1865, the 9th led the advance of the army into Raleigh. Upon the cessation of hostilities, the regiment remained in North Carolina until mustered out in July 1865. The second standard was returned to the state in October and was carried in the 1866 parade.

Presented Flags

The 9th carried at least four additional flags during its term of service. The veterans of Company A received a flag from the ladies of Petersburg (now Duncannon, Perry County) when they came home on furlough in the spring of 1864. It is now owned by VFW Post 255 in Duncannon. Mr. B. M. Greider of Mount Joy, Lancaster County, presented a "stand of colors" to Captain Jacob K. Waltman and his Company G in September 1861.[4] The Second Battalion received a "magnificent flag" from the Union ladies of Calhoun, Kentucky, while it guarded this area in March 1862.[5] Finally, Captain Jacob Bertles of Company D, recruited in Luzerne County, carried a company flag that had been given to Company D, 8th Pennsylvania, in 1861 by Wilkes-Barre citizens.[6]

Flag Presented to Company A
Size: 44 x 46

Notes

1 Rowell, p. 30; "The Lochiel Cavalry," *Pennsylvania Daily Telegraph*, November 25, 1861.

2 Rowell, p. 184.

3 Special Order #2, January 7, 1865, Regimental Letter and Order Book, RG 94.

4 "Handsome Present to Capt. Waltman," *Pennsylvania Daily Telegraph*, September 27, 1861.

5 "Second Battalion of the Lochiel Cavalry . . .," *Pennsylvania Daily Telegraph*, March 18, 1862.

6 "Letter from Capt. Bertles," *Wilkes-Barre Record of the Times*, April 9, 1862.

Bibliography

Ashton, Ross. "The Surrender of Raleigh." *NT*, April 8, 1915.
Bowers, George W. "Memories of a Retreat." *NT*, June 11, 1896.
Ditty, Jesse B. "Entering Raleigh." *NT*, December 29, 1898.
____. "The Fight at Morris Ravine." *NT*, June 8, 1899.
Gibble, Abraham. Memoirs. USAMHI, CWTI Collection.
Herrold, Dewey S. "Brigadier-General Edward Charles Williams." *Snyder County Historical Society Bulletin* 1: 495-519 of reprint.
Jordan, Thomas J. "Battle of Thompson's Station and the Trial of the Spies at Franklin, Tennessee." *United Service* ns 3 (1890): 300-314.
____. "Some Military Reminiscences of the Rebellion." *United Service* ns 2 (1889): 508-521.
Miller, James C. "We Scattered the Rebels." *Civil War Times Illustrated* 8 #5 (August 1969): 508-521.
____. "With Sherman Through the Carolinas." *Civil War Times Illustrated* 8 #6 (October 1969): 35-44.

Prichard, W. W. "The Fight at Dandridge." *Philadelphia Weekly Times*, November 17, 1883.
____. "Pursued by Morgan" *Philadelphia Weekly Times*, January 29, 1887.
Rowell, John W. *Yankee Cavalrymen: Through the Civil War with the Ninth Pennsylvania Cavalry*. Knoxville: University of Tennessee Press, 1971.
Shaw, A. B. "Battle of Perryville, as Seen by a Pennsylvania Cavalryman." *NT*, March 10, 1904.
____. "Hot Chase on a Hot Day." *NT*, July 26, 1900.
____. "Kilpatrick's Version. The Montrose Crossroads Story, as Told of by the General." *NT*, October 4, 1900.
____. "Tullahoma Campaign." *NT*, November 5, 1903.
Stevens, Carlisle. Letters. Susquehanna County Historical Society.
Witmer, Isaac. "He Let the Bears Go." *NT*, May 23, 1912.

93rd Infantry

First State Color

The 93rd Pennsylvania was organized at Lebanon in September and October 1861, the men being recruited in Lebanon, Dauphin, Berks, Montour, Clinton, and Centre counties. Governor Curtin traveled to Camp Coleman to present a state color to the new unit on November 8. The silk banner was given to Private Henry Fittery of Company A to carry.[1] Later that month, the 93rd moved to Washington, where it remained throughout the winter. It was assigned to Darius Couch's division of the Fourth Corps.

In company with the Army of the Potomac, the 93rd was transported by water to Fort Monroe in March 1862, then moved north to take part in the Siege of Yorktown. Its first encounter with Confederate forces occurred on May 5 during the fighting at Williamsburg. In the ensuing struggle at Fair Oaks on May 31, the 93rd suffered more than a hundred casualties while resisting the furious Rebel assaults. During the Seven Days' Battles, the battered Fourth Corps protected the army's left flank and was not heavily engaged.

When the Army of the Potomac was withdrawn from the Peninsula, Couch's division was detached from Fourth Corps and sent north. The division arrived on the battlefield at Antietam too late to take part in the fighting. Shortly thereafter, the division was attached to the Sixth Corps, remaining with that organization until war's end. The 93rd next fought at Fredericksburg on December 13, suffering a mere four casualties. During the Chancellorsville Campaign, the Sixth Corps remained at Fredericksburg, charging and capturing Marye's Heights (May 3), then moving on to fight at Salem Church (May 3-4) where the 93rd lost seventy-nine soldiers.

The Sixth Corps arrived on the Gettysburg battlefield late on July 2 after a thirty-two-mile forced march. Used to bolster the sagging left flank, most units were not heavily engaged, the 93rd included. After taking part in the Bristoe Station and Mine Run campaigns that fall, the 93rd went into winter quarters at Brandy Station. In late December, the 93rd's brigade was sent to Harper's Ferry, where the 93rd remained until sent home for veterans' furlough in February 1864. The first state color was left in Harrisburg when the regiment arrived there and was officially returned to the state in 1866.

Second State Color

A replacement state color was provided to the Commonwealth by Horstmann Brothers in early March 1864. It was probably given to the 93rd when the men reassembled at Camp Curtin before returning to Virginia. During the ensuing campaign, the 93rd fought in the Wilderness (May 5-6), at Spotsylvania (May 9-18), North Anna River (May 23-24), Cold Harbor (June 1-6), and in the initial assaults on Petersburg (June 18-22).

When Confederate General Jubal Early's troops moved north down the Shenandoah Valley to threaten Washington, the Sixth Corps was sent to defend the city in early July. When Early withdrew, Major-General Philip H. Sheridan was placed in command of a new army to drive the enemy from the Valley. The 93rd participated in the subsequent campaign that ousted Early's men from the Shenandoah. The

First State Color
Maker: EH
1985.155

Second State Color
Maker: HB
1985.154

regiment fought at Winchester on September 19, then at Fisher's Hill three days later. In this latter engagement, Sergeant William H. Smith of Company F carried the state color forward as the men surged over the Confederate entrenchments. As Smith planted his banner, a nearby caisson suddenly exploded, fragments of which severely mangled Smith's left leg, forcing amputation. As Smith fell, Corporal Jacob Renkenberger seized the flag and apparently carried it until the end of the war.[2]

Following the victory at Cedar Creek (October 19), the 93rd was sent to Philadelphia for provost duty during the presidential election. After a brief return to the Valley, the regiment, with the Sixth Corps, returned to Petersburg. Here, the command participated in an abortive charge on the Confederate entrenchments on March 25, 1865, then took part in the general assault of April 2 when Petersburg fell to Grant's soldiers. The regiment next fought at Saylor's Creek on April 6. Following Lee's surrender, the 93rd eventually returned to Washington and was mustered out of service on June 27. Colonel Charles W. Eckman turned the state color over to the mustering officer, who in turn sent it to the state in July.[3] It was included in the 1866 ceremony.

Coleman Flags

George Dawson Coleman, a Lebanon iron ore magnate, took a special interest in equipping the 93rd. He provided the regiment with at least two flags. The first, a 37-star national color, was given to the regiment on November 5, 1861. The inscription "Presented to the Coleman Guards of Lebanon, Pa. by G. Dawson Cole-

National Colors Presented by G. Dawson Coleman

man" was painted among the gold stars.[4] This banner was carried alongside the state color until December 1863. Private Fittery carried this color at Fair Oaks, where he was mortally wounded on May 31, 1862.[5]

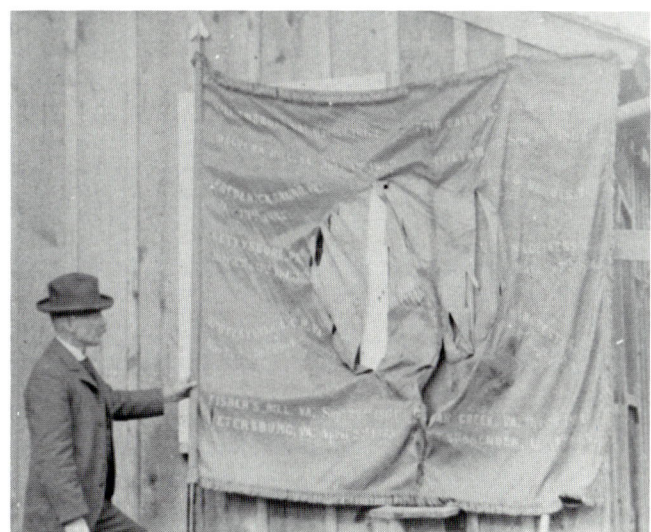

Regimental Color Presented by G. Dawson Coleman

93rd Infantry

Coleman provided a replacement flag to the regiment on Christmas Day, 1863. This 34-star national color was inscribed with battle honors through Mine Run and was carried until the end of the war. Sergeant Charles Marquette of Company F carried the banner during the April 2 attack on Petersburg. Though wounded by accidentally stabbing himself on a piece of abatis, Marquette struggled forward and was one of the first to plant his flag on the enemy line. The sergeant also captured a Confederate Flag. On May 10, he was awarded a Medal of Honor for his courage.[6]

Both national colors were kept by the regimental association and eventually were given to the Coleman family for safekeeping. Heirs of the family donated the flags to the Lebanon County Historical Society in 1935. Both may be seen at the Society. Coleman may also have presented a blue regimental flag to the regiment in December 1863. A contemporary letter describes this flag while a postwar photograph shows what may be this same flag.[7] The banner apparently has not survived.

Danville Flags

The ladies of Danville presented two flags to the 93rd. Company H, the "Baldy Guards" of Danville, received the first flag on October 26, 1861. A regimental circular from Colonel Eckman indicates that a flag from the ladies of Danville was to be presented to the 93rd on June 27, 1865. No other information has been located that describes these flags, which apparently have been lost.[8]

Color-Bearers

Several additional names of bearers have been found in the literature. Sergeant John Hutchison of Company E, carrying one of the regiment's flags, was wounded at Williamsburg on May 5, 1862.[9] Private George K. Stoud of Company C was bearer from December 1862 through July 1863.[10] Private Gideon Mellin of Company H, filling in for a sick bearer, carried one of the flags during the June 18, 1864, attack on Petersburg. Mellin, a nineteen-year-old Danville printer who enlisted in February 1864, thought it a great honor that he had been chosen to carry the flag. Mellin came through the charge unscathed, although he recounted that the banner was pierced by a piece of shell and several bullets.[11]

Sergeant William Risser of Company C was wounded at Winchester on September 19, 1864.[12] Finally, the 1914 register of bearers for the parade lists Private George Imboden of Company A as a bearer until he was wounded at Cedar Creek, the wound resulting in the amputation of his left arm.

Notes

1 William H. Egle, *History of the Counties of Dauphin and Lebanon in the Commonwealth of Pennsylvania* (Philadelphia: Everts & Peck, 1883), p. 78 (Lebanon County section).
2 "From the Ninety-third Regiment," *Lebanon Courier*, October 20, 1864.
3 Receipt from Lieutenant F. T. Bennett, June 30, 1865, Eckman Papers.
4 "Flag Presentation," *Lebanon Courier*, November 7, 1861.
5 Mark, p. 170.
6 *Lebanon Courier*, January 7, 1864; Mark, pp. 239, 322.
7 *Lebanon Courier*, January 7, 1864.
8 *Danville Intelligencer*, November 1, 1861; Regimental Circular, June 27, 1865, Eckman Papers.
9 *Harrisburg Daily Telegraph*, May 30, 1862.
10 Clothing Account for George K. Stoud, Eckman Papers.
11 Mellin to sister, July 4, 1864, Mellin Letters.
12 *Lebanon Advertiser*, October 19, 1864.

Bibliography

Eckman, Charles W. Papers. Robert T. Lyon, Muncy, Pa.
Euston, Edward C. "The 93rd Pa. Vols. at Williamsburg." *NT*, January 24, 1884.
Fernsler, Leonard. "An Incident at Gettysburg." *NT*, December 7, 1905.
____. "Those Singing Girls Again." *NT*, August 16, 1906. (Gettysburg)
Fox, Solomon. Papers. Pennsylvania State Archives.
Gruber, David A. Company K Papers. USAMHI.
Laubaugh, Frederick. Papers. Wyoming Historical & Geological Society.
Lyon, Robert T. *A Photographic Supplement of the Ninety-third Regiment Pennsylvania Volunteers*. Muncy, 1987.
Mark, Penrose G. "Keystone Veterans. The Ninety-third Pennsylvania in the Late War." *Philadelphia Weekly Times*, February 5, 1887.
____. *Red: White: and Blue Badge, Pennsylvania Veteran Volunteers, A History of the 93rd Regiment, Known as the "Lebanon Infantry" and "One of the 300 Fighting Regiments," from September 12th, 1861, to June 27th, 1865*. Harrisburg: Aughinbaugh Press, 1911.
Mellin, Gideon. 1864 Letters. USAMHI, Save the Flags Collection.
Nevin, John I. Papers. Historical Society of Western Pennsylvania.
"The 93rd Pennsylvania Again." *NT*, February 7, 1884. (Williamsburg)
Rogers Family. Letters, 1862, 1864. USAMHI, HbCWRT Collection.
Seibert, Jacob. Letters, 1862-1865. USAMHI, HbCWRT Collection.
Shaaber, Mahlen. "A New Lincoln Story." *NT*, June 18, 1908.
Shuey, Anson B. Letters, 1862-1864. USAMHI.
Uhler, George H. "Army Hardships." *NT*, September 12, 1889.
____. "The Sixth Corps at Chancellorsville." *NT*, November 28, 1901.
____. "The Wilderness." *NT*, May 21, 1891.
____. "With Sedgwick. At Fredericksburg During the Battle of Chancellorsville." *NT*, January 6, 1887.
United States Army Units. Papers. Duke University.
Zerbe, James E. "Battle of the Wilderness." *NT*, April 28, 1910.

95th Infantry

State Color

Organized in Philadelphia by Colonel John M. Gosline, the 95th was first designated the 45th, then the 54th, and finally, in February 1862 as the 95th Pennsylvania. Nicknamed "Gosline's Zouaves," the regiment was formed in the fall of 1861 and immediately went to Washington, where the men spent the winter of 1861-62 in drilling. Because of the initial confusion with the regimental number, a state color was not provided to the regiment until March 18, 1862, when Colonel Gosline acknowledged receipt of the color from the State Agency.[1]

The 95th joined the Army of the Potomac and moved to the Yorktown Peninsula in April 1862. After the Confederate evacuation of Yorktown, the 95th moved in pursuit and first engaged the enemy near West Point on May 7. As part of the new Sixth Corps, the 95th fought at Gaines' Mill on June 27, suffering heavy casualties in the fighting. Scarcely engaged during the remainder of the Seven Days' Battles, the regiment moved north and helped cover the retreat of the Union army from Second Manassas in late August. During the Maryland Campaign, the regiment fought at Crampton's Gap on South Mountain (September 14), and was marginally active at Antietam three days later. At Fredericksburg on December 13, the 95th lost four men wounded. After participating in Burnside's "Mud March" in January 1863, the regiment went into winter camp near White Oak Church.

During the Chancellorsville Campaign, the Sixth Corps remained near Fredericksburg, capturing the Confederate positions there on May 3, 1863. The troops moved on and engaged the enemy at Salem Church before retreating. In this campaign, the 95th sustained more than 150 casualties. The regiment arrived at Gettysburg late on July 2 and was used to bolster the left flank of the line. After taking part in the Bristoe Station and Mine Run campaigns (October-November), the depleted regiment erected winter quarters near Culpeper.

Over the winter, the regiment re-enlisted as veteran volunteers and entered the 1864 campaign greatly strengthened. The regiment fought in the Wilderness (May 5-7), at Spotsylvania (May 8-18), Cold Harbor, and in the initial attacks on Petersburg. Then,

View of State Color

State Color
Maker: HB
1985.158

the Sixth Corps was moved to Washington in time to assist in the city's defense against Jubal Early's Confederates. The corps moved into the Shenandoah Valley and was occupied with Early's men until returning to Petersburg in early December. In this campaign, the 95th fought at Fisher's Hill (September 22) and Cedar Creek (October 19). After returning to Petersburg, the regiment was engaged at Hatcher's Run (March 25, 1865), the capture of Petersburg (April 2), and Saylor's Creek (April 6). Following Lee's surrender, the regiment eventually returned to Washington, and was mustered out of service at Philadelphia on July 24. The remnant of the state color was returned in the 1866 ceremony.

Philadelphia Colors

During its term of service, the 95th received several colors from Philadelphia friends. On November 13, 1861, a deputation of citizens presented two colors to the regiment. Mrs. Mary Ann Gosline was the prime mover in obtaining these flags. The national color bore the number "54" in addition to the regimental nickname. The regimental color was apparently handsewn by Mrs. Gosline. Thirty-four white stars surround a crude representation of the American eagle. It is not known how long these flags were carried by the regiment. The national color was taken home in February 1864 and photographed at that time. Both colors were in the possession of Major Theodore H. McCalla in August 1865, when another officer thought they should be given to the Commonwealth. Apparently, the national color was obtained by the state sometime after August 1865; little remains other than an inscribed "E&H" on the finial base to ascertain its origin. The regimental color is owned by a private collector.[2]

National Color
Maker: EH
1985.157

1861 Presented Color Made by Mrs. Gosline

Regimental Color
1985.156

The Cooper Shop Refreshment Saloon presented a flag to the 95th on February 18, 1864. No further information about this flag has been located.[3]

There are three additional colors for the 95th. The regimental color in the state collection is fairly intact, with a blank red scroll. A second regimental color is in the GAR Museum, Philadelphia. The red scroll on this flag is blank. Finally, a small remnant of a national color obtained by the State Museum from the Union League of Philadelphia may be associated with the 95th, according to a fragmented cardboard tag attached to the staff of this color. With little documentation to rely on, identification of the histories of these colors is impossible.

Advance the Colors!

Color-Bearers

Names of several color-bearers have been located, but none can be matched with a particular flag. Sergeant William Byrnes carried one of the 95th's colors throughout most of the war and although thrice wounded, survived the conflict. Byrnes was first wounded at Gaines' Mill. Lieutenant-Colonel Gustavus W. Town, in his official report, specially mentioned Byrnes " . . . for intrepidity under adverse circumstances retaining his colors and his position under a galling fire which killed or wounded five out of seven [guards] immediately around—he himself having his clothing pierced by numerous bullets and receiving a painful wound in the arm." Byrnes was hit in a leg at Crampton's Pass and hit again in an arm at Cedar Creek.[4]

Sergeant George W. Ulmer of Company A was carrying one of the colors on May 12, 1864, when the regiment attacked Confederate entrenchments at Spotsylvania. The attackers made a temporary lodgement in the enemy line but were finally forced to yield. Ulmer somehow missed the word to retire, and remained lying down in a row of dead and wounded comrades, one of whom told Ulmer of the withdrawal. Although it was suicide to get up and run across over a hundred yards of clear terrain to reach the Union line, Ulmer felt he had no choice; he did not wish to lose the flag. Quickly he sprang to his feet and began running, zigzagging so none of the enemy could aim at him. Ulmer's sudden dash to the rear drew a storm of lead from the Rebels but miraculously he escaped unhurt to receive the gratitude of his comrades, who thought the flag had been captured.[5]

One of the last color-bearers was Albert J. Bannon of Company C. Bannon was promoted to the color-guard on October 22, 1864, and further promoted to sergeant on February 24, 1865. When the 95th assaulted the Petersburg defenses on April 2, 1865, Bannon rushed ahead with the colors and shouted encouragement for the men as they ran forward under a heavy musketry fire.[6] Finally, John B. Cooke was wounded at Saylor's Creek as he seized a flag after its bearer was shot down.[7]

Sergeant Albert J. Bannon's Color-Sergeant's Chevrons

Notes

1 Gosline to Colonel J. H. Puleston, March 18, 1862, Regimental Letter & Casualty Book, RG 94.

2 "Interesting Ceremony," *Philadelphia Inquirer*, November 20, 1861, has the date as November 13. Galloway, in *95th Pennsylvania*, p. 42, cites a diary account as occurring on November 11. See also John Harper to Major W. B. Lane, August 3, 1865, and Lane to Theodore H. McCalla, August 3, 1865, both in RG 25, for the fuss over the flags in McCalla's possession. The handwritten legend on the reverse of a carte-de-visite owned by Ronn Palm contains the photographic information cited in this paragraph.

3 "Flag Presentation," *Philadelphia Public Ledger*, February 19, 1864.

4 Lieutenant-Colonel Town's report, dated July 19, 1862, in Regimental Letter & Casualty Book, RG 94; Town's report of September 25, 1862, ibid.; Captain John Harper's report of October 21, 1864, ibid.

5 Robert W. Patrick, *Knapsack and Rifle* (Philadelphia: Calypso Publishing Company, 1887), pp. 333-43, contains Ulmer's account of Spotsylvania.

6 General Orders #1, October 22, 1864, in Company B Order Book, RG 94; Special Orders #13, February 24, 1865, in Company C Order Book, RG 94; *O.R.* 46.1, p. 939.

7 Cooke obituary in *NT*, February 9, 1939.

Bibliography

Byrnes, William. 1863 Diary. Duke University.

Galloway, George Norton. "At Spotsylvania." *Philadelphia Weekly Times*, January 15, 1881.

____. "Battle of Cedar Creek." *Grand Army Scout and Soldiers Mail*, January 5, 1884.

____. "Battle of Gaines' Mill." *Philadelphia Weekly Times*, February 15, 1885.

____. "Battle of the Wilderness." *Philadelphia Weekly Times*, February 16, 1884.

____. "Capture of the Salient." *Philadelphia Weekly Times*, November 18, 1882.

____. "Cool Arbor. The Part Taken by the Sixth Corps." *Grand Army Scout and Soldiers Mail*, April 26, May 3, 10, 17, 24, 31, 1884.

____. "From Cool Arbor to Petersburg." *Grand Army Scout and Soldiers Mail*, June 7, 14, 1884.

____. "From Petersburg to Washington." *Grand Army Scout and Soldiers Mail*, June 21, 28, July 5, 12, 1884.

____. "Getty's Hard Fight." *Philadelphia Weekly Times*, October 15, 1881.

____. "Hand-to-Hand Fighting at Spotsylvania." *Battles and Leaders* 4:170-74.

____. "Mine Run." *Grand Army Scout and Soldiers Mail*, July 26, August 2, 9, 16, 1884.

____. *The Ninety-fifth Pennsylvania Volunteers ("Gosline's Pennsylvania Zouaves") in the Sixth Corps, and Historical Paper, by G. Norton Galloway (Late Co. "A," 95th P.V.), Read by Charles Snyder, at a Reunion of the Surviving Members of the 95th Pennsylvania Volunteers,*

Held at Germantown, Pa., on the 12th October, 1883, ... Philadelphia: Collins, Printer, 1884.

____. "Storming of Marye's Heights." *Grand Army Scout and Soldiers Mail,* March 29, 1884.

____. "Through the Wilderness." *Philadelphia Weekly Times,* January 8, 1881.

____. "Under the Apple Tree at Appomattox." *Grand Army Scout and Soldiers Mail,* July 19, 1884.

Reed, George E. *Campaign of the Sixth Army Corps, Summer of 1863.* Philadelphia: McLaughlin Brothers, printers, 1864. (poem)

Shaw, J. "Battle of Gaines' Mill." *NT,* February 26, 1891.

____. "Crampton's Gap." *NT,* October 1, 1891.

____. "Salem Church." *NT,* May 7, 1896.

____. "Our Surprise Party." *NT,* June 11, 1896. (Fredericksburg, April 1863)

Treichler, James M. "End of the Battle. Charge of a Brigade of the Sixth Corps At Gettysburg." *NT,* May 4, 1916.

96th Infantry

State Color

The 96th Infantry was composed almost solely of soldiers recruited in Schuylkill County. It was organized in camp near Pottsville by late September 1861. The command remained in camp, drilling, until early November. Governor Curtin and staff arrived in Pottsville and presented a state color to the 96th on November 6.[1] Two days later, the regiment moved to Washington where it wintered.

After taking part in the advance to Manassas, the regiment moved by water to the Yorktown Peninsula. The 96th first engaged the enemy at West Point (May 7) as the Confederate army retreated toward Richmond. Although present on the field, the regiment sustained no loss. Later that month, the regiment was assigned to the Sixth Corps when that organization was formed. As part of the First Division, Sixth Corps, the 96th took part in the Seven Days' Battles, being engaged primarily at Gaines' Mill on June 27. It was also present at Glendale (June 30) and Malvern Hill (July 1), but lost few men. The corps moved to Alexandria in late August, arriving in time to help reinforce the defeated troops falling back from the Second Battle of Manassas.

During the ensuing Maryland Campaign, the 96th fought at Crampton's Pass (South Mountain) on September 14, suffering 91 casualties. Three days later, the regiment was present at Antietam, but was held in reserve and lost only two soldiers. During the Battle of Fredericksburg on December 13, the 96th was actively engaged as skirmishers, having one man wounded. The regiment took part in Burnside's abortive "Mud March" in January 1863, then went into camp near White Oak Church.

The Sixth Corps was engaged at Fredericksburg again during the Chancellorsville Campaign of April-May 1863. After recrossing the Rappahannock River, the corps attacked the thinly-held Confederate positions on May 3, then moved forward toward Chancellorsville, only to be repulsed at Salem Church. The 96th lost 79 officers and men during this fighting. When fighting erupted at Gettysburg on July 1, the Sixth Corps was more than thirty-two miles away at

State Color
Maker: EH
1985.159

Manchester, Maryland. When word reached the corps about the battle, Major-General John Sedgwick marched his 15,000 soldiers non-stop to reach the battlefield on the afternoon of July 2. The brigade to which the 96th was attached was thrown forward to bolster the line just north of Little Round Top. The mere appearance of fresh troops, no matter how tired they were, was a deterrence to a further enemy advance. Thereafter, the 96th participated in the return to Virginia, taking part in the Bristoe Station and Mine Run campaigns (October-November) before taking up winter quarters along the Hazel River.

At this point, the history of the state color becomes hazy. On February 22, 1864, it was sent to Pottsville for safekeeping. No documentation has been found to indicate when it was returned (if at all) to the regiment. During the 1864 campaign, the 96th fought in the Wilderness (May 5-7), at Spotsylvania (where, on May 10, it participated in Colonel Emory Upton's bloody assault on the Confederate entrenchments, suffering more than 170 casualties), Cold Harbor (June 1-3), and in the initial operations around Petersburg. In mid-July, the corps was sent north to protect Washington from a threatened Confederate attack. Although present on the battlefield at Winchester (September 19), the 96th suffered no loss. Three days later, its term of service over, those who had not re-enlisted were sent back to Pennsylvania for mustering out. The veterans who remained were consolidated into a battalion which was later attached to the 95th Pennsylvania. It is unknown when the state flag was returned to state care. It does not appear on any of the lists for the 1866 ceremony, but does appear on the list of flags returned by 1866.

Regimental Color

There is no surviving evidence to indicate the source of this blue regimental color. It was kept by the surviving 96th veterans and presented to the Historical Society of Schuylkill County on December 14, 1913. Later that month, Adjutant-General Stewart requested that this color be given to the Commonwealth for preservation. The veterans assented, and on January 28, 1914, Stewart acknowledged receipt of the "Blue Standard or State Flag" of the 96th Infantry, to be placed beside the "National Standard" presented by Governor Curtin. Stewart's terminology is mysterious, as the surviving pieces of this regimental color clearly indicate that the banner is a blue infantry regimental painted with the national eagle, not the state arms. It was included in the 1914 ceremony.[2]

National Color Presented to 25th Infantry and Used by 96th Infantry
S1984.009

1863 Presented Regimental Color
S1984.010

Regimental Color
1985.160

Pottsville Flags

The 96th Infantry received two flags from admirers in Schuylkill County. On May 25, 1861, Colonel John W. Forney presented a national color to the 25th Infantry on behalf of Pottsville resident Joseph W. Cake. This 34-star national color was subsequently carried by the 96th Infantry through at least September 1862, since Henry C. Boyer wrote that the regiment carried it through the fighting at Crampton's Pass.[3]

On June 11, 1863, a deputation of Pottsville residents presented a regimental color to the 96th on behalf of a group of Pottsville ladies. This regimental color was painted with the state arms on the obverse and the national arms on the reverse. Each was surrounded with the names of the engagements in which the 96th had fought. Together with the state color, this local presentation was sent back to Pottsville on February 22, 1864. Surgeon D. Webster Bland explained that "the massive fringe has already been torn from the silk, the splendid paintings and the historic scroll are separating from the blue field. We cannot but feel, from the value of its association, that it should be placed in safe keeping." There seems to be no surviving evidence to indicate if the flag was carried in any of the 1864 battles. Both this banner and the national color were presented to the Historical Society of Schuylkill County in 1913 and donated to the Capitol Preservation Committee in 1984.[4]

Color-Bearers

Names of several flag-bearers have found, but none can be matched to a particular flag of the four carried by the 96th. Five men were struck down while carrying the state and national colors at Crampton's Pass. Sergeants Solomon McMinzie (Company C) and Charles B. Ziegler (Company H) were both killed. Sergeant Joseph S. Johnson (Company H) and Corporals William Ortner (Company H) and Thomas Oliver (Company C) were each wounded.[5] Zeigler and Ortner apparently carried the same flag. When Ortner fell with a thigh wound, Private Harry H. Hunsicker seized the flag and carried it throughout the rest of the fighting that day.[6] Sergeant J. W. Conrad was wounded at Spotsylvania on May 9, 1864. The very next day, Sergeant George W. Foltz was also wounded while carrying one of the colors.[7] Finally, Sergeant

Corporal George W. Foltz

Ezra Hendley's name appeared in a casualty list in the *Pottsville Miners' Journal* of May 21, 1864. The sergeant received a thigh wound sometime prior to that date; Bates has no such information with Hendley's name.[8]

Notes

1 Wallace, *Schuylkill County*, pp. 108-112.

2 Stewart to Baird Halberstadt, December 19, 1913; Halberstadt to Stewart, December 29, 1913; Stewart to Halberstadt, January 28, 1914, all in RG 25.

3 "Military," *Pottsville Miners' Journal*, October 19, 1861; H. C. Boyer, "An Affair at Crampton's Pass," *Philadelphia Weekly Press*, August 18, 1886.

4 Wallace, *Schuylkill County*, pp. 493-96.

5 *O.R.* 19.1, pp. 395-96; Wallace, *Schuylkill County*, p. 199.

6 Letter from Henry Royer in *Norristown Herald*, September 23, 1862.

7 "Proceedings and Speeches Made at the Transfer of Battle Flags to the Historical Society of Schuylkill County, December 14, 1913," *Publications of the Historical Society of Schuylkill County* 5 (1932): 19, 21. Foltz's obituary in a Pottsville paper of December 29, 1918, mentioned that he was appointed color-sergeant on March 24, 1864, and wounded on May 5.

8 "Casualties in Other Regiments," *Pottsville Miners' Journal*, May 21, 1864.

Bibliography

Boland, Francis. Letters. Historical Society of Schuylkill County, Copies in USAMHI.

Boyer, Henry C. "An Affair at Crampton's Pass." *Philadelphia Weekly Press*, August 18, 1886.

Boyle, John T. "An Outline Sketch of the Ninety-sixth Pennsylvania Volunteers." *Philadelphia Weekly Times*, July 17, 1886.

Delaney, James. "At Petersburg." *NT*, April 16, 1891.

Faust, Daniel. Letters, September 1862-1864. USAMHI, HbCWRT Collection.

Filbert, Peter A. Diary, through December 1862. USAMHI, HbCWRT Collection.

Haas, Jacob W. Papers. USAMHI, HbCWRT Collection.

Henry, Edward. Letters, November 1861-June 1864. USAMHI.

Keiser, Henry. Diary. USAMHI, HbCWRT Collection.

Luckenbill, Lewis. Diaries, 1861-65. USAMHI

McGlenn, Patrick. Letters. Historical Society of Schuylkill County, copies in USAMHI.

Martin, Lewis J. Letters. University of Michigan.

Oestreich, Maurus. *Diary of Maurus Oestreich*. Translated from the German by Rev. William Hammeke, edited and printed by Rev. Emil C. Oestreich. Philadelphia, 1966. Copies in War Library & Museum, USAMHI, plus other libraries.

Potts, Clement D. Letters, September 1861-November 1862. USAMHI, HbCWRT Collection.

Richards, M. Edgar. Letters 1854-March 7, 1864. USAMHI, CWMisc Collection.

Severn, Isaac. 1864 Diary. USAMHI.

Ward, David A. "Amidst a Tempest of Shot and Shell: A History of the Ninety-sixth Pennsylvania Volunteers." M. A. Thesis, Southern Connecticut State University, 1988.

97th Infantry

First State Color

Organized at Camp Wayne near West Chester, the ten companies of the 97th Infantry were recruited in Chester and Delaware counties during the late summer of 1861. The regiment received a state color on November 4, when Governor Curtin and several members of his staff went by rail to Camp Wayne to present the flag. Sergeant John D. Beaver of Company C was the regiment's original color-bearer.[1]

Shortly thereafter, the regiment moved to Washington, then to Fort Monroe. From this point, the 97th was transported south to Port Royal, South Carolina, to serve as part of the garrison at that Federal post. The regiment was present but not engaged during the bombardment and capture of Fort Pulaski, Georgia. From here, the 97th went south to occupy Fernandina, Florida, in early March 1862. The regiment remained here until June, when it became part of an expedition operating against Charleston, South Carolina. It participated in some minor skirmishes but was not seriously engaged during this abortive operation. By July, the 97th was part of the Hilton Head garrison for a short time. Then, the unit again operated against Charleston from April to late September 1863, a time when disease was more deadly than enemy bullets.

In early October, the regiment was back at Fernandina, where it stayed until early April 1864, when it was transferred to Virginia as part of the Tenth Corps, Army of the James. It thus took part in General Butler's Bermuda Hundred Campaign, fighting at Drewry's Bluff (May 16), Foster's Place (May 18), and Green Plains (May 20). The regiment suffered more than two hundred casualties in this heavy fighting. Sergeant Samuel M. McBride was appointed color-bearer on May 19. He was wounded in the regiment's charge the next day, when six bearers were shot down in succession and the flag was riddled by more than a hundred bullets, a few of which broke the staff.

In the confusion of this day, Sergeant John A. Russell seized the flag but was quickly wounded. Russell handed the banner to Captain George Lemaistre, who was soon felled by a piece of shell. Finally, the sole survivor of the color-guard, Corporal Thomas Forsythe, though wounded himself, bore the flag to the rear as the shattered regiment fell back.[2]

The regiment moved north across the James River to fight at Cold Harbor, then returned to take part in the siege operations around Petersburg. Its engagements included the initial attack on the city (June 15-16), Cemetery Hill (June 30), the Crater (July 30), and the operations at Deep Bottom (August 13-20). This latter combat was the last active service for the tattered remnant of the original state color, reduced to less than half its original fabric by the hard service it saw in 1864. When Major Isaiah Price went north with a detachment to recruit for the 97th, he took the old flag along with him. It was left with the 97th's first colonel, Henry R. Guss, who allowed the Chester County Fair to display the banner that October. Guss retained the flag until the July 4, 1866, ceremony, when it was officially returned to the Commonwealth.[3]

Second State Color

On June 21, 1864, Adjutant H. W. Carruthers wrote to Colonel Samuel B. Thomas to request a replacement

First State Color
Maker: EH
1985.162

Second State color
Maker: HB
1985.161

state color. The lieutenant noted that the original flag was "so tattered and worn that it can scarcely be unfurled." The new flag was forwarded to the State Agency and arrived at the 97th's headquarters on September 1, 1864. Corporal Forsythe, who remained color-bearer since the May 20 battle, continued as bearer with the new banner.[4]

The new flag was first involved in battle during the assault on Fort Gilmer (September 29), where the regiment was repulsed with scant loss. By this time, Corporal Forsythe seems to have been relieved of duty as color-bearer and replaced by Sergeant William McCarty of Company D, who was cited for gallantry in the September 29 attack.[5] The regiment's next engagement occurred on October 27-28 during the fighting along the Darbytown Road.

In January 1865, the 97th, now a part of the Twenty-fourth Corps, was included as part of the expedition sent to capture Fort Fisher, the main bastion protecting Wilmington, North Carolina. After a prolonged naval bombardment, the army troops landed and assaulted the sand parapets on January 15. Colonel Galusha Pennypacker, all of twenty years of age, led the 97th forward. As the column reached the fort, Sergeant McCarty was hit in the knee and forced to

Sergeant James McCarty and the Second State Color

drop the flag. Colonel Pennypacker seized the banner and led his men forward. Just as the young colonel placed the flag on the third interior traverse of the fort, he was badly wounded in the right side and hip. Pennypacker refused to be carried off to a hospital until he was able to inform General Alfred H. Terry, the expedition commander, that his regimental flag was the first planted on Fort Fisher. Expected to die, Penny-

Colonel Galusha Pennypacker

97th Infantry

packer clung to life and survived the war. For his gallantry that day, the colonel was awarded a Medal of Honor in 1891. The state color was badly damaged in the assault; it was pierced by 107 bullets and and a canister shot.[6]

After the capture of Fort Fisher, the 97th marched north to occupy Wilmington, then moved on to Raleigh. Remaining here until July 10, the regiment then garrisoned other towns in the Old North State until mustered out of service on August 28. The state color was left in Philadelphia and returned to state care in 1866. Colonel Guss had a small blue banner, emblazoned with battle honors, made for each state color in time for the 1866 parade.[7]

Notes

1 *West Chester Village Record*, November 16, 1861; Price, pp. 78-83.
2 Price, pp. 278-280; "The Colors of the 97th Pa.," *NT*, February 19, 1914; Special Orders #21, May 19, 1864, Regimental Order Book, RG 94.
3 Price, p. 327; Colonel John Wainwright to Adjutant-General A. L. Russell, May 31, 1866, RG 19.
4 Adjutant Carruthers to Colonel Thomas, June 21, 1864, Regimental Letter & Endorsement Book, RG 94; Price, p. 321.

5 "Gallantry of Pa. Soldiers," *Philadelphia Inquirer*, October 26, 1864.
6 Price, pp. 355-356; caption with photograph of Sergeant McCarty and state colors, Chester County Historical Society.
7 Colonel Guss to Major William B. Lane, November 17, 1865, with attachment of May 20, 1866, RG 19; Colonel Wainwright to Adjutant-General Russell, May 31, 1866, RG 19; and Colonel Guss to Russell, June 11, 1866, RG 19.

Bibliography

Brosius, Marriott. "The Siege and Capture of Fort Wayne [Wagner]." *Philadelphia Weekly Press*, May 5, 1886.
"Col. Wainwright and the 97th Pa." *NT*, August 6, 1908.
Fisher, Leonard R. *Story of Fort Fisher*. Ocean City, NJ, 1915.
Garry, Co. C. "In Front of Petersburg." *NT*, September 3, 1885.
Goodwin, John S. Papers. Pennsylvania State Archives.
Guest, John. Letters. January 2, 1863-July 24, 1864. USAMHI.
Guss, Henry R. Letters. Chester County Historical Society.
Harper, Douglas. 5-part regimental history. *West Chester Daily Local News*, August 24-28, 1987.
Pennypacker, Galusha. Letters. Chester County Historical Society.
Price, Isaiah. *History of the Ninety-seventh Regiment Pennsylvania Volunteer Infantry During the War of the Rebellion, 1861-65.* . . . Philadelphia: B. & P., Printers, 1875.

Bibliography

____. "The 97th Regiment Penna. Vols. at Fort Fisher." *Philadelphia Weekly Press*, March 10, 1886.
____. *Reunion of the Ninety-seventh Regiment Pennsylvania Volunteers, October 29th, 1884, "on the Old Camp Ground," at Camp Wayne, West Chester, Pa.*. Philadelphia: Press of Donaldson & Mcgrath, 1884.
Sullivan, Ezra. "The Colors of the 97th Pa." *NT*, February 19, 1914.
Thomas, L. R. "The Capture of Fort Fisher." *NT*, October 30, November 6, 1913.
____. "The 97th Pa. at Fort Fisher." *NT*, September 4, 1913.
Wainwright, John. "The 97th Pa." *NT*, March 2, 1905.
Wayne Family Papers. University of Michigan.

98th Infantry

First State Color

Recruited in Philadelphia in August and September 1861, the 98th Infantry was composed largely of Philadelphians of German ancestry. Many of its soldiers had served previously in the 21st Pennsylvania, a three-month regiment. The 98th moved to Washington in late September, remaining in camp near the city throughout the winter. The initial state color was completed by Horstmann Brothers on December 9 and forwarded to the State Agency for presentation to the regiment.

In late March 1862, the 98th, a part of the Fourth Corps, Army of the Potomac, moved to the Peninsula as McClellan began his advance on Richmond. After taking part in the Siege of Yorktown, the 98th pursued the retreating Confederate troops, fighting at Williamsburg on May 5. The regiment was then detached from its brigade and sent as support for the cavalry advance of the army. The unit moved forward and occupied Mechanicsville and Hanover Junction. After rejoining the corps in late June, the 98th took a minor part in the Seven Days' Battles as the army retreated to Malvern Hill. Here, on July 1, the 98th was actively engaged when the Confederate army attacked McClellan's troops.

The division to which the 98th was attached was sent north to Washington when the main body of the army moved north to reinforce Pope's Army of Virginia in August. Arriving too late to fight at Second Manassas, the division then joined the army for the Maryland Campaign, but was not engaged at Antietam. Thereafter, the division was attached to the Sixth Corps. The regiment was not engaged during the defeat at Fredericksburg (December 13), then went into winter quarters near Falmouth. During the Chancellorsville Campaign, the 98th fought at Fredericksburg and Salem Church (May 3-4, 1863), then marched north and arrived at Gettysburg late on July 2. After returning to Virginia, the 98th took part in the Bristoe Station and Mine Run campaigns before going into the winter camp near Brandy Station.

In December, the brigade moved to Harper's Ferry from whence the regiment returned to Pennsylvania for a furlough in February 1864. The original state color was left in Harrisburg, Colonel John F. Ballier having requested a replacement in September 1863. Ballier noted that the flag was worn out from constant use. At Salem Church, more than thirty bullets and a piece of shell perforated the silk. Ballier, concerned that the "least breath of wind would threaten to annihilate" the flag, thus asked for a new color.[1] Before leaving the flag in state hands, the regiment had the names of its battles inscribed on the worn silk.[2] It was returned to the state in 1866.

First State Color
Maker: HB
1985.163

Second State Color

A replacement color was forwarded to the State Agency in December 1863, and may not have been given to the 98th until the men returned to Virginia in March 1864. During the ensuing 1864 campaign, the regiment fought in the Wilderness, at Spotsylvania, Cold Harbor, and in the initial attacks on Petersburg. In July, the Sixth Corps was sent to Washington to help counter an enemy threat to the city. As part of Major-General Philip Sheridan's command, the 98th then

Second State Color
Maker: HB
1985.164

participated in the Shenandoah Valley Campaign. It fought at Winchester (September 19), Fisher's Hill (September 22), and Cedar Creek (October 19) before the corps returned to Petersburg in December 1864.

During the initial stage of the Valley campaign, Corporal John V. Koch of Company I carried the state color.[3] He was replaced as bearer by Sergeant John Hirschling of Company I on September 26. Hirschling was still bearer when the Southern army attacked Sheridan's men at Cedar Creek. During the fighting, a bullet struck the flagstaff, sending splinters flying. One sharp piece of wood struck Hirschling's right wrist and opened a gash four inches long. The painful injury caused Hirschling to drop the banner, but Sergeant Jacob A. Schmid of Company A quickly seized the color and carried it briefly until Hirschling returned to duty.[4]

After returning to Petersburg, the regiment occupied a section of the trenches for two months, then took part in the April 2, 1865, attack on Petersburg. It then fought at Saylor's Creek on April 6. Following Lee's surrender, the regiment marched south to Danville, Virginia, and went into camp here for a time before returning to Washington. Sergeant Hirschling was relieved as color-bearer on May 1, 1865, his place taken by Sergeant Jacob Herrman of Company C.[5] The 98th was mustered out of service on June 29. The second state color was left in Philadelphia and returned to the state in 1866.

Notes

1 Ballier to Governor Curtin, September 7, 1863, RG 25.
2 Bates 3: 469.
3 Company I Morning Report Book, RG 94.
4 Ibid.; Jacob Hirschling service record, RG 94; Jacob A. Schmid, "Personal Military and Civil History, with Historic Reference," privately published booklet in possession of Harold McElroy, Allentown.

5 Regimental Orders #15, May 1, 1865, Regimental Letter and Order Book, RG 94. However, Company I's morning Report Book lists Corporal Henry Schlacter as detailed for bearer on May 2, 1865. Perhaps the regiment had acquired a second flag that has not survived.

Bibliography

Bramish, A. B. "Battle of Fort Stevens." *Grand Army Scout and Soldiers Mail*, July 10, 1886.
Evan, Charles F. "98th Regiment of Pennsylvania Volunteers." *Grand Army Scout and Soldiers Mail*, May 15, 22, 1886.

Loeble, J. Frederick. "No Doubt of Their Presence. A Veteran of the Sixth Corps has Painful Memories of July 11, 1864." *NT,* April 26, 1900.
Teller, H. R. "Mary Sharpless." *NT,* July 13, 1911. (nurse)

99th Infantry

State Color

Nicknamed the "Lincoln Legion," the 99th Pennsylvania was recruited primarily in Philadelphia, with strong contingents from Lancaster County in several companies. The first three companies of the new unit were dispatched to Washington in August 1861, and by February 1862 the regiment was complete. On behalf of Governor Curtin, Congressman Hendrick B. Wright presented a state color to the 99th on January 5, 1862.[1] Ten days later, Sergeant Samuel Hutton of Company K was appointed the regiment's first official color-bearer.[2] Thereafter, the unit remained in the defenses of Washington until late June 1862.

At this time, the 99th was sent to join the Army of the Potomac at Harrison's Landing, Virginia. Upon reaching the army on July 4, the 99th was assigned to the Second Brigade, First Division, Third Corps. While in camp here, Harvey M. Munsell was promoted to color-sergeant on August 8.[3] Munsell, a Steuben County, New York, native, was managing an uncle's lumber yard in Oil City when war broke out in the spring of 1861. The patriotic Munsell decided to enlist and eventually made his way to Philadelphia, where he joined the 99th in July 1861. The eighteen-year-old recruit was perceived as one of the "youngest, smallest, scrawniest-looking" privates in the regiment. However, by hard work and dedication, Munsell was promoted first to corporal, then to sergeant.[4]

In mid-August, units of the Army of the Potomac were sent north to reinforce General Pope. The Third Corps arrived in time to fight at Second Manassas (August 29-30) and Chantilly (September 1), the 99th suffering comparatively few casualties. Its next engagement was at Fredericksburg on December 13, Here, the division supported several batteries of artillery which were threatened by a Confederate countercharge as the defeated Pennsylvania Reserves fell back. As the enemy closed in on the 99th, Munsell suddenly got the urge to run forward with the colors, forcing the regiment to advance with him to save the flag. Other regiments also moved forward and the enemy was repulsed.[5]

After spending the winter in camp, the 99th took part in the Chancellorsville Campaign, fighting on May 2-3, 1863. Munsell continued to carry the battered state color. In honor of his bravery in this battle, Munsell received the coveted "Kearny Cross," a medal devised earlier by General Phil Kearny to honor the gallantry of selected soldiers in his command.[6]

At Gettysburg on July 2, the 99th occupied the left flank of the Third Corps battleline above the Devil's Den. The regiment maintained its position against heavy odds until ordered to retire late that afternoon. During the fighting, the entire color-guard was killed

State Color
Maker: HB

99th Infantry

or wounded and Munsell's clothing was pierced by eleven bullets. When the regiment fell back, Munsell did not hear the order at first and was one of the last to begin retreating. As he did, an artillery shell hit the ground near his feet and burst, tearing a small hole in the earth. Stunned by the concussion, Munsell pitched forward into the hole, falling on top of the silk banner. Afraid to move because he thought the Rebels would capture him, Munsell played possum until reinforcements came up and drove the enemy back. He then jumped up and ran to the rear, found the regiment, and quietly reported for duty amid the cheers of his comrades, who had suffered 110 casualties.[7]

After taking part in the Bristoe Station and Mine Run campaigns (October-November), the regiment went into winter camp near Brandy Station. Most of the regiment re-enlisted and went home on furlough in February 1864. While in Philadelphia, Munsell was approached one day by some of the officers, who wanted him to accompany them to "a little entertainment." Munsell arrived at the hotel and was disappointed at not finding any ladies there. However, much to his surprise, Colonel Asher S. Leidy, on behalf of the officers of the 99th, presented the courageous sergeant with a national color as a testimonial of his bravery. The flag contained the names of the engagements through which Munsell had been colorbearer. Its present disposition is unknown.[8]

Once home on furlough, Munsell developed a presentiment that he would be killed in the next battle he carried the flag. Munsell earlier had requested Governor Curtin to appoint him lieutenant to fill a vacancy in the regiment, and he again renewed his request. He even attended the Free Military School in Philadelphia and passed a test that would allow him to accept a commission in a black regiment should the opportunity arise. Munsell wished to remain with his comrades, and even managed to see Secretary of War Edwin Stanton about being promoted. He took along his national color and impressed Stanton so much that the Secretary promised to help him obtain a commission. Munsell rejoined to the 99th in June 1864 as lieutenant, and was captured at Deep Bottom in late July. After being exchanged, he returned to the 99th in May 1865, to find he had been promoted to captain of Company C. Munsell received a Medal of Honor in 1866 for gallantry during the war.[9]

Once the 99th rejoined the Army of the Potomac in March 1864, it was assigned to the Second Corps when the Third was broken up. The strengthened regiment fought in the Wilderness (May 5-6), Spotsylvania (May 8-18), North Anna River (May 23-26), Cold Harbor (June 2-3), and in the initial attack on Petersburg. Thereafter, the 99th engaged enemy troops at

National Color Presented to Sergeant Munsell

National Color Presented by William S. Cobb
1985.165

Deep Bottom (July 27-29 and August 13-20), Poplar Spring Church (October 1-2), Boydton Plank Road (October 27-28), as well as numerous smaller skirmishes during the siege operations around Petersburg. After taking part in the Appomattox Campaign, the regiment marched in the Grand Review, then returned to Philadelphia for mustering out on July 1, 1865. Colonel Edwin R. Biles kept the state color, and although instructed to bring it to Philadelphia on July 4, 1866, failed to do so. Its subsequent fate is unknown.[10]

Philadelphia Colors

Friends of the regiment presented two colors to the 99th in March 1864. On March 17, William S. Cobb presented a national color, described as a "splendid silk flag."[11] A few days later, Daniel Dougherty represented a group of donors who presented a "beautiful state flag" to the veterans of the 99th.[12] The use of these flags by the 99th in the last year of the war remains undocumented. The Cobb flag was given to the state and Dougherty color has disappeared.

Color-Bearer

On June 1, 1865, Sergeant Amos Casey of Company K was appointed bearer of one of the regiment's flags.[13]

Notes

1 "From Col. Sweeney's Regiment," *Philadelphia Inquirer*, January 11, 1862; "Flag Presentations to Penna. Troops," *Philadelphia Press*, January 6, 1862.

2 Special Orders #12, January 5, 1862, Regimental Order Book, RG 94.

3 Munsell to Governor Curtin, January 9, 1863, Regimental Correspondence, RG 19.

4 Munsell, "With the Colors," pp. 163-67.

5 *Ibid.*, pp. 174-77.

6 *Ibid.*, pp. 178-82.

7 *Ibid.*, pp. 183-90.

8 *Ibid.*, pp. 195-97; "Flag Presentation," *Philadelphia Daily Evening Bulletin*, February 25, 1864; "Flag Presentation," *Philadelphia Public Ledger*, February 26, 1864.

9 Munsell, "With the Colors," pp. 197-208; Munsell to Curtin, January 9, 1863; Munsell to William Burgwyn, April 23, 1864; Munsell to A. L. Russell, June 22, 1864, all in Regimental Correspondence, RG 19.

10 Biles to A. L. Russell, June 5, 1866, Adjutant-General's Correspondence, RG 19. The GAR Museum in Philadelphia has custody of the remnant of a national color of the 99th Pennsylvania. Not enough remains to positively identify which color this flag might be.

11 "Flag Presentation," *Philadelphia Inquirer*, March 17, 1864.

12 "Flag Presentation," *Philadelphia Inquirer*, March 24, 1864, gives the presentation date as March 21. Both "Flag Presentation," *Philadelphia Public Ledger*, March 23, 1864, and "Presentation of the Flag to the 99th Regiment, P.V.," *Philadelphia Daily Evening Bulletin*, March 23, 1864, give March 22 as the date.

13 Orders #14, June 1, 1864, Regimental Order Book, RG 94.

Bibliography

Ayars, Peter B. "The Capture of the Rebel Pickets in Front of Fort Hell." *NT*, December 11, 1884.

____, and Bradley, Thomas W. "At Gettysburg," *NT*, February 4, 1886.

Graham, W. H. "Arrived Too Late With His Recruits." *NT*, December 17, 1914.

Hanft, John D. (editor). "Letters from a Civil War Soldier." *Tredyffrin-Easttown Historical Club Quarterly* 11 (October 1961): 72-87. (Benjamin F. Kirk)

Hauser, C. B. "Who Killed Jackson? This Correspondent Thinks It was the 99th Pa." *NT*, April 21, 1904.

Kappler, Jacob C. Letters, 1861-62. Historical Society of Pennsylvania.

Munsell, Harvey M. "With the Colors in War Time." In Theophilus F. Rodenbough, *The Bravest Five Hundred of '61*, pp. 163-208. New York: G. W. Dillingham, Publisher, 1891.

Swope, Milton. "The 20th Indiana and 99th Pennsylvania at Gettysburg." *Grand Army Scout and Soldiers Mail*, September 20, 1884.

100th Infantry

First State Color

Nicknamed the "Roundheads" because most of its men were descended from English and Scotch-Irish settlers of southwestern Pennsylvania, the 100th Infantry was organized at New Castle in late August 1861. The new regiment moved to Washington, then went on to Annapolis, where it joined Brigadier-General Thomas W. Sherman's expedition, which sailed south to attack and occupy Port Royal Sound, South Carolina, in November. Here, the 100th occupied Beaufort until June 1862, when it joined an attack on the defenses of Charleston, highlighted by the repulse at Secessionville on June 16. The regiment returned to Hilton Head where it remained until sent north to Newport News, Virginia, in late July, as part of the reinforcements for the Army of the Potomac. While in camp at this location, the state color finished by Horstmann Brothers in December 1861 finally reached the regiment. Brigadier-General Isaac I. Stevens officially presented the flag to the 100th on July 29.[1]

The regiment moved to Aquia Creek in early August in time to participate in the campaign that culminated in the Second Battle of Manassas (August 29-30). As part of the Ninth Corps, the 100th Pennsylvania skirmished at Raccoon Ford on the Rapidan River (August 13-19) before entering the major battle of the campaign. Following the retreat from Manassas, the depleted regiment fought at Chantilly on September 1, suffering a loss of 140 men for the two engagements. During the ensuing Maryland Campaign, the 100th engaged the enemy at South Mountain, where Corporals Richard P. Craven (Company K) and Richard Porter (Company B) both were wounded while carrying the state color.[2] Three days later, the regiment was actively deployed as skirmishers at Antietam and suffered few casualties. In the final battle of 1862, at Fredericksburg on December 13, the regiment was held in reserve but did cover the retreat of the army across the Rappahannock.

In early 1863, most of the Ninth Corps was transferred to the Department of the Ohio, the 100th reaching Lexington, Kentucky, on March 28. The regiment

First State Color
Maker: HB
1985.180

subsequently moved south to Middleburg and Columbia on garrison duty. In June, the 100th was part of the reinforcements sent to Vicksburg, Mississippi, to reinforce General Grant's troops besieging that fortified Southern city. After the July 4 surrender of the garrison, the 100th took part in the capture of Jackson, Mississippi. The regiment then went back to Kentucky. From here, the regiment marched to Knoxville in late September. It fought briefly at Campbell's Station (November 16) before Burnside's command retreated into the city's defenses. Confederate General James Longstreet besieged the city from November 17 to December 4, when his troops retreated into Virginia. The 100th remained near Knoxville until early January 1864, when most of the men re-enlisted and were granted a furlough. To reach home, the regiment had to undergo a mid-winter march over the Cumberland Mountains. The 100th arrived in Pittsburgh in February and went home on leave.

The regiment reassembled at Camp Copeland in early March, then moved to Annapolis to rejoin the Ninth Corps, which had been sent back to Virginia. As part of the corps, the regiment fought in the Wilderness (May 6-7), at Spotsylvania (May 9-18),

Cold Harbor (June 2), and in the first assaults on Petersburg (June 16-18), suffering losses of more than three hundred men.

During the fighting at the Crater on July 30, the 100th was heavily engaged and was one of the last units to leave the shelter of the hole to retreat to the Union lines when Confederate troops recaptured the position. The battered state color suffered extensive damage this day. A large portion of the silk—the top half of the canton and most of the five upper stripes, including the designation "100th Regt. P.V."—was shot away from the remainder of the flag. It fell into the loose dirt of the Crater and was later seized as a war trophy by Captain R. L. Kilby of the 16th Virginia. Meanwhile, when the bearer fell, Richard P. Craven, now a lieutenant in Company K, seized the remnant of the flag and handed it to Captain James L. McFeeters for safekeeping. Moments later, a shell burst nearby and killed the lieutenant. At some point in the action, the staff was broken into three pieces. When the remnant of the 100th scampered back to safety, Captain McFeeters carried back what little was left of the state color.[3]

Thereafter, the regiment fought at the Weldon Railroad (August 19) and at Poplar Spring Church (September 30). A replacement flag arrived in October and the treasured remnant of the first color was sent north for safekeeping. Owing to its condition, it was not used in the 1866 parade. In 1905 the War Department returned the portion captured at the Crater. The veterans' association of the 100th Infantry complained that their flag had never been captured, so Deputy Adjutant-General Frank D. Beary opened the glass case containing the remnant, laid it out on a table, then opened the package from the War Department. Beary and the veterans present then saw that both pieces were from the same flag, and they were placed together.[4]

Second State Color
Maker: EH
1985.181

Second State Color

Evans & Hassall completed this banner on September 28, 1864, and sent it to the State Agency in Washington. The 100th received the flag at some unspecified date, probably sometime in October. It may have been carried by the regiment when it was marginally engaged at the Boydton Plank Road on October 27. After spending a fairly quiet winter, the unit was next engaged at Fort Stedman on March 25, 1865. It was among the troops that moved up to counter the Southern infantry that seized the fort early that morning. As the regiment swept over the parapet into the fort, a Confederate soldier seized hold of the flagstaff and demanded its surrender. Color-Sergeant Charles Oliver of Company M replied "The hell you say," as he knocked his assailant to the ground with his fist. Oliver captured his counterpart and then managed to seize a Confederate flag before the fighting ended.[5]

After Lee's surrender at Appomattox, the depleted regiment moved to Washington where it took part in the Grand Review on May 23. By this time, the state color had been painted with the names of twenty battles.[6] The regiment was mustered out of service on

Lieutenant Richard P. Craven

100th Infantry

National Color of Company C
Size: 48 3/8 x 63 5/8
1985.182

July 24, and the color was included in the 1866 parade.

Company C Flag

On August 7, 1861, the citizens of Portersville and Muddy Creek Township, Butler County, presented a national color to Company C. This flag was carried by the company until October 15, 1864, when it was given to Private Frederick Bauder for safekeeping. It remained with this veteran until his death in 1919 and then was given to Mr. H. E. Haberling of Portersville. This man donated the flag to the Commonwealth in June 1921.[7]

Company M Flag

When the regiment reassembled at Camp Copeland, Pittsburgh, on March 23, 1864, the soldiers of Company M presented a "most beautiful flag" to the regiment to be carried alongside the state color. The company stipulated that it would be returned to the survivors of the company when the war ended. This banner was indeed carried by the 100th throughout the 1864-65 campaigns. It was badly damaged during the fighting in the Crater. Its postwar history and eventual disposition are unknown.[8]

Company C Reunion. Sergeant Phineas Bird Holds the Flag

Notes

1 Elisha Bracken Diary, July 29, 1862, New Castle Public Library.
2 Stevenson manuscript, p. 5, New Castle Public Library.
3 "Flag of the 'Roundheads'," *NT,* August 10, 1916; John W. Morrison to Frank D. Beary, August 11, 1919, RG 19; Label for Captured Flag #33, RG 25.
4 *NT,* August 10, 1916; Morrison to Beary, August 11, 1919, RG 19.
5 J. R. Holibaugh, "Battle Days of the Roundheads," *NT,* October 27, 1898.

6 "Home from the Wars! The Grand National Pageant! Review of the Army of the Potomac," *Philadelphia Inquirer,* May 24, 1865.
7 F. D. Beary to H. E. Haberling, June 9, 1921; January 10, 1927, untitled page with history of Company C flag, both in RG 19.
8 "From the Roundheads," *Washington Reporter and Tribune,* April 6, 1864; Silas Stevenson, *Account of the Crater,* p. 18.

Bibliography

Adams, Alexander. "Fort Sanders." *NT,* August 13, 1891.
Applegate, Henry. Letter, March 7, 1862. USAMHI, HbCWRT Collection.
Bates, Samuel P. *A Brief History of the One Hurdredth [sic] Regiment, (Roundheads).* New Castle: W. B. Thomas, Printer, 1884.
Browne, Robert A. Letters. USAMHI.
Crowl, Philip. "At Fort Stedman." *NT,* October 24, 1912.
"Flag of the 'Roundheads'." *NT,* August 10, 1916.
Gavin, William G. *Campaigning with the Roundheads, The History of the Hundredth Pennsylvania Veteran Volunteer Infantry Regiment in the American Civil War, 1861-1865.* Dayton: Press of Morningside, 1989.
____. *Infantryman Petit.* Shippensburg: White Mane Press, 1990. (Corporal Fred C. Petit's letters, 1862-64)
Holibaugh, J. R. "Battle Days of the Roundheads." *NT,* October 20, 27, 1898.
Huffman, William H. "At South Mountain." *NT,* November 3, 1898.
____. "Criticizes Powell's Chantilly." *NT,* November 19, 1903.
____. "From a Prisoner's Diary." *NT,* October 1903.

____. "On the Firing Line. A Roundhead Who was with Pope's Army at Chantilly." *NT,* April 13, 1899.
Justice, Jefferson. Papers. Historical Society of Pennsylvania.
Kennedy, J.B. "Fort Sanders." *NT,* November 22, 1883.
____. "Fort Sanders." *NT,* October 15, 1891.
Leasure, Daniel. "Personal Observations and Experiences in the Pope Campaign in Virginia." *Glimpses of the Nation's Struggle. Papers Read Before the Minnesota Commandery of the Military Order of the Loyal Legion of the United States,* 1: 135-166. St. Paul: St. Paul Book and Stationery Company, 1887.
Lobingier, C. C. "Without a Countersign. Picketed at Night in a Southern Forest with Orders to Shoot." *NT,* October 28, 1897.
McDowell, M. Gyla. Papers. The Pennsylvania State University, Pattee Library.
McMillin, Edward M. "First Wire Entanglements. The Telegraph Wire Strung in Front of Fort Sanders." *NT,* May 23, 1918.
Magee, John A. *Memoirs of the War of 1861-65.* N.p., n.d.
Morrison, John W. Papers. War Library and Museum, Philadelphia.

Moss, Michael. "Bringing in Deserters." *NT,* April 27, 1899.

100th Pennsylvania Collection. New Castle Public Library.

Pettit, Frederick. Papers. USAMHI, CWTI Collection.

Rodgers, Robert W. 1863 Diary. USAMHI, HbCWRT Collection.

Rounds, J. L. "At the Bloody Angle." *NT,* May 23, 1912.

____. "Fort Stedman." *NT,* September 16, 1909.

Sankey, James P. "Captured Rebel Flags. Four Regiments Took Eight Stands of Colors at the Fort Stedman Fight." *NT,* July 25, 1912.

Smith, R. A. "Death of Gen. Kearny." *NT,* March 19, 1914.

____. "In Front of Petersburg." *NT,* November 10, 1898.

____. "On the Picket Line. A Roundhead's Reminiscences of Rebel Deserters at Petersburg." *NT,* January 26, 1899.

Stevenson, J. H. "One that was of High Rank. How the 'Roundheads' Attended a Military Funeral at Beaufort, S.C." *NT,* August 16, 1900.

Stevenson, James C. "Battle Days of the Roundheads." *NT,* October 13, 1898.

____. "Burnside's Campaign and Siege of Knoxville." *Grand Army Scout and Soldiers Mail,* May 15, 1886.

____. "Fort Stedman." *NT,* October 15, 1885.

Stevenson, Silas. *Account of the Battle of the Mine or Battle of the Crater in Front of Petersburg, Va. July 30th 1864.* New Castle: John A. Leathers, Printer, [1914].

Thomas, Lon. "Gen. John Pope." *NT,* February 20, 1908.

Young, Victor V. (editor). *The Major, Being a Collection of Letters and Notes by James Harvey Cline on the Organization, Experiences and Battles of the Hundredth Round Head Regiment, Pennsylvania Volunteers.* Pittsburgh: Privately printed by Connelley Vocational High School, 1935.

101st Infantry

First State Color

Recruited primarily in the counties of Allegheny, Butler, Lawrence, Adams, Bedford, and Tioga, the 101st Pennsylvania was organized at Camp Curtin in October 1861. The regiment spent most of the winter in camp drilling until its equipment finally arrived in February 1862. On the twenty-sixth of that month, the 101st, together with the 54th, 56th, and 103rd Regiments, marched into Harrisburg to the Capitol, where Governor Curtin presented state colors to the four units.[1] The following day, the 101st moved to Washington and was assigned to a division led by Brigadier-General Silas Casey.

Casey's division, a part of the Fourth Corps, Army of the Potomac, moved to the Peninsula and took a minor part in the Siege of Yorktown. The 101st was present on the field at Williamsburg (May 5, 1862), suffering a few casualties from artillery fire. Its first major engagement with Rebel troops occurred on May 31, when the enemy struck Casey's position at Fair Oaks. When finally forced to retreat, the 101st had suffered 129 casualties, approximately one-third of the men present for duty. Thereafter, the regiment was not engaged during the Seven Days Campaign.

The 101st performed guard duty in the Yorktown area until sent to Suffolk in mid-September. Then, in early December, the 101st's brigade moved to North Carolina in time to participate in Major-General John G. Foster's raid to Goldsboro. Although actively engaged as skirmishers during this brief inland movement, the 101st was largely unscathed. After spending the winter near New Bern, the 101st went to Plymouth, North Carolina, to form part of the garrison of that town. With the exception of occasional forays into the surrounding country to attack suspected guerrilla bases, the 101st enjoyed a quiet 1863. However, a large Confederate force attacked Plymouth in April 1864. The garrison held out for a few days but capitulated on April 20. With the exception of sick soldiers (who had been sent to Roanoke Island) and those on detached duty, the entire regiment was captured, its state color included. Once taken by the enemy, the color disappeared from history.

Second State Color
Maker: HB
1985.183

Second State Color

Horstmann Brothers completed a replacement color for the 101st in December 1863. This flag was at the State Agency in Washington when the regiment was captured at Plymouth. The flag apparently remained in Washington until it was sent back to Harrisburg in early 1866. The surviving 101st soldiers on Roanoke Island were joined by new recruits, and in the spring of 1865 by eight new companies. The regiment was mustered out of service at New Bern in June 1865. The replacement color was officially returned to state care on July 4, 1866.[2]

Company B Flag

Company B was recruited in Mansfield, Tioga County. Before leaving town, the company received a "beautiful company flag" from a number of lady friends of the soldiers. This flag was carried by the company until it was captured at Plymouth in April 1864.[3]

Advance the Colors!

Notes

1 "Military—Presentation of Flags," *Harrisburg Patriot and Union*, February 27, 1862.

2 Colonel Frank Jordan to Commander, 206th Pennsylvania, October 7, 1864, lists the 101st color among those flags at the State Agency. This letter is found in the 206th Pennsylvania Regimental Descriptive, Letter, Order, and Index Book, RG 94.

3 Company B History, pages 6-7, USAMHI.

Bibliography

Bailey, Chester P. *Tioga Mountaineers, Company B, 101st Regiment Pennsylvania Volunteers Infantry 1861-1865.* Mansfield: The author, 1982.

Boots, Edward N. "Civil War Letters of Edward N. Boots: Virginia 1862." *Virginia Magazine of History and Biography* 69 (1961): 194-209.

____. "Civil War Letters of E. N. Boots from New Bern and Plymouth." Edited by Wilfred W. Black. *North Carolina Historical Review* 36 (1959): 205-23.

Brown, Jacob D. "Battle of Kinston." *NT,* March 20, 1890.

____. "Plymouth, N.C." *NT,* October 3, 1889.

Conley, Isaiah. "Captain Isaiah Conley's Escape from a Southern Prison, 1864." Edited by George D. Harmon & Edith B. Hazlehurst. *Western Pennsylvania Historical Magazine* 47 (1964): 81-106, 225-47.

Creelman, Samuel. *Collections of a Coffee Cooler.* Pittsburgh: Press of Pittsburgh Photo-Engraving Company, ca 1889.

____. "Seven Pines." *NT,* January 5, 1893.

Hollands, George. "Andersonville Memories." *NT,* September 27, 1906.

____. "On the *Massachusetts*. The Midnight Collision on the Potomac Between the *Massachusetts* and the *Black Diamond*." *NT,* May 14, 1914.

Kirk, J. B. "From Bondage to Liberty." *NT,* January 9, 1902.

____. "Money to Burn. A Great Find of Bank Notes in a North Carolina Town." *NT,* April 28, 1904.

____. "Pennsylvania Bankers. A Change of Officials in the Elizabeth City Bank," *NT,* November 3, 1904.

____. "Treatment of Prisoners." *NT.* November 5, 1891.

____. "Two Prisoners at Large." *NT,* November 3, 1904.

Mosgrove, George D. "Captain Kirk's Strategics." *NT,* October 31, 1901.

Pennsylvania. 101st Infantry. Company B Collection. USAMHI, CWMisc Collection.

Porter, Samuel W. "Providence Spring." *NT,* January 24, 1907.

Reed, John A., and Dickey, Luther S. *History of the 101st Regiment Pennsylvania Veteran Volunteer Infantry, 1861-1865.* Chicago: L. S. Dickey & Company, 1910.

____. "Union North Carolina Soldiers." *NT,* June 8, 1911.

Re-union of the 101st Reg't. Pa. Vet. Vols., at Leechburg, Armstrong County, Pa., September 10th, 1879. Minutes of Proceedings, Address of Welcome, by H. H. Wray and Oration by Col. A. W. Taylor. Bedford: Jordan & Mullin, Printers, 1879.

Slaybaugh, George H. "Battle of Plymouth," *NT,* August 22, 1889.

____. "His First Three Weeks at the Front." *NT,* August 19, 26, September 9, 16, 23, 1926.

____. "How Cushing Destroyed the *Albemarle. NT,* May 13, 1926.

Stragand, George. *Cemetery Tales and Civil War Diary.* Scottdale: Laurel Group Press, 1978. (Includes 1862-63 diary of John Housholder.)

102nd Infantry

First State Color

The twelve companies forming the 102nd Infantry were raised primarily from the soldiers of the three-month 13th Infantry. All except Company H (Butler County) were from the Pittsburgh area. By the end of August 1861, the regiment had assembled in camp near Washington, where it remained throughout the winter of 1861-62. Colonel J. H. Puleston of the State Agency presented a Horstmann-made state color to the regiment on December 17.[1]

Assigned to Darius Couch's division of the Fourth Corps, Army of the Potomac, the 102nd moved with the Army to the Peninsula in late March 1862. After the Siege of Yorktown, the regiment first engaged the enemy at Williamsburg on May 5. The regiment next fought on the first day of the fighting at Fair Oaks (May 31). Of the fifty-nine casualties suffered that day, four were color-bearers. Sergeant George W. Workman, the initial bearer, was hit in the leg and went down. He refused to relinquish the banner to anyone except one of the guards.[2] Corporal Joseph Hucks of Company M sought permission to raise the flag, but soon after this brave man seized the fallen color he was hit twice, in the groin and shoulder, and fell mortally wounded.[3] Corporal Charles Donohue of Company K then grabbed the flag and safely took it from the field as the regiment fell back under heavy enemy pressure. The fourth bearer listed by Lieutenant-Colonel Joseph M. Kinkead was Sergeant Edwin Anderson (Company B), who bore the "regimental flag" after it had been perforated by a grapeshot.[4]

During the Seven Days' Battles, the division was not engaged until the Battle of Malvern Hill on July 1. Here, Corporal William H. Cowan of Company H was wounded while carrying the flag.[5] Couch's division moved to northern Virginia in August, arriving in time to help cover the retreat of Pope's beaten troops from the Second Battle of Manassas. During the ensuing Maryland Campaign, the division arrived on the Antietam battlefield after the fighting had ended. Soon thereafter, the division was assigned to the Sixth Corps. At Fredericksburg on December 13, most of the corps was not engaged with the enemy.

The regiment's primary fighting in 1863 was during the Chancellorsville Campaign. While most of the army moved with Hooker on a flanking movement to draw Lee's troops away from Fredericksburg, the Sixth Corps remained opposite the city to hold the enemy's attention. When Hooker's plan bogged down, he ordered Major-General John Sedgwick to attack the enemy and then join the main army. Sedgwick's troops attacked the Confederate positions behind Fredericksburg on May 3, capturing the entrenchments and driving away the defenders. The general put his troops in motion towards Chancellorsville, but

Corporal Charles L. Donohue

encountered Rebel troops at Salem Church. During the severe fighting here, Sergeant John B. Devaux, color-bearer since December 26, 1862, was mortally wounded; he died a week later. Then, Corporal John F. Brill of Company L apparently took the flag, but fell wounded as well.[6]

At this point, subsequent events become confused. Defeated in his attempt to join Hooker, Sedgwick pulled back into a defensive perimeter near Banks's Ford across the Rappahannock River. After some desultory combat the next day, Sedgwick recrossed the river on the evening of May 4-5. The 102nd was one of the rearguard units and reached the ford after dark, apparently in some confusion. Confederate troops could be heard closing in and the regiment seems to have disintegrated in the darkness. Some men managed to escape, but more than a hundred were taken prisoner. Captain Orlando M. Loomis of Company I, together with several other paroled prisoners, later claimed that the flag was torn from its staff, tied around some stones, and thrown into the river to prevent the enemy from taking it.[7] Colonel Kinkead reported that the sole survivor of the color-guard told him that the flag was given to a mounted sergeant of the 8th Pennsylvania Cavalry for safekeeping.[8]

On the other hand, Major-General Richard H. Anderson, commanding one of the Confederate divisions opposing Sedgwick, reported the capture of a flag of the 102nd Pennsylvania. "This flag was not actually taken in battle, but was found by General Wilcox's brigade in the river at the point where the enemy had their bridges down."[9] If this flag was the first state color, then it has not resurfaced after its capture. However, Soldiers and Sailors Memorial Hall in Pittsburgh has the remnant of a 102nd Pennsylvania flag that was supposedly fished from the Rappahannock River sometime after the war, kept by Colonel James Patchell, and presented to the Hall by his family after the colonel's death in 1929. Indeed, Patchell himself supported the river story when he verified the missing state color in 1866.[10]

National Color

Following the loss of its state color, the 102nd Pennsylvania took part in the Gettysburg Campaign, arriving on the field late on July 2. It suffered a slight loss during the remainder of the battle. Just before the beginning of the Bristoe Station Campaign (October 1863), the regiment received some type of flag on October 1.[11] A brief reference by the regimental chaplain is the only documentation to this flag located thus far. Of the colors in the state collection, one is marked as a "national" color. The remnant clearly indicates that

National Color
1985.185

the state coat-of-arms was painted in the blue canton. Although evidence is lacking, this flag is most likely not that thrown into the Rappahannock River, as the staff has battle damage that matches breaks in the silk. Quite possibly, the officers raised some money and had a state color made to replace the missing flag, as did the officers of the 56th Infantry. Without more documentation, the origin of this flag must remain speculation. The bearer of this flag was killed on May 5, 1864. Sergeant Lewis C. White of Company H took the flag and carried it until October 19, when he was wounded at Cedar Creek. As the 102nd advanced near the close of the battle, a bullet nicked the flagstaff, another penetrated White's coffee bucket, and a third lead ball smashed the sergeant's right hand, forcing amputation[12]

Second State Color

A replacement color for the 102nd was finished in April 1864. The regiment carried this new banner into the fighting in the Wilderness on May 5, where the 102nd suffered 163 casualties. Following this battle, the unit took part in the fighting at Spotsylvania, Cold Harbor, and the initial attacks on the Petersburg defenses. In July, the Sixth Corps was sent north to bolster the Washington defenses when Jubal Early's Confederates threatened the capital. The 102nd was engaged as skirmishers at Fort Stevens (July 11-12), but suffered no casualties.

During the ensuing Shenandoah Valley Campaign, the 102nd engaged the enemy at Winchester on September 19, losing 62 soldiers. Three days later, the regiment charged the entrenchments on Fisher's Hill. Sergeant William G. Greenawalt of Company A, carrying the state color, was among the first Union col-

Second State Color
Maker: EH
1985.184

or-bearers to plant a flag on the enemy earthworks.[13] On October 19, the regiment fought at Cedar Creek, the last major engagement of this campaign. Here, Sergeant Greenawalt was wounded in the face by a minie ball, which exited near his ear. When the sergeant fell, Corporal Joseph S. Fithean of Company H seized the flag as the regiment advanced.[14]

On December 7, while yet in camp near Winchester, Colonel Patchell requested a new state color from Adjutant-General Russell. Patchell reported that the present colors "have been so badly torn by bullets and exposure to the weather, that it is unsafe to unfurl them for fear of their falling to pieces."[15] The 1864 color was then sent back to Harrisburg and officially returned to state care in 1866. By this time, Colonel Patchell had removed the coat-of-arms, which remained in his family until donated to Soldiers and Sailors Memorial Hall in 1929.

Third State Color

A replacement color was finished in early January 1865 and forwarded to the 102nd, then back in camp near Petersburg. During the last months of the war in Virginia, the 102nd took part in the picket line fighting on March 25th and at Saylor's Creek (April 6). Following Lee's surrender at Appomattox, the Sixth Corps moved briefly to Danville, Virginia, before returning to Washington. The 102nd was mustered out

National Color of Company K

Third State Color
Maker: HB
1985.186

Regimental Color

344

Advance the Colors!

of service on June 28. The third state color was present in the 1866 parade.

Presented Color

This 34-star national color, with the stars arranged in a giant star pattern, was presented by the ladies of Pittsburgh to Major John Poland sometime in 1861. The brass finial is eagle-shaped, and the cords and tassels are red, white, and blue silk rather than the regulation blue and white silk. Poland's son presented the banner to Soldiers and Sailors Memorial Hall in 1929. Nothing else has been found to document its war-time use.

Notes

1 Special Orders #78, December 14, 1861, in Company I Book, RG 94.

2 *O.R.* 11.1, p. 895. Workman's name does not appear in Bates's roster of the 102nd. Company K has a George H. Workman listed.

3 Huck's name has various spellings. Colonel Kinkead's report (*O.R.* 11.1, p. 895), has the name as Hirch. His manuscript report, found in the Regimental Letter, Order, and Miscellaneous Book, RG 94, spells it Huch. "Letter from Colonel Rowley's Regiment," *Pittsburgh Evening Chronicle*, June 9, 1862, also has Huch. Bates 3:691, has Huck.

4 *O.R.* 11.1, p. 895. It is not known if Anderson carried the state color. The 13th Infantry had received at least one color from friends in 1861, and the 102nd may very well have carried a second flag early in the war. One flag of the 13th Infantry was photographed in 1892, when the 102nd's Veterans' Association had custody of the flag.

5 Cowan's obituary in *NT*, July 25, 1907.

6 "List of Killed, Wounded, and Missing, 102nd Regt. Penna. Vols., May 3rd and 4th, 1863," in Regimental Letter, Order, and Miscellaneous Book, RG 94. Devaux's assignment as color-bearer can be found in General Orders #43, RG 94. See also John F. Brill, "At Spotsylvania," *NT*, July 16, 1914, where Brill claims to have taken the flag after Devaux fell. In the casualty list cited above, Brill is included with those wounded on May 3.

7 "The Colors of the 102nd Regiment," *Pittsburgh Evening Chronicle*, May 29, 1863. See also the following letters from the *Evening Chronicle*: "The Colors of the Old 13th," May 22, 1863, and "Letter from the Old 13th," May 26, 1863.

8 *O.R.* 25.1, p. 623.

9 *O.R.* 25.1, p. 853.

10 Patchell to A. L. Russell, May 25, 1866, RG 25.

11 Stewart, pp. 345-46.

12 White Reminiscences; "Mascot Dog Jack," *NT*, September 19, 1912.

13 "Letter from the Old 13th," *Pittsburgh Evening Chronicle*, October 10, 1864; *O.R.* 43.1, p. 203.

14 White Reminiscences.

15 Patchell to A. L. Russell, December 7, 1864, in Regimental Correspondence, RG 19.

Bibliography

"At Fort Sevens." *NT*, August 2, 1900.

Brill, John F. "At Spotsylvania." *NT*, July 16, 1914.

____. "Trading with the Johnnies." *NT*, April 27, 1911.

Duvall, Samuel. 1864 Shenandoah Valley Campaign Diary. USAMHI, Save the Flags Collection.

Evans, J. B. "Did the Letter Arrive? Trade, Commerce and Postal Service Between the Pickets." *NT*, September 29, 1904.

____. "Wheaton's Brigade was in the Lead at the Wilderness." *NT*, August 20, 1891.

Hawk, Isaac A. "Fort Stevens," *NT*, September 27, 1900.

Lord, Francis A. (editor). "Diary of a Soldier in 1864." *North-South Trader* 4 (November-December 1976): 12-28.

McElroy, John H. "Who Stole the Boat?" *NT*, August 3, 1911.

McGrath, F. J. "The 6th Corps at Marye's Heights." *NT*, June 18, 1908.

Niebaum, John H. *History of the Pittsburgh Washington Infantry, 102nd (Old 13th) Regiment, Pennsylvania Veteran Volunteers, and Its Forebears.* Pittsburgh: Burgum Printing Company, 1931.

Porter, John A. 1862 Diary. Pennsylvania State Archives.

Rowe, John A. Letters, November 1864-March 1865. USAMHI.

Stewart, Alexander M. *Camp, March and Battle-field; Or, Three Years and a Half With the Army of the Potomac.* Philadelphia: James B. Rodgers, Printer, 1865.

Studebaker, Daniel, Jr. "Dog-Jack." *Western Pennsylvania Historical Magazine* 62 (April 1979): 187-89.

White, Lewis C. "Mascot Dog Jack." *NT*, September 19, 1912.

____. "President Lincoln and Fort Stevens. *NT*, March 6, 1913.

____. Reminiscences. USAMHI, Save the Flags Collection.

Wilbur, Arad. Letters. Chicago Historical Society.

103rd Infantry

State Color

Organized at Camp Orr near Kittanning in the fall of 1861, the 103rd Infantry moved to Harrisburg in late February 1862 to complete its organization. While at Camp Curtin, the regiment marched into the city and halted at the Capitol. Here, in the afternoon of February 26, in conjunction with the 54th, 56th, and 101st Regiments, the 103rd received a new state color directly from Governor Curtin. The new flag was given to Sergeant James H. Chambers of Company C, who carried the flag for several months.[1]

The 103rd then moved to Washington, where it was assigned to a division commanded by Brigadier-General Silas Casey. In company with the division, the regiment moved to the Peninsula in April 1862. The 103rd took part in the Siege of Yorktown, and was marginally engaged in the rearguard action at Williamsburg as the Confederate army withdrew toward Richmond. When Casey's division was attacked on the first day of the Battle of Fair Oaks (May 31), the 103rd suffered heavy losses as the division was pushed off the field. The flagstaff was shot in two, but Sergeant William N. Barr held on to both pieces and carried the flag as the regiment withdrew.[2]

During the Seven Days' Battles, the 103rd, together with most of the Fourth Corps, guarded the army's left flank and was not seriously engaged. When the main body of the Army of the Potomac moved to northern Virginia, the 103rd was sent to strengthen the garrison of Suffolk, where it remained until early December, occasionally skirmishing with enemy troops. Then, the command moved to New Bern, North Carolina, to reinforce an expedition commanded by Major-General John G. Foster. His force of 12,000 men marched inland to strike the railroad carrying supplies to Lee's army in Virginia. The 103rd took an active part in the fighting at Kinston on December 14. Here, Sergeant Anthony Spangler of Company D received two mortal wounds while carrying the state color. When Spangler fell, a color-guard seized the flag, but when he found himself a conspicuous target, the man dropped the flag and re-

State Color
Maker: HB
1985.187

sumed firing his rifle. At this point, Corporal Robert J. Thompson of Company E grabbed the flag and remained as bearer through 1864.[3]

After returning to New Bern, the 103rd stayed in the District of North Carolina until the end of the war. The regiment took part in several small expeditions, and by the spring of 1864 was part of the garrison of Plymouth when that town was attacked by a Confederate force commanded by Robert F. Hoke in April 1864. Assisted by an ironclad ram, the Confederate forces chased away Union naval support and overwhelmed the garrison, which surrendered on April 20. With the exception of Company C (on duty at Roanoke Island), the entire 103rd was captured and spent the rest of the war in Southern prisons. The state flag escaped capture. It had been sent north earlier in the spring to have battle honors added, and the flag remained in the state until officially returned during the 1866 ceremony.[4]

Company B Flag

When the teacher of the Blaney School in Sugar Creek Township, Armstrong County, enlisted in the 103rd

346

Advance the Colors!

Company B Flag

Infantry, the girls of the school decided to make and present a flag to the company. The hand-sewn, wool bunting flag was stitched in three days by a number of girls, who presented the flag sometime before the regiment left Camp Orr. The flag remained with the regiment until the fall of Plymouth. When it became apparent that the garrison would surrender, Private Conrad Petzinger took the flag from its staff and wrapped it around his body beneath his uniform. Petzinger was taken to Andersonville, where the flag remained undetected until the private was paroled in December 1864. The flag remained in the Petzinger family for many years before it was given to the Regimental Association, which in turn presented the treasured banner to Soldiers and Sailors Memorial Hall in Pittsburgh, where it can be seen today.[5]

Notes

1 "Military—Presentation of Flags," *Harrisburg Patriot*, February 27, 1862; Dickey, pp. 7, 369.

2 Dickey, p. 17; Colonel T. F. Lehmann to Adjutant-General A. L. Russell, June 8, 1862, 103rd Pennsylvania Regimental Papers, RG 19.

3 Dickey, pp. 36, 118.

4 Dickey, p. 118. For additional Correspondence pertaining to the disposition of the state color, see George W. Kelley to Governor Curtin, May 20, 1864, and John C. Harvey to Major G. W. Gibbons, April 14, 1865, both in RG 25.

5 Dickey, p. 79; tag accompanying flag in Soldiers & Sailors.

Bibliography

Alexander, Alvin H. Letters, February 12-November 13, 1863. USAMHI.

Black, Robert P. "Plymouth Pilgrims, and How They Came to be Captured—A Survivors' Story." *NT*, May 1, 1884.

____. "Saw the Monitor-Merrimac Fight." *NT*, May 7, 1914.

Croop, William. Letters, April 29, 1862-January 17, 1864. USAMHI, CWTI Collection.

Dickey, Luther S. *History of the 103d Regiment Pennsylvania Volunteer Infantry, 1861-1865*. Chicago: the author, 1910.

Donaghy, John. *Army Experience of Capt. John Donaghy, 103d Penn'a. Vols., 1861-1864*. Deland, FL: E. O. Painter Printing Company, 1926.

Gibson, S. J. 1864 Diary. Library of Congress.

Kiester, Jacob S. Correspondence. East Carolina University.

____. Letters, March 19-August 31, 1862. USAMHI, CWTI Collection.

King, Spencer B., Jr. (editor). "Yankee Letters from Andersonville Prison." *Georgia Historical Quarterly* 38 (1954): 394-98.

McElhatten, John. "Duty in the Rear. Experiences of a Soldier on Provost Guard in Philadelphia (Summer 1862)." *NT* July 28, 1887.

McNary, Oliver R. "What I Saw and Did Inside and Outside of Rebel Prisons." In *War Talks in Kansas; A Series of Papers Read Before the Kansas Commandery of the Military Order of the Loyal Legion of the United States*, volume 1, pp. 24-44. Kansas City, MO: Franklin Hudson Publishing House, 1906.

Moyer Joseph. "The 'Red Head' at Florence." *NT*, January 19, 1911.

Stoke, George W. "Made His Escape." *NT*, February 3, 1898.

104th Infantry

First State Color

Recruited primarily in Bucks County, the 104th Pennsylvania was organized in a camp near Doylestown during the fall of 1861. Governor Curtin and staff visited the regiment on October 31 to present a state color to the new unit. Colonel William W. H. Davis accepted the banner and gave it to Sergeant James L. Slack of Company C.[1] Colonel Davis formed a color-guard on November 18, appointing eight corporals from the twenty-seven men who volunteered for this duty.[2] By this time, the 104th had moved to Washington, where it spent the winter in camp, constantly drilling and training.

First State Color
Maker: EH
1985.188

The regiment moved to the Yorktown Peninsula in March 1862 as the Army of the Potomac began its campaign against Richmond. Now attached to the Fourth Corps, the 104th took part in the Siege of Yorktown, then moved in pursuit of the retreating Confederate forces. After a brief skirmish with Southern infantry at Savage's Station on May 24, the 104th went into Camp near Fair Oaks, a scant five miles from Richmond.

Confederate General Joseph Johnston's Southern defenders assailed the Federal soldiers at Fair Oaks on May 31, 1862. The 104th was engaged early in the action as the initial enemy attack struck Brigadier-General Silas Casey's division. Colonel Davis moved his regiment (less two companies detached elsewhere) to protect a battery of artillery north of the Williamsburg Road. After fighting for two hours, Davis, seeing yet more enemy soldiers debouching from the woods to his front, determined to charge the Confederates to gain time for the artillery to move to the rear. The men sprang forward, crossing an open field dotted with small bushes. After crossing an old worm fence running diagonally with the line of battle, the 104th halted and managed to stop the enemy advance.

However, with losses running high and no support in sight, Davis's men were forced to retreat. As the regiment began to drift to the rear, Sergeant Slack was badly wounded. As he fell the young sergeant jabbed the flagstaff into the ground, exclaiming, "I have hit the ground, but Old Glory has not."[3] The location of the state color was not immediately seen, but Colonel Davis, observing the stationary color, also saw several Rebel soldiers spring forward to seize the Yankee banner. Davis, already wounded in his left arm, called out for volunteers to save the flag. A number of men led by Major John M. Gries turned about and charged the squad of Confederates. Sergeant Hiram W. Purcell, carrying a flag presented to the regiment by Bucks County friends (see below), leaped back over the worm fence and reached the state color ahead of the Rebels. He grabbed the flag, turned about, and ran for the rear with both flags. As Purcell mounted the fence, a bullet slammed into his left thigh. Purcell fell to the ground, but staggered to his feet and kept running. He finally collapsed from loss of blood, as two other bullets had struck his neck and arm. However, the plucky sergeant had saved both flags. When Purcell finally collapsed, two soldiers took the flags and safely carried them to the rear. General Casey's bugler found the exhausted Purcell and took the wounded man on his horse to the rear. Sergeant Purcell later received a deserved Medal of Honor for his rescue of the colors.[4]

Advance the Colors!

Sergeant Hiram Purcell

During the ensuing Seven Days' Battles, the 104th guarded the army's left flank and was not engaged. The division remained on the Peninsula when the Army of the Potomac was withdrawn to northern Virginia, the 104th moving to Gloucester Point to garrison the earthworks there. In early January 1863, the division moved to Beaufort, North Carolina. After remaining here a month, the troops moved on to Port Royal, South Carolina. From here, the 104th went to Beaufort to serve as part of the garrison, and was engaged in this duty until July 1863, when the regiment was transported to James Island to take part in the siege operations against Charleston. The 104th was engaged in the arduous operations near Charleston until mid-June 1864. At some point during the winter of 1863-64, Colonel Davis went home for a furlough. He took both colors along with him to have battle honors painted on each. The colonel recalled that the flags "had become so tender from long exposure to the weather, that they would hardly bear the weight of the inscriptions."[5]

In June 1864, the 104th moved to Hilton Head for a time, then was transferred to Florida to guard the railroad between Jacksonville and Baldwin. In late August, the regiment was sent to Alexandria, Virginia, where the men who had not re-enlisted were mustered out in early October. The survivors were consolidated into five companies and sent to guard supply trains in the Shenandoah Valley. The battalion was occupied in this duty until November, when it was sent to Philadelphia to act as provost guards during the presidential election. The unit returned to the Valley for a short time, then moved to join the Army of the James in front of Petersburg. Here, the 104th manned the defenses of Bermuda Hundred. While engaged in this duty, Major Theophilus Kephart, then in command of the 104th, wrote to Governor Curtin to request a replacement state color. When this new banner was received, Kephart sent the battered original flag back to Harrisburg. It was officially returned to the Commonwealth in 1866.[6]

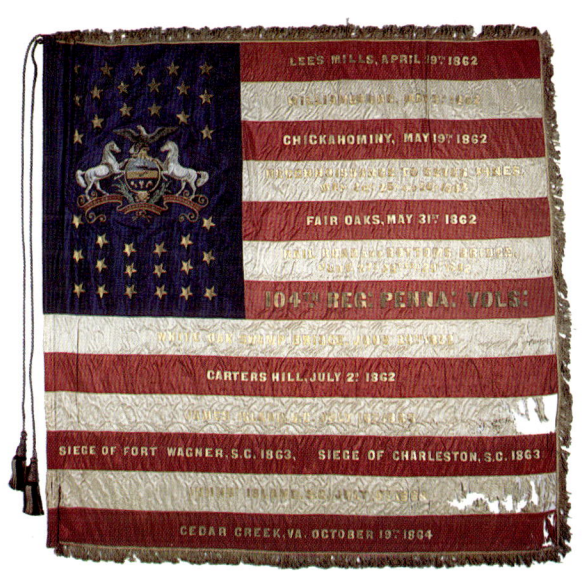

Second State Color
Maker: EH
1985.189

Second State Color

Major Kephart requested this flag on January 12, 1865. This color was received on February 17 and was used by the regiment for the remainder of its term of service.[7] The regiment was strengthened by five new companies in early 1865. It participated in the final attack on Petersburg, then moved to garrison Norfolk and Portsmouth after Lee's surrender. The 104th was mustered out of service on August 25, 1865. The second state color was included in the 1866 parade.

Bucks County Flag

To show their patriotic appreciation for the 104th Pennsylvania, a group of Bucks County women collected $141.00 to purchase a flag for the new regiment. Horstmann Brothers supplied this national color, which contained silver stars in the blue field. "Ringgold regiment, P.V." was inscribed in silver on the center red stripe. This inscription reflected the regiment's nickname, honoring an American officer

104th Infantry

killed in the Mexican War. The banner was presented to the regiment on October 21, 1861. The Rev. Jacob Belville of Hartsville presented the flag on behalf of the ladies. Colonel Davis received the flag and gave it to Sergeant John M. Laughlin of Company A. Laughlin remained bearer until promoted on May 12, 1862. Sergeant Hiram W. Purcell of Company E succeeded Laughlin as bearer. Purcell carried this color at Fair Oaks, when he rescued the state color from capture, as described above. During the fighting, fifteen bullets perforated the silk banner. The Bucks County flag was carried through at least the spring of 1864, and may have been taken home when the majority of the original members were mustered out in the fall of 1864. This flag is now owned by the Bucks County Historical Society.[8]

Notes

1 Davis, p. 17; "Flag Presentation," *Philadelphia Inquirer,* November 1, 1861.

2 General Orders #24, November 18, 1861, Regimental Letter and Order Book, RG 94.

3 Lippincott, *NT,* July 10, 1913.

4 Beyer-Keydel, pp. 41-42; Davis, pp. 101-102; "Rescue of the Colors," p. 580; "The Bucks County Regiment in the Great Battle," *Bucks County Intelligencer,* June 10, 1862.

5 Davis, p. 293.

6 Kephart to Curtin, January 12, 1865, RG 25.

7 Kephart's acknowledgment of receipt, February 17, 1865, RG 25.

8 "Flag for the Ringgold Regiment," *Philadelphia Inquirer,* October 25, 1861; "Flag Presentation," *Bucks County Intelligencer,* October 22, 1861; Special Orders #8, May 12, 1862, Regimental Letter and Order Book, RG 94; "National Flag for the Ringgold Regiment," *Doylestown Democrat,* October 22, 1861; "The Flags of the 104th," *Ibid.,* June 10, 1862.

Bibliography

Davis, W. W. H. "Address in Memory of William Richard Gries, Late Chaplain of 104th Regt. Penna. Vols. . . . at the Unveiling of the Window of St. Paul's P. E. Church, Doylestown, Sunday, Sept. 27th, 1884." N.p., n.d.

____. "The Battle of Fair Oaks." *A Collection of Papers, Bucks County Historical Society* 2 (1909): 337-47.

____. *History of the 104th Pennsylvania Regiment, from August 22d, 1861, to September 30th, 1864.* Philadelphia: James B. Rodgers, Printer, 1866.

____. "The Man Who Stopped a Cannon-Ball." *NT,* February 13, 1896.

____. "The 104th Pa. at Fair Oaks." *NT,* November 14, 1907.

____. "The Siege of Morris Island, S.C." *Philadelphia Weekly Times,* August 18th, 1877. (Also in *Annals of the War,* pp. 95-110).

____. Papers. Duke University; Bucks County Historical Society.

Hopkins, M. S. "A Remarkable Experience. A Man Who Stopped a Cannon-Ball and Still Lives." *NT,* January 30, 1896.

Lippincott, Samuel. "The 104th Pa. at Fair Oaks." *NT,* July 10, 1913.

Marple, Alfred. Letters. University of South Carolina.

"Rescue of the Colors." *A Collection of Papers, Bucks County Historical Society* 2 (1909): 576-88.

Smith, Andrew J. *The Light of Other Days; or, Passing Under the Road.* Edited by J. P. Watson. Dayton: United Brethren Publishing House, 1878.

Torbert, Isaac L. Diary, January-May 6, 1862. Bucks County Historical Society.

Wood, Joseph. Letters, 1862-63. USAMHI, HbCWRT Collection.

105th Infantry

State Color

Composed primarily of soldiers recruited in Jefferson, Indiana, Clearfield, Clarion, and Westmoreland counties, the 105th Infantry was formed in September 1861 to serve for three years. The survivors re-enlisted for a second term and served until the end of the war. With battle deaths totalling 245, the 105th ranks second among Pennsylvania commands in battle-related fatalities. However, this fighting regiment left behind little information concerning its battleflags.

After organizing in camp near Pittsburgh, the regiment moved to Washington, where it spent the winter of 1861-62. On January 5, 1862, Representative James K. Moorhead of Pittsburgh presented a state color to the regiment. One of the boys in blue wrote that his fellow soldiers "felt about as enthusiastic as the chilly blasts of the North wind would permit."[1] By this time, the 105th had been assigned to Phil Kearny's First Division, Third Corps, Army of the Potomac.

The regiment moved with the army to the Peninsula in March 1862. Folllowing the Siege of Yorktown, the 105th was present on the Williamsburg battlefield but suffered no casualties. On May 31, the regiment fought at Fair Oaks, losing 161 soldiers. During the Seven Days' Battles, the 105th was engaged primarily at Glendale on June 30, although the regiment was under fire on numerous occasions during this series of battles. The regiment then fought at Second Manassas (August 29-30). Following this campaign, the Third Corps remained in Washington during the succeeding Maryland Campaign. The 105th's final combat action of 1862 came at Fredericksburg on December 13.

During the Chancellorsville Campaign, the 105th fought on May 3-4, losing 76 of the 347 officers and men taken into the fighting. At Gettysburg on July 2, the 105th was posted north of the Peach Orchard. Most of the 132 men lost that afternoon occurred as the regiment fell back from this line to Cemetery Ridge. After the Bristoe Station and Mine Run Campaigns, the decimated regiment went into camp near Brandy Station, Virginia.

The battered state color seems to have been returned to Harrisburg after the 1863 campaigns. Colonel Calvin A. Craig wrote to Adjutant-General Russell on April 2, 1864, to inform him that he was sending the flag back for preservation.[2] It remained in state care and was officially returned on July 4, 1866.

First National and Regimental Colors

There are no records to indicate that the 105th asked for a replacement state color from the adjutant-general's department. Instead, the regiment seems to have carried a "national" color obtained from a now unidentified source. The remnant of the canton clearly indicates that the state coat-of-arms adorned this section of the new banner. This flag was carried in the 1864 Virginia Campaign. The 105th fought in the Wilderness, losing 160 men here on May 5-6. Then followed combat at Spotsylvania (May 10 and 12 primarily), North Anna River (May 23), skirmishing at Cold Harbor, and the initial assaults on Petersburg (June 18-22). The regiment then participated in the Second Corps expeditions to Deep Bottom (July-August) and was briefly engaged at Poplar Spring

State Color
Maker: HB
1985.190

First National Color
1985.191

Second National Color
Maker: EH
1985.193

First Regimental Color
1985.194

Second Regimental Color
1985.192

Company A Flag
Size: 21 x 25½

Church (October 1-6). In combat at the Boydton Plank Road on October 27, the regiment was struck in the flank and thrown into confusion. Both the national and regimental colors then carried by the 105th were taken by the enemy. Sergeant Thomas F. Richardson of the 12th Virginia received credit for seizing the regimental color.[3] Tagged as Numbers Nine and Sixty-five by the War Department, both were returned to the Commonwealth in 1905.

Second National and Regimental Colors

The condition of these two banners indicates that they were obtained very late in the war. The 35-star national color has an "E & H" engraved on the finial base. No information has been found to indicate the use of these two flags. During the final engagements around Petersburg, the 105th fought at Quaker Road (March 29, 1865) and Saylor's Creek (April 6). After marching in the Grand Review on May 23, the regiment stayed near Washington and was mustered out of service on July 11.

Company A Flag

Gettysburg National Military Park has custody of a guidon-sized national flag attributed to Company A.

352

Advance the Colors!

During the fighting at Gettysburg, the bearer of this flag was wounded. To prevent its capture, Cassius E. McCrea stripped it from the staff and saved it. The flag remained in the McCrea family until presented to the park museum.

Notes

1 A. J. Davis (editor), *History of Clarion County, Pennsylvania* (Syracuse, NY, 1887), p. 264; letter in *Pittsburgh Evening Chronicle*, January 11, 1862. The article "Flag Presentations to Pennsylvania Troops," *Philadelphia Press*, January 6, 1862, does not mention Moorhead's part in the ceremony.

2 Craig to Russell, April 2, 1864, Regimental Correspondence, RG 19. "The Battle Flag of the 105th," *Brookville Republican*, January 20, 1863, indicates that the state color was in town at this time. The article contains no details on why or how the flag was in Brookville.

3 Captured Flags Document, p. 13.

Bibliography

Armstrong, J. A. "The 105th Pa. at Fair Oaks." *NT*, November 1, 1888.

Brown J. B. "The Way His Premonition Began." *NT*, April 2, 1914.

Craig, Samuel A. "Captain Samuel A. Craig's Memoirs of Civil War and Reconstruction." *Western Pennsylvania Historical Magazine* 13 (1930): 215-36, 14 (1931): 43-60, 115-37, 191-206, 258-79.

Criswell, David. "Boydton Plank Road," *NT*, April 25, 1901.

Fatout, Paul (editor). *Letters of a Civil War Surgeon*. West Lafayette, IN: Purdue University Press, 1961.

Rich, G. W. "A Comrade of the Wildcat Regiment Places the Troops in the Peach Orchard." *NT*, May 7, 1891.

Roster of the Surviving Members of the One Hundred and Fifth Pennsylvania Infantry Serving from 1861-1865 . . . . Brookville: Republican Office, 1901.

Scott, Kate M. *History of the One Hundred and Fifth Regiment of Pennsylvania Volunteers, A Complete History of the Organization, Marches, Battles, Toils, and Dangers Participated in by the Regiment from the Beginning to the Close of the War, 1861-1865*. Philadelphia: New-World Publishing Company, 1877.

____."Many Brothers in This Regiment." *NT*, November 6, 1902.

____. "The Mountain Men. The Famous 'Wild-Cat' Regiment in the Civil War. Record of Hard Fights. The Gallant One Hundred and Fifth Pennsylvania Veterans." *Philadelphia Weekly Times*, March 19, 1887.

____. "The Wild Cats. Some Random Sketches of the 105th Pa." *NT*, January 26, 1888.

Vasbinder, Darius J. "Battle of Seven Pines." *NT*, July 18, 1901.

____. "Fair Oaks." *NT*, April 11, 1889.

106th Infantry

First State Color

Recruited primarily in Philadelphia, the 106th Pennsylvania also included large contingents of soldiers from Lycoming and Bradford counties. Sent to Poolesville, Maryland, in the fall of 1861, the 106th was attached to the "Philadelphia Brigade," composed of the 69th, 71st, 72nd, and 106th Pennsylvania. Although present during the Ball's Bluff disaster on October 21, the 106th was not engaged. The regiment then spent the winter of 1861-62 on guard duty in this same area. A state color was finished by Horstmann Brothers in December and presented to the regiment at some unspecified time thereafter.

Attached to the Second Division, Second Corps, Army of the Potomac, the 106th moved to the Peninsula in late March and took part in the Siege of Yorktown. It was engaged briefly during the Battle of Fair Oaks, then fought at Savage's Station (June 29) and Glendale (June 30) during the Seven Days' Battles. During the ensuing Maryland Campaign, the 106th was engaged at Antietam on September 17, as the division marched forward into the West Woods. Here, Confederates hit the attackers from three sides, causing heavy losses as the three brigades broke and fled. At Fredericksburg on December 13, the 106th participated in the unsuccessful attacks on Marye's Heights.

After wintering near Falmouth, the Second Division, Second Corps, supported the Sixth Corps during the Chancellorsville Campaign. The division reoccupied Fredericksburg and was not heavily engaged with the enemy. At Gettysburg, the 106th fought on July 2, helping to repulse Confederate attacks on the center of the Union line, then moved to support the Eleventh Corps on Cemetery Hill. Following the Bristoe Station and Mine Run campaigns, the regiment went into winter camp near Brandy Station. The original state color was retired at this time and was officially returned to state care in 1866.

Second State Color

Lieutenant-Colonel William L. Curry requested a replacement color on August 27, 1863.[1] This flag was received by the regiment on December 26, when the original banner was sent north.[2] The regiment carried this new flag in the 1864 Virginia battles. After fighting in the Wilderness on May 6, the regiment participated in the grand assault on the Confederate earthworks at Spotsylvania on May 12. Then, after engaging the enemy briefly at the North Anna River, the 106th fought at Cold Harbor in early June.

During the initial operations at Petersburg, the 106th, now down to a field strength of about 125 officers and men, took part in the movement to cut the Weldon Railroad. On June 22, as the brigade lay in line of battle behind some earthworks, the enemy attacked and broke through on the left of the brigade. The grayclad attackers then swept around behind the Union troops and surrounded many of the defenders. Most of the soldiers in the 106th were captured before they had a chance to flee. Corporal John Houghton of Company F was carrying the state color. When he saw that there was no chance to escape, he and a comrade tore the flag from its staff and tried to hide it, but they were spotted by the enemy and a fight broke out. In the end, the color was ripped to

First State Color
Maker: HB
1985.195

Regimental Color

pieces by the men of the 106th to avoid surrendering it. The staff was even broken in two and discarded.[3]

Other Colors

In addition to the state-issued colors, there are three other infantry colors for the 106th that have survived. Two are owned by the War Library and Museum in Philadelphia. Although little remains of each flag, it appears that one is a national color and the other a blue regimental color. They were given to the library by Philip M. Allen, a veteran of the 106th. The War Library also has custody of a flank marker for this regiment. A framed blue regimental color is on display in the Canton Junior-Senior High School in Bradford County. Captain John W. Lynch took this flag home and presented it to a friend in Canton shortly before his death in 1913.[4]

No evidence has been found to document how and when these flags were carried by the 106th. After the debacle at the Weldon Railroad, the survivors were organized into a three-company battalion and attached to the 69th Pennsylvania. Most of the regiment had not re-enlisted. Those who had not were sent to Washington in late July, where they spent a month on garrison duty. They were sent to Philadelphia and mustered out of service on September 10.

Color-Bearers

Sergeant Benjamin F. Slonaker of Company C was appointed color-bearer on October 6, 1861. He carried a flag until after the fighting at Antietam. Because of his gallantry at this battle, he was promoted to lieutenant and the flag given to Corporal Joseph N. Radcliff of Company C, who then performed this duty for an unspecified period.[5] One of those killed in the Wilderness on May 6, 1864, was Sergeant Charles Hickok, then a color-bearer.[6] Eight men carried the

Sergeant Charles H. Hickok

colors during the May 12 fighting at Spotsylvania. One was Sergeant William C. Wagner of Lebanon, who was thrice wounded. When the regiment finally retreated, Corporal S. Macey Smith carried a flag from the field.[7] In 1914, Sergeant Rufus G. Brown carried the original state color. He was described as a previous color-bearer in the book listing those who were contacted about this ceremony.

Notes

1 Curry to A. L. Russell, August 27, 1863, RG 25.
2 Information in caption of photograph of state color in Ward, opposite p. 232.
3 Ward, pp. 276-77; *O.R.*, 40.1, p. 387.
4 When the survivors returned to Philadelphia in 1864, "the tattered flag of the regiment was saluted with cheer." Later that day (August 29), the flag of Company B was presented to the Union Volunteer Refreshment Saloon. Neither flag is described in detail. See "Reception of the 106th Reg. Penna." and "Flag Presentation," both in the *Philadelphia Public Ledger*, August 30, 1864.
5 Ward, pp. 317-18.
6 Ward, p. 318.
7 Ward, pp. 249-50; letter from Jacob Y. Ely in *Lebanon Courier*, July 1, 1864.

Bibliography

Lynch, John W. Papers. Historical Society of Pennsylvania.
Manley, William H. Letters. Historical Society of Pennsylvania.
Myers, William H. Letters, December 1861-August 1864. USAMHI.
Pyewell, Jacob. Letters, November 1861-May 1862. USAMHI.
Sanders, Richard A. "Civil War Diary." *Now and Then* 4 (1929-32): 232-34, 276-77, 302-3; reprinted in 12 (1961-62): 36-43, 151-62.
Ward, Joseph R. C. "Another Letter About Fredericksburg." *Grand Army Scout and Soldiers Mail*, December 30, 1882.
____. *History of the One Hundred and Sixth Regiment Pennsylvania Volunteers, 2d Brigade, 2d Division, 2d Corps, 1861-1865*. Philadelphia: Grant, Faires & Rodgers, 1883; revised edition, Philadelphia: F. McManus Jr. & Company, 1906.
____. "Not Long Learning." *NT*, April 26, 1923.
____. "The Philadephia Brigade at Federicksburg." *Grand Army Scout and Soldiers Mail*, November 10, 1883.
White, G. W. "Colonel Baker's Californians." *NT*, November 29, 1901.

107th Infantry

State Color

Formed by the consolidation of two under-strength regiments, the soldiers comprising the 107th Infantry came from more than sixteen of the Commonwealth's central and eastern counties. The unit was formed in early March 1862. Governor Curtin presented a state color to the 107th on March 8, the day before the new command departed for Washington.[1] After remaining near Washington for two months, the 107th joined the corps commanded by Major-General Irvin McDowell, which eventually became the Third Corps of Pope's Army of Virginia. Following some maneuvering in northern Virginia, the 107th arrived on the Cedar Mountain battlefield (August 9) but was not engaged. During the Second Manassas Campaign, the regiment was constantly under enemy fire, but suffered few casualties until it was engaged at Second Manassas, where it lost 117 officers and men.

Upon the army's withdrawal to Washington, McDowell's command was assigned to the Army of the Potomac as its First Corps, now led by General Hooker. The 107th next fought at South Mountain on September 14, then participated in the bloody fighting in the Cornfield at Antietam three days later. Here, of 190 men present for duty, the 107th suffered 64 casualties. Five color-bearers were shot down and the two colors were barely rescued before the shattered regiment fell back over the Cornfield to allow fresh troops to enter the battle. The regiment fought at Fredericksburg on December 13, charging forward with the division to support General Meade's Pennsylvania Reserves, losing 56 of 171 officers and men that day.

After spending the winter near Falmouth, the 107th played a minor role in the Chancellorsville Campaign, since the First Corps was barely engaged with Confederate troops. At Gettysburg, the corps defended McPherson's and Seminary ridges on July 1, 1863, before being forced back through the town to the high ground to the south. The depleted 107th lost 165 men, more than half of these captured during the confusion of the retreat. Two color-bearers were slain in

State Color
Maker: HB
1985.196

this battle. Following the Bristoe Station and Mine Run campaigns (October-November), the 107th went into winter camp along the Orange & Alexandria Railroad to act as guards over the winter. In February 1864, most of the men in the regiment re-enlisted and the soldiers went home on furlough in April.

The 107th rejoined the Army of the Potomac on May 16, 1864, and was assigned to the Fifth Corps. After brief skirmishing with the enemy here and along the North Anna River, the 107th then was only marginally engaged at Cold Harbor before taking part in the initial attacks on the Petersburg defenses. Then, the regiment manned a section of the trench line before taking part in the Federal move against the Weldon Railroad. During the fighting here on August 19, Brigadier-General Samuel W. Crawford's division was outflanked and lost heavily in prisoners, the 107th losing 151 soldiers to the enemy. Thereafter, the remnant of the 107th again garrisoned a section of the trenches until returning to destroy the Weldon Railroad in December.

The 107th fought at Hatcher's Run (February 5-7, 1865), suffering a loss of 81 soldiers of the 275 engaged. During this engagement, the staff of the state color was broken by an enemy bullet.[2] During the Appomattox Campaign, the regiment fought in the series of engagements collectively known as Five Forks (March 29-April 1), losing very few men in these victories. Following Lee's surrender, the 107th returned to Washington, took part in the Grand Review on May 23, and was mustered out of service on July 13. The remnant of the state color was officially returned in 1866.

Regimental Color

This infantry regimental color was apparently carried alongside the state color during the 107th's term of service. There are several references to the 107th carrying two flags during the war; this blue color is most likely the second color. The staff was apparently broken when the flag was rescued from capture at Antietam (see below). It was given to the state when the 107th's survivors went home in 1865.

Regimental Color
1985.197

Color-Bearers

Names of fourteen men who carried the state and regimental colors of the 107th have been located. Because the regiment carried two flags and the nature of the sources are vague, in most cases it is impossible to identify which bearers carried which of the two flags.

During the Battle of Antietam, the 107th almost lost both of its colors. The regiment advanced across the Cornfield to the fence at the southern edge, then formed behind the fence and engaged the enemy for a short time. When the brigade battleline began to fall back, the 107th was the last unit to do so. By the time the left wing of the regiment retreated, several color-bearers had been hit. Brigadier-General James B. Ricketts, commanding the Second Division, First Corps, listed the names of five color-bearers of the 107th who deserved recognition. Three of these men—Sergeant Solomon R. Hough, Company A, who was wounded; Corporal Henry W. Smyser, Company E, also wounded; and a Sergeant Pike, whose name does not appear in Bates—seem to have already been casualties by the time the 107th reached the southern edge of the Cornfield.[3]

When the regiment began to retreat, Captain Henry J. Sheafer and Private John C. Delaney of Company I both noticed that the two colors lay in the hands of their bearers. Both men sprang to rescue the flags even as a Confederate battleline could be seen advancing toward the fence. Private James Kennedy, Delaney's tentmate, also ran to help. Captain Sheafer pried the state color from the dead Private Cornelius Regan of Company A, and ran to the rear. Delaney, a mere fourteen-year-old, seized the fallen regimental color from the dying Thomas Kehoe of Company C. Then, he and Kennedy followed their captain toward the rear as the Rebels shouted at them to drop the flags and surrender. Strangely, the approaching Southerners failed to immediately fire at the trio of fleeing Yankees. Captain Sheafer recalled that some of the enemy did fire shots at them. One bullet broke off the spearpoint of the state color as he ran for dear life. When most of the way across the field, Delaney encountered a wounded comrade who begged for his assistance. The youngster threw the flag to Kennedy and began to assist the wounded man to the rear. All managed to get to safety as reinforcements arrived and repulsed the enemy.[4]

During the fighting at Fredericksburg, Corporal Henry Sunniver and Private George Henthorne, both of Company B, carried the regiment's colors.[5] The two color-bearers killed at Gettysburg on July 1, 1863, were Corporal Thomas Breash of Company C and his successor, Corporal George A. McConnelly, Company H.[6] During the engagement at Hatcher's Run, Sergeant Francis J. Swoyer of Company C was cited in the official report of Major Sheafer, who wrote that Swoyer "behaved with his usual courage until compelled to relinquish the [colors], being wounded in the hand."[7] Finally, Corporal John M. Hileman of Company C carried a flag during the fighting at Five Forks.[8]

Notes

1 "The Last Flag to the Last Regiment," *Pennsylvania Daily Telegraph*, March 8, 1862.

2 Bates 3: 865.

3 *O.R.* 19.1, p. 260.

4 This reconstruction of the rescue of the colors is based upon Delaney's March 27, 1891, letter to "My Dear Capt." and an undated letter from Captain Sheafer to Thomas B. McCamant; both in Antietam Collection, Dartmouth College. The major discrepancy between these two accounts is whether or not the Rebels fired at the fleeing Unionists—Delaney wrote that they did not, while Sheafer recalled that the spearpoint was shot off his flag and another bullet broke the staff the other man was carrying. Also, in "A Brave Act at Antietam," *NT*, November 14, 1912, Delaney changed his 1891 tale by claiming that Edward Bretz, not Kennedy, was the man who helped him rescue the fallen banners. Kennedy soon came to help, while Sheafer did not play a direct role in the rescue.

5 *O.R.* 21, p. 495.

6 *Pennsylvania at Gettysburg* 2: 559.

7 *O.R.* 46.1, pp. 294-95.

8 *O.R.* 46.1, p. 895.

Bibliography

Byrnes, William. "An Artillery Fight at Close Range." *Blue and Gray* 2 (1893): 160-62.

____. "Jackson Defeated Twice?" *NT*, September 3, 1925.

____. "The 107th Pa." *NT*, March 15, 1928.

Cauler, Samuel Y. Letters, June 22, 1864-July 8, 1865. USAMHI, HbCWRT Collection.

Delaney, John C. "A Brave Act at Antietam." *NT*, November 14, 1912.

____. "The First Corps at Gettysburg." *NT*, October 1, 1914.

____. "The 107th Pa. at Gettysburg." *NT*, September 19, 1912.

____. "Robinson's Division." *NT*, September 17, 1908. (Gettysburg)

Hernbaker, Henry. *True History. Jefferson Davis Answered. The Horrors of Andersonville Prison Pen. The Personal Experience of Henry Hernbaker, Jr. and John Lynch.* Philadelphia: Merihew & Son, Printers, 1876.

Linn, George W. *An Echo of the Civil War. From Richmond to Appomattox, Some Account of the Evacuation of Richmond and Petersburg and the Surrender of General Robert E. Lee, By an Eyewitness in the Advance Column.* Lebanon: Press of Sowers Printing Company, 1911.

McCoy, Thomas. Diaries. Mifflin County Historical Society.

____. Papers. In Frank McCoy Papers. Library of Congress.

____. "At the Weldon Railroad." *NT*, March 13, 1890.

____. "Five Forks." *NT*, June 26, 1890.

____. "In the Wilderness." *NT*, September 1, 1887.

____. "The 107th Pennsylvania Veteran Volunteers at South Mountain, Antietam, and Fredericksburg." *Philadelphia Weekly Press*, January 4, 1888.

McPherson, Theodore H. N. Collection. Library of Congress.

Roath, Emanuel D. Diaries, 1863 & 1865. Lancaster County Historical Society.

Shuler, Samuel. "A Stunner." *NT*, April 26, 1923.

Weiser, Albert. Letters, March-August 1862. In George Miller Collection. USAMHI.

11th Cavalry (108th Regiment)

State Standard

Organized at Philadelphia during the autumn of 1861, the 11th Cavalry included soldiers from Iowa, Ohio, New York, and New Jersey, as well as from more than fifteen Commonwealth counties. The new regiment moved to Washington in October, and by December was in camp near Fort Monroe, Virginia. A state standard sent to the State Agency by Horstmann Brothers was presented to the regiment at some unspecified date after mid-December.

The 11th Cavalry remained at Fort Monroe until mid-May 1862. At this time, several companies were detached to the Suffolk area, while the remainder of the regiment guarded the supply trains of the Army of the Potomac. The regiment was united at Suffolk in mid-August. While forming part of this city's garrison the 11th was engaged in numerous skirmishes with enemy cavalry and guerrilla forces, most notably at Franklin (October 31), Beaver Dam Church (December 2), Deserted House (January 30, 1863), and Franklin (March 17). After taking an active part in the Siege of Suffolk by General Longstreet's Confederates (April 11-May 2), the regiment was ordered to Yorktown. While changing ships there on June 23-24, the state standard disappeared, considered stolen by the regimental historian.[1]

Unidentified Standard

After the loss of the state standard, it is likely that the 11th Cavalry obtained some type of replacement standard. After moving to Yorktown, the regiment continued on to White House, then marched inland to Hanover Court House. It raided to the crossing of the Virginia Central Railroad over the South Anna River, where a convalescing General W. H. F. Lee (Robert E. Lee's son) was seized as a prisoner. The unit destroyed the depot at Ashland Station on July 5, as Union troops feinted toward Richmond during the Gettysburg Campaign.

Following this short campaign, the 11th Cavalry was sent back to Suffolk. From July 25 to August 2, the regiment participated in a raid through North Carolina toward the Weldon Railroad, which included a skirmish at Jackson on July 29. After returning from this raid, the cavalry built a new camp near Portsmouth and remained in the area throughout the fall and winter, taking part in several expeditions into the surrounding countryside in search of elusive Confederate irregular detachments.

The regiment briefly was stationed at Williamsburg (January 23-April 8, 1864) before returning to Portsmouth to join the Cavalry Division, Army of the James. Leaving Portsmouth on May 5, the division hit the railroads south of Petersburg, destroying part of the Weldon Railroad, the 11th engaging enemy troops at Jarrett's Station (May 8). Upon returning to the Union lines on May 10, the division immediately set off on a second expedition, tearing up part of the Danville Railroad at Coalfield on May 12. The 11th fought at Flat Creek Bridge (May 14). After striking the Southside and Weldon Railroads, the command returned to rest and resupply. The regiment was next engaged on June 9 and 15, aiding in the initial attacks on Petersburg.

Union Cavalry leader James H. Wilson launched another cavalry raid on June 22, hoping to destroy the Southside Railroad. Wilson's command was occupied in this raid until July 1, covering 335 miles and fighting several engagements with enemy cavalry sent to thwart the Yankees. The 11th fought at Staunton River (June 25) and Stony Creek-Reams's Station (June 28-29), the unit suffering almost two hundred casualties. Following this raid, the regiment was engaged in picket duty, then fought at Reams's Station on August 25.

It went north of the James River in late September to screen the Union assault on the Confederate entrenchments at Forts Harrison and Gilmer. It remained in this area for the rest of the year, fighting at the Darbytown Road (October 7 and 13). In late March 1865, the division returned to the left flank of the army and fought at Five Forks on April 1. Following the Appomattox Campaign, the 11th Cavalry moved to Lynchburg, then marched to Richmond in late April. The regiment occupied Charlottesville in May, remaining there until late July, when the regiment returned to Richmond. The survivors were sent north to Philadelphia, where the regiment was disbanded on August 17.

Regimental Color
1985.198

Regimental Color

The infantry regimental color in the collection was carried by veterans of the 11th Cavalry in the 1866 ceremony. Otherwise, no documentation has been located to specify any other use by the regiment.

Company B Flag

Company B Guidon

Sergeant James E. McFarland of Company E carried the guidon shown in the accompanying photograph while acting as guide sergeant. McFarland, who later was brevetted lieutenant-colonel, preserved the flag and carried it home with him at the war's end. It was recently acquired by a private collector.

Notes

1 *History of the Eleventh Pennsylvania Cavalry*, p. 75.

Bibliography

Aughinbaugh, James. Papers. USAMHI, HbCWRT Collection.
Ayres, James C. "Twenty-eight Brothers." *NT*, July 11, 1918.
Brink, John B. "Three Long and Destructive Raids by Kautz's Cavalry." *Grand Army Scout and Soldiers Mail*, January 31, 1885.
Cruikshank, G. L. *Back in the Sixties: Reminiscences of the Service of Company A, Eleventh Pennsylvania Regiment*. Fort Dodge, IA: Times Job Printing House 1892.
____. "The Contraband. How the Cavalry Brought a Colored Man into Suffolk." *NT*, April 20, 1893.
____. "Fort Dodge Soldiers in the East." *Annals of Iowa* s3 6 (1905): 571-80.
____. "Swift Retribution. A Severe Lesson Taught Rebel Bushwackers." *NT*, April 2, 1891.
Frantz, J. H. "Stopped the Murder." *NT*, July 11, 1918.
History of the Eleventh Pennsylvania Volunteer Cavalry, Together with a Complete Roster of the Regiment and Regimental Officers. Philadelphia: Franklin Printing Company, 1902.
Lyle, Henry. Letters. USAMHI, HbCWRT Collection.
McRae, Robert P. "The Andersonville Raiders." *NT*, November 4, 1897.
____. "A Raider in Dixie." *NT*, June 2, 1887.
Porter, W. B. "Captured Fitz-hugh Lee." *NT*, January 21, 1897.
Register of the Commissioned Officers of the Eleventh Regiment of Pennsylvania Cavalry Volunteers . . . with an Appendix Containing Historical Memoranda of the Regiment During the Same Period. Philadelphia: J. B. Lippincott & Company, 1866.
Shirley, William J. "Capture of the Famous Rocket Battery." *Grand Army Scout and Soldiers Mail*, December 29, 1883.
____. "Capture of the 'Rocket' Battery." *NT*, March 17, 1887.
____. "Charge of the 11th Pennsylvania Cavalry at Franklin, Va." *Grand Army Scout and Soldiers Mail*, December 27, 1884.
____. "'Draw Saber—Charge!' A St. Patrick's Day Dash of the 11th Penna. Cavalry at Franklin, Va." *NT*, May 26, 1887.
____. "Duty Around Suffolk and Norfolk." *Grand Army Scout and Soldiers Mail*, November 27, 1884.
____. "Kelley's Store." *NT*, February 11, 1886.
____. "A Raid Near Richmond. Burning of Ashland Station." *Grand Army Scout and Soldiers Mail*, October 25, 1884.
____. "A Raid of the 11th Penna. Cavalry. Capture of Gen. Fitz Hugh Lee." *Grand Army Scout and Soldiers Mail*, January 19, 1884.
____. "Siege of Suffolk, as Taken from a Comrade's Diary." *NT*, May 13, 1886.
Stalb, J. B. "A Brilliant Charge." *NT*, January 10, 1907. (August 23, 1864)
____. "The 11th Pa. Cavalry. Scouting and Fighting Around Suffolk, Va." *NT*, December 6, 1906.
____. "The 11th Pa. Cavalry. The Time that it did Not Go to Richmond." *NT*, August 9, 1906. (February 1864)

___. "Had Been There Before." *NT*, November 8, 1906.
___. "The Siege of Suffolk." *NT*, March 16, 1911.
Stratton, Samuel R. "The 11th Pa. Cavalry." *NT*, December 1, 1887.
___. "The Night of Appomattox." *NT*, July 1, 1915.
Tripp, Stephen. "The Cavalry at Appomattox." *Maine* Bugle 5 (1898): 212-16.
___. "A Difference." *NT*, May 25, 1916. (Appomattox)
___. "Fitzhugh Lee's Capture." *NT*, June 4, 1896.

___. "The Wilson Raid." *NT*, September 21, 1899.
___. "With the Sailor Boys." *NT*, July 4, 1912.
Watson, W. W. "One of the Unfortunates." *NT*, October 26, 1911. (Andersonville)
Weaver, A. J. "The 11th Pa. Cavalry." *NT*, October 18, 1906.
Weaver, J. S. "Ready for a Raid. Some of the Exploits of the 11th Pa. Cav." *NT*, October 23, 1884.

109th Infantry

State Color

The 109th Pennsylvania was organized near Philadelphia, in a camp at Nicetown, over the winter of 1861-62. On May 7, 1862, former Pennsylvania Governor James Pollock arrived to present a state color to the regiment.[1] The 109th moved to Washington, then was ordered to Harper's Ferry. When the Army of Virginia was organized that summer, the 109th was assigned to the Second Corps, led by Major-General Nathaniel P. Banks. The regiment's first engagement with Confederate troops occurred at Cedar Mountain on August 9. Here, Color-Sergeant Lewis Shaw of Company C was killed.[2] During the ensuing Second Manassas Campaign, this corps guarded the army's supply train and was not engaged. Now assigned to the Twelfth Corps, Army of the Potomac, the 109th remained on guard duty and did not fight at Antietam. During the Fredericksburg operation, the corps was part of the force guarding the army's supply line and was not engaged.

The Twelfth Corps was part of General Hooker's force that took part in the initial flanking movement of Chancellorsville in late May 1863. During the fighting on May 3, Colonel Henry J. Stainrook was killed and the regiment was thrown into confusion. The senior captain, a number of the men, and the colors "ran ignobly from the field" and did not rejoin the regiment until after the battle. The captain was shamed into resigning and the colors were given to a more worthy bearer.[3]

The 109th arrived at Gettysburg late on July 1, then took position on Culp's Hill the next morning. The regiment was engaged that evening as Rebel troops assaulted the positions on the hill, and fought again on July 3 as the Twelfth Corps drove the enemy out of captured entrenchments. Although the 109th suffered only ten casualties, two of these were color-bearers. Sergeant John Greenwood was killed and Sergeant William McNally wounded.[4]

Following the Gettysburg Campaign, the Twelfth Corps was part of the reinforcements sent to relieve the Union troops under siege at Chattanooga. The regiment participated in the short but severe combat

State Color
Maker: HB
1985.200

at Wauhatchie on October 28, then was held in reserve during the November fighting at Chattanooga. Most of the 109th re-enlisted and went home on furlough in late January 1864.

When the regiment returned to the Army of the Cumberland, it became a part of the Second Division, Twentieth Corps. Commanded by Brigadier-General John W. Geary, this division participated in Sherman's Atlanta Campaign (May-September 1864). During the initial phase of this campaign, the 109th fought at Resaca (May 15), Pumpkin Vine Creek (May 25-31), and Pine Knob (June 15-22). Sergeant Fergus Elliott of Company G carried the state color during this period. Elliott, not quite twenty-one years of age, was an Englishman who came to America in 1857. He was given the state color just after Gettysburg and was still bearer when the Atlanta Campaign began.[5]

When the Confederate army fell back into Atlanta's defenses, Sherman's troops followed. Geary's division, together with the rest of the corps, crossed Peach Tree Creek on July 19. Geary's troops halted on a low ridge and built a defensive line with fence rails and other materials at hand. On July 20, Confederate

Sergeant Fergus Elliott

General John B. Hood launched an attack on the Twentieth Corps, hoping to crush it before reinforcements could arrive. Union skirmishers were quickly driven in and Southern troops found a gap on Geary's right. Soon, grayclad infantry began to envelop Geary's position as the 5th and 29th Ohio fell back to avoid an enfilade musketry fire.

At this time, the 109th was in reserve behind the front line. When the troops began to fall back in confusion, most of the 109th was carried along to the rear. Elliott tried to help reform some of the fugitives, but was unable to do so. As he turned to see how close the advancing Rebels were, a friend fell dead close by.

Seeing this, Elliott decided to make a stand and stopped his rearward motion. A few 109th comrades saw Elliott halt and rallied on the flag. At the same time, a handful of artillerists of the 13th New York Battery had turned two cannon toward the enemy and were attempting to load and fire the guns. Elliott and his comrades ran to the cannon and helped man them. Meanwhile, Captain Henry Bundy of the battery had rallied about twenty-five additional soldiers and led them forward to save his guns from capture. The pointblank canister fire from these two cannon, together with the arrival of reinforcements, helped stall and eventually repulse the Confederate attack on this part of the battlefield. Sergeant Elliott always believed he had helped turn the tide of battle that day. He applied for a Medal of Honor in the 1890s but his claim was rejected.[6]

Following the engagement of Peach Tree Creek, the 109th played a minor role during the rest of the Atlanta Campaign. The regiment accompanied the army on the March to the Sea. During this campaign, Sergeant Bernard J. Drury carried the colors, having been prompted to color-bearer when Elliott was promoted to First Sergeant of Company G.[7] The regiment then participated in the Carolinas Campaign, but saw no major fighting. On March 31, 1865, the badly-understrength 109th was consolidated with the 111th Pennsylvania and served with that unit until July 19, when the 111th was mustered out of service. The 109th's state color was listed as returned by February 5, 1865, and was in the 1866 ceremony.

Presented Colors

Existing documentation indicates that the 109th received at least one additional flag during its term of service. On April 5, 1864, as the 109th was returning from furlough in Philadelphia, the regiment stopped

Regimental Color

364

Advance the Colors!

briefly in Pittsburgh. On that date, in front of the Monongahela House, former Chaplain John W. McMillan presented the regiment with a "stand of colors."[8] Corporal John M. Valleau of Company C was selected to carry this new flag, which he described as a "blue, or state color." Valleau carried it throughout the Atlanta campaign. The flag was struck repeatedly by bullets at Resaca on May 15. Another lead ball passed through Valleau's cap and burned the hair from his scalp. The corporal later recalled that it felt like someone had laid a rod of hot iron on his head. At Pine Knob (June 15) the spearpoint was shot off; Valleau thought it a miracle that both he and Sergeant Elliott escaped, but the rest of the guard was laid hors-de-combat.[9]

Valleau was still carrying this color at Peach Tree Creek. When the 109th was thrown into confusion and began to drift to the rear, Valleau and his flag went along, the corporal informing Elliott that it was madness to remain under such a heavy fire. Captain Bundy, while rallying anyone he could, grabbed the staff and demanded the flag. Valleau remonstrated with the captain and told him he would advance with the flag. The corporal and a few men accompanying him then moved forward and supported the two cannon manned by Elliott and those with him. A regimental color of the 109th is currently owned by a private collector, and may be the same flag carried by Valleau during the Atlanta Campaign.[10]

Sergeant Elliott alluded to other flags in his personal writing of the war period. On September 8, 1863, the sergeant informed his family that he had charge of three stands of colors, but only carried one. On January 22, 1864, Elliott recorded in his diary that the "national flag" was given to Sergeant John Storey of Company F. However, the sergeant was drunk so John Valleau received the honor of carrying this flag. Elliott also briefly referred to guide flags, when he wrote that the "small ones" were put out to dry after a rain.[11] Without further documentation, the identity of these other flags must remain a mystery.

Notes

1 "Flag Presentation to the Curtin Light Guards," *Philadelphia Daily Evening Bulletin*, May 7, 1862.

2 Casualty list in *Philadelphia Press*, August 20, 1862.

3 *Pennsylvania at Gettysburg* 2:565.

4 *O.R.* 27.1, p. 848.

5 Elliott Diary, July 4, 1863, USAMHI.

6 For details on Elliott's actions at Peach Tree Creek, see the following, all in the Elliott Papers, USAMHI: John M. Valleau to Secretary of War Russell A. Alger, undated; Affidavit of Fergus Elliott, Alfred B. Croasdale, and Thomas Why to Secretary of War Daniel S. Lamont, October 13, 1894; and John R. Patton statement and affidavit, March 16, 1900. Captain Bundy's report *(O.R.* 38.2, p. 482) makes no mention of Sergeant Elliott. For other non-109th Pennsylvania accounts, see: F. M. Lee (13th N.Y. Battery), "Peach Tree Creek," *NT*, May 5, 1892; and Henry E. Clark (29th Ohio), "Peach Tree Creek," *NT*, November 26, 1891.

7 Special Orders #3, September 14, 1864, in Regimental Letter & Order Book, RG 94.

8 "The 109th Regiment," *Pittsburgh Gazette*, April 5, 1864, indicates a "stand of colors." However, "The 109th Regiment," *Pittsburgh Gazette*, April 6, 1864, states that a "flag" was presented.

9 Valleau, "Gallant Soldier Sons," *NT*, August 23, 1900; Idem., "Keeping the Flag to the Front," *NT*, December 29, 1898.

10 Valleau to Alger, cited above in Note 5.

11 Elliott to family, September 8, 1863; Elliott 1864 diary, entries of January 22, April 26; both in Elliott Papers, USAMHI.

Bibliography

Durin, James L. Papers. University of Virginia.
Elliott, Fergus. Papers. USAMHI.
____. "Fergus Elliott's Savannah." *Civil War Times Illustrated* 14 (June 1975): 10-16
____. "Peach Tree Creek." *NT*. July 14, 1892.
Sage, Samuel. "At Cedar Mountain." *NT*, December 12, 1907.
Stevenson, George. "The 109th Pa." *NT*., September 12, 1912.
Storey, J. H. R. "Geary at Wauhatchie." *NT*, January 3, 1907.
Valleau, John M. "The Doctor's Medicine Chest." *NT*, September 27, 1900.
____. "Gallant Soldier Sons. Bright Record of the 109th Pa. in Armies East and West." *NT*, June 21, 28, August 23, 30, September 6, 1900.
____. "Gettysburg." *NT*, May 9, 1901.
____. "Keeping the Flag to the Front." *NT*, December 29, 1898.
____. "On Sherman's March." *NT*, August 18, 1898.
____. "Saved the Day. How Infantrymen Turned Artillerists at Peach Tree Creek." *NT*, September 1, 1898.
____. "A Soldier's Presentiment. How It Bore Fruit at the Chancellorsville Battle." *NT*, October 6, 1898.
____. "Their Baptism of Fire. The Story of the 109th Pa. at Cedar Mountain Battle." *NT*, September 29, 1898.
Zeitler, A. E. "Peach Tree Creek, Ga." *NT*, January 28, 1892.

110th Infantry

First State Color

Initially organized at a camp near Huntingdon, the companies that eventually formed the 110th Infantry were transferred to Camp Curtin, where the regiment was finally organized in December 1861. On the last day of 1861, the regiment marched into Harrisburg and formed in front of the Capitol. Here, Governor Curtin presented a new state color to Sergeant Davidson Martin of Company E.[1] Two days later, the regiment, as yet unarmed, boarded a train for Hagerstown, Maryland. At this time, Southern troops led by Stonewall Jackson were threatening the Union position at Hancock, Maryland, and the 110th was sent as reinforcements.

Half of the 110th was recruited in Philadelphia, the remaining companies in Blair, Huntingdon, Bedford, and Centre counties. The city companies were generally understrength, but in the election of officers, all but the lieutenant-colonel were Philadelphians. Sergeant Martin's selection as color-bearer "created a bitter feeling among the country portion of the regiment," several of whom determined to take the flag from Martin at the first opportunity. When the train arrived in Hagerstown on January 3, the soldiers were left to fend for themselves in obtaining rations. Many Yanks headed for the saloons, and reinforced by whiskey, several enterprising country boys accosted Martin and a general fight broke out. The officers had difficulty getting the men into line. They marched the 110th out of the city along the National Pike, newly-repaired with crushed limestone. Once the regiment halted for bivouac, a regimental melee broke out, as city boys and country boys pelted each other with pieces of limestone. Provost guards finally arrived and quelled the riot, but more than forty soldiers were killed or maimed. The regimental historian recording this event failed to write whether or not the state color was given to another bearer.[2]

After helping repel Jackson's maneuvers against Hancock, the 110th was part of a division of Union troops that guarded the Baltimore & Ohio Railroad before moving to Winchester in March 1862. Here, Stonewall Jackson's Confederates attacked Brigadier-General James Shields's troops on March 23. The 110th participated in the successful charge on a section of stone wall protecting some of the grayclad soldiers. Losses for the 110th totalled fifty. The state color was pierced by three bullets while another tore off the finial.[3]

After spending several weeks on guard duty near Winchester, the 110th marched to Fredericksburg, then tramped back into the Shenandoah Valley, fighting at Port Republic on June 8-9. Then, worn out from weeks of constant service, the 110th went to Alexandria to rest and refit. As part of Irvin McDowell's First Corps, Army of Virginia, the regiment was present at Cedar Mountain on August 9, suffering few casualties. At Second Manassas, the regiment was engaged on August 30, losing heavily. As twilight fell, the 110th became scattered and mixed with the advancing enemy. Sergeant William A. Norton of Company I, fearing the loss of the flag, tore the silk from the staff and safely carried the banner as the survivors fell back.[4]

After retreating to Washington, the 110th became a part of the Third Corps, Army of the Potomac, fighting at Fredericksburg on December 13. The regiment

First State Color
Maker: HB
1985.201

participated in the Chancellorsville Campaign (April-May 1863), engaging Confederate troops on May 3 especially. Then followed the Gettysburg Campaign. Here, the 110th fought in and near the now-famous Wheatfield on July 2. After taking part in the Bristoe Station and Mine Run campaigns (October-November), the regiment went into winter camp near Brandy Station. Many of the survivors re-enlisted and went home on furlough during the winter. The state color may have been taken along and deposited in Harrisburg at this time. It was officially returned to the Commonwealth in 1866.

Second State Color

Captain Franklin B. Stewart acknowledged receipt of this flag on May 5, 1864.[5] On this same day, the regiment, now attached to the Second Corps, crossed the Rapidan River as Meade's troops pushed into the Wilderness, fighting here on May 6-7. At Spotsylvania, the 110th engaged the enemy on May 9, then took part in the May 12 grand charge of the Second Corps. Thereafter, the depleted regiment fought at the North Anna River, Cold Harbor, and the initial assault on Petersburg (June 16 and 18).

The 110th was actively engaged during the ensuing operations at Petersburg. It fought at Deep Bottom (July 27-29) and there again on August 13-20. At Poplar Spring Church (Peebles's Farm) on October 2, the regiment participated in an abortive attack on a Confederate position. The regiment next fought at the Boydton Plank Road (October 27-28), where it helped recapture some abandoned Union cannon. After a fairly quiet winter in the Petersburg trenches, the 110th fought at Hatcher's Run (February 5-7, 1865),

Second State Color
Maker: EH
1985.203

Fort Stedman (March 25), and Amelia Springs (April 6). Following Lee's surrender at Appomattox, the few survivors of the 110th moved to Washington and took part in the Grand Review on May 23. The regiment was mustered out of service on June 28. The second state color was officially returned in 1866.

Regimental Color

The remnants of this blue infantry regimental color indicate it as a standard national eagle design. Nothing has been found to document its acquisition and use by the 110th.

Regimental Color
1985.202

Color-Bearers

Owing to the possibility that the 110th carried the blue regimental color in addition to its state color, the names of color-bearers are included here. On January 30, 1863, Color-Sergeant William H. Hill was promoted to second lieutenant of Company E.[6] Corporal Joseph White of Company E was appointed color-sergeant on February 9, 1863.[7] This soldier may have carried the state color throughout 1863 and possibly until he was discharged on October 6, 1864. Among the few casualties at Poplar Spring Church was Sergeant Valentine Stewart of Company B. Stewart was instantly killed when a bullet passed through the flag and pierced his heart.[8] On February 6, 1865, when the regiment charged the enemy field works at Hatcher's Run, Color-Sergeant Mike Feather of Company H was the first Yankee color-bearer to plant his flag on the enemy line. He was awarded a thirty-day furlough for his efforts.[9] Finally, Sergeant George G. Tate of Company B was appointed color-bearer on June 2, 1865.[10]

Color-Party of the 110th Infantry
Although All Soldiers are Unidentified, the Sergeant is Probably William H. Hill

Notes

1 Hamilton manuscript, p. 5. Hamilton does not mention Martin's first name, only his company. Bates (3: 999) has a Davidson Martin listed as a private, but has no additional information about this man.

2 Hamilton manuscript, pp. 6-7.

3 Colonel William G. Lewis, Jr. to Governor Curtin, March 30, 1862, RG 19, 110th Pennsylvania Regimental Papers.

4 Hamilton manuscript, pp. 59-60.

5 Frank Stewart to A. L. Russell, May 5, 1864, RG 25.

6 Special Orders #2, January 30, 1863, Regimental Papers, RG 19.

7 Special Orders #7, February 9, 1863, in Regimental Letter, Indorsement, and Order Book, RG 94.

8 Hamilton manuscript, p. 208.

9 Ibid., p. 221.

10 Unnumbered Regimental Order, June 2, 1865, RG 94. The Hamilton manuscript, p. 225, indicates that Sergeant Tate carried a flag on March 25, 1865.

Bibliography

Anderson, William. Reminiscences. Western Reserve Historical Society.

Apgar, Naum. Papers. Huntingdon County Historical Society.

Applebaugh, Charles E. "Concerning Shields's Division." *NT*, May 12, 1887.

Duram, James C., and Duram, Eleanor A. (editors). *Soldier of the Cross: The Civil War Diary and Correspondence of Reverend Andrew Jackson Hartsock*. Manhatan, KS: MA/AH Publishing for the American Military Institute, 1979.

Hamilton, James C. M. Manuscript History of the 110th Pennsylvania. War Library and Museum, Philadelphia.

____. "Chancellorsville." *Philadelphia Weekly Press*, May 25, 1887.

____. "Marching to Battle. Laborious Time the 110th Pa. had in Getting to Gettysburg." *NT*, October 7, 1909.

____. "The 110th Regiment in the Gettysburg Campaign." *Philadelphia Weekly Press*, February 24, 1886.

Hartman, J. P. C. and George L. Letters, July 1862-August 1863. USAMHI, CWMisc Collection.

Huyette, Samuel L. "A Premonition." *NT*, December 8, 1927.

Lanny, Joseph. "At Petersburg." *NT*, March 30, 1916.

Leighty, Joseph H. Letters, September 1862-April 1865. USAMHI, CWMisc Collection.

McCarthy, Miles. Letters. Huntingdon County Historical Society.

Swaney, David R. P. 1865 Letters. USAMHI, CWMisc Collection.

111th Infantry

First State Color

Recruited in Erie, Crawford, and Warren counties, the companies of the 111th Pennsylvania assembled at a camp near Erie in September 1861. The new regiment stayed in this camp, drilling, until late February 1862, when they were summoned to Harrisburg. On March 1, Governor Curtin personally gave the 111th a state color as the regiment was drawn up in line in front of the State Arsenal.[1] Later that same day, the regiment entrained for Baltimore. It remained in this city on guard duty until late May, when it was ordered to Harper's Ferry to reinforce Major-General Nathaniel Banks's troops.

The 111th remained in the Shenandoah Valley until the Army of Virginia was organized in June. Assigned to Banks's Second Corps, the regiment took part in the engagement at Cedar Mountain (August 9), suffering ninety casualties. During the ensuing Second Manassas Campaign, Banks's corps guarded the army's trains and was not actively involved in the fighting. Banks's corps then became the Twelfth Corps, Army of the Potomac. The 111th fought at Antietam on September 17, losing 110 soldiers, its heaviest loss of the war. The bearer of the state color was seriously wounded in this battle and the battered flag was given to Sergeant Alonzo Foust of Company I.[2] Thereafter, the corps remained near Harper's Ferry on guard duty until it rejoined the army just after the December battle at Fredericksburg.

In 1863, the 111th first engaged the enemy at Chancellorsville on May 1-3, fortunately escaping with few casualties during the fighting in the woods near the Chancellor House. At Gettysburg, the regiment fought on July 2-3 at Culp's Hill, again escaping with a short casualty list. In September, the Twelfth Corps was sent to Chattanooga to bolster the Union defenders of that important city. Together with other Twelfth Corps regiments, the 111th heroically sustained the attack of a superior number of Confederate soldiers in the October 28-29 night action at Wauhatchie, Tennessee. During the fighting around Chattanooga, the regiment was engaged at Lookout Mountain (November 24) and at Ringgold, Georgia, three days later.

In late December, most of the survivors re-enlisted for another three-year term and the regiment re-

State Color
Maker: HB
1985.205

State Color
Maker: HB
1985.206

turned home on furlough. A correspondent of the *Erie Weekly Gazette* covered the veterans' triumphal return, noting that the two colors borne by the regiment were "ribboned and almost totally destroyed."³ The state color was sent to Harrisburg and officially returned in 1866.

Second State Color

A replacement state flag was authorized by the State Legislature on April 11, 1863, as part of Joint Resolution #11.⁴ Sergeant Foust was given the new flag on February 26, 1864, when the regiment arrived in Pittsburgh on its way back to Chattanooga. Sergeant Foust would carry this color throughout the 1864 campaigns.

Now a part of the Twentieth Corps, the 111th took part in many of the battles and skirmishes of the Atlanta Campaign (May-September 1864). It fought at Resaca (May 14-15), where the regiment gallantly charged a battery, planted its colors at this position, then had to fall back. During the operations near Dallas (May 25-June 2), the regiment sustained more than fifty casualties. The 111th suffered more losses during the fighting at Pine Knob (June 15 and 17), then lost a few more soldiers during the pursuit of the retreating enemy. During the July 20 fighting at Peach Tree Creek, the 111th lost about eighty comrades. When General Hood's troops evacuated Atlanta, the 111th was part of the first Union column to enter the city. Together with the 60th New York, the 111th raised its flags from the city court house.⁵

The regiment remained in the city on provost guard duty until General Sherman began his now-famous "March to the Sea." The Twentieth Corps—and the 111th—accompanied Sherman on this campaign, which culminated in the capture of Savannah on December 21. Then followed the successful Carolina Campaign, during which the 111th sustained few casualties. After marching north to Washington, the regiment took part in the Grand Review (May 24, 1865), then remained on guard duty until mustered out of service on July 19. The remnant of the second state color was returned in 1866.

Presented Colors

During its term of service, the 111th carried at least three flags in addition to the two state colors. In appreciation for its gallantry at Antietam, brigade commander Colonel Henry J. Stainrook of the 109th Pennsylvania presented the 111th with an "elegantly finished flag" shortly after the battle.⁶

When the regiment returned to the field in 1864, the veterans brought along a national color the 111th

Regimental Color
1985.204

had carried earlier in he war. Thus, the regiment carried three stands of colors according to Corporal Calvin H. Blanchard of Company D, the man chosen from among the many volunteers desirous of carrying the tattered stars and stripes.⁷ During the Atlanta Campaign, all three bearers went out on the skirmish line with their flags rather than remain in reserve as was the customary army procedure. Blanchard had many close calls as bullets flew thick about the flag he carried.

In addition to the two state colors in the collection, there is the remnant of a blue regimental color returned in 1865 when the regiment was mustered out. A collector has custody of the remnant of a blue regimental color that came from Colonel George A.

Remnant of One of the 111th's Presented Colors

Cobham's family.

Color-Bearers

In addition to Sergeant Foust and Corporal Blanchard, names of other bearers have been located. At Cedar Mountain, Corporal E. V. Sedgwick of Company C was killed while carrying one of the regiment's flags.[8] When the regiment came home in early 1864, Corporal Frank Guy of Company E posed with Sergeant Foust for a photograph with two of the regiment's colors. Guy apparently retained his status as bearer throughout the 1864 campaigns.[9] On December 22, 1864, all three bearers—Foust, Guy, and Blanchard—were reduced to the ranks for drunkenness and desertion of their colors. Three new bearers were appointed in their places. These men were Sergeants Alfred E. Harper (Company E), Myron P. Good (Company C), and Lewis Minium (Company G).[10] According to Bates, it seems that the three men busted to the ranks were restored to their former ranks prior to mustering out.

Notes

1 "Flag Presentation," *Pennsylvania Daily Telegraph*, March 1, 1862. Boyle, on page 20, writes that the presentation date was February 27.

2 Boyle, p. 61.

3 "Return of the 111th Regiment," *Erie Weekly Gazette*, January 16, 1864.

4 *Laws of Pennsylvania, 1863*, p. 610.

5 Boyle, p. 246.

6 "The 111th Regiment, *Erie Weekly Gazette*, October 2, 1862; Boyle, p. 65.

7 Blanchard Reminiscences. Blanchard's appointment is Special Orders #23, March 23, 1964, Company D Book, RG 94.

8 Information from Patrick Knierman.

9 Photograph in Boyle, plus information on Guy on p. 341.

10 Special Orders #77, December 22, 1864, in Regimental Order & Court Martial Book, RG 94.

Bibliography

Blanchard, Calvin H. Reminiscences. Crawford County Historical Society.
Boyle, John R. *Soldiers True, The Story of the One Hundred and Eleventh Regiment Pennsylvania Veteran Volunteers, and of Its Campaigns in the War for the Union, 1861-1865*. New York: Eaton & Mains, 1903.
Clark, Edwin. "An Andersonville Prisoner." *NT*, November 23, 1905.
Cobham, George A. Papers. Warren County Historical Society.

Frank Guy (left) and Alonzo Foust (right) with the Regimental Colors
A December 1863 Photograph Taken in Pittsburgh

Dyke, L. J. "Lookout Mountain." *NT*, September 22, 1887.
———. "The 'White Star' Still Shining Where It did 23 Years Ago at Lookout." *NT*, February 17, 1887.
Harper, Alfred C. Diaries, 1863-65. Crawford County Historical Society.
Lang, C. A. " 'Old Ben,' and How He Silenced the Guns of a Rebel Battery." *NT*, January 6, 1887. (Lost Mountain, GA)
Lowell, N. W. "The Record of the One Hundred Eleventh Pennsylvania Volunteers." *Philadelphia Weekly Times*, May 15, 1886.
Miller, James T. Letters. University of Michigan.
Moore, Sheldon M. "The 111th Pa. A Comrade Tells How It, Too, had a Hand in the Fight on Lookout Mountain." *NT*, May 5, 1887.
Swineford, George W. "On Culp's Hill.'" *NT*. April 29, 1915.
———. "On Culp's Hill." *NT*, August 3, 1916.
Watkins, J. P. "Peach Tree Creek." *NT*, October 13, 1892.
Wells, J. F. "Lookout Mountain." *Philadelphia Weekly Press*, July 20, 1887.
Winslow, Frederick S. "The First in Atlanta." *NT*, October 23, 1924.

2nd Heavy Artillery (112th Regiment)

State Color

Recruited from volunteers who enlisted throughout the Commonwealth, the 2nd Heavy Artillery was the largest Federal regiment during the Civil War, its enrollment exceeding five thousand men. The regiment was organized during the fall and winter of 1861-62. The first three companies were sent to Fort Delaware for duty in January 1862. The remainder of the 112th went to Washington in late February, where it was joined by the companies from Fort Delaware. Thereafter, until the spring of 1864, the regiment garrisoned part of the Washington defenses north of the Potomac River.

A state color manufactured by Horstmann Brothers was sent to the regiment with Captain Gustavus L. Braun of Battery I in April 1862.[1] The second colonel of this regiment, Augustus A. Gibson, returned the flag to the state. Gibson claimed that since the unit had been mustered into Federal service, it should carry the government flag with which it was already supplied rather than the state color. However, the colonel was subsequently informed that all Pennsylvania commands were supplied with state flags, so he requested Colonel Puleston to return the flag in a ceremony to be mutually agreed upon.[2]

In late May 1864, the regiment was ordered to report to the army in the field, and joined the Eighteenth Corps, Army of the James, at Cold Harbor. Since the regiment mustered well over a thousand men at this time, each of its three battalions maneuvered separately in line of battle. The regiment participated in the June 18 assault on Petersburg, suffering more than a hundred casualties. After arduous duty in the Petersburg trenches, the regiment attacked Fort Gilmer at Chaffin's Farm on September 29. Before the charge was sounded, the men requested that the colors be sent to the rear for safekeeping.[3] The loss in the unsuccessful charge totalled 237.

The regiment then garrisoned the captured earthworks north of the James River until early December, when it returned to Bermuda Hundred. After the evacuation of Petersburg in April 1865, the 2nd Artillery was distributed by companies throughout southern Virginia to perform provost guard duty. The regiment was mustered out of service at City Point on January 29, 1866. The men returned to Philadelphia and were sent home from that point. The state color was left in Philadelphia and officially returned on July 4, 1866.

State Color
Maker: HB
1985.207

State Standard
Maker: HB
1985.209

State Standard

This small flag was supplied to the state by Horstmann Brothers in May 1865. It was sent to Adjutant-General Russell's Office in Harrisburg. It is not known if the unit actually received the flag while it was employed on guard duty in Virginia. The standard appears on Major Lane's April 1866 list of flags at his Philadelphia office and apparently was in the 1866 ceremony.

Regimental Color

Although the use of this yellow artillery color is largely undocumented, it appears that this flag was acquired by the 2nd Artillery at some point prior to the

Regimental Color
1985.208

state color. It was apparently carried throughout the war and then returned in 1866. Surviving evidence shows that this flag was manufactured in Philadelphia, but the tattered section of this flag does not include the name of the supplier. The cord has a piece of black crepe attached.

Battery Guidons

On May 25, 1922, S. B. Rambo, the superintendent of the Department of Public Grounds, acknowledged receipt of a Battery F Guidon from the state adjutant-general's office. It was subsequently installed in Case Three in the Capitol Rotunda.[4] On August 11, 1862, Captain David Schooley's artillery company, which became Battery M, received a flag from the ladies of

Battery F Guidon
Size: 18 3/4 x 31
1985.210

Pittston, Luzerne County. The presentation took place that evening at the Eagle Hotel, where Theodore Strong presented the flag on behalf of its donors. No further information on this flag has been located.[5]

Color-Bearers

Names of six color-bearers appear in the regimental books in the National Archives. Regimental Orders #26, dated June 5, 1863, appointed a guard of ten corporals for Sergeants Stephen H. Witt (Company F) and Charles Link (Company G). On May 10, 1864, Link's name appears in Regimental Orders #23, but Witt was replaced by Sergeant Henry F. Rutledge of Company E. On November 16, 1864, Regimental Orders #52 continued Rutledge as bearer and replaced Link with Sergeant James B. Furness of Company M. Three bearers appear in Regimental Orders #22 of January 17, 1866. In addition to Rutledge, the remaining two were Sergeants Lewis Wagner (Company H) and Thomas Hackney (Company C).[6]

2nd Provisional Heavy Artillery (189th Regiment—4th Artillery)

Since the 2nd Heavy Artillery contained almost two thousand men in early 1864, the War Department authorized the formation of a new regiment to be composed of volunteers from the original. Numbered the 2nd Provisional Heavy Artillery, this new command was also dubbed the 189th Regiment (4th Heavy Artillery) by Governor Curtin, who entered into a controversy with Colonel Gibson over the appointment of officers for the new unit. When organized in late April, the regiment joined the Ninth Corps. It suffered negligible casualties in the Wilderness, at Spotsylvania, and the North Anna River.

After fighting at Cold Harbor on June 1-2, the regiment charged the Confederate fortifications at Petersburg on June 17, suffering more than two hundred killed and wounded. Color-Sergeant John Wareing fell when a grapeshot mangled his leg. Minus Devins, who retrieved the fallen banner, was also shot and later died from his wounds. In less than forty minutes of combat, the regiment suffered a loss of 246. When the survivors fell back, the flag was left behind. It was found by Bernard Strasbaugh of the 3rd Maryland, who returned it to the 2nd Provisional Artillery later that night. Strasbaugh received a Medal of Honor for his rescue of the flag.[7]

The regiment then took an active part in the siege operations at Petersburg. On July 30, the regiment fought at the Crater, again suffering heavily. It engaged the enemy on August 20-21 during the foray against the Weldon Railroad. By this time, the regiment had

2nd Heavy Artillery

373

lost over half its strength. Later in August the survivors were returned to the 2nd Heavy Artillery.

There are no surviving flags carried by the 2nd Provisional Artillery. Evans & Hassall furnished a state artillery standard to the Commonwealth in January 1865. However, the regiment no longer existed and the flag remained at the State Agency until the building was closed in 1866. Thereafter, the standard disappeared from any documentation.

Notes

1 "Flag Memorandum" document, RG 25; Colonel Charles Angeroth to Captain Braun, April 25, 1862, in Regimental Letter & Indorsement Book, RG 94; A. L. Russell to Colonel Angeroth, April 19, 1862, in Adjutant-General Letter Book, 1861-63, RG 19.

2 Gibson to J. H. Puleston, October 15, 1862, ibid.

3 Ward, p. 108.

4 S. B. Rambo receipt, May 25, 1922, RG 25.

5 "Departure of Schooley's Battery," *Pittston Gazette*, August 14, 1862.

6 All orders are in the Regimental Order & Roster Book, RG 94.

7 Ward, p. 190; *O.R.* 40.1, p. 748; C. Wilson, "The 2nd Pa. Provisional H.A.," *NT*, December 29, 1910.

Bibliography

Alexander, Joseph M. "Army of the James. Fighting and Suffering Around Bermuda Hundred." *NT*, July 31, 1890.

Beller, James W. "The Mine Explosion." *NT*, June 20, 1889.

De Nio, G. F. "An Incident of the Mine Explosion." *NT*, October 1, 1914.

Fosnot, Lewis C. This veteran was editor of the *Watsontown Record and Star*. Beginning in January 1887, he began to use the paper as the unofficial organ of the veterans of the 2nd Heavy Artillery. For more than twenty years thereafter, this paper contained, in most issues, articles by veterans and notes on reunions and other activities of the regiment's survivors.

Gramlich, C. F. "To Settle a Dispute." *NT*, July 30, 1908. (Mine)

Grugan, Florance W. Letters, March 31-November 26, 1864. USAMHI.

Guest, William A. Letters. USAMHI, CW Misc Collection.

Hadsall, Charles. Diary. Nebraska State Historical Society.

Knapp, Chauncey L. "Notable Regiments." *NT*, December 31, 1903.

____. "2nd Pa. Heavy Artillery." *NT*, March 21, 1912.

Lawrence, Henry J. "The Petersburg Crater." *NT*, January 31, 1907.

Lee, George S. "The Jefferson Davis Guards." *NT*, May 30, 1918.

Pippit, J. Henry. "Before Richmond. Battle of Chaffin's Farm—Capture of Fort Harrison." *NT*, October 10, 1918.

____. "Cold Harbor to Petersburg." *NT*, August 6, 1914.

____. "In Front of Petersburg. Bermuda Hundred and Chaffin's Farm. Incidents on the March, Etc., and Last Engagement with the Enemy Near Chester Station." *NT*, October 15, 1914.

____. "The Last Engagement with the Retiring Enemy from the Vicinity of Petersburg, April 3, 1864 [5]." *NT*, February 18, 1909.

____ "Marching to Cold Harbor." *NT*, August 25, 1910.

Price, O.D. "Veterans Saw Man Killed in Crater Buried in Trench." *NT*, August 27, 1931.

Sanderson, Joseph W. *Memoirs and Memoranda of Forty and Fifty Years Ago*. Milwaukee: Burdick & Allen, Printers, 1907.

Smith, Cyrus. "The Colonel's Grasshopper Step." *NT*, April 25, 1912.

Ward, George W. *History of the Second Pennsylvania Veteran Heavy Artillery, (112th Regiment Pennsylvania Volunteers), from 1861 to 1866, Including the Provisional Second Penn'a Heavy Artillery*. Philadelphia: George W. Ward, Printer, 1904.

Wells, Stephen F. "Camp Doings." *NT*, September 28, 1911.

____ "Captured Four Confederates." *NT*, February 23, 1911.

____. "Forts Harrison and Gilmer." *National Tribune Scrap Book* 3: 32.

Wilson, Clarence. "At Cold Harbor." *NT*, August 17, 1893.

____. "The Crater Fight." *NT*, September 28, 1899.

____. "Exploding a Mine." *NT*, May 14, 21, 1896.

____. "In Front of Petersburg." *NT*, August 4, 1898.

____. "In the Trenches. Ninth Corps Man Tells of Storming Petersburg." *NT*, January 6, 1898.

____. "The Petersburg Mine." *NT*, September 22, 1904.

____. "The Petersburg Mine." *NT*, July 3, 1919.

____. The 2d Pa. Prov. H. A." *NT*, May 1, 1919.

____. "The 2d Pa. Provisional H. A. Fighting with Grant from the Wilderness to Petersburg." *NT*, December 29, 1910.

____. "Where was the Plantation that Afforded Such Lovely Foraging?" *NT*, November 19, 1914.

12th Cavalry (113th Regiment)

State Standards

This cavalry regiment, composed of soldiers recruited in more than fourteen counties spread across the state, was organized at a Philadelphia camp in late November 1861. It remained in camp until late April 1862, when the regiment was sent to Washington. Here, another lengthy camp period ensued. Horstmann Brothers completed a standard for the regiment in early May; on the twentieth of that month, Adjutant-General Russell forwarded the flag to the State Agency.[1] Thereafter, this flag disappears from the existing written record. It was never returned to the state. When the state military department queried officers about missing flags prior to the 1866 ceremony, the 12th Cavalry was apparently never contacted about this missing flag.

The regiment remained in Washington until late June, when it was sent to guard a section of the Orange & Alexandria Railroad. During the Second Manassas Campaign, Confederate General Ambrose P. Hill's division encountered the 12th Cavalry at dark on August 27, as the regiment was engaged in scouting near Manassas Junction. In the ensuing struggle in the dark, the regiment lost more than 260 of its men, primarily captured. Thereafter, the regiment joined the Army of the Potomac and was engaged in scouting and skirmishing during the Maryland Campaign that culminated in the fighting at Sharpsburg on September 17.

The 12th was then assigned as guards for a section of the Baltimore & Ohio Railroad. The regiment was engaged in this activity until June 1863, when it fought at Winchester as part of Major-General Robert H. Milroy's command. Milroy's division was attacked by Lee's Second Corps and suffered severely, the 12th losing 172 troopers, again mostly captured. The regiment then participated in some of the small engagements as Lee retreated from Gettysburg. Then, until the spring of 1864, the regiment served as guards in the northern Shenandoah Valley before re-enlisting and returning home on furlough.

During the 1864 Valley operations, the 12th Cavalry skirmished with Jubal Early's advancing troops as that general swept north to threaten Washington. The regiment engaged the enemy at Winchester (July 20 and 24), then fought in several skirmishes at the opening of Sheridan's campaign. Owing to excessive duty, the regiment was then sent to the rear to obtain fresh horses. Headquarters was established at Charleston, West Virginia, where the regiment entered guard and garrison duties.

On February 18, 1865, Colonel Marcus A. Reno, the regiment's new commander, wrote to request a state standard. Reno indicated that the regiment did not have one at the time, and thought that such a symbol might help with morale.[2] The requested standard was finished by Horstmann Brothers in late April and was sent to Reno via Harper's Ferry. This flag also was not returned to state care and remains unaccounted for.

National Standard
1985.211

National Standards

In his February 1865 letter, Colonel Reno mentioned that his command carried only a United States standard, presumably the one present in the collection. In the early spring of 1865, the regiment engaged enemy irregular forces in the Shenandoah Valley. Upon the cessation of hostilities, the 12th remained in the Valley on provost duty until it was sent to Philadelphia and mustered out of service on July 20. The national standard was left at Camp Cadwalader and given to state custody. The Historical Society of Pennsylvania owns a national standard attributed to the 12th Cavalry. It was acquired by donation in 1943 without any attached history.

Presented Flags

The regiment was the recipient of three flags presented by friends. On February 21, 1862, Mrs. Colonel William Frishmuth presented the men with a "handsome silk flag."[3] On March 12, Mr. A. V. Zane of Philadelphia presented a "handsome regimental flag" to the 12th Cavalry.[4] Finally, on April 28, Philadelphia Mayor Alexander Henry presented "colors" with an appropriate speech.[5] Nothing else has been found to document the use or eventual disposition of these flags.

Notes

1 A. L. Russell to Colonel J. H. Puleston, May 20, 1862, in Adjutant-General's Letter Book, 1861-63, RG 19.

2 Reno to Colonel Samuel B. Thomas, February 18, 1865, RG 25.

3 Untitled story in *Philadelphia Daily Evening Bulletin*, February 22, 1862.

4 "Flag Presentation," *Philadelphia Press*, March 13, 1862.

5 James A Congdon to William T. Bishop, April 28, 1862, Congdon Letters.

Bibliography

Bookmyer, Edwin. "Second Bull Run." *NT*, October 19, 1905.
Casner, John. "On the Scout." *NT*, December 15, 1898.
Congdon, James A. Letters, 1862-65. Historical Society of Pennsylvania.
Cramer, G. W. "A Few Recollections." *NT*, January 17, 1901.
Darling Family Papers. Western Reserve Historical Society.
Gilmer, R. A. "Saved Train from Mosby." *NT*, September 26, 1912.
McAteer, Simon. 1864 Diary. Historical Society of Pennsylvania.
Scott, Scott W. "A Rebel Stampede. How the Johnnies were Driven from Frederick, Md." *NT*, April 8, 1886. (1864)
Valentine, Malden. "Saved Philadelphia. Milroy's Stubborn Resistance Gave Time for the Army of the Potomac to Get Up." *NT*, November 19, 1908.
Weirick, Charles. Letters. USAMHI.

114th Infantry

State Color

In August 1861, Captain Charles H. T. Collis raised in Philadelphia an independent company of infantry known as the "Zouaves D'Afrique." This unit served in the Shenandoah Valley with Major-General Nathaniel P. Banks during the 1862 Valley Campaign. Because of the gallantry of the company, Collis was authorized to recruit an entire zouave regiment. Collis returned to Philadelphia in late July 1862 and in less than five weeks raised nine additional companies.

The new regiment, known as the 114th Pennsylvania, then moved to Washington and joined the Third Corps, Army of the Potomac. It is not known when the unit received a state color. Horstmann Brothers & Company had completed a color for the 114th in March 1862, long before the regiment was recruited. Presumably, the 114th obtained its flag when Colonel Samuel B. Thomas visited the army in October to distribute flags to the new Pennsylvania regiments.

On December 13, the regiment met the enemy at Fredericksburg. It helped support two artillery batteries covering the retreat of Meade's Pennsylvania Reserves. Losses totalled fifty-two men. The regiment next fought at Chancellorsville on April 30, 1863, then again on May 2-3, suffering almost two hundred casualties. Two months later, on July 2, the regiment was posted just north of the now-famous Peach Orchard at Gettysburg. The 114th fell back under pressure from Confederate units from Longstreet's First Corps, leaving 155 of their number slain, wounded, or captured. After taking part in the autumn campaigns in Virginia, the regiment went into winter quarters near Brandy Station.

In the spring of 1864, the 114th was transferred to army headquarters, remaining in this service until April 1865. During this period, the regiment guarded army headquarters, acted as provost guards, escorted prisoners to the rear, and performed other such duties. On April 2, 1865, the 114th took part in the successful assault on the Petersburg defenses. After the engagement at Saylor's Creek (April 6), the regiment guarded the captured grayclad soldiers. Following Lee's surrender, the regiment returned to Washington, took part in the Grand Review (May 23), and was mustered out of service six days later. The state color was left in Philadelphia with Major William B. Lane, but was apparently appropriated by Colonel Collis sometime later. The colonel still had the flag when contacted in 1866. He promised to bring the flag to the July 4 ceremony but failed to do so.[1] Its present whereabouts is unknown.

Regimental Color

This blue color was turned in by the regiment upon mustering out of service. It was carried in the 1866 parade.

Regimental Color
1985.212

Presented Colors

Sometime during August 1862, the 114th was given two colors by groups of friends. Both presentations took place the same day while the regiment occupied Fort Slocum in the Washington defenses. One flag was described as "a handsome State flag, of blue silk, with a dark-blue ground-work, the coat of arms of the Keystone State beautifully emblazoned thereon." The second flag, presented by a group of Germantown citizens, was a national color.[2] The subsequent history and disposition of these flags is unknown. There are two 114th Pennsylvania colors at Grant's Tomb in New York City. Quite possibly, these flags were given to the tomb by Colonel Collis, but both flags are in bad condition, making reconstruction impossible.

Color-Bearers

At Gettysburg, Sergeant Benjamin Baylitts (Company C) carried "the United States flag." Corporal Michael Cannon (Company C) was bearer of "the State flag" until wounded, when Corporal Harry Hall of Company I took the flag for the rest of the battle, and carried it for "some time afterwards."[3] Sergeant Thomas Melsom's name appears as bearer in an 1866 newspaper article.[4] His name does not appear in Bates.

Notes

1 Major W. B. Lane to Governor A. G. Curtin, June 14, 1865; Colonel Collis to Adjutant-General A. L. Russell, May 25, 1866, both in RG 19.
2 Babcock article in the *Philadelphia Weekly Times*.
3 Bowen article in the *Philadelphia Weekly Press*. Baylitts's name also appears in a roll of honor article in the *Philadelphia Inquirer*, May 20, 1863.
4 "Fire Braves. The Hibernia's Heroes," *Philadelphia Sunday Mercury*, March 4, 1866.

Bibliography

Babcock, William A. "The 114th Regiment, Pennsylvania Volunteers, in the Late War." *Philadelphia Weekly Times*, April 24, 1886.
Bowen, Edward R. "Collis' Zouaves. The 114th Pennsylvania Infantry at Gettysburg." *Philadelphia Weekly Press*, June 22, 1887.
Cavada, Frederick F. *Libby Life, Experiences of a Prisoner of War in Richmond, Va., 1863-64*. Philadelphia: J. B. Lippincott & Company, 1865.
____. Letters. Historical Society of Pennsylvania
Collis, Charles H. T. "The Affair at Guiney's Station." *Century Magazine* 54 (1897): 318.
____. *Case of F. F. Cavada*. Philadelphia: King & Baird, Printers, 1866.
____. Letterbooks, 1863-68. Historical Society of Pennsylvania.
Collis, Septima M. *A Woman's War Record, 1861-1865*. New York: G. P. Putnam's Sons, 1889.
Fox, Isaac. Papers. Historical Society of Pennsylvania.
Naylor, Samuel M. "Capture of Fort Mahone." *NT*, March 4, 1909.
Rauscher, Frank. *Music on the March, 1862-'65, With the Army of the Potomac, 114th Regt., P.V. Collis' Zouaves*. Philadelphia: Press of William F. Fell & Company, 1892.

115th Infantry

First State Color

Recruited primarily in Philadelphia, the 115th Infantry was organized in a camp near Hestonville in January 1862. The regiment then moved to Camden, New Jersey, where it remained until the end of May. The unit then went to Harrisburg to guard Confederate prisoners. A state color was sent to Harrisburg by Horstmann Brothers in March 1862. The presentation list indicates that Governor Curtin gave the flag to the 115th at some unspecified date.

By the end of June, the regiment was transported to the Peninsula, where it was assigned to the Third Corps, Army of the Potomac. Together with the corps, the 115th moved north to Alexandria in late August as most of the army was sent to join Pope's Army of Virginia, then maneuvering in northern Virginia. The regiment skirmished with enemy troops at Bristoe Station on August 26, then fought at Second Manassas on August 29-30. During the repeated attacks on Jackson's position behind a railroad cut, Sergeant Hugh Barr "behaved with great gallantry, bearing his colors without falter into the thickest of the fight."[1] Defeated at

First State Color

First State Color
Maker: HB
1985.213

Manassas, the Union troops retreated to Washington, where the Third Corps remained until November. At Fredericksburg on December 13, the 115th lost a single man wounded as most of the corps was held in reserve.

After spending the winter near Falmouth, the 115th took part in the Chancellorsville Campaign of April-May 1863. Here, during the fierce struggle on May 3, the 115th's brigade fought with the enemy over possession of a line of breastworks in the woods near the Orange Plank Road. The brigade fell back only after its ammunition was exhausted. The 115th lost 111 officers and men of less than 250 taken into the fight. Sergeant Benjamin Williams of Company K was wounded while carrying the state color. Before the flag could touch the ground, Color-Corporal Patrick Kenney seized the banner and carried it throughout the rest of the fighting. Major John P. Dunne reported that the flag was torn into shreds during this struggle.[2]

Following the Chancellorsville Campaign, the regiment moved north to fight in the Wheatfield at Gettysburg on July 2. Then, after taking part in the Bristoe Station and Mine Run campaigns that fall, the surviving men of the 115th went into winter quarters at Brandy Station. Just before this latter campaign, Dunne requested a replacement state color, which was delivered to the regiment sometime in December.[3] The original color was sent back to Harrisburg and officially returned to the Commonwealth in 1866.

Second State Color

This new flag, completed by Horstmann Brothers on December 1, 1863, was sent to the State Agency for distribution shortly thereafter. Sergeant James Doyle of Company B was selected as bearer of this flag on February 13, 1864.[4] The 115th was transferred to the Second Corps in time for the opening of the 1864 campaign. After fighting in the Wilderness and at Spotsylvania, the depleted regiment engaged the enemy at Cold Harbor, then took part in the initial operations at Petersburg (June 1864). Late that month, the survivors, numbering fewer than a hundred soldiers, were consolidated into three companies and attached to the 110th Pennsylvania. Adjutant Thomas E. Stevens took the second color along home with him. It remained in his family until 1986, when it was purchased by a private collector.

Second State Color
Maker: HB

Philadelphia Flag

According to several newspaper accounts, a deputation of Philadelphia friends purchased a "silk American flag" for the 115th. The flag was supposed to measure five by eight feet. One side depicted a harp and shamrock, while the other portrayed General Sarsfield, mounted and in full uniform. The motto "No retreat from sword or bayonet" was emblazoned somewhere on the ornamental eagle finial. Gold cords and tassels completed this magnificent color. The mid-June 1862 reports about this flag are supplemented by information that the flag had been sent to Fort Monroe the following month. Nothing else has been found to document the use or disposition of this flag.[5]

Notes

1 *O.R.* 12.2, p. 464.

2 Major Dunne to Adjutant-General A. L. Russell, May 10, 1863, Regimental Papers, RG 19.

3 Dunne to Russell, October 28, November 5, 1863, RG 25.

4 General Order #1, February 13, 1864, Regimental Order and Guard Report Book, RG 94.

5 "Flag Presentation to the 115th Regiment, "*Philadelphia Inquirer,* June 13, 1862; "Flag Presentation to the 115th Regiment," *Pennsylvania Daily Telegraph,* June 14, 1862; "The 115th Regiment," *Philadelphia Inquirer,* July 10, 1862; "The Flag for Col. Patterson's Regiment," *Philadelphia Inquirer,* July 11, 1862.

Bibliography

No letters, diaries, or published materials have come to the attention of the author.

116th Infantry

First State Color

Primarily recruited among the Irish population of Philadelphia, the 116th Infantry was organized during the late summer of 1862. Its organization still incomplete, the new regiment was rushed to Washington in early September when worry over the defeat at Manassas was still at its height. The regiment remained near Washington until early October when it moved to Harper's Ferry to join the Second Corps, Army of the Potomac. It was assigned to the famous "Irish Brigade" (28th Massachusetts, 63rd, 69th, 88th New York). Colonel Samuel B. Thomas presented a state color to the 116th later that month when he visited the army to distribute state flags to the many new Pennsylvania commands.[1]

The 116th's first battle was at Fredericksburg on December 13. Here, the brigade formed part of one of the many Union charges against the entrenched Confederates on Marye's Heights. Artillery and musketry fire swept the blueclad ranks and plowed gaps in the oncoming troops. Most of the 116th's field officers quickly became casualties. Color-Sergeant William H. Tyrrell of Company C was struck in the leg

Fragments of First State Color Taken by Sergeant Tyrrell

but kept the flag aloft for a short time. The intrepid sergeant was hit by five bullets while another broke the flagstaff. When the regiment finally yielded and broke for the rear, Lieutenant Francis T. Quinlan ran back to pull the color from underneath the wounded sergeant. Quinlan grabbed the flag as scores of the enemy fired at him. He clutched the silk banner to his breast, threw himself to the frozen ground as bullets flew past him, and rolled back down the hill to rejoin his men.[2]

Having suffered heavy casualties at Fredericksburg, the emaciated 116th was reduced to a four-company battalion. After spending the winter near Falmouth, the battalion took part in the Chancellorsville Campaign, fighting on May 3, 1863. At Gettysburg, the 116th took part in the fighting in the Wheatfield. After charging through the grain field, the brigade halted on the wooded, rocky hillock to its west. The First Division of the Second Corps had driven the enemy back on its front, but the salient angle at the Peach Orchard collapsed as the Yankees were successful in the Wheatfield. Victorious rebels soon appeared on

First State Color
Maker: HB
1985.215

the right flank and rear of the troops near the Wheatfield. Major St. Clair A. Mulholland saw what was happening and passed the word to his men to break ranks and run to save themselves. Mulholland collared Sergeant Abraham Detweiler of Company C, color-bearer since Fredericksburg, and two or three other men, to make sure the flag remained safe. The fleeing Unionists successfully recrossed the Wheatfield and saved the state color from capture.[3]

The much-reduced regiment then took part in the Bristoe Station and Mine Run campaigns (October-November) before going into winter quarters near Brandy Station. Sergeant Detweiler carried the flag until promoted to lieutenant on November 9.[4] The battered original color was returned to Harrisburg in the spring of 1864 and officially presented to state care in 1866.

Second State Color

A replacement flag was provided to the 116th by Evans & Hassall in April 1864. During this period, the regiment was rebuilt by the addition of six new companies. The command took an active part in the 1864 Virginia campaign. It fought in the Wilderness (May 5-6), then at Spotsylvania (May 8-18). On the last day of the fighting at Spotsylvania, the regiment charged the entrenched enemy and was repulsed. Corporal William Wertz of Company H carried the state color and managed to plant it on the Rebel earthworks before the regiment fell back. Wertz was killed as the 116th retreated, but his body could not be recovered. To compensate a grieving mother for the loss of her brave son, Captain David W. Megraw of Company H cut a star off the flag and mailed it to Mrs. Wertz, an Allegheny City resident.[5]

After fighting at the Totopotomoy Creek (May 31-June 1), the 116th participated in the June 3 charge at Cold Harbor. Color-Sergeant Timothy A. Sloan of Company E was wounded by a bursting shell during the attack. Private James M. Seitzinger of Company G leaped forward to grab the fallen banner. A seventeen-year-old volunteer from Pottsville, young Seitzinger had been in the service only two months, having enlisted with his father in one of the new companies. As he seized the flag the lad cried out, "Come on, pop, I am all right." Colonel Mulholland recalled that Seitzinger's bravery was the talk of the regiment that night. Considered too small and slight to carry the flag, Seitzinger was promoted to sergeant, a rank already held by the lad's father. In 1906, Seitzinger was awarded a Medal of Honor for his gallantry at Cold Harbor.[6]

Following the defeat at Cold Harbor, Sergeant Peter Kelly of Company D volunteered to be color-bearer.[7] This man bravely carried the state flag during the initial Petersburg assaults (June 16-18), at Deep Bottom (July 27-28 and August 13-18), Reams's Station (August 25), and the December reconnaissance to Hatcher's Run. The regiment was under fire again at Hatcher's Run (February 5, 1865) but suffered no loss. After fighting in the engagement at the White Oak Road (March 31), the 116th was engaged at Five Forks on April 1. The next day, the regiment fought at Sutherland's Station, where Sergeant Kelly was wounded. The flag was taken up by Sergeant Edward S. Kline (Company F) until the firing ceased. The banner was then given to Sergeant Charles Maurer of Company F, the regiment's last bearer.[8]

Following Lee's surrender, the 116th moved to Washington and took part in the Grand Review (May 23). The four original companies were disbanded on June 3, the remaining companies on July 14. The remnant of the second color was kept by Colonel Megraw, who returned it to the state prior to the 1866 parade.[9]

Third State Color

On April 2, 1865, Colonel Mulholland requested a new flag, which was to include the battle honors credited to the regiment by the Army of the Potomac's March 7, 1865, order.[10] Horstmann Brothers completed this flag in mid-May and sent it to the State Agency in Washington. Together with the second state color, this new banner was also kept by Colonel Megraw until June 1, 1866. It too was included in the 1866 parade.

Second State Color
Maker: EH
1985.217

Third State Color
Maker: HB
1985.214

National Color
1985.216

National Color

This 35-star national flag was turned over to the state adjutant-general's department on August 15, 1865. No information as to its historical use has been located. Judging from its condition, it may have been acquired at the end of the conflict to carry in the victory parades.

Notes

1 Mulholland, p. 33, writes that the flag was presented by Samuel P. Bates, the then-Deputy Secretary of the Commonwealth. However, the "Flag Memorandum" in RG 25 lists Colonel Thomas as the presenter.

2 Mulholland, p. 66.

3 *Ibid.*, p. 71; Affidavits of Abraham F. Detweiler and S. D. Hunter, in 116th vs. 140th Pennsylvania manuscript book, War Library & Museum, Philadelphia.

4 Mulholland, p. 71.

5 Megraw to Mrs. Eliza Wertz, in Pension Files, RG 94.

6 Mulholland, p. 226; Statement of Colonel Mulholland, December 20, 1905, in James M. Seitzinger Medal of Honor File, RG 94.

7 Mulholland, p. 226.

8 *Ibid.*, p. 306.

9 Colonel Mulholland to A. L. Russell, May 24, 1866, RG 19.

10 Mulholland to Russell, April 2, 1865, in Regimental Papers, RG 19.

Bibliography

Alotta, Robert I. *Stop the Evil, A Civil War History of Desertion and Murder*. San Rafael, CA: Presidio Press, 1978.

Barnard, Jeremiah. "Everybody Captured Everybody." *NT*, May 31, 1923.

Hunter, S. D. "The Battle of Fredericksburg." *Grand Army Scout and Soldiers Mail*, October 6, 1883.

Hutton, William L. "The Hangings in 1864-5." *NT*, June 30, 1910.

Knapp, Solomon. "Germans in the Irish Brigade." *NT*, March 13, 1913.

Landis, Allen. Papers. Library of Congress.

McCarter, William. "Fredericksburg, As Seen by One of Meagher's Irish Brigade," *NT*, July 29, 1886.

____. "Fredericksburg's Battle." *Philadelphia Weekly Times*, September 8, 1883.

____. 1862 Reminiscences. Historical Society of Pennsylvania.

Menge, W. Springer, and Shimrak, J. August (editors). *The Civil War Notebook of Daniel Chisholm: A Chronicle of Daily Life in the Union Army, 1864-1865*. New York: Orion Books, 1989.

Mulholland, St. Clair A. Papers. War Library & Museum, Philadelphia.

____. "Battle of Fredericksburg." *Philadelphia Weekly Times*, April 23, 1881.

____. "The Gettysburg Campaign." *Philadelphia Weekly Times*, February 14, 1880.

____. *The Story of the 116th Regiment, Pennsylvania Infantry, War of Secession, 1862-1865*. Philadelphia: F. McManus, Jr. & Company, Printers, 1899.

____. *The Story of the 116th Regiment Pennsylvania Volunteers in the War of the Rebellion, The Record of a Gallant Campaign*. Philadelphia: F. McManus, Jr. & Company, Printers, 1903.

Smith, William A. Letters. USAMHI, Lewis Leigh Collection.

13th Cavalry (117th Regiment)

State Standard

Recruited originally as a squadron to be attached to the Irish Brigade, the original companies of the 13th Cavalry were upgraded to a full regiment in September 1861. Composed of troopers recruited in Philadelphia, Allegheny, Cumberland, and Lycoming counties, the regiment was organized near Philadelphia. With its organization still incomplete, the 13th was ordered to Baltimore, where it remained until late September 1862. At this time, the regiment moved out to patrol the Potomac River crossings near Point of Rocks, Maryland. The regiment was engaged in this duty until February 1863, when it was sent to Winchester, Virginia, to join the Federal troops stationed there. A state standard completed by Horstmann Brothers in January 1863 and forwarded to the State Agency in May was sent to the regiment at some unspecified date.[1]

The 13th Cavalry was at Winchester when Lee's Army of Northern Virginia attacked the garrison on June 13-15. The blue-clad troops were driven from the town, the 13th Cavalry losing more than two hundred men captured as the regiment retreated to Harper's Ferry. In early July, the regiment was assigned to the Second Division, Cavalry Corps, Army of the Potomac, and took part in the Bristoe Station Campaign in October, fighting primarily near Sulphur Springs on October 12. After the Mine Run Campaign (November), the regiment went into winter quarters near Bristoe Station. The regiment helped guard the Orange & Alexandria Railroad from Confederate guerrilla attacks throughout the winter.

During the 1864 Virginia campaign, the 13th cavalry was engaged in the operations in the Wilderness and at Spotsylvania, then fought at Haw's Shop on May 28. The regiment then went on Sheridan's Trevilian Raid (June 7-26), engaging the enemy at Saint Mary's Church on June 24. After the initial operations around Petersburg, the unit fought in the movement to the Weldon Railroad (August 13-20) and at Reams's Station on August 25. During the autumn maneuvers, the regiment engaged the enemy at Poplar Spring Church (September 29) and along the Boydton Plank Road (October 27-28). The regiment screened both movements to Hatcher's Run, fighting there on December 8-9, and again on February 5-7, 1865.

State Standard
Maker: HB
1985.218

In mid-February, the 13th Cavalry was transferred to Wilmington, North Carolina. Soon after arrival at this city, the regiment moved inland to open communications with Sherman's approaching troops. The regiment met Sherman's troops at Fayetteville and joined his cavalry. On April 13, the regiment was among the first Federal units to occupy Raleigh. Although Bates writes that the regiment displayed its tattered standard from the state capitol's dome, other evidence suggests that some of the officers procured a small national flag to place atop the capitol.[2] After the end of hostilities, the regiment moved to Fayetteville and garrisoned the town until mid-July, when the regiment began a northward rail journey to Philadelphia, where it was mustered out of service on July 27. The state standard was included in the 1866 parade.

Advance the Colors!

Notes

1 Colonel R. B. Roberts to Adjutant-General A. L. Russell, May 6, 1863, RG 19.

2 Bates 3: 1271; but see L. McMakin, "Flag on the Raleigh Capitol," *NT*, March 23, 1911, and L. McMakin, "Entering Raleigh, N.C.," *NT*, March 6, 1913.

Bibliography

Caldwell, D. "Planting the Flag at Raleigh, N.C." *NT*, June 18, 1885.

Dougherty, Michael. *Prison Diary of Michael Dougherty, Late Co. B, 13th Pa. Cavalry, While Confined in Pemberton, Barrett's, Libby, Andersonville, and Other Southern Prisons.* Bristol: C. A. Dougherty, Printer, 1908.

____. *Diary of a Civil War Hero, Michael Dougherty.* New York: Pyramid Books, 1960.

Erskine, Charles M. "The Battle of Winchester." *Grand Army Scout and Soldiers Mail*, March 14, 1885.

____. "Brave David Samuels." *Grand Army Scout and Soldiers Mail*, April 5, 1884.

____. "Experiences and Sufferings of a Prisoner of War." *Grand Army Scout and Soldiers Mail*, February 7, 14, 21, 28, 1885.

____. "Getting to the Front Under Difficulties." *Grand Army Scout and Soldiers Mail*, April 4, 1885.

____. *Life in a Rebel Prison; Or, The Experience of a Prisoner of War.* Philadelphia: Craig, Finley & Company, Printers, 1883.

____. "Recapture of the 2nd Maryland Cavalry." *Grand Army Scout and Soldiers Mail*, May 10, 1884.

Everill, S. R. "About that Running." *NT*, June 6, 1895.

____. "All Stand Up for Milroy." *NT*, March 31, 1910.

____. "As to Milroy." *NT*, September 16, 1909.

____. "At Hawes' Shop." *Grand Army Scout and Soldiers Mail*, December 6, 1884.

____. "The Boy Who Took the Flag from the Capitol at Raleigh." *NT*, January 3, 1889.

____. "The Burning of Columbia." *NT*, May 23, 1907.

____. "Gen. Milroy at Winchester." *NT*, November 29, 1888.

____. "He was Not the President." *NT*, January 24, 1901. (Fort Stevens)

____. "New York at Fort Stevens." *NT*, October 9, 1913.

____. "Stony Creek." *NT*, July 19, 1894.

____. "Those Awful Cavalrymen." *NT*, June 3, 1915.

Hollis, John. "How He Lost His Liberty." *NT*, December 15, 1898.

Kilhool, Denis. "Winchester Battle, and Something of the Last Days at Raleigh Under Sherman." *NT*, September 17, 1896.

Linn, S. T. "The Cavalry at Winchester." *NT*, March 31, 1910.

McElhinny, R. H. "Milroy at Winchester." *NT*, May 20, 1909.

McMakin, Louis. "Custer in Action." *NT*, September 8, 1910. (Haw's Shop)

____. "Entering Raleigh, N.C." *NT*, March 6, 1913.

____. "Flag on the Raleigh Capitol." *NT*, March 23, 1911.

____. "Gregg's Cavalry." *NT*, January 18, 1912. (Gettysburg)

____. "Hancock the 'Superb'." *NT*, February 9, 1911. (Weldon Railroad)

____. "Kilpatrick and Hampton." *NT*, October 12, 1911.

____. "Not Quite Over." *NT*, February 15, 1912. (Raleigh)

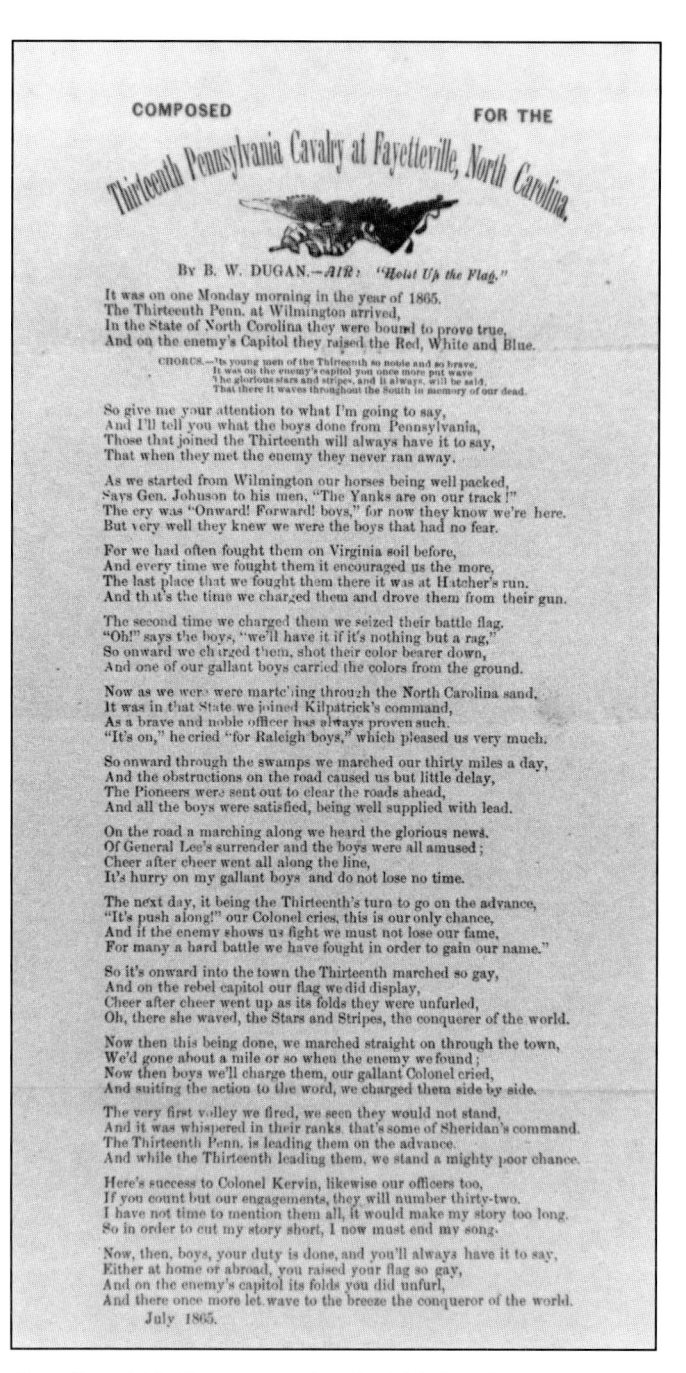

Song Broadside Commemorating the 13th Cavalry

"A Rousing Reunion. Gen. Gregg Attends that of the 13th Pa. Cavalry, Which was Exceptionally Interesting." *NT*, November 3, 1898.

"With the Army of the Potomac." *NT*, July 25, 1901. (Signed S.C., Co. G)

118th Infantry

Company H Flag

The "Corn Exchange Regiment" was recruited by that Philadelphia business concern primarily in August 1862 to serve for three years. During the recruiting period, Mrs. Sophia Donaldson contributed a national color to Company H, which was led by her nephew, Frank A. Donaldson. When the regiment was not yet fully organized, it was called to Washington in the wake of the defeat at Second Manassas. Since the 118th had not obtained a national flag, Donaldson's banner was appropriated for this purpose.

When the Army of the Potomac moved into Maryland to counter General Lee's invasion, the 118th marched to join the Fifth Corps, which was held in reserve during the struggle at Antietam. On September 20, the regiment crossed the Potomac at Shepherdstown, Virginia, as McClellan's troops probed Lee's retreating army. Once across the river, the 118th was unsupported and was assailed by a vastly superior force of Rebel soldiers. In the resulting confusion, the green recruits were literally swept down the bluffs and into the river. Colonel Charles M. Prevost seized the flag to rally his men but was wounded and taken to the rear. Of the 737 officers and men in action that day, 269 were casualties.

Following the Shepherdstown disaster, the 118th fought at Fredericksburg on December 13, losing 98 soldiers. After wintering near Falmouth, the regiment embarked on the Chancellorsville Campaign. Although the Fifth Corps was heavily involved in this engagement, the 118th suffered a mere eight men wounded. Just before this campaign, the regiment finally received a regulation national flag. Donaldson's flag, "battle scarred and bullet rent," was retired from active duty. The captain took the flag from its staff and gave it to Sergeant Henry Q. Cobb for safekeeping. The sergeant carried it in his knapsack until he was discharged in October 1863.

Donaldson kept the flag until 1877, when he loaned it to GAR Post 2, where it remained for many years. However, the captain lost track of the flag when the post transferred its headquarters to another building. He began to search for the flag and finally, in late 1914, located the banner at a trust company where a 118th veteran worked. The captain reclaimed his banner and had its remnants framed and suitably labelled. It remained in the Donaldson family until it was given to the War Library and Museum, where it is presently displayed.[1]

State Color

When Colonel Samuel B. Thomas visited the Army of the Potomac in October 1862 to present state flags to all the new Pennsylvania regiments, he brought the 118th's along. He presented this banner to the unit on October 16.[2] Thereafter, the regiment carried this flag until the end of hostilities. Following the engagements at Fredericksburg and Chancellorsville, the 118th fought at Gettysburg on July 2, at first in the Wheatfield area, then moved to Big Round Top early the next morning. After participating in the Bristoe Station and Mine Run campaigns (October-November), the regiment went into winter camp near Brandy Station.

Remnant of National Color Presented by Sophia Donaldson

State Color
Maker: EH
1985.222

National Color
1985.220

During the 1864 Virginia Campaign, the 118th fought in most of the battles from the Wilderness to Appomattox. After suffering 65 casualties in the Wilderness (May 5-7), the regiment engaged the enemy in the Spotsylvania fighting (primarily on May 8 and 10-12). Following the crossing of the North Anna River and the combat here, the 118th was engaged at Cold Harbor (June 1-2). The army then moved south, crossed the James River, and attacked Petersburg. Here, the 118th was under fire on June 16 and 21.

At Pettersburg, the 118th participated in the August 18-21 Weldon Railroad battle, then at Poplar Spring Church on September 30. In this latter action, the division charged and captured an enemy fort, the 118th suffering 48 casualties. Although present during the fighting along the Boydton Plank Road (October 27-28), the unit escaped with few casualties. Then followed the December expedition to interdict the Weldon Railroad.

In 1865, the 118th fought at Hatcher's Run (February 6), then participated in the Five Forks operation, fighting at the Quaker Road (also known as Lewis's Farm, March 29), White Oak Road (March 31), and Five Forks (April 1). Following Lee's surrender, the brigade to which the 118th was attached remained at Appomattox to superintend the actual surrender proceedings. It then returned to Petersburg. When news of President Lincoln's death reached camp, the regiment was unable to procure the black crepe required to drape its flags. Some of the veterans took their white handkerchiefs, dyed them with writing ink, and attached them to the flag staffs.[3] The 118th took part in the Grand Review (May 23), then went into camp for a short time. The regiment was mustered out of service on June 1. The state color was left in Philadelphia and was present in the 1866 parade.

National Color

According to Captain Donaldson, the 118th received a national flag during the spring of 1863.[4] There seems to be no additional documentation available on this flag. The remnant of the national color in the state collection was left in Philadelphia in 1865 and has been in state custody since that time. It is quite possible that this is the same flag acquired by the 118th in 1863.

Regimental Colors

When the 118th joined the Army of the Potomac in September 1862, it carried a blue regimental color in addition to the Donaldson flag. John L. Smith, the regimental historian, described this flag as a "state flag," probably meaning that it was a standard federal regimental color with the unit designation added to the red scroll.[6] Smith wrote that this flag was carried from Shepherdstown to Appomattox. When the survivors returned to Philadelphia in June 1865, they deposited this banner with the Corn Exchange, which later gave it to Colonel Prevost.[7] The 103rd Engineer Battalion has custody of the remnant of a blue regimental color attributed to the 118th; it may be this same banner carried during the war.

If Smith was accurate in writing that the blue regimental color given to the colonel was borne throughout the war, then the history of the regimental color in the state collection must remain a mystery. It may

118th Infantry

Regimental Color
1985.221

simply have been requisitioned at war's end to carry in the victory parade. Without further written evidence, this theory must remain conjectural.

Presented Flags

In October 1863, the Corn Exchange displayed three flags for the 118th. Made of blue and red silk, one was inscribed on the obverse with battle honors surrounding a wheat sheaf, while the reverse side sported the Philadelphia city coat-of-arms. The second flag contained the state arms on one side with the presentation inscription on the opposite. The third flag was a national color.[8] No further documentation has been located on the subsequent fate of these banners, although quite possibly the national color may be the same as that in the state collection.

Color-Bearers

The 118th carried three colors—state, national, regimental—during its term of service. Perhaps all three flags were carried into action. During the fight at Shepherdstown, as Major Charles P. Herring reached a dam across the Potomac, he found one of the bearers. The soldier was afraid to cross with the flag, so Herring took the silk banner and gave it to Private William Hummel (Company D), who escaped with the flag.[9] Captain Donaldson saw the 118th's other color floating in the river near the dam. After spending some time calling for someone to get the flag, Donaldson was pleased to see a man finally retrieve it.[10]

On June 25, 1863, as the regiment marched north to Gettysburg, Color-Sergeant David L. Ware (Company F) was promoted to First Sergeant. Sergeant John H. Williamson (same company) took his place as bearer.[11] During the charge on September 30, 1864, Corporal William H. Wild (Company C) was the first Yankee to plant a national flag on Fort McRae as the attackers surged over the parapets. Wild was shot in both legs, eventually succumbing to his mortal wounds a month later. When he fell, Captain Isaac H. Seesholtz of Company K seized the flag but was soon shot through the wrist. Thomas Crealy (Company C) then carried the flag during the remainder of this action.[12]

During the combat at Hatcher's Run (February 6, 1865), Color-Sergeant Samuel F. Delaney (Company E) was cited for remaining with the colors when the battleline was broken. He then advanced with his banner and planted it on the enemy breastworks.[13]

Flank Marker
Size: 18 x 23

Notes

1 Information about this flag is taken from "Concerning the Original Flag of the 118th Pennsylvania Infantry," Donaldson Papers.

2 Lieutenant-Colonel James Gwyn to General Fitz-John Porter, October 16, 1862, in Regimental Letter and Indorsement Book, RG 94.

3 John L. Smith to mother, April 20, 1865, Smith Papers.

4 Donaldson, "Original Flag."

5 Smith, p. 22.

6 Donaldson, "Original Flag."

7 Smith, p. 6.

8 "Handsome Flags," *Philadelphia Daily Evening Bulletin*, October 9, 1863.

9 Smith, p. 68.

10 Donaldson to Jacob A. Donaldson, September 23, 1862, Donaldson Papers. It is my conjecture that the captain noticed the blue regimental color floating in the river. Although he did not describe the flag in this letter, it seems likely that he would have been more specific had the flag been that presented by his aunt.

11 Special Order #74, June 25, 1863, in Regimental Letter and Order Book, RG 94.

12 Smith, p. 517. Smith, as well as Bates (3: 1324) has William H. Wild. However, in a November 6, 1864, letter to his mother, Smith referred to Jonathan Wild (Smith Papers). On December 27, 1864, Major James B. Wilson wrote to an unidentified captain to request a medal for Jonathan Wild so his family would have a memento to remember him by. (In Regimental Letter and Indorsement Book, RG 94)

13 Lieutenant-Colonel Henry O'Neill to Captain George F. Morgan, February 12, 1865, in Regimental Letter and Indorsement Book, RG 94.

Bibliography

Cattell, Alexander G. "An Address at the Unveiling of the Monument Erected by the Commercial Exchange Association of Philadelphia (Late Corn Exchange Association) to Commemorate the Heroic Services of the Corn Exchange Regiment, 118th Penn'a. Volunteers, Delivered at "Round Top," on the Gettysburg Battlefield, September 8, 1884." Philadelphia: Commercial List Printing House, 1884.

Cole, A. V. "118th Pa. at Shepardstown." *NT*, July 14, 1910.

Company C Muster Roll Collection. Historical Society of Pennsylvania.

Donaldson, Frank A. Papers. War Library & Museum.

Greene, C. W. "The 118th Pa. The Bloody Fight at Shepherdstown Ford." *NT*, January 14, 1886.

Herring, Charles P. Papers. War Library & Museum.

"Journal of the 118th Regiment." In *Eleventh Annual Report of the Corn Exchange Association of Philadelphia, January 31, 1865*, pp. 45-72. Philadelphia: E. C. Markley & Son, printers, 1865. Concluded in 1866 report, pp. 35-39.

Smith, John L. *History of the Corn Exchange Regiment 118th Pennsylvania Volunteers, From Their First Engagement at Antietam to Appomattox, To Which is Added a Record of Its Organization and a Complete Roster*. Philadelphia: The Author, 1888. Later editions with differing titles printed in 1892 and 1905.

____. Papers. Historical Society of Pennsylvania.

Spear, Ellis. "The 118th Pa." *NT*, May 13, 1915. (Shepherdstown)

119th Infantry

State Color

Recruited primarily in Philadelphia by Colonel Peter C. Ellmaker, the 119th Infantry was organized in August 1862 to serve for three years. The new unit immediately moved to Washington to strengthen the garrison during the aftermath of the defeat at Second Manassas. It remained in the city's defenses until ordered to the Army of the Potomac in October 1862, being assigned to the Sixth Corps. The regiment was engaged at Fredericksburg on December 13, suffering the loss of eight men.

After wintering near Falmouth, the 119th participated in the Chancellorsville Campaign, fighting at Marye's Heights and Salem Church (May 3-4, 1863), losing 122 officers and men. The command arrived at Gettysburg on July 2 and was used to strengthen the left of the battleline. Following the Bristoe Station Campaign (October), Colonel Ellmaker's brigade was one of the commands that successfully charged and captured the Confederate bridgehead at Rappahannock Station on November 7. Following this action, the regiment took part in the November campaign at Mine Run before going into winter quarters near Brandy Station.

A state color for the 119th had been ordered from Evans & Hassall on September 24, 1862. For a now unexplained reason, the color was not forwarded to the State Agency until May 6, 1863, when Colonel R. Biddle Roberts acknowledged its receipt.[1] The flag was still in Washington in mid-November when Colonel Ellmaker remarked that although he had known the flag was at the Agency for several months, he had not found the time to obtain it for the regiment.[2] Once the Mine Run Campaign was over, however, the colonel probably was able to have the flag delivered to the winter camp.

During the 1864 campaign, the 119th was first engaged in the Wilderness, where it lost four color-bearers during the fighting on May 5.[3] At Spotsylvania, the 119th was part of Colonel Emory Upton's May 10 assault on the Rebel line, which although breached, managed to repulse Upton's soldiers when reinforcements failed to support the initial breakthrough. Following the combat along the North Anna River, the 119th fought at Cold Harbor (June 1-3), then participated in the initial attacks on the Petersburg defenses.

In July, the Sixth Corps was transferred to Washington to counter General Jubal Early's movement toward the capital city. That general withdrew to the Shenandoah Valley, followed by a new army led by Phil Sheridan. The 119th took part in the initial battle of the campaign at Winchester on September 19, then was detached as part of the Winchester garrison until November. By this time, the Valley Campaign was effectively over, and the Sixth Corps returned to Petersburg in early December.

After returning to Petersburg, the 119th was present at Hatcher's Run (February 6-7, 1865) and Fort Stedman (March 25) but not engaged in either battle. The regiment participated in the final assault on Petersburg (April 2), then engaged the enemy at Saylor's Creek four days later. Following Lee's surrender at Appomattox, the Sixth Corps marched to Danville, Virginia, before moving to Washington to take part in the

State Color
Maker: EH
1985.223

Advance the Colors!

Grand Review. The 119th returned to Philadelphia and was mustered out of service on June 19. The battered state color was officially returned in the 1866 ceremony.[4]

eage back to the 119th Infantry. At least one color o the 119th was formerly owned by GAR Post 2 in Philadelphia; this color may be one of them.[5]

Regimental Color

A painted regimental color is displayed in the armory of the 103rd Engineer Battalion, which traces its lin-

Color-Bearers

On October 25, 1863, Sergeant William M. Laughlin of Company G was replaced as color-bearer by Sergeant George G. Lovett of the same company.[6]

Notes

1 Roberts to General A. L. Russell, May 6, 1863, RG 19.
2 Ellmaker to Russell, November 15, 1863, Regimental Correspondence, RG 19.
3 Bates 4:4.
4 *Philadelphia Inquirer*, July 5, 1866. Two colors for the 119th appear on the April 20, 1866, list, but not on the list of colors gathered at Philadelphia for the ceremony. The second flag is listed as a regimental color.
5 "Pennsylvania Battleflags," *NT*, August 13, 1903.
6 Special Orders #15, October 25, 1863, Regimental Index, Order and Miscellaneous Book, RG 94.

Bibliography

Allich, Robert. "The 119th Pa. at the Battle of Rappahannock Station." *NT*, November 3, 1887.
Barwis, Howard. "The 119th Pa." *NT*, September 4, 1884.
____. "Spotsylvania." *NT*, September 3, 1891.
Broadbelt, Franklin. "A Gettysburg Picture." *NT*, June 8, 1911.
____. "Raid to Madison Court House, Va." *NT*, June 30, 1910.
____. "War Recollections. The First Division, Sixth Corps, Makes a Raid to Culpepper." *NT*, January 6, 1916.
Diedersheim, John A. "The Death of Sedgwick." *NT*, July 12, 1923.
Gordon, Harmon Y. *History of the First Regiment Infantry of Pennsylvania and Antecedent and Successor Echelons to the 103rd Engineer Battalion (Infantry Division) Pennsylvania Army National Guard (the Dandy First), 1777-1961*. Philadelphia: Legal Intelligencer, 1961.
Latta, James W. Papers. Library of Congress.
Ployd, William. "On the Mud March." *NT*, February 17, 1898.
Springer, James D. Letters, February 1862-May 1864. Lancaster County Historical Society.
Stackhouse, William. Diaries, 1863-65. Historical Society of Pennsylvania.

121st Infantry

State Color

Formed by the merger of two understrength units, the 121st Pennsylvania included soldiers recruited in Venango and Philadelphia counties. The regiment was organized near Philadelphia during the first week in September 1862. It was dispatched to Washington on the sixth of that month. Colonel Chapman Biddle appointed Sergeant Erskine W. Hazard, Jr., of Company D as the regiment's first color-bearer. The thirty-five-year-old Hazard was the son of a prominent Philadelphia merchant family. In early October, the regiment moved to join the Pennsylvania Reserves, then encamped near the Antietam battlefield. Here, on October 16, Colonel Samuel B. Thomas presented an Evans & Hassall-made state color.[1]

The 121st marched with the Army of the Potomac south to Fredericksburg. It took part in the charge of Meade's troops against Stonewall Jackson's position at Hamilton's Crossing. Of the 576 officers and men in line that morning, 138 became casualties. Sergeant Hazard was slain during the fighting. As the regiment fell back, Lieutenant Joseph G. Rosengarten, aided by Sergeant William H. Honor, rescued the fallen banner and safely brought it from the battlefield. Lieutenant-Colonel Elisha W. Davis issued a special order to acknowledge the rescue of the state color.[2]

State Color and Postwar Banner
Maker: EH
1985.226

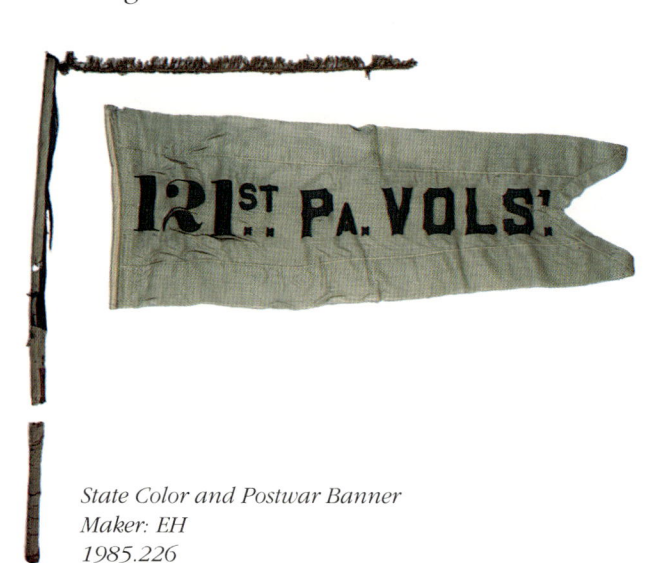

Following the Fredericksburg defeat, the regiment went into winter quarters near Belle Plain. On March 27, 1863, Major Alexander Biddle appointed Sergeant William Hardy of Company B as color-bearer. A Phoenixville native, Hardy was a former Reading railroad employee, a veteran of the three-month service, and a government hospital worker before he enlisted in the 121st. Prior to his appointment as state color-bearer, Hardy had borne the blue regimental color of the 121st.[3]

As part of the Third Division, First Corps, the 121st participated in the Chancellorsville Campaign (April-May 1863), but was only marginally engaged. At Gettysburg on July 1, the 121st fought Southerners of A. P. Hill's Third Corps on McPherson's Ridge before being pushed back to Seminary Ridge later that afternoon. During the fierce fighting, Sergeant Hardy escaped unscathed, but the flagstaff was shot into three pieces, which Hardy carried off the field as the regiment retreated into the town of Gettysburg. The sergeant picked up a loose shingle on the way through town and splinted the broken staff that night. The regiment took 263 blueclad soldiers into the battle; 179 were killed, wounded, or captured.[4]

Following the Bristoe Station Campaign (October), the 121st was detached to guard a bridge on the Orange & Alexandria Railroad. It remained on this duty until it moved to Culpeper to erect winter quarters.

When the First Corps was discontinued in March 1864, the 121st became part of the Fifth Corps, remaining in that organization until the war's end. The 121st fought in most of the major battles of Grant's 1864 campaign. After fighting in the Wilderness (May 5-6), the regiment took part in the operations around Spotsylvania (May 8-21). Here, on May 11, Sergeant Hardy was killed.[5]

Sergeant Alfred Clymer of Company I was the next man appointed to carry the tattered state color. The regimental historian described Clymer as a "mere lad, brim full of enthusiasm, fearing nothing and reckless beyond limit, cheerful under the most adverse circumstances, he and his youthful associates, by their song and laughter, their jests and merry pastimes,

Sergeant William Hardy and the State Color

drove despondency from the heads of their older and more austere companions." Clymer carried the flag during the remainder of the fighting at Spotsylvania, then at the North Anna River (May 23-25), and at Bethesda Church (June 1). Here, the regiment suffered a mere five casualties. One of these was Clymer, who was struck in his leg by a cannonball. The badly wounded sergeant struggled for life but died on July 17.[6]

After Clymer was wounded, the flag was passed to Sergeant James B. Graham of Company B, an eighteen-year-old who had enlisted in December 1863.[7] This man carried the state color as the 121st took part in the June 18 attack on Petersburg. Then, after spending time in the trenches around Petersburg, the regiment participated in the Weldon Railroad engagements (August 18-21). During the fall of 1864, the much-reduced 121st fought at Poplar Spring Church (October 1) and the Boydton Plank Road (October 27-28). Over the winter, it helped in the Fifth Corps raid on the Weldon Railroad in December, which, although unopposed by the enemy, took place during a terrible rain and hail storm. On February 6-7, 1865, the regiment fought at Hatcher's Run.

In March 1865, Graham was elected a lieutenant in the new 214th Pennsylvania and departed for his new assignment. When he left, the state color was given to Sergeant Louis Clapper of Company C. The new bearer carried the flag during the Appomattox Campaign and the Grand Review.[8] The regiment was mustered out of service on June 2, 1865. Colonel Biddle retained the state color until contacted about its re-

Three of the 121st's Color-Bearers
William G. Graham (left), James B. Graham (center), Louis Clapper (right)

121st Infantry

393

Regimental Color
Maker: EH
1985.224

National Color
1985.225

turn in May 1866.[9] Extant records do not reveal whether or not this banner was present during the 1866 proceedings. Clapper was still alive in 1914 and carried the remnant of the state color for the last time on that occasion.

Regimental Color

This blue infantry color was obtained for use early in the regiment's term of service. Sergeant William Hardy was the first bearer. He carried this flag until transferred to custody of the state color sometime after the battle of Fredericksburg. At that time, Sergeant William G. Graham of Company D took charge of the regimental flag. At age twenty-one, Graham was "full of vigor, a capital soldier, tall, manly, quiet and true as steel." His younger brother James enlisted in the 121st in late 1863. William Graham carried the regimental flag until May 5, 1864, when he was killed in the Wilderness. Shortly after Graham's death, the blue flag was retired from field use. It was in Major William B. Lane's Philadelphia office in April 1866.[10]

National Color

There seems to be no documentation for this 35-star national flag. Judging from the lack of mention in the regimental history, the veterans of the 121st apparently did not hold this flag in high esteem. It was probably acquired late in the war and possibly saw no combat action. In 1866, it, too, was in Major Lane's office.

Notes

1 Regimental history (revised edition), pp. 24, 172; General Orders #1, September 7, 1862, in Regimental Letter, Order & Courts Martial Book, RG 94.

2 Regimental history, p. 39; General Orders #16, December 30, 1862, in Regimental Letter, Order & Courts Martial Book, RG94.

3 General Orders #12, March 27, 1863, RG 94; Regimental history, p. 172.

4 Regimental history, pp. 172-73.
5 *Ibid.*
6 *Ibid.*, p. 173.
7 *Ibid.*
8 *Ibid.*, pp. 173-74.
9 Biddle to A. L. Russell, May 25, 1866, RG 19.
10 Regimental History, pp. 172-73.

Bibliography

Baird, Henry C. "Memoir of Col. Alexander Biddle." *Proceedings of the American Philosophical Society* 1 (1900): 196-205.

Biddle, Chapman. "The First Day of the Battle of Gettysburg, An Address Delivered Before the Historical Society of Pennsylvania, on the 8th of March, 1880." Philadelphia: J. B. Lippincott & Company, 1880.

Biddle, Walter L. C. "Address P. V. 121st Regiment, by Walter L. C. Biddle, July 2d, 1886, at Gettysburg." N.p., n.d.

Lang, Nathaniel. "Crossing the Rappahannock." *NT*, July 23, 1925.

____. "Saw Wadsworth Fall." *NT*, April 15, 1926.

____. "Wadsworth and Sedgwick. How the Two Gallant Soldiers Met Their Deaths at the Wilderness and Spotsylvania." *NT*, May 10, 1923.

Leland, Charles G. "A Memoir of Chapman Biddle, Read Before the Historical Society of Pennsylvania." Philadelphia: Collins, Printer, 1882.

Memorial of Thomas M. Hall. Philadelphia: King & Baird, Printers, 1865.

Strong, William W. *Addenda to History of the 121st Regiment Pennsylvania Volunteers, by the Survivors' Association. "An Account from the Ranks."* Philadelphia: Press of Burk & McFetridge Company, 1893.

____. *History of the 121st Regiment Pennsylvania Volunteers, by the Survivors' Association. "An Account from the Ranks."* Philadelphia: Press of Burk & McFetridge Company, 1893; revised edition, Philadelphia: Catholic Standard and Times, 1906.

122nd Infantry

State Color

Organized entirely in Lancaster County, the 122nd Infantry was recruited in August 1862 for a nine-month period of service. After moving to Washington that same month, the regiment was assigned to the Third Division, Third Corps. A state color was probably presented to the regiment when Colonel Samuel B. Thomas visited the army in mid-October to distribute flags to the new Pennsylvania regiments. The 122nd was present on the Fredericksburg battlefield (December 13) but was not engaged; a single man was listed as missing. It fought at Chancellorsville on May 2-3, 1863, as the Third Corps engaged Stonewall Jackson's soldiers after his men broke the Eleventh Corps. Here, the 122nd suffered more than a hundred casualties. Brigadier-General Amiel W. Whipple, the division commander, was mortally wounded. When his body was sent back to Washington, the 122nd escorted the funeral train. From the capital, the regiment went on to Harrisburg where it mustered out of service by May 16. The state color was officially returned to state care on July 4, 1866.

State Color
Maker: EH
1985.227

Unidentified Color

The 122nd carried a second flag, most likely a local presentation. This flag was present at the 1892 national encampment of the Grand Army of the Republic, where it was temporarily misplaced. The flag was returned to Post 84 in Lancaster and was destroyed when the post building burned to the ground on February 10, 1910.[1]

Notes

1 "Information Asked and Given," *NT*, January 26, 1893; "War Veterans' Great Loss," *Lancaster Daily News*, February 11, 1910.

Bibliography

Morrow, Isaac. Letters. USAMHI, HbCWRT Collection.
Smith, J. S. "Gen. Whipple's Death." *NT*, August 6, 1885.
Sprenger, George F. *Concise History of the Camp and Field Life of the 122nd Regiment, Penn'a. Volunteers*. Lancaster: New Era Print, 1885.

Transactions of the First Annual Reunion of the 122d Regiment Pennsylvani Volunteers, Held at Lancaster, Pa., Thursday, May 17, 1883. Lancaster: New Era Printing House, 1884.

123rd Infantry

State Color

The 123rd Infantry was another of Pennsylvania's nine-month units organized under the president's call for 300,000 soldiers on July 7, 1862. Composed entirely of Allegheny countians, the regiment was in large part recruited by the Reverend John B. Clark, a Pittsburgh Presbyterian minister who became the regiment's colonel. After organizing in Pittsburgh, the regiment moved to Harrisburg, then was immediately transported to Washington in late August. Here, the new 123rd became a part of the Third Division, Fifth Corps, Army of the Potomac. The eight Pennsylvania regiments comprising this division remained in the Washington defenses until September 14, when the division marched to join the army. It arrived on the Antietam battlefield soon after the fighting ended. The troops then went into bivouac near the battlefield, remaining here until the army moved into Virginia in November. While in camp, Colonel Samuel B. Thomas, representing Governor Curtin, presented a state color to the 123rd on October 15.[1]

The regiment's major engagement during its term of service was at Fredericksburg on December 13. The division, led by Brigadier-General Andrew A. Humphreys, charged the Confederate position on Marye's Heights beyond the town. During this unsuccessful attack, the 123rd sustained a loss of 134 officers and men. Sergeant Samuel Caldwell safely carried the state color through this battle. The silk was pierced by twelve bullets while a thirteenth crashed into the center of the wooden flagstaff.[2]

Although the division was present on the Chancellorsville battlefield, the 123rd was only lightly engaged, suffering a mere eight casualties. The regiment then returned to Harrisburg and was mustered out of service on May 13, 1863. Colonel Clark kept the state color but returned it in time for its inclusion in the 1866 parade.[3]

National and Regimental Colors

Both flags appear on the 1865 return list, but there is no documentation to indicate how they were used by

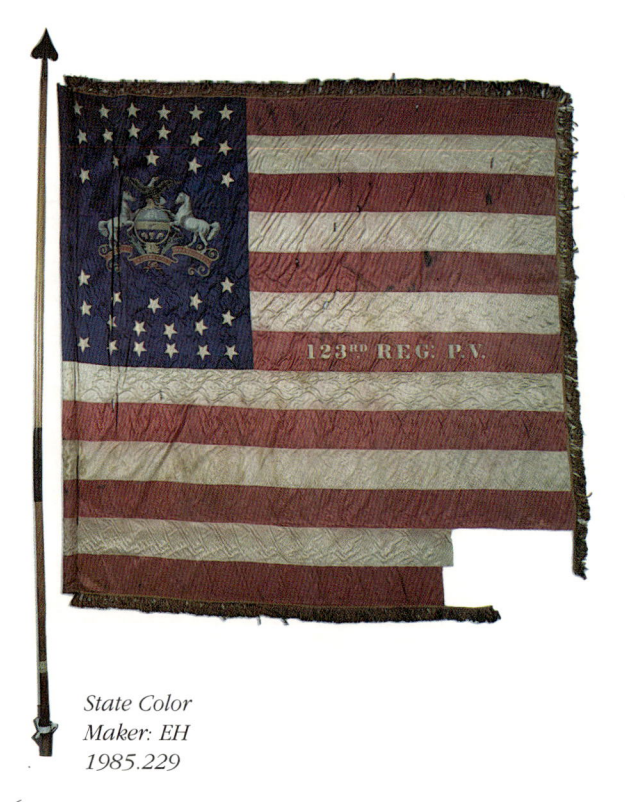

State Color
Maker: EH
1985.229

National Color
1985.230

Regimental Color
Maker: EH
1985.228

Presented Flags

Five of the ten companies of the 123rd received flags from local admirers. On August 16, the Cass Infantry, which became Company C, received a "beautiful stand of colors" from James Reno and William Dill.[4] The Howe Engineers (Company I) received a "silk flag" from Mrs. Fannie Bailey of Manchester on August 8.[5] The three original companies of the 123rd raised by Reverend Clark all were the recipients of flags. Company A (later Company C of the 123rd), was given a "beautiful and costly flag" by a group of friends on August 12.[6] Company B (later Company E) received an "elegant stand of colors" from the Allegheny Greys on August 15.[7] Finally, also on August 15, Company C (later Company H) was given a "splendid set of colors" by a Professor Wilson.[8] No documentation to indicate if these flags were carried by the 123rd, or their eventual fate, has been located.

the 123rd. The regimental color was manufactured by Evans & Hassall. The national color contains 34 stars arranged in an oval pattern.

Notes

1 M. H. Borland diary, October 15, 1862.
2 *O.R.* 21, p. 445.
3 Clark to A. L. Russell, June 9, 1866, RG 19.
4 "Presentations," *Pittsburgh Gazette*, August 19, 1862.
5 "Flag Presentation," *Pittsburgh Post*, August 12, 1862.
6 "Flag Presentation," *Pittsburgh Gazette*, August 12, 1862.
7 "Colors Presented," *Pittsburgh Post*, August 18, 1862.
8 "Flag and Sword Presentation," *Pittsburgh Gazette*, August 16, 1862.

Bibliography

Borland, M. H. Diary. Historical Society of Western Pennsylvania.
Rheim, Christian. "The 123d Pa." *NT*, July 11, 1907.
Ross, James B. Diary. Historical Society of Western Pennsylvania.
Whiston, Benton. "Drawing Water at Fredericksburg." *NT*, December 25, 1913.
___. "Helping the Wounded." *NT*, April 4, 1912.

124th Infantry

State Color

Another of the state's nine-month regiments, the 124th was recruited in Chester and Delaware counties. After being organized at Camp Curtin in August 1862, the regiment moved to Washington and was assigned to the Twelfth Corps, Army of the Potomac. It fought at Antietam on September 17, suffering sixty-four casualties. The 124th received a state color on October 13, when Colonel Samuel B. Thomas presented the new banner to the troops.[1]

State Color
Maker: EH
1985.231

The Twelfth Corps remained in the Harper's Ferry area until early December, when it moved into northern Virginia to rejoin the army. After wintering near Stafford Court House, the 124th took part in the Chancellorsville Campaign, being engaged with the enemy on May 1-3, 1863, sustaining few losses. Then, its term of service about over, the regiment was sent back to Harrisburg, where it was disbanded on May 17. The state color was officially returned in 1866.

National Color

During its term of service, the 124th also carried a national color. A photograph of this flag, misidentified as the state color, appears in the regimental history. This flag was retained by the veterans of the 124th and was used in postwar reunions.[2] It was owned by Colonel Joseph W. Hawley's family until 1933, when his daughter presented it to the Commonwealth. The flag was received by the adjutant-general's office, who in turn sent it to the State Arsenal for safekeeping. Its present whereabouts has not been ascertained.[3]

National Color

Advance the Colors!

Notes

1 Green, p. 38.
2 Ibid., p. 215.
3 "Flag Data—Information concerning flags that have been returned to the custody of the Commonwealth of Pennsylvania," letter in RG 19.

Bibliography

Green, Robert M. *History of the One Hundred and Twenty-fourth Regiment Pennsylvania Volunteers in the War of the Rebellion, 1862-1863. Regimental Re-unions, 1885-1906. History of Monument.* Philadelphia: Ware Brothers Company, Printers, 1907.

Guest, William A. Letters. USAMHI, CW Misc Collection.

Secretary's Report of Annual Re-union of the Survivors' Association 124th Regiment, P.V., from 1885 to 1890 (Inclusive). Wilmington: Delaware Printing Company, 1890.

125th Infantry

National Color

Comprised of soldiers from Huntingdon and Blair counties, the 125th Pennsylvania was organized in August 1862 at Camp Curtin to serve for nine months. The new command immediately went to Washington, where it was assigned to the First Division of the Twelfth Corps, Army of the Potomac. The regiment accompanied the corps to the Antietam battlefield, where it engaged the enemy on September 17.

Regimental Monument at Antietam, Showing Sergeant Simpson

During the fighting that morning, the 125th advanced across the Cornfield into the West Woods. It held a position here for some time, repelling several enemy attacks. Then, fresh Rebel soldiers forced the battered recruits to fall back. Sergeant George A. Simpson of Company C, carrying a now-unidentified flag, was hit in the temple and fell lifeless onto the banner, his blood oozing onto the silk. Most of the guards had also been shot down as the regiment turned to withdraw. At this point, Private Eugene Boblitz of Company H seized the fallen color and carried it a short distance when he was struck in the leg, making him a cripple for life. Then, Sergeant Walter W. Greenland of Company C rescued the banner from the fallen Boblitz. Greenland took the flag through the Cornfield and entered the East Woods, where he found Captain William W. Wallace trying to rally the men. Wallace appropriated the flag and called the survivors together behind a nearby artillery battery.[1]

Captain Wallace appreciated Greenland's bravery and asked that he be appointed color-sergeant. However, Greenland declined the honor. As the wrote to a friend: "It was a position that suited George (Simpson) but did not suit me." When Greenland stepped aside, Captain Wallace asked for a volunteer. After a moment's hesitation, Sergeant Lewis F. Wattson of Company C stepped forward and was given the flag. Wattson carried this flag until promoted to a lieutenancy in February 1863.[2]

The color borne by the 125th at Antietam has not been located. Apparently, the regiment gave the flag to George Simpson's sister Annie. The author of a biographical pamphlet on Annie Simpson recalled that she retained the flag for many years, then gave it to the "trophy room in the Capitol."[3] However, this flag is not in the Commonwealth collection. When the regiment erected its monument at Antietam in 1904, Annie Simpson was chosen to unveil the monument, which featured a sculpture of George Simpson heroically carrying the color of the 125th.

State Color

After suffering a heavy loss at Antietam, the regiment, together with the Twelfth Corps, went into camp near

Advance the Colors!

Harper's Ferry. Here, on October 13, Colonel Samuel B. Thomas presented a state flag to the 12th.[4] The corps finally marched south to rejoin the Army of the Potomac in December. It arrived too late to fight at Fredericksburg and went into winter quarters near Stafford Court House. The regiment was next engaged at Chancellorsville on May 1-3, 1863, suffering forty-nine casualties. After this campaign, the regiment returned to Harrisburg and was mustered out of service on May 18. The state color was included in the 1866 ceremony.

Color-Bearer

A Soldiers Memorial of Company C, 125th Pennsylvania, owned by the Huntingdon County Historical Society, lists the name of Charles E. Campbell as color-bearer.

State Color
Maker: EH
1985.232

Notes

1 Regimental history (1906 edition), pp. 74, 172-73; "Who Bore the Colors at Antietam?" *Huntingdon Globe*, March 4, 1863; biographical sketch of Greenland in *NT*, April 4, 1895.

2 Regimental history (1906), p. 174; Greenland to J. R. Simpson, September 27, 1862, Simpson Letters; L. F. Wattson to adjutant-general, February 22, 1863, RG 19, Regimental Correspondence.

3 Warren B. Simpson, *Recollections of a Centenarian*.

4 "Letter from 'Sykesy'," *Huntingdon Journal and American*, October 22, 1862.

Bibliography

Dunigan, Edward R. "Battle of Antietam." *NT*, November 3, 1892.
Greene, Edward M. "The Huntingdon Bible Company." *Civil War Times Illustrated* 3 #1 (April 1964): 22-24.
Hicks, J.D. "Death of Gen. Mansfield." *NT*, December 27, 1917.
Higgins, Jacob. "At Antietam." *NT*, June 3, 1886.
History of the One Hundred and Twenty-fifth Regiment Pennsylvania Volunteers, 1862-1863, by the Regimental Committee. Philadelphia: J. B. Lippincott Company, 1906; second edition, 1907.
Hobart, B. "Battle of Antietam." *NT*, February 16, 1893.
Huyette, Miles C. "At Harper's Ferry." *NT*, January 30, 1913.
____. "Fort Dunker Church." *NT*, September 9, 1909.
____. *The Maryland Campaign and the Battle of Antietam*. Buffalo, 1915.
____. "On a Bloody Field. An Argument as to the Advance of William's Division Through the Cornfield at Antietam." *NT*, November 30, 1893.
____. "Reminiscences of a Private." *National Tribune Scrapbook* 1: 83-103.
____. *Reminiscences of a Soldier in the American Civil War*. Buffalo: Vosburgh & Whiting Company, 1908.
Keatley, John H. Across the Occoquan." *NT*, March 18, 1897.
____. "Ill-Timed Bravery. How One Competent General Lost His Life Through Carelessness." *NT*, November 16, 1893.
McCamant, Wallace. Papers. University of Oregon.
Moore Family Papers. USAMHI, Save the Flags Collection.
Morrison, John B. "Message from the Past." *NT*, March 4, 1897.
"Saving the Colors. Boblitz Tells a Thrilling Tale of the Battle of Antietam." *Pittsburgh Commercial Gazette*, March 5, 1892.
Simpson, James R. Letters. Huntingdon County Historical Society.
Wallace, William W. "War Reminiscences of a Presbyterian Elder." *The Presbyterian* 81, May 10-June 21, 1911.

125th Infantry

126th Infantry

State Color

Recruited primarily in Franklin and Juniata counties, the 126th was formed in August 1862 to serve for a nine-month enlistment. The regiment left Harrisburg for Washington, where it was assigned to the Third Division, Fifth Corps, Army of the Potomac. The division remained in Washington until General Lee invaded Maryland. It then moved to join the army, arriving on the Antietam battlefield after the fighting had ended. The command then went into bivouac near the field. On October 18, Colonel Samuel B. Thomas presented a state color to the 126th.[1]

The regiment first was engaged in battle at Fredericksburg on December 13. Here, the 126th suffered a loss of ninety-two soldiers during one of the unsuccessful attacks on the enemy position on Marye's Heights. Then, after wintering near Falmouth the regiment took part in the Chancellorsville Campaign, fighting on May 1-3, 1863, losing seventy-seven casualties. Then, its term of service nearly complete, the regiment returned to Harrisburg and was mustered out of service on May 20. The state color was returned in 1866.

Presented Colors

Surviving evidence indicates two additional flags were carried by the 126th. On October 1, 1862, the Honorable Edward McPherson, the House of Representatives member whose district included most of the 126th's soldiers, presented a flag to Company E on behalf of the ladies of Waynesboro. Company E, the "Waynesboro Sharpshooters," was the regiment's color company. The flag was described as having the state arms on one side and the national eagle on the opposite, but was also called the stars and stripes by Lieutenant-Colonel David W. Rowe. His words indicate that this color was some type of national flag with the two different arms painted in the blue canton.[2] This flag was apparently carried at Fredericksburg, since Brigadier-General Andrew A. Humphreys, commanding the division, indicated that the regiments in his First Brigade each carried two colors.[3] No other documentation has been found to verify its use or eventual disposition.

The Kittochtinny Historical Society has custody of a 34-star national color attributed to the 126th. There seems to be no surviving evidence to document how this flag was used by the regiment.

Color-Bearers

At Fredericksburg, Corporal Thomas Daily was one of the unit's two bearers. When the brigade began to fall back, Daily retrieved the fallen color of the 134th Pennsylvania and carried both flags to the rear. General Humphreys spied the corporal and asked him why he had two flags in addition to his musket. After hearing Daily's explanation, Humphreys commented: "Give me your musket, it is honor enough to carry the colors of two regiments."[4]

Corporal Solomon B. Kauffman of Company F was listed as a color-bearer in the regimental history, but no evidence was supplied to indicate when he was a bearer.[5]

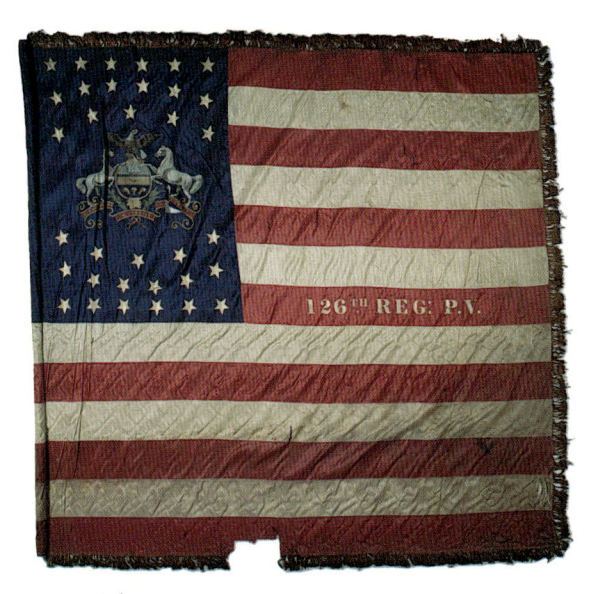

State Color
Maker: EH
1985.233

Notes

1 *Chambersburg Valley Spirit and Times*, October 22, 1862.

2 *Ibid.*, October 8, 1862. "Our Hagerstown Letter," *Philadelphia Inquirer*, October 4, 1862, indicates the presentation date as September 30.

3 Humphreys to General Darius N. Couch, February 10, 1863, Humphreys Papers, Historical Society of Pennsylvania, copy in RG 25.

4 "Worthy of Mention," *Chambersburg Valley Spirit and Times*, January 14, 1863. Daily is mentioned as one of the regiment's bearers in *O.R.* 21, pp. 440-441. However, Colonel Rowe (*Ibid.*, p. 441) mentioned a Corporal George E. Jones of Company H as the man who carried the 134th's flag off the field.

5 Alexander, p. 88.

Bibliography

Alexander, Ted. *The 126th Pennsylvania*. Shippensburg: Beidel Printing House, Inc., 1984.

Groninger, William H. "Chasing a Cannon Ball." *NT*, December 24, 1925.

____. "Jackson at Chancellorsville." *NT*, August 20, 1925.

____. "Lincoln's Visit to the Antietam Battlefield." *NT*, April 7, 1927.

____. "Story of Frank Mayne." *NT*, November 1, 1923.

____. "With Gen. Burnside at Fredericksburg." *NT*, April 1, 1926.

MacCauley, Clay. "From Chancellorsville to Libby Prison." In Military Order of the Loyal Legion of the United States, Minnesota Commandery, *Glimpses of the Nation's Struggle* 1: 179-201. St. Paul: St. Paul Book and Stationery Company, 1887.

____. "Through Chancellorsville, Into and Out of Libby Prison." In Rhode Island Soldiers and Sailors Historical Society, *Personal Narratives of Events in the War of the Rebellion*, Series 6, Number 7.

____. *Memories and Memorials: Gatherings from an Eventful Life*. Tokyo: Fukuin Printing Company, 1914.

McGill, Paul. "A Soldier's Tale." *Pennsylvania Folklife* 35 #3 (1986): 127-29.

North, Samuel W. Letters. USAMHI, CW Misc Collection.

Rowe, David W. *A Sketch of the 126th Regiment Pennsylvania Volunteers*. Chambersburg: Cook & Hays, Publishers, 1869.

Trogler, William A. "Hard Trials of a Recruit." *NT*, March 8, 1928.

Welsh, George W. and Philip R. "Civil War Letters from Two Brothers." *Yale Review* 18 (1928): 148-61.

127th Infantry

State Color

Organized at Camp Curtin in August 1862, the 127th Infantry was recruited in Dauphin, Lebanon, and Adams counties, to serve for nine months. Immediately upon organization, the regiment moved to Washington, where it was posted to guard the Chain Bridge. Colonel Samuel B. Thomas unexpectedly arrived in the regimental camp on October 22 to present a state color on behalf of Governor Curtin. Colonel William W. Jennings hastily assembled the soldiers then in camp and the men joyfully received the new flag.[1]

In December, the regiment was relieved from guard duty and joined the Second Corps, Army of the Potomac. As part of the corps, the 127th fought at Fredericksburg, suffering more than a hundred casualties. Sergeant Schaeffer carried the color in this battle.[2] Then, after spending the winter opposite the city, the regiment participated in the Chancellorsville Campaign by aiding in the recapture of the city, which it held on May 3-4, 1863, before withdrawing. The 127th returned to Harrisburg and was mustered out of service on May 16. The state color was included in the 1866 ceremony.

Company Flags

On August 13, 1862, several Harrisburg ladies presented a flag to Captain John J. Ball's Company G, the "Harrisburg City Guards." Sometime in September, a Mr. Hummel presented a flag to Company A. The use and eventual disposition appear to be undocumented.[3]

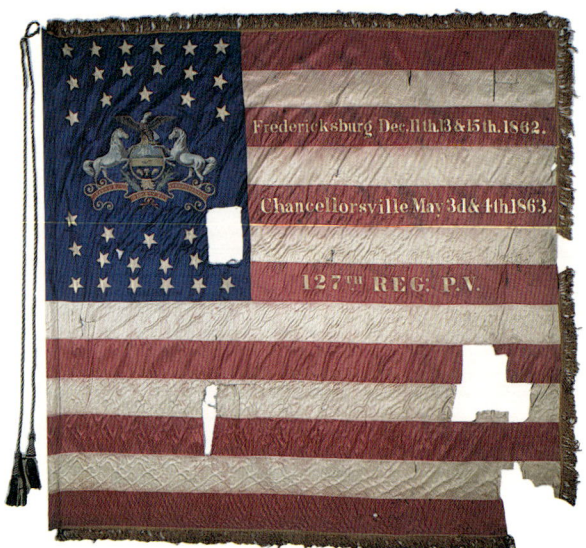

State Color
Maker: EH
1985.234

Notes

1 Regimental history pp. 155-159; "From the 127th Regiment," *Lebanon Courier*, October 28, 1862. The *Pennsylvania Daily Telegraph* ("The 127th Pa. Regt.," October 27, 1862) indicates that the state color was presented on October 21 rather than the twenty-second.

2 Regimental history, p. 132. The text does not indicate who this Sergeant Schaeffer was. Bates has two men: William E. Shaffer of Company H, and Samuel G. Sheaffer of Company I. Both were wounded at Fredericksburg.

3 "Flag Presentation," *Harrisburg Patriot & Union*, August 14, 1862; Untitled story in *ibid.*, September 18, 1862.

Bibliography

Alleman, Hiram C. Papers. Pennsylvania State Archives.
Awl, F. Asbury. Papers. Pennsylvania State Archives.
Gregg, John C. *Life in the Army, in the Departments of Virginia, and the Gulf, Including Observations in New Orleans, With an Account of the Author's Life and Experience in the Ministry.* Philadelphia: Perkinpine & Higgins, 1866, 1868.
Guilford, S. H. "The 127th Pennsylvania Infantry at the Capture of Fredericksburg." *Philadelphia Weekly Press*, June 16, 1886.

History of the 127th Regiment Pennsylvania Volunteers, Familiarly Known as the "Dauphin County Regiment." Lebanon: Press of Report Publishing Company, 1902.
Reed, William W. Diary, August 2-October 16, 1862. Historical Society of Pennsylvania.

128th Infantry

State Color

Recruited in Berks, Bucks, and Lehigh counties, the 128th Infantry was organized at Camp Curtin in August 1862. The new unit immediately was dispatched to Washington, where it helped construct fortifications. In early September, the 128th was assigned to the Twelfth Corps and fought at Antietam on September 17, losing 118 soldiers in the Cornfield. Colonel Samuel B. Thomas presented a state color to the regiment on October 21, as the 128th lay in camp on Maryland Heights opposite Harper's Ferry.[1]

The Twelfth Corps guarded the Army of the Potomac's rear and was not engaged at Fredericksburg. It did fight at Chancellorsville, where, on the evening of May 2, the regiment blundered into Confederate troops that occupied Union entrenchments abandoned earlier in the day. More than half the 128th was captured, but Sergeant Henry S. Lovett of Company C escaped with the flag.[2] The survivors returned to Harrisburg and were mustered out of service on May 16. The state color was left in Harrisburg, but was temporarily loaned to the regiment for use in a ceremony honoring Colonel Joseph A. Mathews. The June 2 ceremony, held in Reading, featured the return of the paroled prisoners. A reporter noted that the flag "is much weather-stained, but bears no marks of having been in battle." The wooded terrain at Chancellorsville prohibited Sergeant Lovett from unfurling his banner, so it did not receive any battle damage.[3] The color was officially returned in 1866.

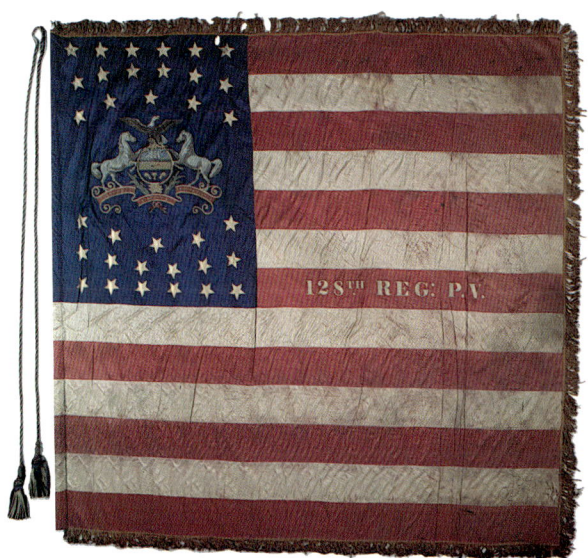

State Color
Maker: EH
1985.235

Company D Flag

On October 20, 1862, Captain J. P. Dillinger of Company D acknowledged receipt of a flag paid for by subscription by a number of Allentown ladies. No further information has been located about its use.[4]

Notes

1 "From the 128th Regiment," *Bucks County Intelligencer*, November 4, 1862.
2 *Berks and Schuylkill Journal* (Reading), June 13, 1863.
3 Ibid.
4 "Flag Presentation," *Allentown Democrat*, November 5, 1862.

Bibliography

Mattern, Carolyn J. (editor). "A Pennsylvania Dutch Yankee: The Civil War Letters of Private David William Mattern (1862-1863)." *Pennsylvania Folklife* 36 (Autumn 1986): 2-19.
Pickering, H.A. "At Richmond." *NT*, February 27, 1913.
Wilcox, William J. (editor). "Civil War Letters of William J. Reichard, 1862-1868." *Lehigh County Historical Society Proceedings* 22 (1958): 136-280.

129th Infantry

State Color
National Color

Another of the state's nine-month regiments, the 129th was recruited in Schuylkill, Northampton, and Montgomery counties during August 1862. After organizing at Camp Curtin, the new unit was rushed to Washington, where the regiment's first duty was to provide an escort for an ammunition train heading for Pope's army, then engaged at Second Manassas. Upon returning to the city's defenses, the 129th was assigned to the new Third Division, Fifth Corps, composed of eight Keystone regiments. Led by Andrew A. Humphreys, this division arrived at Antietam after the fighting was over, then went into camp near the battlefield. On October 18, Colonel Samuel B. Thomas presented a state color on behalf of Governor Curtin.[1]

At Fredericksburg on December 13, the 129th participated in the division's unsuccessful charge against the enemy position on Marye's Heights. As the regiment moved forward, the color-bearers and most of the guards were shot down. When the state color fell, Colonel Jacob G. Frick quickly ran forward and seized the fallen banner. Already covered with blood when a nearby horse was torn to pieces by an artillery shell, Frick grabbed the flag and led his command forward. Soon, a bullet broke the flag staff and the color drooped over the colonel's head. When the command finally retired from the field, Frick carried the flag safely to the rear. The 129th suffered 139 casualties during the brief time it was engaged.[2]

After wintering near Falmouth, the division took part in the Chancellorsville Campaign of April-May 1863. The 129th was engaged primarily on May 3. When the battleline near the Chancellor House retired, the 129th was one of the last units to fall back, its ammunition low. The line became somewhat mixed in the wooded terrain, and a large group of grayclad soldiers charged forward into the retiring Yankees in an effort to capture the regiment's two colors. Initially successful in their impetuous assault, the enemy seized both colors and some of the men around them.

Colonel Frick quickly saw the danger. He rallied some of his men and charged his flags. Captain John Stonebach of Company K, a "tall, powerfully-built man of dark complexion," lunged forward toward the

State Color
Maker: EH
1985.237

National Color
1985.236

406

Advance the Colors!

Colonel Jacob G. Frick

flags. Frick, right behind him, deflected a Rebel's swordthrust at the captain, who then felled his opponent with a staggering blow from his fist. Both flags were retaken by their owners and carried safely off the field as the regiment fell back to the main line. Twenty-seven years after the war, Colonel Frick was awarded a Medal of Honor for his feats at Fredericksburg and Chancellorsville.[3]

Shortly after the end of the Chancellorsville Campaign, the 129th returned to Harrisburg, where it was mustered out of service on May 18. Both colors were left in Harrisburg. The state color was included in the 1866 festivities.

Color-Bearers

At Chancellorsville, the regiment's colors were carried by Sergeants Lewis S. Boner (Company E) and Peter M. Miller (Company F).[4] In addition to these two names, that of William Gressang (Company B) appears on the staff of the state color. The name was branded into the wood just below the finial base at some now-undocumented time. The author has not found any information that links Gressang with either flag as bearer.

Notes

1 Letter in *Chambersburg Valley and Spirit*, October 22, 1862.

2 Mulholland, p. 171; Beyer-Keydel, pp. 117-18. Apparently the staff was later replaced. There is a break in the pole sleeve at the lower edge of the blue canton, but no corresponding damage to the existing staff.

3 Ibid.; *O.R.* 25.1, pp. 554-55; Frick, "Chancellorsville," *NT*, January 5, 1893.

4 *O.R.* 25.1, p. 554.

Bibliography

Armstrong, William H. *Red-Tape and Pigeon Hole Generals, as Seen from the Ranks During a Campaign in the Army of the Potomac, by a Citizen-Soldier.* New York: Carleton, 1864.

Davis, Isaac. "A Friend of Lincoln." *NT*, March 5, 1925.

Falls, C. F. "Sunday at Chancellorsville." *Philadelphia Weekly Times*, December 24, 1881.

Frick, Jacob G. "Chancellorsville." *NT*, January 5, 1893.

Haas, Jacob. Letters. Northampton County Historical Society.

Horn, Luther. Letters. Northampton County Historical Society.

Rice, William H. Papers. Historic Bethlehem, Inc.

Rudy, Joseph P. Letters, August-September 1862. USAMHI, HbCWRT Collection.

Williams, W. H. "At Chancellorsville." *NT*, August 11, 1892.

130th Infantry

State Color

Another of the nine-month regiments organized at Camp Curtin in August 1862, the 130th Infantry immediately moved to Washington to help man the defenses during the waning stage of the Second Manassas Campaign. It was then attached to the Third Division, Second Corps, and

State Color
Maker: EH
1985.238

Postwar View of State Color

Bullet Gash in Staff of State Color

moved north into Maryland to counter the Confederate invasion of that state. The raw recruits were thrown into battle at Antietam on September 17. Still without a flag, the 130th carried flank markers only.[1] Almost two hundred men were felled as the regiment attacked the enemy position in the Bloody Lane. The regiment then went into camp near Harper's Ferry, receiving its state color sometime in mid-October when Colonel Samuel B. Thomas visited the army to present flags to the new Keystone units.

The regiment next engaged Southern troops at Fredericksburg on December 13. During one of the assaults on Marye's Heights, the 130th encountered a storm of shot and shell. One volley swept through the color company, decimating it. When the flag fell, Colonel Henry I. Zinn, five days past his twenty-eighth birthday, seized the silk banner and attempted to rally his faltering regiment. "Stand here till those colors leave," the colonel bravely commanded, but the musketry from behind the stone wall was too much for the attackers. Seeing that other regiments were retreating, Zinn took the flag and turned to order his men to the rear when a bullet struck him just below the eye. Both the flag and the colonel were carried to the rear. The flag had thirty-two bullet holes in it; Zinn died in less than half an hour from his fatal wound.[2]

After spending the winter near Falmouth, the 130th took part in the Chancellorsville Campaign, fighting in the woods near the Chancellor House on May 2-3. The regiment was mustered out of service on May 21 at Harrisburg. The state color was included in the 1866 ceremony, when Sergeant Charles A. Smith of Company A carried the banner.

Company D Flag

On August 14, 1862, a delegation of Shippensburg ladies presented a "splendid silk flag" to Captain James Kelso and the men of Company D. The ceremony took place at Camp Simmons, Harrisburg. No additional information about this flag has been located.[3]

Notes

1 Fisher, "Battle of Antietam," *NT*, January 3, 1907.
2 Bates 3: 206; "Death of Col. H. I. Zinn," *York Gazette*, December 30, 1862; Wiley, "Charging at Marye's Heights," *NT*, December 30, 1897. Wiley includes a story in this latter article about the 130th's color-bear, who laid down when the regiment halted and kept the flag flying. Wiley calls this bearer "Pat," an Irishman from one of the companies, but does not further identify this man.
3 "Flag Presentation," *Carlisle American Volunteer*, August 21, 1862.

Bibliography

Brehm, Samuel H. Diary, August 9, 1862-May 8, 1863. Cumberland County Historical Society.
Fisher, Edward. "Battle of Antietam." *NT*, January 3, 1907.
Hays, John. "The 130th Regiment, Pennsylvania Volunteers in the Maryland Campaign and the Battle of Antietam, An Address Delivered June 7, 1894, Before Capt. Colwell Post 201 G.A.R., by John Hays, Late 1st Lieut. and Adjt." Carlisle: Herald Printing Company, 1894.
One Hundred and Thirtieth Regiment Pennsylvania Volunteer Infantry. Ceremonies and Addresses at Dedication of Monument at Bloody Lane, Antietam Battlefield, September 17, 1904. Letters of Colonel Henry I. Zinn. Roster of Survivors. N.p., 1904.
Spangler, Edward W. *My Little War Experiences With Historical Sketches and Memorabilia.* York: York Daily Publishing Company, 1904.
Wiley, John T. "Charging at Marye's Heights." *NT*, December 30, 1897.
____. "Marye's Heights." *NT*, April 21, 1898.

131st Infantry

State Color

Composed of men recruited in central Pennsylvania, the 131st Infantry assembled at Camp Curtin in August 1862 and soon after moved into the defenses of Washington. When the Maryland Campaign began, the regiment was assigned to the Third Division, Fifth Corps, Army of the Potomac, which arrived at Antietam too late to take part in the battle. A state color was presented to the 131st by Colonel Samuel B. Thomas sometime in October when he distributed colors to the new Pennsylvania units.

The 131st accompanied the army when it finally crossed the Potomac River in late October. It fought at Fredericksburg on December 13, losing 175 men in one of the assaults on the stone wall at Marye's Heights. After spending the winter in camp near Falmouth, the regiment participated in the Chancellorsville Campaign, where it was only marginally engaged. Then, its term of service over, the regiment returned to Harrisburg and was disbanded on May 23. The state color was officially returned in 1866.

State Color
Maker: EH
1985.239

At some point during the regiment's service, Sergeant Henry H. McLaughlin of Company D served as color-bearer.[1]

Notes

1 McLaughlin to unidentified recipient, December 16, 1864, in 21st Pennsylvania Cavalry correspondence, RG 19. McLaughlin served as a lieutenant in Company C of this regiment.

Bibliography

Noll, Emanuel. "Allabach's Brigade. It Attacked at Fredericksburg Before Tyler's Brigade, and Went Farther." *NT*, October 1, 1908.

Orwig, Joseph E. "War Reminiscences 1861-5. Co.A, 131st Regt. Pa. Vol." *Lewisburg Chronicle*, most issues from March 9, 1895, to May 9, 1896.

Orwig, Joseph R. *History of the 131st Penna. Volunteers, War of 1861-5*. Williamsport: Sun Book and Job Printing House, 1902.

Papers in Civil War Collection. Iowa State Department of Archives & History.

Thurner, Arthur W. (editor). "A Young Soldier in the Army of the Potomac: Diary of Howard Helman, 1862." *Pennsylvania Magazine of History and Biography* 87 (1963): 139-55.

Wertz, William. "A Story of the War, with Co. A, 131st Regt. Pa. Vol." *Lewisburg Chronicle*, December 12, 1896.

132nd Infantry

National Color
Regimental Color

A nine-month regiment organized in August 1862, the 132nd Pennsylvania was composed of soldiers from the counties of Montour, Wyoming, Bradford, Columbia, Carbon, and Luzerne. Soon after formation, the regiment moved to Washington. In early September, the 132nd was assigned to the Third Division of the Second Corps, Army of the Potomac. By this time, the regiment apparently had received a set of national and regimental colors, each painted with the name of the unit. There is no surviving documentation to indicate the source of these flags.

In company with the Second Corps, the 132nd entered action at Antietam on September 17. The 132nd was one of the Federal units that attacked the now-famous Sunken Road, suffering 152 casualties. Lieutenant-Colonel Vincent M. Wilcox wrote that the regiment planted its colors on the enemy position and brought them back "riddled by his balls."[1]

Regimental Color
Maker: EH
1985.241

Following the Maryland Campaign, the army moved back to Virginia and next encountered Lee's Confederates at Fredericksburg on December 13. Here, one of these flags became the center of a post-battle controversy. During one of the assaults on Marye's Heights, the regiment suffered a loss of 107 of its members. Five men and two officers were shot down while carrying the colors. One of the officers was Lieutenant Henry H. Hoagland of Company H; he was mortally wounded and died the next day.[2]

Sometime after Hoagland went down, Lieutenant Charles M. McDougall (Company C) grabbed one of the banners and called to the regimental adjutant, Frederick L. Hitchcock, to help him replace the fallen color-guard so the colors could be kept aloft. As McDougall handed one of the flags to Hitchcock, a bullet crashed into his arm and wrist, spattering warm blood over Hitchcock's face. Hitchcock took the staff as McDougall fell, only to see another bullet cut the pole in half just below his hand. Seconds later, Hitchcock was struck on the head by a shell fragment and fell unconscious. When he awoke, the battlefield was strewn with dead and wounded all around him. The shell fragment had opened a nasty wound that effused

National Color
1985.242

132nd Infantry

411

Frederick L. Hitchcock
(Shown Here as Colonel of the 25th USCT)

blood and covered his left side. Weakened from the loss of his precious fluid, Hitchcock decided to run for it. He suddenly jumped up and zig-zagged to the rear, all the while under fire from Rebel soldiers. However, the lieutenant managed to escape safely, although a bullet did hit his right leg just above the ankle. Hitchcock recalled that this flesh wound only accelerated his speed.[3]

When the regiment retired, the flag taken by Hitchcock was apparently left behind. Later events showed that Corporal William Parks of Company H, though badly wounded, found the flag and crawled off the field with it. Parks was taken to a field hospital, then sent to Washington, where he died on December 28. The survivors of the 132nd at first thought that the Confederates had captured the flag. However, a few weeks later, Hitchcock was riding past the camp of the 34th New York. He noticed something odd—the regiment was at dress parade with three flags. Upon closer examination, the lieutenant saw clearly that one of the flags belonged to the 132nd. When Hitchcock confronted Colonel James A. Suiter and asked where he got the flag, the New Yorker retorted that "Those are the colors of a damned runaway regiment which my men picked up on the battlefield of Fredericksburg." As Hitchcock recalled: "My hair and whiskers were somewhat hot in color those days, and I have not kept a record of my language to that colonel for the next few minutes. I sincerely hope the recording angel has not."[4]

Hitchcock immediately rode at top speed to the 132nd's camp. He informed Lieutenant-Colonel Charles Albright of his discovery. Albright, whose temper was shorter than his adjutant's, promptly visited the New York camp. After berating Colonel Suiter, Albright refused his offer to return the flag. Instead, Albright sought and received a court of inquiry from Major-General Oliver O. Howard, the Second Corps commander. The 132nd was found blameless and Corporal Parks's deed was especially commended in a general order read before the entire corps. Lieutenant Hitchcock could never understand why Colonel Suiter mistreated the flag in such a way. He found that a company captain had rescued the flag from the hospital and brought it safely across the Rappahannock when the army fell back to Falmouth. Following the court of inquiry, the beloved flag was returned to the 132nd in an official ceremony.[5]

Following the winter of 1862-63, the 132nd participated in the Chancellorsville Campaign, fighting primarily on May 3, 1863. Soon after the end of this operation, the 132nd was sent home and mustered out of service on May 24.

It is not known when these flags were given to the Commonwealth; both are listed in the 1866 inventory lists. It is not apparent which one was the sub-

State Color
Maker: EH
1985.240

412

Advance the Colors!

ject of the controversy detailed above. Both colors have replacement staffs and both are battle-damaged. A logical assumption is that the national color was retired when the state color was issued. Hitchcock wrote that he found it odd that the 34th New York carried three flags. This indicates that the 132nd did not carry both flags alongside the state color. Without further information, both flags remain somewhat of a mystery as to source and exact use during the 132nd's term of service.

State Color

The regiment probably received its state color when Colonel Samuel B. Thomas visited the Army of the Potomac in October 1862 to present flags to all the new Pennsylvania regiments. Its field use remains a mystery. The flag seems to be in good physical condition, indicating light use. If the regiment actively carried this flag, it was probably substituted for the national color received earlier in its term of service. This color was included in the 1866 parade.

Notes

1 *O.R.* 19.1, p. 331.
2 *O.R.* 21, p. 309; Bates 4: 258.
3 Hitchcock, pp. 121-23.
4 *Ibid.*, pp. 141-42; *O.R.* 21, p. 275.

5 Hitchcock, pp. 142-45; "Letter from Virginia," *Bradford Reporter*, March 5, 1863; Colonel Albright to Governor Curtin, February 7, 1863, RG 19; *O.R.* 21, p. 275.

Bibliography

Fourth Re-union of the Regimental Association of the 132nd Pennsylvania Volunteers, Antietam, Md., September 17th, 1891. N.p., n.d.

Hitchcock, Frederick L. *War from the Inside, The Story of the 132nd Regiment Pennsylvania Volunteer Infantry in the War for the Suppression of the Rebellion 1862-1863.* Philadelphia: Press of J. B. Lippincott Company, 1904.

Kitchen, D. C. "Burnside's Mud March." *Philadelphia Weekly Times*, March 4, 1882.

Maycock, John. Diary, 1862-63. USAMHI, HbCWRT Collection.

Oakford, Richard A. Papers. Pennsylvania State Archives.

Wilcox, Vincent M. "An address by Vincent M. Wilcox, Colonel, 132d Regiment Pennsylvania Volunteers, Delivered at the First Re-union of the Regiment on the 26th Anniversary of the Battle of Antietam, at Danville, Pennsylvania, September 17th, 1888." New York: Albert B. King, 1888.

Wright, Orestes B. "The Record of a Nine Months Regiment." *National Tribune Scrapbook* 1: 125-26.

133rd Infantry

State Color

The 133rd Pennsylvania included men recruited in Cambria, Somerset, Bedford, and Perry counties. After the regiment was assembled at Camp Curtin, it moved to Washington in late August 1862. When the Maryland Campaign began, the regiment joined the Third Division, Fifth Corps, Army of the Potomac. This division arrived on the Antietam battlefield the day after the bloody fighting, then went into camp for some time. Colonel Samuel B. Thomas presented a state color to the 133rd during his October visit to the army.

Engaged at Fredericksburg on December 13, the 133rd participated in the division's charge on the enemy soldiers positioned on Marye's Heights. Casualties in this unsuccessful attack totalled 184 for the regiment. Then, after wintering near Falmouth, the unit took part in the Chancellorsville Campaign, fighting on May 3. Soon after the end of the campaign, the regiment went back to Harrisburg, where it was mustered out of service by May 26. The state color was returned in 1866.

State Color
Maker: EH
1985.243

Bibliography

Duram, James C. and Eleanor A. (editors). *Soldier of the Cross: The Civil War Diary and Correspondence of Reverend Andrew Jackson Hartsock.* Manhatan, KS: MA/AH Publishing for the AMI, 1979.

Ross, Orville. Letter, November 1862. USAMHI, CWTI Collection.

Scott, John W. "Battle Incidents. Some Things Out of the Usual at Chancellorsville." *NT,* May 24, 1906.

____. "A Fighting Regiment." *NT,* March 22, 1906.

134th Infantry

State Color

Organized at Camp Curtin in August 1862, the 134th Infantry included soldiers from Lawrence, Butler, and Beaver counties. The regiment was ordered to Washington during the Second Manassas Campaign, joining what became the Third Division, Fifth Corps, Army of the Potomac, in September. This division of eight Pennsylvania regiments arrived at Antietam too late to take part in the battle. The men then went into camp near the battlefield. Colonel Samuel B. Thomas, representing Governor Curtin, presented a state color to the 134th on October 18.[1]

During the Battle of Fredericksburg on December 13, the division was in one of the assaults on Marye's Heights. The 134th suffered 148 casualties. After the color-bearer was shot down and the regiment was falling back, Private George E. Jones of the 126th Pennsylvania rescued the fallen banner and later returned it to the 134th.[2] After spending the winter near Falmouth, the 134th took part in the Chancellorsville Campaign, engaging the enemy on May 3, 1863. The regiment then returned to Harrisburg and was mustered out of service on May 26. Corporal William Flugga of Company E carried the state color in the 1866 parade.

Regimental Color

This blue infantry color was probably obtained from a government depot and was carried at Fredericksburg, the 134th being the lone unit in the division to carry a regimental color.[3]

State Color
Maker: EH
1985.245

Regimental Color
Maker: EH
1985.244

Notes

1 *Chambersburg Spirit of the Times,* October 22, 1862.
2 Alexander, *126th Pennsylvania,* pp. 46-47.
3 Andrew A. Humphreys to D. N. Couch, February 10, 1863, copy in RG 25.

Bibliography

No material on the 134th Infantry has come to the author's attention.

135th Infantry

State Color

Composed of companies from the counties of Westmoreland, Indiana, Jefferson, and Lancaster, the 135th Pennsylvania was organized at Camp Curtin in mid-August 1862. The regiment immediately moved to Washington, where it remained on provost guard duty until February 1863. A state color supplied by Evans & Hassall was sent to the State Agency and presented to the 135th at some unspecified date. Finally relieved from guard duty, the regiment joined the Army of the Potomac near Fredericksburg and was assigned to the Third Division, First Corps. It took part in the opening stages of the Chancellorsville Campaign on April 29, 1863, by supporting artillery batteries placed along the Rappahannock River. It remained on this duty until it rejoined the corps at Chancellorsville, where it was employed as skirmishers, losing a number of men captured. Upon the end of the campaign, the 135th returned to Harrisburg and was discharged from service on May

State Color 1985.246
Maker: EH

24. Corporal Samuel B. Harrison of Company I carried the state color in the 1866 parade.

Bibliography

McClune, Hugh H. *Miscellanea*. York: Gazette Company, 1907.

136th Infantry

State Color

Comprising soldiers recruited in ten Commonwealth counties, the 136th Pennsylvania was organized at Camp Curtin on August 20, 1862. The new regiment then moved to Washington, where the men formed part of the city's garrison until September 27. At this time, the regiment began moving to join the Army of the Potomac, then encamped between Sharpsburg, Maryland, and Harper's Ferry. When the command arrived, it was assigned to the Second Division, First Corps. Colonel Samuel B. Thomas presented a state color to the 136th on October 16, during his visit to the army.[1]

During the Battle of Fredericksburg on December 13, the division moved to support the charge of the Pennsylvania Reserves on Stonewall Jackson's position near the right flank of the Confederate line. When Meade's troops began to retreat, Brigadier General John Gibbon ordered his division forward to cover the withdrawal. As the men of the 136th reached a railroad, the color-bearer was wounded and dropped the flag. Colonel Thomas M. Bayne called for a volunteer to raise the fallen banner. Corporal Philip Petty recalled the events of the next few moments:[2]

Sergeant Philip Petty

State Color
Maker: EH
1985.247

> At the time the colonel made this request I was busy taking charge of and marching to the rear the Confederates whom we had captured in the battle, and as no one else responded, I stepped up and told him I would pick up the colors, and carried them in the advance until we were repulsed by a flank movement of the enemy and were ordered to retreat.
>
> I had advanced a little beyond the railroad track with the colors when the retreat was ordered, and, as I could not very well retreat with a gun and the colors in my hands, I planted the flagstaff in the ground and fired about thirty rounds into the rebels, then broke my gun by striking it on the rails, and carried the colors safely off the field. The colonel formed what was left of the regiment in a hollow square, and when

136th Infantry 417

he told the boys what I had done, they gave me three rousing cheers, after which the colonel promoted me to be color-sergeant.

Petty, originally from England, was a twenty-year-old farmer living near Jackson Summit, Tioga County, when the war began. He enlisted in the 12th Pennsylvania Reserves, but caught typhoid fever and was discharged in March 1862. He re-enlisted in the 136th as a musician, but then was "put into the ranks from musician at his own request." Petty received a Medal of Honor in 1893 for his gallantry at Fredericksburg.[3]

After spending the winter near Falmouth, the 136th took part in the Chancellorsville Campaign, suffering a few casualties from artillery fire on April 30, 1863, and skirmishing with enemy infantry on May 2. Then, its term of service over, the 136th returned to Harrisburg and was mustered out of service on May 29. Sergeant Jacob Johnston of Company C carried the state color in the 1866 parade.

Notes

1 "From the 136th Pa. Regiment," *Wellsboro Agitator,* November 16, 1862.
2 Beyer-Keydel, p. 122.
3 "For His Adopted Country," *NT,* November 8, 1894; information in Petty's Medal of Honor file, RG 94. Captain John J. Mitchell of Company A recalled that the color-sergeant dropped the flag and deserted the battle line when several of the guards were wounded before Petty seized the flag. (statement of February 25, 1893, RG 94).

Bibliography

No letters, diaries, or published accounts have come to the author's attention.

137th Infantry

State Color

The last of the nine-month regiments organized in August 1862, the 137th Infantry moved to Washington, where it was assigned to the Sixth Corps, Army of the Potomac. Although present on the battlefields of South Mountain (September 14) and Antietam (September 17), the regiment suffered no casualties. When Confederate cavalry raided into Maryland and Pennsylvania in October, the 137th was one of the regiments sent in fruitless pursuit of the horsemen. After halting near Hagerstown, Maryland, the command rejoined the army, but was then detached to help garrison the supply depot at Aquia Creek. The 137th was relieved from this duty in January 1863, when it was assigned to the First Corps. Again under fire at Chancellorsville in April-May 1863, the unit suffered no loss. It returned to Harrisburg and was mustered out of service on June 1.

The colors of the 137th pose a mystery over a hundred years later. The state color, finished by Evans & Hassall in September 1862, apparently was not sent to the State Agency until May 6, 1863, when Colonel Roberts acknowledged its receipt.[1] On May 10, Colonel Joseph B. Kiddoo sent to Adjutant-General Russell a letter regarding the number of flags in his command. Kiddoo noted that two state colors were given to the 137th when it left Harrisburg. Since the existing state color was not even completed until September, it is not known what type of flag the colonel referred to. One flag was returned when the regiment was near Hagerstown, and when Kiddoo wrote in May 1863, he remarked that the regiment then carried both state and United States flags.[2] The state color was carried in the 1866 parade by Corporal William H. Chilson of Company H.

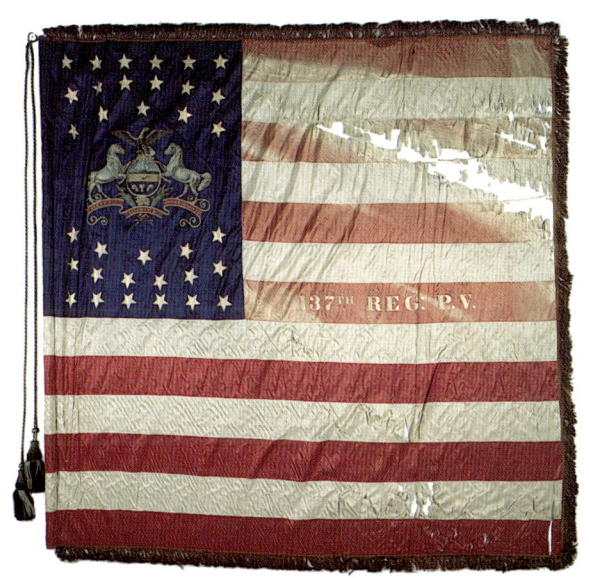

State Color
Maker: EH
1985.248

Notes

1 Roberts to Adjutant-General Russell, May 6, 1863, RG 19.

2 Kiddoo to Russell, May 10, 1863, RG 25.

Bibliography

Barnes, George N. Papers. Crawford County Historical Society.

138th Infantry

State Color

This regiment was organized at Camp Curtin in August 1862 to serve for three years. The companies were recruited in Montgomery, Adams, Bedford, and Bucks counties. Shortly after being organized, the regiment moved to Baltimore and was assigned to duty at Relay House, a junction on the Baltimore & Ohio Railroad. While acting as railroad guards, the regiment received a state color, probably in October when Colonel Samuel B. Thomas visited most of the new Pennsylvania units to present colors to each. The 138th remained on guard duty along the railroad until mid-June 1863, when it was sent to Harper's Ferry to join the garrison there. Most of these troops became the Third Division, Third Corps, Army of the Potomac, in the latter stage of the Gettysburg Campaign. The 138th was first under fire at Wapping Heights (July 23) but suffered no loss. After participating in the Bristoe Station and Mine Run campaigns, the regiment went into winter camp near Brandy Station.

During the winter, the division was transferred to the Sixth Corps, and took part in the 1864-65 campaigns with that body of troops. The 138th fought in the Wilderness (May 5-6), where two color-bearers—Sergeant John F. Biesecker (Company B) and Corporal John H. Ashenfelter (Company K)—were slain while carrying the regiment's two flags.[1] After fighting at Spotsylvania (May 8-20) and briefly on the North Anna River, the regiment took part in the engagement at Cold Harbor (June 1-2). Thereafter, the division was largely held in reserve and did not take an active part in the initial operations around Petersburg.

In July, the Sixth Corps was sent north to Washington to reinforce the city garrison when Jubal Early's Confederates threatened the capital. The Third Division fought in the delaying action along the Monocacy River (July 9) before retreating into the city fortifications. During the ensuing Shenandoah Valley Campaign, the 138th Pennsylvania fought at Winchester (September 19), Fisher's Hill (September 22), and Cedar Creek (October 19). The regiment was sent to Philadelphia during the week of the 1864 presidential election to help maintain law and order. It then returned to the Sixth Corps encampment near Winchester. With the Confederate threat in the Valley erased, the corps returned to Petersburg in early De-

State Color
Maker: HB
1985.250

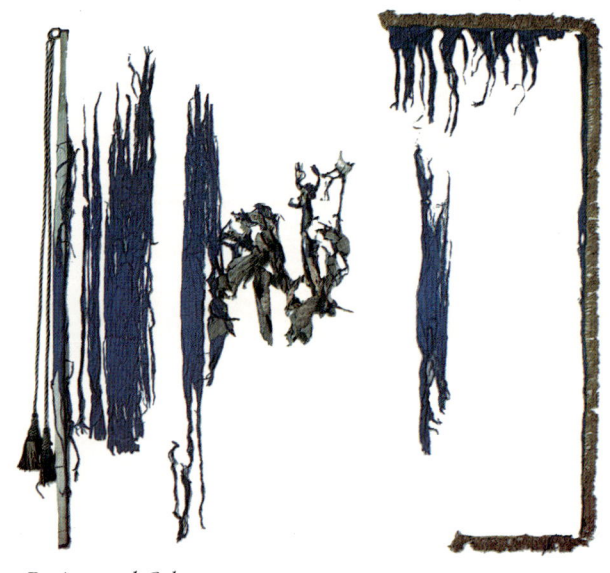

Regimental Color
1985.249

420

Advance the Colors!

obverse *reverse*

Color Presented to 138th in December 1864

cember. At this time, the 138th retired its state color, "being much tattered and nearly unserviceable."[2] It was officially returned to state care in 1866.

Regimental Color

This blue infantry flag was apparently carried side-by-side with the state color from 1862 through December 1864, when it was retired from active service.

Montgomery County Flags

The 138th Infantry received three flags from Montgomery Countians during its term of service. On August 29, 1862, a Dr. Wetherel of Montgomery presented a "splendid flag" to the regiment. No other details have been located to shed further light on this flag.[3]

The "loyal citizens of Norristown and Bridgeport" presented a stand of colors to the regiment on December 23, 1864. Money for the two colors was raised by subscription and the work was done by Evans & Hassall at a cost of $250. One banner was a 35-star national color with "138th Regiment P.V." added. The second flag was a blue regimental color, with the state coat-of-arms on the obverse and the national eagle on the reverse. Scrollwork surrounding the arms contained the names of four battles—Wilderness, Monocacy, Locust Grove, and Spotsylvania. An oval plate on the flagstaff listed the engagements of Bristoe Station, Petersburg, Cold Harbor, Opequan [sic], Fisher's Hill, and Cedar Creek. Two square blue flank markers completed the handsome gift.[4]

These presented colors were carried by the regiment in the capture of Petersburg (April 1, 1865) and in the action at Saylor's Creek (April 6). Following Lee's surrender, the 138th eventually returned to Washington, where it was mustered out of service on June 23. The 1864 flags were finally deposited in GAR Post 52 in Norristown. When the post broke up, the flags were acquired by at least one collector before being purchased by the War Library and Museum in Philadelphia. This museum has custody of the regimental color plus one of the flank markers. A private collector recently acquired the national color.

Notes

1 Bates 4: 353; *Personal War Sketches Presented to Anna M. Ross Post 94, Philadelphia, Department of Pennsylvania, by Mrs. W. H. Kemble*, volume 1, p. 222 (available in the GAR Museum, Philadelphia).

2 Colonel Matthew R. McClennan to Quartermaster-General James L. Reynolds, July 20, 1865, RG 25.

3 "Colonel Sumwalt," *Gettysburg Compiler*, September 1, 1862.

4 "Colors for the 138th," *Bucks County Intelligencer*, December 13, 1864; McClennan to Reynolds, July 20, 1865, RG 25.

Bibliography

Ashenfelter, John H. Diary, April 1-May 4, 1864. Historical Society of Montgomery County.
Bortz, Samuel S. Papers, 1864-65. Historical Society of Western Pennsylvania.
Davis, James W. 1864 Diary. USAMHI.
Gray, Richard A., Jr. (editor). *Pocket Diary of Private George R. Imler*. N.p., 1963.
Griffith, John H. "The Hardships of Prison Life." *NT,* March 9, 1911.

Harrold, John. *Libby, Andersonville, Florence, the Capture, Imprisonment, Escape and Rescue of John Harrold* . . . . Philadelphia: William B. Selheimer, Printer, 1870.

Lewis, Osceola. *History of the One Hundred and Thirty-eighth Regiment, Pennsylvania Volunteer Infantry*. Norristown: Wills, Iredell & Jenkins, 1866.

Lowery, John E. 1863 Diary. USAMHI, HbCWRT Collection.

Markley, John H. Diary, August 1862-November 1863. Historical Society of Pennsylvania.

Mauk, John W. "The Death of Gen. A. P. Hill." *NT*, May 24, 1888.

____. "The Man Who Killed General A. P. Hill. Statement of Mr. Mauk, Who Says He Fired the Fatal Shot." *Southern Historical Society Papers* 20 (1892): 349-51.

Roberts, Frank. 1863 Letters. USAMHI, HbCWRT Collection.

Tate, John M. *Half Hour With an Andersonville Prisoner. Delivered at the Reunion of Post 9, G.A.R., at Gettysburg, Pa., Jan. 8th, 1879*. The author, 1879.

Wood, Joshua. 1862-64 Letters. USAMHI HbCWRT Collection.

139th Infantry

Presented Colors

The 139th Infantry was recruited in Allegheny, Armstrong, Mercer, and Beaver counties during the month of August 1862 to serve for three years. Pittsburgh businessman William Semple took a special interest in helping recruit and equip this new unit. On August 11, Mr. Semple presented a national color to Company I, which was one of four companies in the 139th named the "Semple Infantry" in honor of their benefactor. This color was then used as the regimental flag when the 139th was dispatched to Washington on September 1.[1]

After arriving in the capital, the 139th was sent out to the Manassas battlefield to help inter the dead, who had been largely left unburied following the battle there on August 29-30. Having completed this gruesome task, the regiment was sent to join the Army of the Potomac. It arrived at Antietam during the battle but was not engaged. The 139th was assigned to the

Regimental Officers Photographed Sometime in Early 1864. State Color on Left, Presented National Color on Right

Sixth Corps, remaining with that organization its entire term of service. During the engagement at Fredericksburg on December 13, the corps was held in reserve and the 139th suffered a few casualties from long-range artillery fire.

During the Chancellorsville Campaign, the 139th was first engaged at Marye's Heights on May 3. Here, Color-Sergeant James S. Graham of Company E was severely wounded as the regiment charged forward. Two corporals were hit in succession before a third color-guard grabbed the flag and kept it aloft.[2] The regiment moved on and fought at Salem Church before the Sixth Corps was forced to withdraw. At Gettysburg, the 139th arrived on the field late on July 2 and was sent to bolster the Union left flank, helping to repel the final Confederate attack of the day.

Once the armies returned to Virginia, Mr. Semple, acting upon Colonel Frederick Collier's request for a new flag, purchased a replacement color for the 139th. He arrived at the regiment's camp and presented the flag in person on October 8, 1863. This second flag was a national color inscribed with the battle honors of Antietam, Williamsport, Fredericksburg, Marye's Heights, Salem Heights, and Gettysburg.[3] This color was carried side-by-side with the state colors until the regiment went home in 1865. Both Semple colors were apparently kept by the 139th's veterans until September 21, 1916. On that date, the survivors presented the two flags to Soldiers & Sailors Memorial Hall in Pittsburgh, where they remain today.[4]

First State Color

Although a state color was finished by Horstmann Brothers on September 24, 1862, it somehow became lost and was not forwarded to the State Agency until May 6, 1863.[5] It was obtained by the 139th sometime after Chancellorsville and possibly carried at Gettysburg. Following the Bristoe Station and Mine Run campaigns (October-November 1863), the 139th went into winter camp near Brandy Station until late December. At this time, the brigade to which the 139th was attached was sent to Harper's Ferry for the winter, rejoining the Sixth Corps in mid-March 1864.

During the 1864 campaign, the 139th fought in the Wilderness on May 5-7, suffering almost two hundred casualties in the bitter struggle in the tangled woods. Another 116 officers and men were lost in the fighting at Spotsylvania on May 8-21. The regiment was not engaged in the combat along the North Anna River, but did participate in the fighting at Cold Harbor on June 2-3. After taking part in the initial Union assaults on Petersburg, the Sixth Corps was sent to Washington to reinforce the garrison when Jubal Early's Confederates threatened the city in mid-July. The

Second State Color
Maker: HB
1985.251

Sergeant David W. Young

corps then marched into the Shenandoah Valley and eventually defeated Early's small army. During this campaign, the 139th was engaged at Winchester (September 19), Fisher's Hill (September 22), and Cedar Creek (October 19).

The corps returned to Petersburg in December. At some point during the winter of 1864-65, the commander of the 139th apparently requested a replacement state color. The initial color was never returned to the state and its subsequent fate is thus unknown.

Second State Color

A replacement color was forwarded by Horstmann to the State Agency in early February 1865. On February 22, Major James McGregor requested Colonel Jordan to forward the color to City Point, Virginia, the main Federal supply point for the armies besieging Petersburg and Richmond.[6] The regiment carried this new color during the final assault on Petersburg (April 2) and at Saylor's Creek (April 6). Following Lee's surrender, the Sixth Corps marched on to Danville before returning to Washington, where the 139th was mustered out of service on June 21. The second state color was officially returned to the Commonwealth on July 4, 1866.

Color-Bearers

During the Battle of Winchester (September 19, 1864), one of the 139th's color-bearers was badly wounded and the entire guard was hors-de-combat, when Major Robert Munroe retrieved the fallen banner and carried it from the field. He was breveted lieutenant-colonel for this act of gallantry.[7]

David W. Young of Company E was another of the regiment's flag-bearers. Young enlisted as a private and was promoted to corporal in November 1863. On March 30, 1864, he was promoted to color-sergeant. Young was wounded slightly during the fighting in the Wilderness, hit again at Fisher's Hill, and struck a third time on April 2, 1865. Shortly after the end of the war, Young was honored by General Grant for his gallantry in the Petersburg assault. The general had received a donation of $460 from a group of patriotic citizens who wished the money to be given to the man who raised the first flag over Richmond when the city would be taken by assault. Since Richmond was evacuated and not taken by force, Grant decided to split the money among the three soldiers most conspicuous for gallantry at Petersburg. Young's name was sent forward by Major-General Horatio G. Wright, and on July 22, 1865, Young received the sum of $153.33 for his gallant act of planting the first Yankee flag on Petersburg's defenses.[8]

Notes

1 "Flags Presentation—Semple Infantry," *Pittsburgh Post*, August 12, 1862; unsigned letter in *Pittsburgh Evening Chronicle*, May 21, 1863; "The Semple Infantry," *Pittsburgh Gazette*, August 12, 1862.

2 "Casualties—Col. Collier's Regiment," *Pittsburgh Evening Chronicle*, May 15, 1863; *Pittsburgh Evening Chronicle*, May 21, 1863.

3 "Flag for the 139th," *Pittsburgh Gazette*, October 3, 1863; Regimental Circular, October 8, 1863, Regimental Letter & Order Book, RG 94.

4 "139th Pa.," *NT*, October 19, 1917.

5 Colonel R. B. Roberts to A. L. Russell, May 6, 1863, RG 19. See also Colonel F. H. Collier to Russell, April 12, 1863, in Regimental Papers, RG 19, complaining that the 139th had not yet received a state color.

6 McGregor to Jordan, February 22, 1865, Regimental Letter & Order Book, RG 94.

7 Entry for Robert Munroe in *Personal War Sketches of the Members of Colonel John B. Clark Post No. 162, of Allegheny* (Philadelphia: Louis M. Everts, 1890), found in the library of Soldiers & Sailors.

8 David W. Young Pension Records, RG 94; Bates 4: 381-2; *O.R.* 46.1, 965-6, 1262; "The Killed and Wounded in the 139th," *Pittsburgh Evening Chronicle*, May 13, 1864.

Bibliography

Aber, W. H. "The 139th Pa." *NT*, July 11, 1912.
Armstrong, Edward. "In the Wilderness." *NT*, November 26, 1891.
Borland, Joseph. "Gettysburg." *NT*, January 27, 1887.
Brown, Abraham. "As a 139th Pa. Man Saw It. First Brigade of Wheaton's Division at Cedar Creek." *NT*, January 13, 1898.
Dunlap, William. Letters, June 1863-April 1864. USAMHI, CWMisc Collection.
"Fine Record of 139th at Gettysburg." *Pittsburgh Gazette-Times*, October 10, 1909.
George, Harold C. Collection. Library of Congress.
George, W. "In the Wilderness." *NT*, April 28, 1892.
____. "Wheaton's Brigade. Its Splendid Advance at Gettysburg on the Afternoon of July 2." *NT*, February 11, 1909.
Guyton, Robert. Papers. Duke University.
____. "Facing Early." *NT*, March 29, 1900. (Fort Stevens)
Haines, John J. "Deserted by Their Corps." *NT*, July 17, 1924.
Harbison, Matthew L. "The Eighth Corps. A Sixth Corps Man Testifies to Their Gallantry at Fort Hill." *NT*, May 19, 1892.

Harper, John. Papers. Historical Society of Western Pennsylvania.
Heaslett, James B. Papers. Duke University.
Hildebrand, S. F. "Brothers in One Company." *NT*, March 27, 1902.
____. "Inducements to Confederate Deserters." *NT*, July 13, 1905.
McConnell, Edward N. "A Brief History of Company A, 139th Regiment, Pennsylvania Volunteers." *Western Pennsylvania Historical Magazine* 55 (1972): 307-18.
Schoyer, William T. (editor). *The Road to Cold Harbor. Field Diary, January 1-June 12, 1864, of Samuel C. Schoyer, Captain, Company G, 139th Pennsylvania Volunteer Regiment. Supplemented by Accounts of Other Officers and a Brief History of the Regiment.* Apollo: Closson Press, 1986.
Schrecongast, Joseph M. "Picketing Before Petersburg." *NT*, September 17, 1914.
Snyder, A. H. Papers. Mercer County Historical Society.
Young, David W. "Three Shining Names. The Men Who Bore Off the Honors at Petersburg." *NT*, March 20, 1884.

140th Infantry

State Color

This regiment was composed of companies recruited in Washington, Greene, Beaver, and Mercer counties. It was organized at Camp Curtin in early September 1862 to serve for three years. The new regiment moved south to Parkton, Maryland. All ten companies were then spread along the Northern Central Railroad for about twenty miles to guard this vital link to Baltimore. On November 21, 1862, Colonel Samuel B. Thomas arrived at the 140th's central camp (named Seward) to present a state color to the unit. Sergeant Robert Riddle of Company F was given the honor of bearing this new banner.[1]

The 140th remained on railroad guard duty until mid-December, when the regiment went south to join the Army of the Potomac. Upon arriving near Falmouth, the 140th was assigned to the Third Brigade, First Division, Second Corps. It first engaged the enemy during the Chancellorsville Campaign, fighting on May 1-3, 1863. At Gettysburg, the regiment charged forward with the division through the Wheatfield to the wooded hillock just west of the field. Here, Sergeant Riddle was badly wounded when a bullet

Sergeant Robert Riddle

*State Color
Maker: HB
1985.253*

Advance the Colors!

Corporal Power   Corporal Taggart

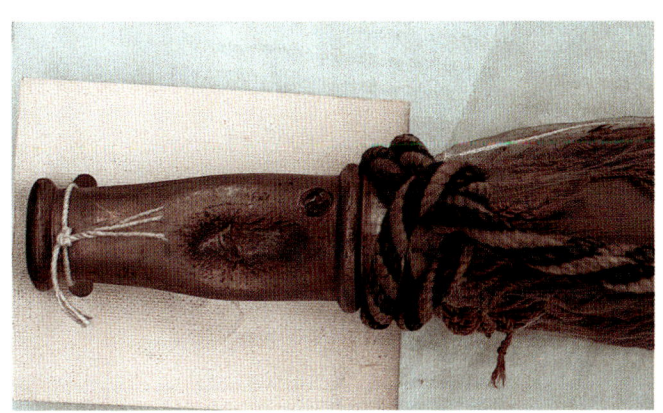

Dent in Finial Base Caused by Bullet on May 12, 1864

crashed through his left lung. He fell on top of the flag, which was pulled from beneath him by Corporal Joseph Moody of Company H. Moody gave the flag to Corporal Jesse Power of Company E, then attempted to place Riddle in a more comfortable position. The battleline soon fell back through the Wheatfield as the Confederates counterattacked. Losses for the 140th totalled 241 killed, wounded, and missing.[2]

Following the Gettysburg Campaign, the 140th took part in both the Bristoe Station and Mine Run campaigns (October-November) before going into winter quarters near Brandy Station.

During the ensuing 1864 Virginia campaign, the regiment fought in all the important battles, beginning with the Wilderness (May 5-7). At Spotsylvania, the 140th fought on May 8 and 10, then participated in the May 12 charge of the Second Corps on the salient. Here, Sergeant Power received two wounds and fell. Sergeant A. G. Beeson of Company E found the fallen banner and was making his way along a line of captured earthworks when a bullet entered his cheek and went completely through his neck. As soon as Beeson went down, Corporal David Taggart of Company G seized the flag. As Taggart recalled: "I had been watching for an opportunity to get hold of the colors, and when Beeson fell with them I picked them up and was the color-bearer from that moment until the end of the war."[3]

Taggart further wrote:

> The battle flag had a broad spear on top of the staff, which was shot off at Spotsylvania. It got another welt on the brass ring, near the top, the same morning. Another welt was made by a bullet in the flagstaff while in my hands at Cold Harbor. Altogether there were three welts made by bullets in the staff. No bullet ever struck me and I was a good bit bigger than a flagstaff.[4]

After Spotsylvania, the regiment engaged the Rebels at the North Anna River (May 27) and at Cold Harbor (June 3). During the initial attack on Petersburg, the 140th fought primarily on June 16-17. Then followed the operations along the Jerusalem Plank Road (June 21-22), at Deep Bottom (July 28-29 and August 14-20), Reams's Station (August 25), and Hatcher's Run (December 9). During the final campaign in 1865, the regiment took part in the March 25 assault at Hatcher's Run, then fought at Sutherland's Station on April 2. As the Second Corps pursued Lee's retreating army toward Appomattox, the 140th fought at Farmville (April 7). After taking part in the Grand Review, the regiment was mustered out of service on May 31. The remnant of the state color was officially returned in 1866.

Regimental Color

The small remnant of what appears to be a blue regimental color makes documentation impossible. Together with the state color, this flag appears on the 1865 quartermaster return list in Record Group 25.

Regimental Color
1985.252

140th Infantry

Company Flags

Existing records indicate that three companies of the 140th received flags during the war. Company C, the Brady Infantry, received a flag from Nathan F. Brabst. The presentation took place on August 29, 1862, in front of the Washington County Courthouse.[5] Company D, the Ten Mile Infantry, was the recipient of a "splendid flag" from the ladies of Amwell Township, Washington County. The presentation occurred on September 4, 1862.[6] Finally, the men of Company E were given a flag by the citizens of Monongahela, Washington County. This banner was presented to the company when it stopped in Pittsburgh en route to Harrisburg in 1862.[7] There seems to be no existing documentation to indicate how and when these three flags were carried by the 140th. Company C's flag was present at the regiment's 1874 reunion, when it was owned by Mrs. A. W. Acheson.[8]

The remnant of the unidentified national color in the state collection was brought to Harrisburg by Harry J. Boyde in 1914. The flag was then placed alongside the other two colors of the 140th. Since Boyde brought the flag at the last minute, it was not encased with a chiffon sleeve. No records pertaining to Boyde have been located. His name does not appear either in Bates, the regimental history, or the card file in the State Archives. A bit of black crepe attached to the flag indicates that this banner may have been carried late in the war.

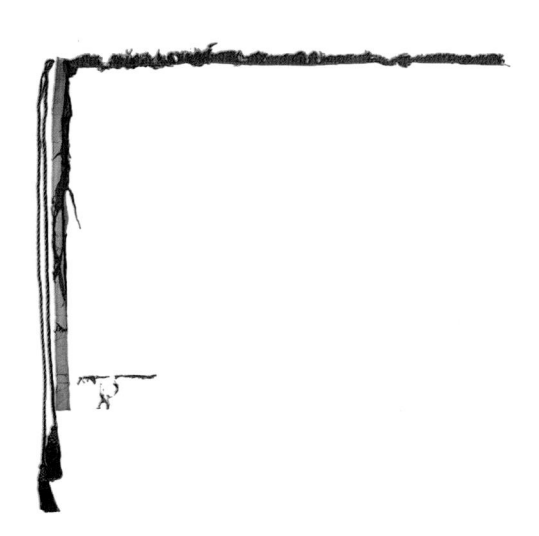

National Color Brought to Harrisburg in 1914
1985.254

Notes

1 *Washington Reporter and Tribune*, November 27, 1862; Stewart, pp. 19, 442.
2 Stewart, pp. 106, 442.
3 *Ibid.*, pp. 198, 442-44.
4 *Ibid.*, p. 444.
5 "Flag to Capt. Acheson's Company," *Washington Reporter and Tribune*, September 4, 1862; Stewart, p. 303.
6 "Departure of Companies," *Washington Reporter and Tribune*, September 11, 1862; Stewart, p. 304.
7 Stewart, p. 291.
8 *Ibid.*, pp. 410-11.

Bibliography

Acheson, Alexander W. "At Spottsylvania Court House." *Philadelphia Weekly Press*, October 27, 1886.
____. "History of the 140th Pennsylvania Volunteers." *Beaver Radical*, December 11, 1868-January 28, 1870.
Collins, Isaiah L. "A Prisoner at the Windup. A Story of the Pursuit of the Enemy to Appomattox, and Observations as a Prisoner." *NT*, March 19, 1914.
Fulcher, Jane M. *Family Letters in a Civil War Century*. Avella, PA, 1986. (Includes letters of Alexander W. and David Acheson)
Graham, James S. Reminiscences. In Janice McFadden Papers. Historical Society of Western Pennsylvania.
Hopkins, D.S. Reminiscences. Pennsylvania State Archives.
Kelley, John. "The Burned Chancellor House. It was the 140th Pa. Who Took Out the Wounded Soldiers." *NT*, January 28, 1909.
____. "Burning of the Chancellor House. The 140th Pa. Saved Part of the Guns of Lepine's (sic) Battery." *NT*, July 8, 1909.
____. "The North Anna Engagement." *NT*, September 8, 1910.
Linton, C.L. "Saving the Guns. It was Part of the 140th Pa. that Saved the Battery at Chancellorsville." *NT*, December 23, 1886.
Linton, E. H. "Chancellorsville Incidents." *Philadelphia Weekly Times*, May 7, 1881.

Moody, Joseph. Letters. USAMHI, Lewis Leigh Collection.
Paul, Philo V. Diary, November 16, 1863-May 11, 1864. USAMHI, Save the Flags Collection.
Paxton, John R. *Sword and Gown, by John R. Paxton, Soldier and Preacher, a Memorial Volume, a Gift to His Friends, Issued by His Daughter, Mary Paxton Hamlin*. Edited by Calvin D. Watson. New York: Knickerbocker Press, 1926.
Potter, Samuel. Papers. Library of Congress.
Powelson, Benjamin F. *History of Company K of the 140th Regiment, Pennsylvania Volunteers (1862-'65)*. Steubenville, OH: Carnahan Printing Company, 1906.
Purdy, J. J. "Her Objection." *NT*, July 9, 1914.
Purman, J. J. "The Authorship of 'Tenting Tonight on the Old Camp Ground'." *NT*, June 18, 1908.
____. "Gen. Zook at Gettysburg." *NT*, March 25, 1909.
Ray J. J. "Cold Harbor." *NT*, December 31, 1891.
Stewart, Robert L. *History of the One Hundred and Fortieth Regiment, Pennsylvania Volunteers*. Philadelphia: Franklin Bindery, 1912.
White, Andrew G. *History of Company F, 140th Regt. Penna. Vols.* Greenville: Beaver Printing Company, 1908.
Wright, John A. "Two Remarkable Coincidences." *NT*, February 12, 1914.

141st Infantry

State Color

Recruited in Bradford, Susquehanna, and Wayne counties during August 1862, the 141st Infantry was formed at Camp Curtin late that month. It then moved to Washington, remaining in the city's defenses until mid-September. The regiment was then attached to the First Division, Third Corps, Army of the Potomac. For the next month, the 141st picketed the Potomac River in the vicinity of Poolesville, Maryland. On October 23, Colonel Samuel B. Thomas arrived in camp to present a state color to the regiment.[1]

After rejoining the army, the regiment was lightly engaged at Fredericksburg on December 13, then went into winter quarters near Falmouth. It next fought at Chancellorsville on May 1-3, suffering more than fifty percent casualties. Here, on May 3, the entire color-guard was felled by enemy bullets. Sergeant George C. Beardsly of Company C, although severely wounded in the thigh, clung to the flag until he fell. Captain Abram J. Swart, commanding the color company (C), grabbed the flag and was instantly killed. Major Israel P. Spaulding then seized the color, but Colonel Henry J. Madill had seen the flag go down twice. The colonel dismounted, elbowed his way through the battle line, and took the flag from Spaulding, declaring that if the flag went down a fourth time, he would go with it. However, Madill safely took the flag as the remnant of his command retreated.[2]

The regiment fought at Gettysburg on July 2. Stationed just behind the Peach Orchard, the 141st initially helped repel the attack of Brigadier-General Joseph B. Kershaw's South Carolinians on some nearby artillery batteries. Then, a Mississippi brigade led by William Barksdale assaulted the Peach Orchard and compelled the defenders to fall back. As the fighting reached the 141st, its casualties mounted. Of the 209 officers and men answering roll call that day, 149 were killed, wounded, or missing in action. Again, the entire color-guard was annihilated in the bloody combat. Private John J. Stockholm of Company H recalled his own action: "I picked up the State Colors when the second man was shot. Just as I raised it, while it

State Color
Maker: HB
1985.256

was gathering in my hands, a musket ball cut about half of the staff away, made a line of holes the length of the flag and went through my hat rim."[3]

Following the Gettysburg Campaign, the survivors of the 141st took part in the Bristoe Station and Mine Run campaigns (October-November) before going into winter camp near Brandy Station. The regiment received many replacements over the winter and entered the 1864 campaign greatly strengthened.

During this protracted campaign, the 141st fought in most of the major engagements with Lee's grayclad soldiers. After fighting in the Wilderness (May 5-6), the regiment took part in the Spotsylvania operations, fighting primarily on May 11 and 12. Then, the survivors fought at the North Anna River (May 23) before moving to Cold Harbor, where the 141st suffered few casualties. At Petersburg, the regiment took part in the June 18 assault. During the ensuing siege operations, the regiment engaged the enemy twice at Deep Bottom (July 28-29 and August 14-20), then at Poplar Spring Church (October 2) and the Boydton Plank Road (October 27-28).

The final campaign opened in March 1865. The 141st fought on March 25 and again on April 6-7, at Saylor's Creek and Farmville. Following Lee's surrender, the regiment returned to Washington, took part in the Grand Review (May 23), then was mustered out of service five days later. The remnant of the state color was officially returned in 1866.

Regimental Color

This federal-issue regimental color was carried side-by-side with the state color during the regiment's term of service. Apparently, Corporal Morton Berry of Company D carried this banner at Gettysburg. Already thrice wounded, Berry refused to relinquish the flag until hit a fourth time. The corporal died of his wounds on July 10. When Berry fell, J. J. Stockholm, already carrying the state color, reached out and grabbed the blue flag with his left hand. Colonel Madill relieved Stockholm of this flag and took it from the field as the survivors retreated to Cemetery Ridge.[4] This flag was carried in the Grand Review. A Philadelphia reporter remarked that the 141st "carried two flags in shreds hanging from the staffs."[5] The regimental color was returned to Harrisburg in June 1865, together with the state color. It still has a piece of black crepe attached.

National Color
1985.255

Color-Bearers

During the 1864 campaign, Private Abner W. Forest of Company K carried one of the regiment's colors. Forest was mortally wounded in the Wilderness on May 6. The wound, incurred in his elbow, eventually con-

Regimental Color
1985.257

National Color

There seems to be no documentation to verify the use of this flag. The thirty-five stars are arranged in an oval pattern. This flag too was sent to Harrisburg in June 1865.

Sergeant Stephen B. Canfield Sits in Front of the Battered Colors of the 141st, May 1865
Regimental Color on the Left, State Color on the Right

tributed to his death on June 29. When Forest went down, Lieutenant Elisha B. Brainerd of Company F took the flag, then passed it on to Sergeant John Seagraves (Company G) for safekeeping.[6]

At Spotsylvania, the 141st took part in the great attack on the morning of May 12. Sergeant Charles Scott of Company C bore one of the flags during this fighting. The regiment became disorganized during the charge, and when Captain Benjamin M. Peck (Company B) chanced upon Scott, the sergeant had only a few men with him. Fearing the advancing enemy might capture the flag, Peck ordered Scott to make his way rearward to save the flag, which he did.[7]

Captain Charles H. Weygant of the 124th New York apparently saw the "State flag" of the 141st at some point during this confused fighting. The banner was accompanied by a lieutenant and eight or ten men. Weygant requested the color to be advanced in an effort to get the stalled Union troops moving forward again. However, the bearer quickly fell. The unidentified lieutenant seized the flag but was also disabled by a bullet. Weygant, angered over the subsequent wavering of the troops, called the nearby men "cowards," whereupon a corporal of the 141st stepped forward, handed the flag to the New Yorker, and told him that his comrades would follow the flag to the "infernal regions" if he would carry it there. A moment later, about fifty soldiers sprang forward; Weygant planted the flag on the next line of enemy works but soon fell wounded. Thereafter, he was carried to the rear and did not learn what happened to the flag.[8]

Notes

1 Craft, p. 17.
2 *Ibid.*, pp. 79-80, 83, 86; J. D. Bloodgood, "Chancellorsville," *NT*, October 17, 1901; O.R. 25.1, p. 428.
3 Craft, p. 122.
4 *Ibid.*; OR. 27.1, p. 505. This is a tentative reconstruction of which flag each man was carrying. Craft, p. 122, writes that Stockholm picked up the "State colors" when a second bearer was shot down. Berry was carrying the "stars and stripes" when he fell. It is unlikely that the national color in the state collection is this "stars and stripes" because 35-star colors were not officially carried until after July 4, 1863. Stockholm remembered that a bullet cut the staff of his flag; the state color in the collection has a broken staff. There is no damage to the staff of the blue regimental color. Thus, Stockholm may have been mistaken about Berry and his "stars and stripes," unless the regiment had another flag which has not survived. There is one other possibility to disentangle this evidence: given the propensity of some writers to refer to inscribed regimental colors as "state colors," Stockholm may have taken hold of the blue flag, but again, the staff is not broken.
5 "Home from the Wars! The Grand National Pageant . . .," *Philadelphia Inquirer*, May 24, 1865.
6 Craft, p. 186.
7 *Ibid.*, pp. 193-94.
8 Charles H. Weygant, *History of the One Hundred and Twenty-Fourth Regiment, New York State Volunteers* (Newburgh: Journal Printing House, 1877), p. 324.

Bibliography

Adams, A. J. "The Fight in the Peach Orchard." *NT*, April 23, 1885.
Birchard, Albert. Letters, March, 1862-October 1864. Susquehanna County Historical Society.
Bloodgood, John D. "Chancellorsville." *NT*, October 17, 1901.
____. *Personal Reminiscences of the War*. New York: Hunt & Eaton, 1893.
Coburn, James P. Papers. USAMHI.
Craft, David. *History of the One Hundred Forty-first Regiment, Pennsylvania Volunteers, 1862-1865*. Towanda: Reporter-Journal Printing Company, 1885.
Delamarter, Jacob. Letters, August 1862 - June 1863. Susquehanna County Historical Society.
Kent, Richard. Diary, January-May 4, 1863. Susquehanna County Historical Society.
Kilmer, George W. "The Bloody Angle at Spotsylvania." *NT*, September 4, 1924.
____. "A Captive at Richmond." *NT*, October 9, 1924.
____. "Chancellorsville and Gettysburg." *NT*, August 25, 1921.
____. "The 141st Pa. Vols. at Chancellorsville." *NT*, July 5, 1923.
____ "The Stand at the Peach Orchard." *NT*, December 27, 1923.
____. "With Grant in the Wilderness." *NT*, July 17, 31, 1924.
Lee, A. Papers. Library of Congress.
Loring, William E. "Gettysburg. The 141st Pa. at the Battle—A Graphic Narrative by a High Private." *NT*, July 9, 1885.
____. "Going to the Front. A Graphic Description of the Young Recruit's Experiences." *NT*, December 31, 1896; January 7, 1897.
____. "How Gen. Graham was Captured at Gettysburg." *NT*, January 1, 1885.
____ "On the Second Day. The 141st Pa. in the Gettysburg Battle—A Loss of Over 75 Per Cent." *NT*, July 5, 1894.
____ "A Rough Hospital." *NT*, October 22, 1885.
Madill, Henry J. Diary, September 1862-April 1865. USAMHI, HbCWRT Collection.
Millard, H. J. 1863 Diary. Susquehanna County Historical Society.
Thompson, J. W. "Fredericksburg." *NT*, August 7, 1890.
Ward, Lester F. *Young Ward's Diary, A Human and Eager Record of the Years Between 1860 and 1870*. Edited by Bernhard J. Stern. New York: G. P. Putnam's Sons, 1935.

142nd Infantry

State Color

Comprised of troops recruited in ten scattered counties, the 142nd Infantry was formed at Camp Curtin in late August 1862. It moved to Washington and spent a month on garrison duty before moving to join the Army of the Potomac, then camped near the Antietam battlefield. Upon arrival, the 142nd was assigned to General Meade's Pennsylvania Reserves. On October 19, Colonel Samuel B. Thomas, during his trip to distribute colors to all the new Keystone regiments, presented a state color to the 142nd.[1]

State Color
Maker: HB
1985.259

The 142nd's first battle was at Fredericksburg on December 13. Here, almost 250 officers and men were casualties during the division's charge against Stonewall Jackson's troops posted at Hamilton's Crossing. After spending the winter in quarters erected near Belle Plain Landing, the regiment, now attached to the Third Division, First Corps, took part in the Chancellorsville Campaign, suffering no casualties. At Gettysburg on July 1, 1863, the First Corps sustained horrendous losses during its day-long defense of McPherson's and Seminary ridges west of the town. Here, the 142nd lost 211 men killed, wounded, and captured. At some point during the fighting, the color-bearers were shot down and apparently the flag was left on the ground, where it was found by a mounted staff officer. This man mistakenly brought the flag to the 151st Pennsylvania, whose colonel was at first shocked that his command had lost its flag until he was able to read the inscription on the center red stripe.[2]

After Gettysburg, the regiment took part in the Bristoe Station Campaign (October) before retiring to winter quarters near Brandy Station. In the spring of 1864, the regiment was transferred to the Fifth Corps when the old First Corps was broken up. As part of this corps, the 142nd engaged the enemy at the Wilderness (May 5-6), Spotsylvania (May 8-18), North Anna River, Cold Harbor, and in the initial assaults on Petersburg (June 18 and 21). During the ensuing operations around Petersburg, the regiment fought at the Weldon Railroad (August 18-21), the Boydton Plank Road (October 27-28), and Hatcher's Run (February 5-7, 1865). After engaging the enemy at Five Forks (April 1), the regiment marched in pursuit of Lee's troops to Appomattox Court House. Following Lee's surrender, the 142nd eventually returned to Washing-

Regimental Color
1985.258

Advance the Colors!

ton, took part in the Grand Review, and was mustered out of service on May 29. The survivors returned to Harrisburg, where the remnant of the state color was presented to Governor Curtin on June 3.[3] It was officially returned to state care in 1866.

Regimental Color

The remnant of this blue regimental flag was also returned to state care in 1866.

Color-Bearers

At Gettysburg, J. Robinson Balsley of Company H was in the act of retrieving one of the regiment's fallen colors when he was struck by two bullets and fell wounded. Balsley lay between the battlelines as the outnumbered bluecoats fell back to Seminary Ridge. Later that afternoon, as he lay watching the fighting, Balsley was struck by yet another bullet, while other lead projectiles sliced through his haversack and cartridge box. He eventually was rescued and treated at a field hospital.[4]

The names of two other bearers have been located. Sergeant Daniel Young carried a flag in the fall of 1864.[5] Finally, at Hatcher's Run on February 6, 1865, the entire color-guard save one was killed or wounded. The lone survivor, Corporal James X. Walter of Company H, seized the fallen banner and carried it with "perfect coolness" throughout the fighting. He was promoted to sergeant for his gallantry that day.[6]

Notes

1 "From Gen. Hooker's Division," *Philadelphia Inquirer*, October 20, 1862.
2 Lieutenant-Colonel George F. McFarland to John B. Bachelder, August 13, 18??, Bachelder Papers, New Hampshire Historical Society.
3 "Harrisburg. A Proud Day in Our History . . . ,"*Philadelphia Inquirer*, June 5, 1865.
4 J. R. Balsley, "A Gettysburg Reminiscence," *NT*, May 19, 1898.
5 Special Orders #8, October 18, 1864, in Regimental Letter, Indorsement, Order & Guard Report Book, RG 94.
6 *O.R.* 46.1, p. 296.

Bibliography

Balsley, J. Robinson, "Burnside's Mud March." *NT*, January 14, 1915.
____. "A Gettysburg Reminiscence." *NT*, May 19, 1898.
____. "Not So Kind." *NT*, April 7, 1910.
Boyts, Hiram. Letters. Historical and Genealogical Society of Somerset County.
"Captain Dushane's Company." *NT*, January 10, 1907.
Dushane, J. M. "From Libby to Liberty." *Keystone Courier*, March 28, 1888.
Fisher, T.S. "Recollections of Belle Isle." *NT*, May 23, 1918.
Gearhart, Edwin R. *Reminiscences of the Civil War*. Stroudsburg: Daily Record Press, 1901.
James, David. Papers. University of Wyoming.
Lohr, Harrison. "Preferred the Front to the Hospital." *NT*, April 19, 1900.
McCalmont, Alfred B. *Extract from Letters Written by Alfred B. McCalmont . . . from the Front During the War of the Rebellion*. Franklin, PA, 1908.
Ness, Charles H. (editor). "Home to Franklin! Excerpts from the Civil War Diary of George Randolph Franklin." *Western Pennsylvania Historical Magazine* 54 (1972): 158-66.
Prothero, Thomas. "One of the Youngest." *NT*, August 27, 1891.
Walker, Joseph. "About Fort Stevens." *NT*, September 16, 1915.
____. "At Fort Stevens." *NT*, October 30, 1913.
Warren, Horatio N. *The Declaration of Independence and War History, Bull Run to Appomattox*. Buffalo: Courier Company, Printers, 1894.
____. *Two Reunions of the 142d Regiment, Pa. Vols., Including a History of the Regiment, Dedication of the Monument, a Description of the Battle of Gettysburg, Also a Complete Roster of the Regiment*. Buffalo: Courier Company, Printers, 1890.
Wilkins, D. S. "A Personal War History." Westmoreland-Fayette Historical Society.

143rd Infantry

First State Color

This regiment, recruited in the Wyoming Valley during the summer and fall of 1862, was organized at a camp near Wilkes-Barre in early October. Upon arrival in Washington a month later, the 143rd encamped near Fort Slocum, remaining in the city's defenses until mid-February 1863. A state color, supplied by Horstmann Brothers in early November, probably was sent to the regiment while at Washington.

In February 1863, the 143rd joined the Army of the Potomac and was assigned to the Second Brigade, Third Division, First Corps. This brigade, led by former Bucktail Colonel Roy Stone, consisted of two other Pennsylvania regiments—the 149th and 150th—organized as new Bucktail units. Both regiments initially looked down upon the outsiders assigned to their brigade, and at times the 143rd received the worst camping ground and most menial details from the brigade commander. Although the regiment was under fire during the Chancellorsville Campaign (April - May), it was not seriously engaged with the enemy.

However, the 143rd fought gallantly in its first major battle at Gettysburg on July 1. Here, with the other regiments of Stone's brigade, the 143rd contested with the grayclad troops of Lieutenant-General Ambrose P. Hill's Third Corps of Lee's army. Posted near the Chambersburg Pike west of town, the regiment held on until forced to retreat by more numerous enemy troops. As the 143rd began to retire, Color-Sergeant Benjamin Crippen (Company E) kept turning around to shake his fist at the oncoming Confederates, daring them to take his flag. Young Crippen paid with his life, and all but two of the guards went down as well. General Hill, accompanied by his staff and some foreign observers, saw Crippen at a distance and praised his bravery. Hill also regretted Crippen's demise.[1]

When Crippen fell dead, Corporal Owen Phillips of Company B, the only unscathed member of the color-guard, retrieved the fallen state color. He also seized the fallen blue regimental color and took both flags as the survivors fell back. In addition to his burden, Phillips neglected to throw down his rifle. Colonel Edmund L. Dana spied the brave corporal struggling to carry all three items and asked why he had not discarded his musket. Phillips replied that he was more familiar with his musket than with a flag. Dana, impressed with the man's coolness under fire, lightened Phillips's load by taking one of the flags. In recognition of his bravery, Phillips was promoted to sergeant to rank from July 1.[2]

Although the regiment was under fire both on July 2 and 3, it suffered negligible loss. Of the 465 officers and men present in the ranks on July 1, 253 were casualties. However, the regiment saved both its flags, the only regiment in the brigade to do so.

Following the Gettysburg Campaign, the regiment took part in the October Bristoe Station Campaign. During the ensuing November operations at Mine Run, the division was detached to guard the supply base at Manassas Junction. Winter quarters were erected near Culpeper. When the First Corps was discontinued in March 1864, the brigade was incorporated into the Fifth Corps, with which it remained during the 1864-65 Virginia Campaign.

First State Color
Maker: HB
1985.261

James E. Taylor Painting of Sergeant Crippen at Gettysburg

When this campaign opened, the 143rd engaged the enemy in the Wilderness (May 5-6), suffering more than two hundred casualties. Sometime during this struggle, Sergeant Phillips fell mortally wounded. He fell into Rebel hands and lingered perhaps three days before expiring.[3] During the Spotsylvania operations (May 8-18), the 143rd fought primarily on May 8, 10-11, and 13, losing seventy-three soldiers.

During the fighting along the North Anna River on May 23, the regiment almost lost its flag to the enemy. A Confederate attack hit the brigade line and caused a temporary setback. Owing to several factors, the 143rd split into two sections. The main part of the unit retreated, but a number of the men failed to hear the order to retire. Sergeant Patrick DeLacy of Company A rallied these men about the colors at an old fence running at right angles to the main line. Although the foot soldiers managed to halt the enemy advance, Union artillery began to fire also, endangering DeLacy's detachment. To add to their predicament, blueclad infantry also started firing at the enemy as the afternoon sun set. Risking his life, DeLacy ran out between the lines and stopped the friendly fire. When he reached the main line, DeLacy had the

Sergeant Owen Phillips

143rd Infantry 435

Wartime Photograph of the First State Color

pany K) stepped up and asked for the banner. This soldier had gotten into some sort of trouble previously and had been reduced in the ranks. He wished to redeem his reputation, and carried the flag throughout the rest of the fighting. DeLacy's party remained in the line until the morning of the twenty-fourth, when they rejoined the regiment. Major Chester K. Hughes was overjoyed to see DeLacy and the flag, which he had thought was lost.[4]

After fighting at Cold Harbor, the regiment took part in the initial assaults on the Petersburg defenses (June 18). Thereafter, the 143rd took its turn in the trench lines dug by the Union troops, occasionally taking part in Fifth Corps maneuvers against the enemy railroads supplying Petersburg. The regiment fought at the Weldon Railroad (August 18-21) and Boydton Plank Road (October 27-28). A few days after the combat at Hatcher's Run (February 5-7, 1865), the regiment, together with three other understrength regiments from the brigade, was withdrawn from the front and sent north. The 143rd went to Hart's Island,

flag and a few 143rd comrades with him. At that moment, the color-bearer was shot down. The sergeant retrieved the flag when Private Merrit Coughlin (Com-

The Colors and Bearers of the 143rd at Harrisburg, Flag Day 1914
Left to Right: Patrick DeLacy, James A. Stettler, Francis Furman, Nathan Vosler, Mark B. Perigo

Advance the Colors!

New York, to guard the draft rendezvous camp located there. It remained in this service until mustered out of service on June 12. The state color was initially left in Harrisburg, but borrowed by Colonel Dana for use in the Independence Day ceremonies in Wilkes-Barre. It was returned to the adjutant-general's office and was present in the 1866 Philadelphia ceremony.[5]

Second State Color

This replacement color was completed by Horstmann Brothers in late January 1865. It was sent to the Honorable John Reichard, an associate judge of Luzerne County, whose son served in the 143rd.[6] Judge Reichard in turn forwarded the flag to the regiment.[7] It, too, was present in the 1866 ceremony.

Second State Color
Maker: HB
1985.260

Regimental Color
Maker: EH
1985.262

Regimental Color

This blue flag was apparently the one carried at Gettysburg and retrieved by Corporal Phillips. It was carried by the 143rd until the opening of the 1864 Virginia Campaign. At this time, Oliver K. Moore, formerly a captain in the regiment until he resigned due to ill health, visited the regiment just before the campaign started. When he returned to Wilkes-Barre, he brought this banner along with him, in accordance with the wishes of Colonel Dana and his men. It remained in Wilkes-Barre until August 1865, when Dana sent it to the state together with the first state color.[8]

Wilkes-Barre Color

This flag was presented to the regiment in 1865 by a group of Wilkes-Barre ladies. Corporal Rogers W. Cox

Corporal Rogers W. Cox

Presented "State" Color
1985.263

143rd Infantry

437

of Company E was detailed as bearer. Many years later, Cox recalled that this duty "was about the biggest undertaking I ever had on my hands, as I only weighed about 125 pounds then, and a flag is a hard thing to carry anyway, specially thru woods."[9] The pristine "state" color in the collection may be this same flag. The staff is marked "national," and this banner was turned over to the state in February 1868.

Company B Flag

On September 4, 1862, the citizens of Schultzville presented a "beautiful and costly" silk flag to Captain Joseph H. Sornberger's company.[10] No other documentation has been found to shed additional light on this banner.

Color-Bearers

In addition to the names mentioned in the text, two others have been identified as bearers for one of the regiment's flags. Sergeant W. H. Harden's 1906 obituary lists this man as a bearer.[11] In 1866, Sergeant Thomas Dakin of Company C was one of the bearers.

Notes

1 Bates 4: 488-89.

2 Harris manuscript, pp. 90-91.

3 *Ibid.*, pp. 169-70. Harris was inconclusive about Phillips's death. On page 169, he wrote that the sergeant was mortally wounded and died the next day in rebel hands. On page 170, he wrote that Phillips was shot on May 6 and lingered three days. Bates (4: 495) indicates that Phillips died from wounds on May 9.

4 Autobiographical sketch written by Patrick DeLacy, in Gary Roche collection.

5 Colonel E. L. Dana to Adjutant-General A. L. Russell, June 19, 1865, RG 25. Dana describes the color as "the regimental flag." A written note on the letter indicates a return date of August 14. The author assumes that the flag in question is the first state color, returned in tandem with the blue regimental color now in the state collection.

6 Information about Reichard is from George B. Kulp, *Families of the Wyoming Valley*, 3 volumes (Wilkes-Barre, 1890), 3: 1299.

7 Reichard to Adjutant-General A. L. Russell, February 4, 1865, RG 25.

8 "The Flag of the 143rd," *Luzerne Union*, May 11, 1864. There is no physical description of the banner in this article. Since the regiment carried their first state color during the 1864 campaign, the blue regimental in the state collection must be the flag mentioned in this article, unless there is another 143rd color unaccounted for. The blue regimental color appears on the February 10, 1865, list, with its appendages, under the August 14 date. The author firmly believes that this is the same flag sent home in May 1864.

9 R. W. Cox article in *NT*, December 19, 1907.

10 Untitled article in *Wilkes-Barre Record of the Times*, September 10, 1862.

11 Obituary can be found in *NT*, August 2, 1906.

Bibliography

Cox, Rogers W. "Fought Fire in the Wilderness." *NT*, December 19, 1907.

Dana, Edmund L. Papers. Wyoming Historical and Geological Society.

Foster, Frank E. "How He Escaped Death. Comrade was Too Sick to Go North on the 'General Lyon' and was Saved." *NT*, January 6, 1927.

Fulton James. "Gettysburg Reminiscences." *NT*, October 20, 1898.

Harris, Avery. "As to Carroll's Brigade." *NT*, February 9, 1911. (Wilderness)

——. Personal Reminiscences. USAMHI.

Keys, William F. Diary, 1863-64. Rutgers University.

Lyon, Robert T. "The Civil War Record of Lt. Col. John D. Musser." *Now and Then* 19 (January 1980): 207-15.

143d Regt. Pa. Vols. 2d Brigade, 3d Division, 1st Army Corps. Historical Address of the Late M. D. Roche, Historian of the Regiment. Dedication of Monument and Re-union at Gettysburg, September 11 and 12, 1889. Scranton: Sunday News, 1889.

Shafer, John. "First in at Gettysburg." *NT*, August 25, 1887.

Wolfe, Josiah M. "An Old Andersonville Comrade." *NT*, July 13, 1905.

Zierdt, William H. *Narrative History of the 109th Field Artillery, Pennsylvania National Guard, 1776-1930.* Wilkes-Barre: E. B. Yordy Company, 1932.

145th Infantry

First State Color

Comprised of soldiers from Erie, Warren, Crawford, and Mercer counties, the 145th Infantry was organized at Erie on September 5, 1862. Six days later, the regiment, still lacking equipment and training, was rushed south to Chambersburg as the Maryland Campaign developed. The raw recruits arrived on the Antietam battlefield on September 17 but were not engaged. After helping to bury the dead, the 145th moved south and went into camp on Bolivar Heights, opposite Harper's Ferry. Here, Colonel Samuel B. Thomas presented a state color to the regiment on October 14.[1] While in camp here, the 145th was assigned to the First Division, Second Corps, Army of the Potomac.

The regiment first engaged Confederate troops at Fredericksburg on December 13. Eight companies participated in one of the bloody assaults on the Marye's Heights position. About half of the five hundred men engaged were casualties. The state color was pierced by eighteen bullets before the survivors withdrew.[2] After spending the winter in camp near Falmouth, the 145th took part in the Chancellorsville Campaign (April-May 1863), fighting near the Chancellor House on May 2-3. At Gettysburg on July 2, the 145th charged through the Wheatfield, again suffering heavy casualties. Following the Bristoe Station and Mine Run campaigns (October-November), the battered 145th went into camp near Brandy Station.

During the 1864 campaign, the 145th skirmished briefly in the Wilderness (May 5-6), then lost heavily in the fighting at Spotsylvania (May 8-20). The regiment was not seriously engaged at the North Anna River, and lost comparatively few men at Cold Harbor. However, the regiment was largely destroyed on June 16, when the division launched a disjointed attack on the outer defenses of Petersburg. With darkness approaching, the 145th charged forward across an open field under heavy fire from cannon and muskets. The survivors dropped to the ground in an effort to avoid further needless casualties. When Colonel David B. McCreary perceived grayclad infantry starting to flank his command, the colonel consulted other officers and all decided to surrender rather than attempt a hazardous retreat to friendly positions. Before the 145th gave up, McCreary took the state color and had the remnants divided up among the guards and a few officers.[3]

Second State Color
Maker: HB
1985.264

Second State Color

It is not known if the survivors obtained a color to use during most of the remainder of their term of service. Following the debacle on June 16, the 145th fought at Weldon Railroad (June 22), Deep Bottom (July 27-29 and August 13-20), and Reams' Station (August 25), together with the constant strain of picket duty in the trenches around Petersburg. Following Lee's surrender, the regiment moved to Washington. On May 16, 1865, Horstmann Brothers sent a new state color to the State Agency. Major Charles M. Lynch obtained the flag four days later, in time for the 145th to display it in the Grand Review (May 23).[4] Thereafter, the men returned to Harrisburg and were disbanded on May 31. The second color was present in the 1866 ceremony.

Presented Flags

The 145th received four colors by local presentation in 1862. Company F, recruited in Warren County, received a silk flag from the ladies of Tidioute on August 16.[5] The Conneautville Soldiers' Aid Society presented a "beautiful flag" to Company H, recruited in Crawford County, on September 3.[6] Neither flag seems to have survived the years since the war.

A deputation of Erie citizens presented a national color to Company A on September 11. This banner was given to the museum of GAR Post 67 in 1932 and is presently housed in the Erie County Library System building in Erie.[7]

The ladies of Erie presented a blue regimental color to the 145th on September 30 while the command lay in camp near Harper's Ferry. Lieutenant-Colonel McCreary presented the flag on behalf of the absent donors. This flag was carried at Fredericksburg, where it suffered heavy damage. Thirteen bullets and a large piece of railroad iron (probably fired as canister) pierced the silken banner. Another piece of shell broke the staff and a bullet clipped off part of a wing of the eagle-shaped finial. Considering the flag too damaged to carry into another battle, the regiment sent it back to Erie in April 1863. It is now owned by the Erie County Library System.[8]

Color-Bearer

John P. Ferguson of Company K carried one of the 145th's colors sometime prior to the 1864 campaign.[9]

Notes

1 Robert A. Kerr diary, October 14, 1862. The October 25, 1862, issue of the *Warren Mail* indicated October 16 as the presentation date.

2 *O.R.* 21, p. 239.

3 McCreary to Adjutant-General Russell, June 1, 1866, RG 19. Sergeant J. C. Veit, Company B, later claimed that he ripped the remnant of the silk from the staff and hid the flag under his uniform, successfully concealing the flag from prison guards until released. See "Battle Flag of the 145th," *Erie Daily Times*, February 14, 1906. Veit's letter elicited a defense of McCreary's story in the March 6, 1906, issue of the same paper. Both clippings are in a scrapbook in the Erie County Historical Society.

4 Moorhead diary entry for May 20, 1865.

5 "War Meeting at Tidioute," *Warren Mail,* August 30, 1862.

6 *Crawford Journal* (Meadville), September 7, 1862.

7 Information taken from inscription card accompanying the flag.

8 "Flag for Col. Brown's Regiment," *Erie Weekly Gazette*, September 25, 1862; *Ibid.*, October 16, 1862; *Ibid.*, April 23, 1863; *O.R.* 21, p. 239; *Erie Daily Times,* March 6, 1906, letter cited above; Kerr diary, September 30, 1862.

9 *The History of Erie County, Pennsylvania* (Chicago: Warner and Beers, 1884), p. 17 of the township biographies section. Ferguson resided in Conneaut Township at the time. He served as a lieutenant in 1864.

Bibliography

Black, John C. "Reminiscences of the Bloody Angle." In *Glimpses of the Nation's Struggle. Papers Read Before the Minnesota Commandery of the Military Order of the Loyal Legion of the United States,* 4: 420-36. St. Paul: H. L. Collins Company, 1898.

____. Papers. Pennsylvania State Archives.

Hill, W. W. "Soldierly Honesty." *NT,* April 28, 1904.

Kent, Daniel. Letters. University of Michigan, Bentley Historical Collection.

McCreary, D. B. "The 145th Pa. The True Story of that Affair at Chancellorsville." *NT,* December 17, 1885.

____. Papers. Erie County Historical Society.

Reed, George E. (editor). *Civil War Diary of Private Robert Scott Moorhead of Erie County, Pennsylvania, 145th Regiment of Pennsylvania Volunteers, 4th Brigade, 1st Division, 2nd Army Corps, Army of the Potomac.* Harrisburg, 1988.

Stuckenberg, J. H. W. Diary. Gettysburg College.

Trine, D. "Battle of Five Forks." *NT,* September 4, 1902.

Yeakle, Amos A. Diary. Schwenkfelter Library, Pennsbury, PA.

147th Infantry

First State Color

In the fall of 1862, the War Department ordered all infantry regiments in excess of ten companies to disband or transfer all extra companies. The 28th Pennsylvania, which fielded fifteen companies, was accordingly pared to the prescribed ten. Its extra companies became the first five of the new 147th Infantry, which was augmented by three new companies raised that fall. Later in the war, two more companies were added to bring the regiment up to full strength.

The three new companies joined the five veteran companies at their camp near Harper's Ferry in November 1862. When these companies left Camp Curtin, they brought along a new state color for the 147th. This flag was unfurled by the regiment on November 27; Sergeant Samuel Henry of Company C was appointed bearer.[1] The 147th was brigaded with the 28th and four Ohio regiments as a component of the Twelfth Corps, Army of the Potomac. The corps remained near Harper's Ferry until early December, when it marched south to join the army near Fredricksburg.

The regiment's first battle was at Chancellorsville, where it fought on May 1-3, 1863. Among the 94 casualties was Sergeant Henry. During the close fighting in the woods on May 3, the regiment stubbornly contested its breastworks with the advancing enemy. At one point, the 147th attached and retook its works. Henry had just planted the colors on the works when he was killed, either by a rifle bullet or an artillery shell that decapitated him and splattered his brains over the flag. Lieutenant-Colonel Ario Pardee, Jr., then seized the banner and carried it until the regiment fell back.[2]

At Gettysburg, the 147th took position on Culp's Hill on July 2 and 3, suffering light casualties while defending its breastworks. Following the Gettysburg Campaign, the Eleventh and Twelfth Corps were sent by rail to join the Army of the Cumberland, then under siege at Chattanooga. The 147th played a minor role in the fighting on Lookout Mountain (November 24) and Ringgold (November 27). Once this campaign

First State Color
Maker: HB
1985.266

was over, the regiment went into winter quarters, at first near Wauhatchie, then at Bridgeport, Alabama. The battered state color was retired and apparently kept by Colonel Pardee until August 1865. The colonel returned the flag without its staff; a replacement was added prior to the 1866 ceremony.

Second State Color

A replacement color was furnished by Horstmann Brothers in March 1864. Captain Nelson Byers of Company G obtained the flag while home on furlough and brought it to the 147th when he returned in the spring of 1864.[3] The regiment carried this new flag during the ensuing Atlanta Campaign. The regiment fought at New Hope Church (May 25), then skirmished with the enemy for the next week. Following the engagement at Pine Knob (June 15-18), the 147th suffered more casualties in the operations near Kenesaw Mountain later in June. On July 20, the 147th engaged the enemy at Peach Tree Creek, retaining its position behind fieldworks when the right of the division was turned briefly by John B. Hood's attacking Rebels.

In early September, Hood abandoned Atlanta. The 147th remained near the city until November, then accompanied Sherman on his now-famous March to the Sea. After capturing Savannah, the army turned north through the Carolinas, the regiment sustaining very few losses during these two campaigns. The troops marched north to Washington, where they took part in the Grand Review (May 24, 1865). The 147th remained near Washington until mustered out of service in mid-July. The second state color was sent to Harrisburg and officially returned in 1866. Sergeant Jesse K. Pryor of Company C was color-bearer at muster out and also carried his flag on July 4, 1866.[4]

Second State Color
Maker: HB
1985.265

Notes

1 Lumbard sketch, Chapter 14; Special Orders #1, November 28, 1862, in Regimental Order Book, Part One, RG 94.

2 Pardee's official report *(O.R. 25.1, p. 747)* indicates that Henry was killed by a bullet. However, both Lumbard (Chapter 39) and Schroyer (page 348) state that Henry was decapitated by an artillery shell.

3 A Horstmann bill in RG 25 has the date March 12, 1864, for completion of the flag. On April 9, 1864, Colonel Pardee wrote to Adjutant-General Russell, asking for a replacement flag. This letter is also in RG 25. Schroyer, page 389, writes that this new flag was received at the regiment's Bridgeport camp.

4 Letter of Captain William J. Mackey, Company C, July 3, 1866, authorizing Sergeant Pryor as one of the color-bearers, RG 25.

Bibliography

Johnston, Gertrude K. (editor). *Dear Pa and So It Goes.* Harrisburg: Business Service Company, 1971. (letters of Ario Pardee)

King, Josiah E. Letters. University of Michigan.

Lumbard, Joseph A. "The 147th Regiment at Chancellorsville." *Snyder County Tribune*, July 16, 1891.

____. "The White Stars, and Their Splendid Defense of Culp's Hill, Gettysburg," *NT*, September 20, 1883.

____. "Sketch of Company G, 147th P.V.I." *Snyder County Tribune*, issues of January 13, 1876-January 27, 1878.

Moore, Joseph A. Papers. USAMHI, Save the Flags Collection.

____. "After the Battle. Removing the Wounded from Ringgold to Chattanooga." *NT*, November 26, 1891.

____. "Lookout Mountain." *NT*, December 15, 1887.

____. "Personal Recollections of the Battle of Gettysburg." *Grand Army Scout and Soldiers Mail*, November 3, 1883.

Pettit, J. F. "Wounding of a Young Lady." *NT*, April 7, 1910. (Peach Tree Creek)

Rankin, William. "His Last Letters." *NT*, May 25, 1905.

Russ, William A. (editor). "Civil War Letters Concerning Members of Co. G, 147th Reg. P.V.I." *Susquehanna University Studies* 5 (1953-56): 179-220.

Schroyer, Michael S. "Company 'G' History." *Snyder County Historical Society Bulletin*, pages 336-428 of volume two reprint.

148th Infantry

State Color

Comprised of seven companies from Centre County, and one each from the counties of Clarion, Jefferson, and Indiana, the 148th Pennsylvania was formed at Camp Curtin in early September 1862. The regiment moved by rail down the Northern Central Railroad, and was dispersed over a twelve-mile stretch of that route to guard against sabotage. On November 14, Colonel Samuel B. Thomas visited the regiment's headquarters to present a Horstmann-made state color to the regiment.[1]

The regiment joined the Army of the Potomac in mid-December. It was assigned to the First Brigade, First Division, Second Corps. After wintering near Falmouth, the command fought at Chancellorsville on May 1-3, 1863, suffering 164 casualties. At Gettysburg, the regiment fought in the Wheatfield on July 2 as the division counter-attacked across the field. Here, 125 officers and men were added to the casualty list, but Sergeant John F. Benner of Company C, bearer of the state color, escaped unscathed.[2] Following the Bristoe Station and Mine Run campaigns (October-November), the regiment went into winter camp near Stevensburg, Virginia.

During the 1864 campaign, the 148th participated in all the major battles. The unit was deployed as pickets during the Wilderness fighting and escaped with a solitary man killed. At Spotsylvania, the regiment was principally engaged on May 10 and 12, with 301 officers and men listed as casualties. Then followed the operations along the North Anna River (May 23-26), Cold Harbor (June 3), and the initial assaults on Petersburg (June 16-18). The regiment then engaged the enemy at the Jerusalem Plank Road (June 22), and participated in both moves of the Second Corps north across the James River to Deep Bottom (July-August).

When the corps returned to Petersburg, it marched west to strike the Weldon Railroad at Reams's Station. Here, on August 25, the corps was attacked and fared badly in the ensuing battle. The 148th lost its state color during the fighting. Captain James F. Weaver reported the loss as follows:

One of the Regimental Colors was lost at the Battle of Reams' Station, August 25th, 1864, by a Sergeant who was ordered to remain and keep it with the line of battle, the Regiment having been ordered on the skirmish line. It is not known whether the colors fell into the hands of the enemy or not, although it has been definitely ascertained that the Sergeant is a prisoner of war.[3]

Apparently captured by the Confederates, the state color was not on the 1905 list of returned flags.

First National Color

The origin of this flag is undocumented, but it most likely was obtained to replace the captured state color. The remnant clearly indicates that it was some type of national color with a circular star pattern. The 148th apparently carried this flag throughout the remainder of its term of service. Following the Reams's Station affair, the regiment returned to Petersburg and performed trench duty until the last campaign that began in March 1865. It engaged the enemy at the White Oak Road on March 31. Here, Corporal Joseph J. Shotstall of Company E was killed. Corporal Isaiah P. Leightley of Company F then seized the fallen banner and safely carried it during the remainder of the battle.[4] During the Appomattox Campaign, the regiment fought

First National Color
1985.268

at Sutherland's Station (April 2). The 148th returned to Washington, took part in the Grand Review, and was mustered out of service on June 3. This national color, in company with the other national and regimental colors, was returned by the 148th in June 1865. One of these three colors was carried in the 1866 Philadelphia parade. In 1914, Isaiah Leightley carried this national color for the last time. At some point during the day, he penciled his name on the staff label.

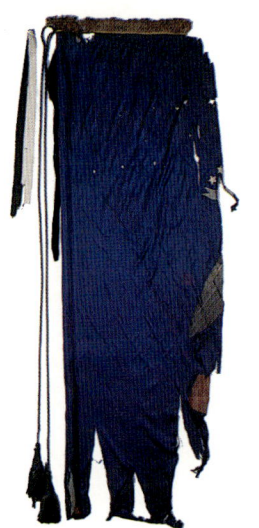

Second National Color

The history of this 35-star Alexander Brandon contract flag is undocumented. At some point after the war, this flag was misidentified as one belonging to the 118th Pennsylvania because of the faded staff label that can be read either as "118th" or "148th." However, "148th P.V." is penciled on two of the white stripes on the pole sleeve.

Regimental Color
Maker: W. F. Scheible
1985.267

Second National Color
1985.219

Regimental Color

This flag was apparently carried side-by-side with the state color throughout the war. At Gettysburg its bearer was killed. When the flag fell, Lemuel Osman of Company C seized the flag for a time, then gave it to Sergeant Benner as the regiment fell back.[5] The small bit of surviving red scroll indicates that this flag was a product of William F. Scheible. Some black crepe is still attached to the flag.

Color-Bearers

During the fighting at Chancellorsville on May 3, 1863, Corporal Hugh S. Neil of Company K, one of the flag-bearers, was killed.[6] On May 10, 1864, Corporal David H. Swyers of Company B carried one of the flags. The flag was a tempting target for the enemy who opposed the 148th that day. Swyers had his cap shot off, then his knapsack. Both his canteen and blouse were riddled with bullets. Finally, a musket ball entered his left breast and came out beneath his shoulder. Swyers was taken to a hospital for treatment. Later wounded at White Oak Road, Swyers was promoted to a lieutenancy. The other color-bearer that day, Sergeant Robert A. Henry of Company F, was not so lucky; he was killed outright, together with six of the eight corporals comprising the color-guard.[7]

On June 16, 1864, the 148th participated in an unsuccessful assault on the Petersburg defenses. When the regiment began to retreat, Sergeant William Ward of Company H, one of the flag-bearers, was well in the advance. Worried that the pursuing Rebels might take his flag, Ward buried it in the sand. Although the sergeant was soon taken prisoner, the flag survived and was dug up next day by comrades who had witnessed Ward's act. The brave sergeant did not survive his captivity; he died at Andersonville on December 1.[8] The other color-bearer became temporarily separated from the 148th and eventually brought the flag in after the regiment fell back.[9]

Notes

1 Muffly, p. 65.
2 *Ibid.*, p. 603.
3 Weaver to Lieutenant J. W. Muffly, September 28, 1864, in Regimental Letter, Indorsement & Index Book, RG 94.

4 Muffly, pp. 690, 972.
5 *Ibid.*, p. 603.
6 *Ibid.*, p. 438. On page 1029, the spelling appears as Neal.
7 *Ibid.*, pp. 165, 636.

8 *Ibid.*, pp. 157, 740, 1005.

9 *Ibid.*, p. 157. Bates, 4: 580, mentions the name of a Sergeant Cochrane as the other color-bearer. However, Cochrane's name does not appear in the roster. Private Isaac G. Cochran's name appears in Company G's roster.

Bibliography

Barr, C. T. "The Second Corps. A Comrade Tells of Some of the Victories They Won After Hancock Left Them." *NT*, November 3, 1892.

Beaver, James A. Papers. Pennsylvania State Archives.

Blair, William. "Patriotism and Protest." *Town & Gown* 23 (July 1988): 50-54, 56, 62, 64, 66.

Burr, Frank A. *Life and Achievements of James Addams Beaver, Early Life, Military Services and Public Career.* Philadelphia: Ferguson Brothers & Company, Printers, 1882.

Campbell, Henry C. Memoir. USAMHI.

Law, D. C. "Asleep on Post." *NT*, March 1, 1923.

____. "That Dark Night of May 11." *NT*, June 30, 1910.

McIvison, J. Thomas. Letters, 1862-63. Pennsylvania State University.

Muffly, Joseph W. *The Story of Our Regiment, A History of the 148th Pennsylvania Vols., Written by the Comrades.* Des Moines: Kenyon Printing & Manufacturing Company, 1904.

Sloan, S. H. "At Petersburg." *NT*, July 11, 1912.

Williams, John. 1864 letters. University of Virginia.

Wilson G. A. "Conscripts Versus Drafted Men." *NT*, May 23, 1918.

____. "Who was to Blame?" *NT*, May 29, 1919. (Spotsylvania)

149th Infantry

State Color
Regimental Color

Recruited in nine Pennsylvania counties, the 149th Infantry was one of two "Bucktail" units recruited in August 1862 by Roy Stone, major of the original Bucktails (42nd Infantry). Immediately upon organization at Camp Curtin, the 149th, in company with the 150th Infantry, proceeded to Washington, where the regiment remained on provost duty until it was assigned to the Third Division, First Corps, Army of the Potomac, in mid-February 1863. On October 21, 1862, Colonel Samuel B. Thomas presented State colors to both Bucktail regiments.[1] The 149th took part in the Chancellorsville Campaign of April-May 1863, but was not engaged with the enemy.

Colonel Stone's brigade arrived at Gettysburg on July 1, 1863, and took position near the McPherson farm on the ridge of the same name west of town. There was a lull in the fighting as the Pennsylvanians took position about noon. By 1:30 p.m., newly-arriving Confederate troops were deploying and artillery fire began to descend on the Bucktails. To prevent needless casualties, Colonel Stone ordered Captain John C. Bassler, commanding Company C (the color-company), to send his flags off into a wheatfield located between the Chambersburg Pike and the unfinished railroad cut to the northwest of the brigade battle line. By doing so, the enemy noticed the movement of the colors and shifted the artillery to shoot at the flags, all alone in the wheat except for the bearers and guards.[2]

Captain Bassler's Company C was recruited in the Myerstown area of Lebanon County. The regimental color-guard included two flag-bearers and four guards that fateful day. Sergeant Henry Brehm, a twenty-nine-year-old tailor, carried the state color. Corporal Franklin Lehman carried a regimental color, while four corporals—Frederick Hoffman, John Hammel,

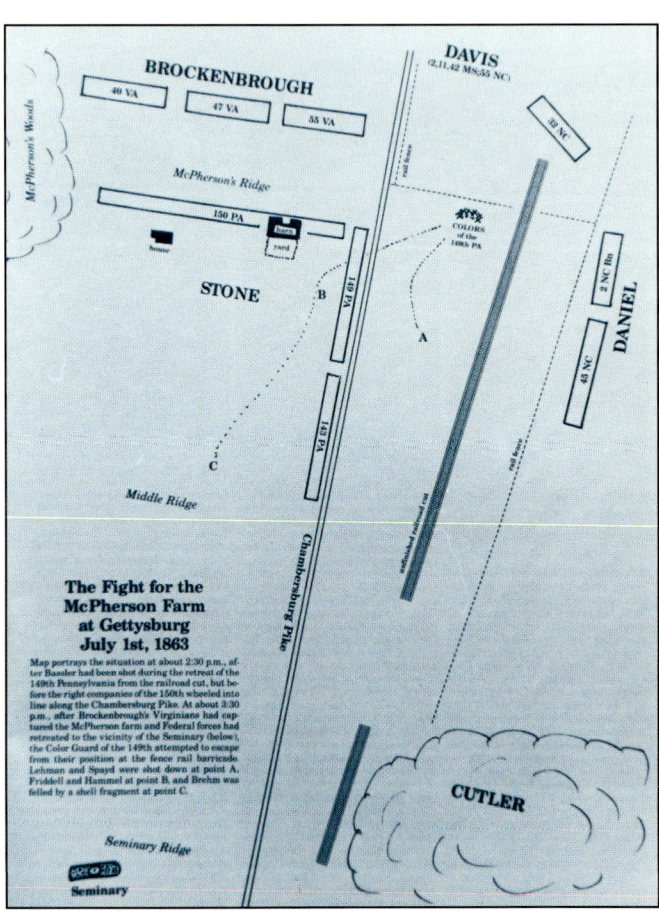

Map Showing Gettysburg Color Episode of the 149th

State Color
Maker: HB
1985.270

446

Advance the Colors!

Four Members of the Color-Party Involved in the Gettysburg Action
From Left to Right: Sergeant Brehm, Corporals Spayd, Lehman, and Friddell

Henry Spayd, and John Friddell—comprised the guards present for duty. When ordered to take the flags out into the wheatfield, Brehm led his squad through the tall stalks until he found a pile of fence rails that apparently had been heaped together by some of Buford's cavalrymen earlier in the day. The guard placed the flags upright and then crouched down behind the rails for protection as artillery projectiles began to fall in the field.[3]

As the color-guard nervously awaited events, Confederate troops began to attack the position of the First Corps. By 3:15 p.m., Stone's brigade was attacked from the north and west and forced to retreat to Seminary Ridge to avoid destruction. When it became apparent that troops were moving about and it looked like Confederate infantry was approaching, several members of the guard asked Brehm to return to the regiment. But Brehm, a good soldier, said he had orders and would not retire unless Captain Bassler approved. Since the sergeant also was a bit apprehensive over their lack of subsequent orders, he allowed Corporal Hoffman to leave, find the regiment, and obtain fresh instructions. Hoffman finally located the 149th as it was beginning to retreat, but since enemy soldiers could be seen between the regiment and the colors, Hoffman had no opportunity to return and order his comrades to retreat.[4]

Meanwhile, advancing Mississippians of Joseph C. Davis's brigade saw the two Yankee colors floating above the wheatfield. Soon, five volunteers led by Sergeant Frank Price of the 42nd Mississippi cautiously approached the wheatfield, crawling on all fours to avoid detection. The grayclad soldiers expected to see a line of Federal infantry protecting their silk banners. As they came nearer and nearer to the flags, they spied the rail pile and surprisingly saw no defending Yankees.[5]

With a Rebel yell, the Mississippians sprang forward to the rail pile and the prized flags. The sudden yelling startled the color-guards, still waiting behind the rails. Corporal Lehman stood up to run, but collided with Sergeant Brehm. Lehman fell as one of the Mississippians grabbed the staff of the regimental flag and tried to wrench the banner from Lehman's grasp. A second enemy soldier rammed his musket into the bearer's chest. Before he could shoot, Corporal Spayd fired his Enfield and dropped the Confederate. Spayd then clubbed his musket and threw it at the Rebel who had seized the flagstaff, causing the enemy soldier to drop the flag. Lehman apparently was deafened by the rifle shot and had relaxed his grip on the flag. Spayd, now weaponless, grabbed the flag and sprinted toward the rear with Lehman close behind him.[6]

Meanwhile, Sergeant Price lunged forward for the state color, but Brehm retained his grip and the two antagonists pitched forward together into the fence rails. Brehm let go of the flag and began fisticuffs with Price. Another Rebel seized the fallen banner but was shot by Corporal Friddell while Hammel fired point-blank at yet another assailant. By this time, Brehm had knocked Price down and reclaimed the state color. The three surviving members of the guard then took off for the rear as Spayd and Lehman had already done.[7]

As Spayd and Lehman ran toward the last noted position of the 149th, they saw nothing but the advancing battleline of Colonel J. M. Brockenbrough's

149th Infantry

Virginia brigade. The two fleeing Yankees veered off to the north toward the railroad cut, hoping to pass around the enemy left flank. However, the flag proved a tempting target. Quickly, both men were hit in the legs and fell less than a hundred feet from the rail pile. Spayd fell on the flag and hoped to shield it from view, but it was pulled out from underneath him by pursuing Confederates. The flag was later given to Sergeant Price for his efforts to capture both colors. The captured regimental color has not reappeared since 1863.[8]

Sergeant Brehm, followed by Corporals Hammel and Friddell, also sprinted for the last reported position of the 149th. The three ran south across the Chambersburg Pike, then cut through the meadow behind the McPherson barn. Here, they saw a battle line directly ahead of them, half-hidden by musketry smoke. As Brehm's party approached at a run, they discovered that the line of battle was Confederate, not Union. It was too late to stop, so the three Yankees bowled into the Rebel line. As they passed through and continued their flight across the meadow, Hammel was shot in the bowels (he died on September 23) and Friddell fell with a hideous chest wound. Brehm miraculously escaped the hail of gunfire and ran on toward the retreating Union line. However, a piece of a nearby exploding shell struck Brehm in the back and knocked him down. The flagstaff was also broken. The shell fragment severely bruised the plucky sergeant's back and also must have caused internal injuries, for Brehm died on August 9.[9]

Captain Bassler was lying wounded by the McPherson barn and witnessed Sergeant Brehm's attempt to save the colors. Brehm passed out of Bassler's view before he was wounded. Shortly thereafter, Bassler saw "a red haired rebel approaching on his way to the rear bearing aloft our beloved colors." This soldier was apparently Private John Lumpkin of the 55th Virginia, who received official credit for the capture of the state color.[10] The postbattle history of this flag is somewhat confused. The flag was returned to Pennsylvania in 1905. In 1907, Ralph E. Gambell wrote to Bassler and included the statement that the state color was recaptured at Falling Waters, Maryland, by the 6th Michigan Cavalry on July 14, when Lee's rearguard was attacked by Union cavalrymen.[11] No other documentation has been located to corroborate Gambell's letter.

Presented Color

The 149th Pennsylvania suffered seventy-five percent casualties at Gettysburg—336 of 450 officers and men engaged. The wounded Corporal Spayd returned to duty in November 1863 just before the regiment went into winter quarters near Culpeper. During Spayd's absence, the decimated 149th took part in the Bristoe Station campaign. The regiment had also procured a replacement flag from a source unknown to Spayd. This flag resembled the state color, but there are no bills for it in the State Archives. The lists of state-issued flags indicate that only one was issued to the 149th, so this color was probably bought by subscription within the regiment, or so theorized Spayd in 1907.[12]

National Color
1985.271

Spayd was promoted to sergeant and carried this flag throughout the remainder of the 149th's term of service. During the 1864 campaign, the regiment fought in the Wilderness on May 5-6, suffering 215 casualties. The regiment then engaged the enemy at Spotsylvania (May 8-18), North Anna River (May 23-26), and Cold Harbor (June 1-5) before crossing the James River to take part in the June 18 attack on Petersburg. Thereafter, the 149th fought in the August 18-21 Weldon Railroad engagement, at the Boydton Plank Road (October 27), and finally at Hatcher's Run (February 6-7, 1865). At this time, the 149th and 150th were detached from active service and sent to Elmira, New York, to guard the draft rendezvous located there. The regiment remained on this duty until mustered out of service on June 24, 1865. The replacement color was given to state care in 1866.

Notes

1 Chamberlin, *150th Pennsylvania* (1905 edition), p. 46.

2 Bassler, "Color Episode," p. 6.

3 Pfanz, p. 38; Bassler, "Color Episode," pp. 10-12. In Bassler's accounts, Brehm carried the "national" color, while Lehman was bearer of the "state" color. The state color in the collection contains information that it was captured by the 55th Virginia. In order to reconcile this information with the written record, I believe that when Bassler used the term "national color," he referred to the state color (national flag with state coat-of-arms). When referring to the "state color," Bassler probably meant a blue regimental color with the regimental inscription added. Since this captured flag has never reappeared, my theory cannot be substantiated, but given the information at hand, it appears to be the most plausible reconstruction of events.

4 Bassler, "Color Episode," pp. 11-12; Henry H. Spayd statement to John B. Bachelder, undated, Bachelder Papers, New Hampshire Historical Society.

5 Matthews, p. 23; Pfanz, pp. 36-37; Price to Bachelder, January 27, 1878, Bachelder Papers.

6 Matthews, pp. 23-24; Pfanz, p. 39; Spayd to Captain Ralph E. Gambell, February 22, 1907, 149th Pennsylvania Collection; Spayd to Bassler, February 20, 1907, 149th Collection; Spayd Statement to Bachelder; F. W. Lehman to John B. Bachelder, January 26, [?], Bachelder Papers.

7 Ibid.

8 Spayd letter, February 22, 1907; Spayd statement to Bachelder.

9 Pfanz, pp. 39-40; Matthews, p. 24; Bassler, "Color Episode," pp. 12-13; Bassler to Bachelder, December 17, 1881, Bachelder Papers.

10 Bassler to Bachelder, September 5, 1881, Bachelder Papers; Pfanz, p. 40.

11 Gambell to Bassler, May 8, 1907, 149th Collection. In connection with the 149th's flags, it should be noted here that Bassler wrote his "Color Episode" in response to postbattle writings that suggested the 150th Pennsylvania had recaptured the colors of the 149th, then lost them before they could be taken off the field with the retreating troops. Bassler spent years researching this rumor and corresponding with veterans, and a large part of his pamphlet refutes convincingly this rumor. For a summary of all of this, see Matthews, pp. 24-25. Several additional letters in the collections cited above refer to this controversy.

12 Spayd to Gambell, February 22, 1907.

Bibliography

Bassler, John H. "The Color Episode of the One Hundred and Forty-ninth Regiment Pennsylvania Volunteers in the First Day's Fight at Gettysburg, July 1st, 1863." *Papers and Addresses of the Lebanon County Historical Society* 4 (1907): 77-110; also in *Southern Historical Society Papers* 37 (1909): 266-301; reprint, Baltimore: Butternut and Blue, 1986.

———. "Reminiscences of the First Day's Fight at Gettysburg, An Address Delivered by J. H. Bassler Before the Faculty and Students of Albright Collegiate Institute, June '95, by Invitation of the Principal, E. W. Chubb." Myerstown: Press of Myerstown Enterprise, 1895.

———. Papers. Whitmoyer Public Library, Myerstown, PA.

Beaty, Miles. Papers. State University of Iowa.

Clark, James L. Letters. USAMHI, Lewis Leigh Collection.

Foust, Samuel D. Diary, January-October 1864. USAMHI, HbCWRT Collection.

Goshorn, George. "Two Days in the Wilderness." *NT*, April 5, 1900.

Harshberger, Abraham, Memoirs. USAMHI, CWTI Collection.

Irvin, John. Diaries, 1863-1865. Historical Society of Pennsylvania.

Matthews, Richard. "The Jackson Guards, Company C, 149th Pennsylvania Infantry at Gettysburg." *Military Images* 7 #6 (May-June 1987): 16-25; as "Bassler and His Jackson Guards." *Lebanon County Historical Society* 17 #1 (1987): 21-51.

Neely, David R. P. 1864 Diary. Pennsylvania State Archives.

Nesbit, John W. "The Bucktails on July 1." *NT*, February 26, 1914.

———. "Cross Roads in the Wilderness." *NT*, March 22, 1917.

———. *General History of Company D, 149th Pennsylvania Volunteers and Personal Sketches of the Members*. Oakdale, CA: Oakdale Printing and Publishing Company, 1908.

———. "Recollections of Pickett's Charge." *NT*, November 16, 1916.

Pennsylvania Infantry. 149th Regiment. Collection. USAMHI, CWMisc Collection.

Pfanz, Harry W. "The Regiment Saved, The Colors Lost." *By Valor and Arms* 3 #2 (1977): 36-41.

Proceedings of Reunion and Dedication of State Monument Held by the Survivors of the 149th P. V. Regiment at Gettysburg, Pennsylvania Day, Sept. 11th and 12th, 1889. Pittsburgh: Ferguson & Company, Printers, 1889.

150th Infantry

State Color

The second of two "Bucktail" regiments recruited by Roy Stone, the 150th included soldiers from Philadelphia, Crawford, McKean, and Union counties. Soon after organizing at Camp Curtin in September 1862, the regiment was ordered to Washington, where it was detailed for guard duty in the city. While in camp at Meridian Hill near the city, Colonel Samuel B. Thomas arrived to present colors to both Bucktail units (149th and 150th) on October 21, 1862.[1]

In mid-February 1863, the 150th moved to join the Army of the Potomac near Fredericksburg. Together with the 143rd and 149th Pennsylvania regiments, the 150th formed the Second Brigade, Third Division, First Corps. The division was not actively engaged during the Chancellorsville Campaign of April-May, and the 150th suffered no casualties.

At Gettysburg on July 1, the Bucktail Brigade covered itself with glory as it repulsed several Confederate attacks on its position on McPherson's Ridge. By three o'clock that afternoon, enemy pressure along the corps battleline forced the entire defensive line to give way and retreat. The remnant of the brigade retired to an orchard, where it made a brief stand before again falling back under heavy enemy pressure. During this last stand, Color-Sergeant Samuel Phifer of Company I was shot dead while carrying the state color. The guard was nearly wiped out by this time; perhaps Corporal Joseph Gutelius of Company D was the sole unwounded survivor. Gutelius seized the fallen banner and followed the 150th to the rear. As the regiment entered Gettysburg, the survivors became sep-

Corporal Joseph S. Gutelius

*State Color
Maker: HB
1985.273*

450

Advance the Colors!

arated and subsequent events became shrouded in controversy.²

According to one story, which is perhaps the truest, Gutelius was severely wounded during the retreat but insisted on carrying the flag to the rear. As he stopped a moment to rest on a door step, a squad of grayclad soldiers rounded the corner and spied the flag. Gutelius was killed and Lieutenant F. M. Harney of the 14th North Carolina (Ramseur's Brigade, Rodes's Division, Ewell's Second Corps) seized the banner as a trophy. Soon thereafter, Harney fell mortally wounded himself. The lieutenant's last request was that the flag he had captured should be presented in his name to President Jefferson Davis. In acknowledging the receipt of the color to Governor Zebulon Vance of the Old North State, Davis wrote that the flag "will be treasured by me as an honorable memento of the valor and patriotism and devotion which the soldiers of North Carolina have displayed on many hard fought fields."³

The captured flag remained with Davis even when he fled Richmond in April 1865. The 150th's state color was found in the President's baggage when he was captured by Union cavalrymen near Milledgeville, Georgia, in May. It was taken to Washington and incorporated in the War Department's collection of recaptured flags. Several prominent Pennsylvanians, among them Simon Cameron, made repeated attempts to release the flag to state care. Finally, the War Department relented and released the banner on October 25, 1869. The flag, together with the letter returning it to the state, was installed in the new flag room when it opened in 1873.⁴

National Colors

Following the capture of the state color, the 150th seems not to have requested a replacement flag from the state government. Instead, the regiment appears to have used three national colors for the remainder of its term of service. The first was probably acquired soon after Gettysburg. Of the 417 officers and men taken into the July 1 fighting, 264 were casualties. The survivors took part in the Bristoe Station Campaign (October) before going into winter camp near Culpeper.

The 150th formed part of the Fifth Corps when the old First Corps was discontinued in the spring of 1864. The regiment fought in the Wilderness (May 5-6), Spotsylvania (May 8-18), North Anna River (May 23), and in the Cold Harbor area (May 30-June 1) before taking part in the initial attacks on the Petersburg defenses (June 18-21). The regiment next fought the Rebels at the Weldon Railroad (August 18-21). Six weeks later, on October 6, the regiment retired its flag,

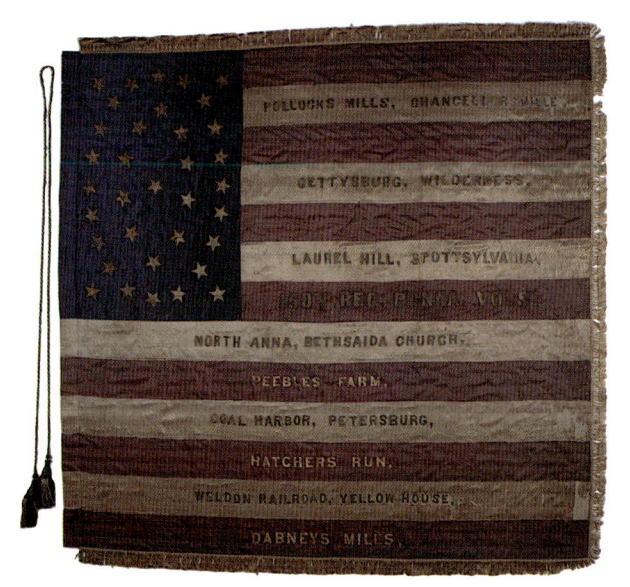

National Color Presented in October 1864

*National Color
1985.272*

"having been too much exhausted by storm and battle to hold together longer. Its retirement was the subject of much regret in the regiment."⁵ This flag seems not to have survived its eventual postwar disposition.

A 35-star national color served as replacement. This flag included a listing of battle honors. The 150th carried this flag on the field at Boydton Plank Road (October 27) and Hatcher's Run (February 5-7, 1865). Shortly after this latter affair, both the 149th and 150th were relieved from active duty and sent north to guard the draft rendezvous camp at Elmira, New York. The 150th was mustered out of service here on June 21, 1865. Apparently, Major George W. Jones took this national color home with him. It remained with his heirs until recently sold at auction. It is now owned by a private collector.

The 35-star national color in the state collection was carried in the 1866 ceremony. Nothing else has been found to document its use by the 150th.

Company K Flag

While the regiment spent time in Washington during the fall of 1862, Company K was detached to guard the Soldier's Home, about three miles north of the White House. President Lincoln spent most of his time at this place during the summer, and the men of this Crawford County unit kept a watchful eye on the President and any guests he might have. Sometime in 1865, Tad Lincoln presented a 34-star wool bunting flag to the company. This 6x10' flag eventually came into the possession of Henry W. Hoffman, one of the company's privates. It has remained in the family and is currently on loan to the Venango Museum of Art, Science and Industry, located in Oil City, Pennsylvania.[6]

Notes

1 Chamberlin, *150th Pennsylvania* (1905 edition), p. 46.
2 Chamberlin, 1895 edition, p. 128.
3 O.R. 27.2, pp. 451, 555; O.R. 51.2, p. 756; Mary A. Livermore, *My Story of the War* (Hartford: A. D. Worthington and Company, 1890), pp. 42-43; *Pennsylvania at Gettysburg* 2: 738 (monument address of Major Chamberlin in 1889). Chamberlin later changed his mind, for in both editions of the regimental history, he wrote that Corporal Rodney Conner of Company C lost the color at the corner of Washington and High streets in the town. Conner, who survived the war, wrote Chamberlin that when Phifer went down, Corporal Samuel Gilmore took the banner. Since Gilmore was not a member of the color-guard, Conner, though wounded, demanded the flag and Gilmore gave it to him to carry during the retreat. Conner said he lost the flag to pursuing Confederates and had kept quiet because he was embarrassed about the incident. See the 1905 edition, pp. 137-39, and George P. Ryan, "The Colors of the Old Bucktails at Gettysburg," *Meadville Tribune-Republican*, February 17, 1904. As a contradiction to this account, Corporal J. Monroe Reisinger of Company H recalled that the flag was captured from his person at Gettysburg. Reisinger applied for and received a Medal of Honor in 1907. But see a protest to this in the *NT*, February 18, 1904, for an untitled story in which another newspaper supported Conner's tale rather than Reisinger's.
4 Varina Howell Davis, *Jefferson Davis, Ex-President of the Confederate States of America, A Memoir by His Wife*, 2 volumes (New York: Belford Company, Publishers, 1890), 2: 473; Cornelius C. Widdis to Governor Curtin, June 2, 1866, RG 25; E. D. Townsend to Adjutant-General of Pennsylvania, October 25, 1869, RG 25.
5 Chamberlin, 1905 edition, p. 281.
6 Tag attached to flag in Venango Museum.

Bibliography

Ashhurst, Richard L. "Address to the Survivors' Association of the 150th Regiment, Pennsylvania Volunteers, Read at Gettysburg, September 25, 1896." Philadelphia: Printing House of Allen, Lane & Scott, 1896.
____. "Remarks on Certain Questions Relating to the First Day's Fight at Gettysburg, A Paper Read February 10th, 1896, Before the Pennsylvania Commandery of the Loyal Legion." Philadelphia: Press of Allen, Lane & Scott, 1897.
Association of the 150th Regiment Pennsylvania Volunteers. *Account of the Proceedings at the Dedication of the Regimental Monument and Annual Meeting of the Association, at Gettysburg, September 11, 1889.* N.p., n.d.
Carpenter, John Q. Letters, September 14, 1862-May 2, 1864. USAMHI, Alexander Chamberlin Collection.
Chamberlin, Thomas. *History of the One Hundred and Fiftieth Regiment Pennsylvania Volunteers, Second Regiment, Bucktail Brigade.* Philadelphia: J. B. Lippincott Company, 1895; second edition, Philadelphia: F. McManus, Jr. & Company, Printers, 1905.
____. "Major Chamberlin at Gettysburg." *Philadelphia Weekly Times*, March 31, 1883.
____. "A Would-Be Incompetent." *Philadelphia Weekly Times*, January 27, 1883.
Cutter, Willard A. Letters, 1862-65. Allegheny College.
Frey, Charles A. "Was He Loyal?" *NT*, July 14, 1910.
Haskins, J. H. "A Guard at the White House." *NT*, April 14, 1910.
Huidekoper, Henry S. "Gettysburg." *Book of the Royal Blue* 5 (August 1902): 1-7.
____. "A Short Story of Gettysburg Forty Years After the Battle." *Book of the Royal Blue* 6 (July 1903): 1-13.
____. *A Short Story of the First Day's Fight at Gettysburg.* Philadelphia: Bicking Print, 1906.
Kensil, John C. "The Bucktail Brigade in the Battles of Gettysburg and the Wilderness." *Grand Army Scout and Soldiers Mail*, February 17, 1883.
____. "A Gettysburg Coincidence." *NT*, January 21, 1882.
____. "When They Went Out." *NT*, April 8, 1897.
Kieffer, Henry M. "An Address Delivered at the Second Reunion of the Survivors of the 150th Regiment Pennsylvania Volunteers, 'Bucktails,' Held at Meadville, Pa., September 10th, 1890." Philadelphia: Allen, Lane & Scott, Printers, 1890.
____. *The Recollections of a Drummer-Boy.* Boston: James R. Osgood and Company, Printers, 1884, plus numerous subsequent editions.
____. "Tale of a Turkey." *NT*, December 20, 1900.
Marshall, James W. "At Gettysburg." *NT*, April 27, 1916.
Perry, William L. Diary. USAMHI, Save the Flags Collection.
Ramsey, William R. "The 'Bucktails'." *NT*, April 9, 1885.
____. "The First Corps at Gettysburg." *NT*, April 30, 1908.
____. "History of the 150th Pa. Regiment of the Bucktail Brigade." *Grand Army Scout and Soldiers Mail*, April 28, May 5, 12, 19, 1883.
____. "Prisoners at Libby." *NT*, August 31, 1905.
____. "Stannard's Brigade." *NT*, October 1, 1908.
See, A. N. "Lincoln in War Times." *NT*, April 8, 1915.
Tyler, J. E. "Made a Bow and Arrow." *NT*, March 6, 1913.

151st Infantry

State Color

The 151st Infantry was organized at Camp Curtin in September 1862, to serve for a period of nine months. Its soldiers came from six counties, with more than a hundred schoolteachers among them, including most of the instructors and teachers from McAlisterville Academy in Juniata County. While at Camp Curtin, the regiment received a state color from the governor in person before leaving for Washington in late November.

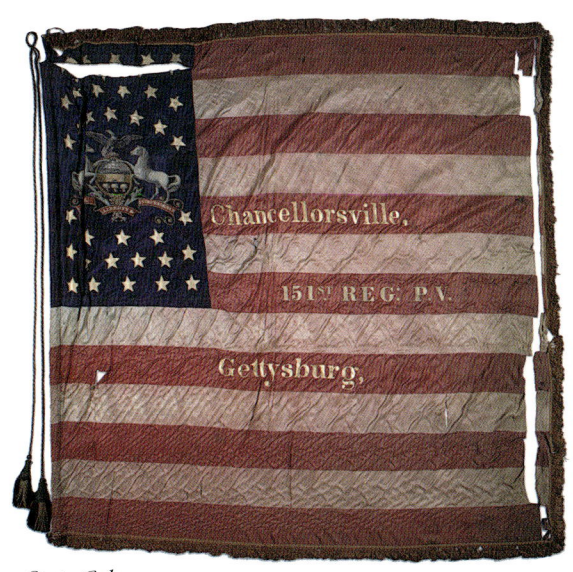

When the 151st arrived in Washington, it first camped near Arlington, then moved out to Union Mills to perform guard duty. In mid-February 1863, the 151st was assigned to the Third Division, First Corps, Army of the Potomac. The regiment took part in the Chancellorsville Campaign, skirmishing with Confederate troops on May 3-4, suffering sixteen casualties.

The division arrived at Gettysburg on the morning of July 1 and took position on the left flank of the First Corps. Initially held in reserve, the 151st moved forward to fill a gap in the line that afternoon when the superior number of Southern troops began to move forward all along the battle line. Exposed to a withering enemy fire, the regiment suffered heavy casualties before retreating. Four color-bearers were shot down. Among them was Sergeant Adam Heilman of Company E, by profession a clerk in a Reading store. Heilman was badly wounded while carrying the state color. A bullet struck his arm, another hit him in the breast, while yet another passed through his cap.[1] After falling back to Cemetery Hill, the remnant of the 151st was briefly engaged during the remaining two days of the battle. Casualties for all three days totalled 337 of the 467 officers and men taken into the fighting. The regiment was relieved from duty on July 19, and sent back to Harrisburg, where it was mustered out of service on July 27. Sergeant Heilman recovered from his wounds and proudly carried the state color in the 1866 parade.

State Color
Maker: HB
1985.274

Notes

1 *Reading Daily Times*, July 11, 1863.

Bibliography

Beebe, Lyman. Letters, October 12, 1862-June 8, 1863. USAMHI.
Chase, Theodore. Collection. Warren County Historical Society.
McFarland, George F. "Teachers in the Army." *Pennsylvania School Journal* 11 #9 (March 1863): 269-70.
McKelvey, C. W. "Was Right There." *NT*, March 23, 1911. (Gettysburg)
Miller, Robert E. Letters. In Miller Brothers Letters. University of Michigan.
Morrow, William C. 1863 Diary. In Morrow-Hittle Collection. Pennsylvania State Archives.
Potts, Charles P. "A First Defender in Rebel Prisons." *Publications of the Historical Society of Schuylkill County* 4 (1914): 341-52.
Sayre, R. D. "A Day at Gettysburg." *NT*, April 13, 1899.
Stoudt, Alfred D. "Diary of Alfred D. Stoudt." *Historical Review of Berks County* 41 (Winter 1975-76): 14-16, 33.

3rd Heavy Artillery (152nd Regiment)

State Color
Regimental Color

The 3rd Heavy Artillery was formed in the spring of 1863 by the consolidation of two independent artillery battalions. The twelve companies forming the regiment were recruited from various sections of Pennsylvania and originally rendezvoused at camps in Philadelphia and Camden, New Jersey. There were some problems in the formation of the regiment, primarily those involving the duping of many recruits of their bounty money. As a result, Battery H mutinied and was sent under arrest to Fort Delaware. Major-General Robert C. Schenck investigated the mutiny and decided that the men had indeed been wronged. He freed the battery and stationed it in the defenses of Baltimore. Mounted as light artillery, a section of Battery H joined the Army of the Potomac's Second Cavalry Division in June 1863 and was engaged at Gettysburg on July 2-3.

Regimental headquarters for the 3rd Artillery was established at Fort Monroe, but the remaining eleven batteries usually were separated, performing all sorts of various duties. Battery F was detached at nearby Camp Hamilton to guard Confederate prisoners of war. When General James Longstreet advanced against the Union troops garrisoning Suffolk in April-May 1863, Batteries A, B, F, and G were sent to man some of the city's fortifications. Battery A then went on to North Carolina to service the heavy guns on some of the Federal gunboats plying the Carolina sounds.

Other batteries, notably D, E, G, and M, served with the Army of the James during the 1864-65 operations around Petersburg. These batteries acted as heavy artillery with the siege batteries, as light artillery with field batteries, as gunboat artillery with the army's naval brigade, as guards for prisoners, and in many other duties. Battery I was detailed as headquarters guard for the Army of the James and was present when Lee surrendered at Appomattox. The bat-

Regimental Color
Maker: HB
1985.276

State Color
Maker: HB
1985.275

454

Advance the Colors!

teries were mustered out of service between July and November 1865.

Colonel Joseph Roberts acknowledged receipt of the yellow regimental color on July 11, 1863.[1] The Horstmann-made state color was sent to regimental headquarters in late October 1863. Both colors were left in Philadelphia when the regiment disbanded and both were officially given to the Commonwealth on July 4, 1866.

Notes

1 Roberts to Horstmann Brothers & Company, July 11, 1863, in Regimental Letter Book, RG 94.

Bibliography

Beatty, William. Letters. Temple University.
Bowman, E. J. "Entering Richmond." *NT*, September 12, 1907.
Emery, J. M. "The Fight at Chuckatuck." *NT*, July 16, 1908.
Fisher, William D. "A Jeff Davis Guard." *NT*, January 2, 1913.
Groundwater, Frank. "Jeff Davis's Guard." *NT*, January 25, 1912.
Holcomb, M. A. "Guarded Davis." *NT*, December 26, 1912.
McLaughlin, Levi. "A Jeff Davis Guard." *NT*, December 5, 1912.
Mohler, H.S. "Jeff Davis's Guard." *NT*, November 30, 1911.
Nevitt, James M. Diary, June 1863-January 1865. USAMHI, CWTI Collection.
Ogle, John J. "Jeff Davis at Fortress Monroe." *NT*, April 4, 1912.
Platt, William D. "Jeff Davis Guards." *NT*, May 30, 1918.
Rodgers, Thomas W. "The Smithfield Disaster." *NT*, April 23, 1908.
Sanderson, Joseph W. *Memoirs and Memoranda of Forty and Fifty Years Ago*. Milwaukee: Burdick & Allen, printers, 1907; Cincinnati: Lotz Printing Company, 1910.
Settle, William S. "The Burning of Richmond." *NT*, January 19, 1905.
_____. *History of the Third Pennsylvania Heavy Artillery and One Hundred and Eighty-eighth Pennsylvania Volunteer Infantry*. Lewiston: First Reunion Association, 1886.
Turner, Thomas F. "The Death Roll of the 188th and 3rd Pa. Heavy Artillery for the Past Two Years." *NT*, January 3, 1907.
von Schilling, Franz Wilhelm. Papers. Virginia Historical Society.

153rd Infantry

National Color

Recruited in Northampton County during the late summer of 1862, the 153rd Pennsylvania formed at Camp Curtin and was mustered into service in early October. At some point early in its existence, the regiment acquired some type of national flag; the surviving fragments indicate the stars comprised a circular pattern. Sergeant John Henning of Company I became the flag's only carrier throughout the regiment's nine-month term of service.[1]

After receiving uniforms and equipment, the 153rd proceeded to Washington, where it was attached to the First Brigade, First Division, Eleventh Corps, Army of the Potomac. The corps remained in northern Virginia until mid-December, when it marched south to join the main army near Fredericksburg.

The 153rd then fought in the next two major battles in the eastern theater of the war. At Chancellorsville, the regiment was posted near the right flank of the Eleventh Corps. It received the first shock of Stonewall Jackson's surprise attack on the corps late in the afternoon of May 2, 1863. The regiment managed to fire one volley as the onrushing Confederates struck the Union line and drove it from the field. Colonel Charles Glanz was captured, both the lieutenant-colonel and major were wounded, and casualties totalled eighty-five, a remarkably low sum for the circumstances. During this fighting, the staff of the flag

National Color
1985.278

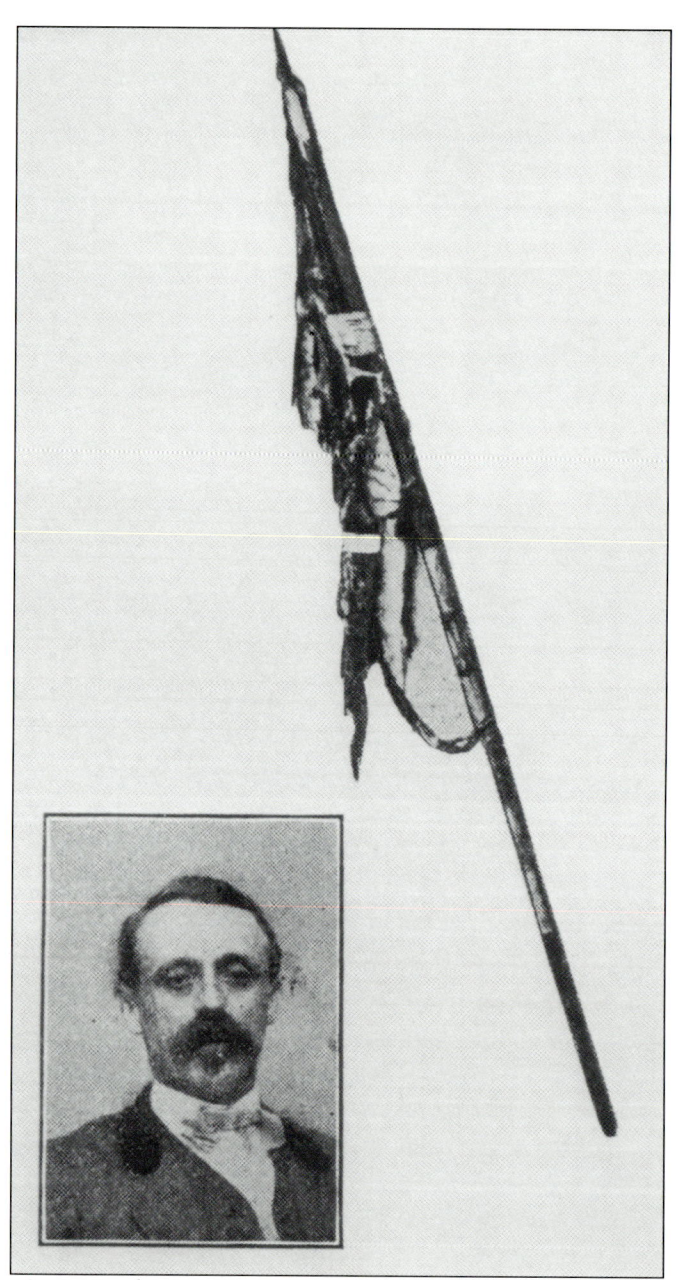

Sergeant John Henning and National Color

Advance the Colors!

was broken, but Henning escaped capture when the regiment fell back.[2]

At Gettysburg, the regiment was engaged on July 1, suffering heavy losses when the corps was attacked north of the town and driven back through the streets to Cemetery Hill. The next evening, the 153rd engaged the Southern troops assaulting Cemetery Hill. Casualties for the two days numbered 211 of about 500 officers and men present. Following the pursuit of Lee's army to the Potomac River, the regiment returned to Harrisburg and was disbanded on July 24.

The national color was kept by Colonel Glanz for many years. It was often displayed during regimental reunions and parades. Sometime between 1896 and 1909, the remnant was given to the flag collection, apparently upon the request of state authorities.[3]

State Color

This flag was sent to the regiment sometime in October 1862. It was then sent to the State Agency to have some "necessary work" performed on it. The flag remained in Washington and was never carried by the 153rd. It was yet in Washington in 1866. A detachment of men from the 153rd carried it during the 1866 ceremony.[4]

State Color
Maker: HB
1985.277

Notes

1 Kiefer, p. 112.
2 *Ibid.*
3 *Ibid.*, pp. 112, 172. The flag does not appear on the 1896 adjutant-general's list of flags, and had been returned when Kiefer's book was published.
4 Glanz to Adjutant-General A. L. Russell, June 8, 1866, RG 19.

Bibliography

Coddington, Edwin B. *The Role of the One Hundred and Fifty-third Regiment, Penna. Vols. Infantry, in the Civil War, 1862-1863.* Easton: Northampton County Historical & Genealogical Society, 1949.

Kiefer, William R. *History of the One Hundred and Fifty-third Regiment Pennsylvania Volunteers Infantry, Which was Recruited in Northampton County, Pa., 1862-1863.* Easton: Press of the Chemical Publishing Company, 1909.

____. Diary. Easton Public Library.

Melick, Philip W. Diary. Easton Public Library.

Millar, J. C. "Another of the Eleventh Corps Takes Up for the Part They Performed." *NT*, September 22, 1892.

Myers, J. S. "The Eleventh Corps at Gettysburg." *NT*, June 3, 1886.

Rice, Owen. "Afield with the Eleventh Army Corps at Chancellorsville." Cincinnati: H. C. Sherick & Company, 1885; also printed in *Sketches of War History, 1861-1865. Papers Read Before the Military Order of the Loyal Legion of the United States, Ohio Commandery,* 1: 358-91. Cincinnati: Robert Clarke and Company, 1888.

Simmers, William. *The Volunteers Manual; Or, Ten Months with the 153rd Penn'a. Volunteers, Being a Concise Narrative of the Most Important Events of the History of the Said Regiment.* Easton: D. E. Neiman, Printer, 1863.

Stofflet, Francis. Diary. Easton Public Library.

Strickland, C. V. "What a Drummer Boy Saw at Chancellorsville." *NT*, May 14, 1908.

Wallace, Stephan A. Diary. Pennsylvania State Archives; Easton Public Library.

Weaver, Ethan A. *Owen Rice, Christian, Scholar and Patriot, A Genealogical and Historical Memoir.* Germantown, 1911.

153rd Infantry

155th Infantry

State Color

This regiment, composed of seven companies from Allegheny County, two from Clarion, and one from Armstrong, was recruited during the month of September 1862 to serve for three years. After organizing at Camp Curtin, the new regiment was sent to Washington, arriving there in the wake of the Second Manassas defeat. The 155th was assigned to the Third Division, Fifth Corps, Army of the Potomac. This division arrived on the Antietam battlefield just after the end of the struggle, then went into camp near Sharpsburg. Here, on October 17, Colonel Samuel B. Thomas presented a new state color to the 155th. Colonel Edward J. Allen appointed Sergeant Thomas Wiseman of Company C color-bearer.[1]

The regiment first engaged the enemy at Fredericksburg on December 13. The division formed one of the attacking columns against the Rebels shielded by the stone wall on Marye's Heights. During the un-

State Color
Maker: HB
1985.279

Two Views of the 155th's Color-Party, 1862 and 1864-65, showing Sergeants Wiseman (left) and Marlin (right)

458   *Advance the Colors!*

Sergeant Thomas C. Lawson

successful charge, Sergeant Wiseman was mortally wounded. As he swayed to keep his feet and prevent the color from falling, two of the color-corporals—Charles Bardeen (Company F) and George W. Bratten (Company E)—seized the flag in succession, only to be shot down. Finally, Corporal Thomas C. Lawson (Company H) grabbed the flag and carried it to the rear as the regiment fell back, leaving sixty-eight of its men on the field of carnage.[2]

The state color was heavily damaged at Fredericksburg. The staff was broken in two places, while fourteen bullets sliced through its silken folds. Considered too badly damaged to carry again, the flag was sent back to Pittsburgh for repairs. The colonel's wife, assisted by other ladies, repaired the rents in the silk. J. R. Reed, a well-known jeweler, spliced the broken wood. The flag was then exhibited in the windows of John W. Pittock's bookstore before Private Samuel W. Hill, home on leave, carried the flag back to the 155th.[3]

Following the Fredericksburg battle, the regiment was only marginally engaged during the Chancellorsville Campaign (April - May 1863). During the northward march to Gettysburg, Thomas C. Lawson, since promoted to sergeant and color-bearer, in a "broken down and exhausted condition," was forced to leave the ranks for an ambulance. His place was taken by Corporal Matthew Bennett (Company I), who carried the state color safely through the battle of Gettysburg, where the regiment again suffered few casualties.[4]

Following the Gettysburg Campaign, the 155th participated in the Bristoe Station and Mine Run campaigns (October-November), then went into winter quarters near Warrenton. Over the winter, Colonel Alfred L. Pearson changed the regiment's dress to the Zouave pattern of dark blue trimmed with yellow. Meanwhile, shortly after Gettysburg, Sergeant Thomas I. Marlin of Company K was appointed color-bearer, a position he would hold until war's end.[5]

The regiment fought in most of the major engagements of the 1864-65 Virginia Campaign. After fighting in the Wilderness (May 5-6), the regiment became embroiled in the series of engagements at Spotsylvania, fighting primarily on May 8 at Laurel Hill. The 155th fought at the North Anna River (May 23-24), then at Bethesda Church and Cold Harbor. It also fought at Petersburg on June 18. In this charge, Sergeant Marlin received a slight wound on his chin and was off duty for a few days. Corporal Lemuel E. McPherson (Company C) carried the flag during Marlin's absence.[6]

During the operations around Petersburg, the 155th fought at the Jerusalem Plank Road (June 22), Weldon Railroad (August 18-21), and Peebles' Farm (September 30). Here, the regiment charged the entrenched Confederates. Sergeant Marlin was in the lead, vying with another color-bearer to see who would first reach the enemy works. Being almost exhausted, Marlin called upon Sergeant Thomas C. Anderson (Company I) to help, and the two men planted the regiment's colors ahead of the others.[7] Then followed the fighting at Hatcher's Run (October 27) and a raid on the Weldon Railroad in mid-December.

In 1865, the 155th engaged enemy troops at Hatcher's Run on February 6. The regiment next fought at the Quaker Road on March 31. Here, as the brigade was advancing, it received a withering fire from gray-clad soldiers sheltered behind breastworks. There was some temporary confusion in the Union ranks. Colonel Pearson saw the momentary wavering and decided to act quickly to keep the troops moving forward. He galloped to the color-guard and demanded the flag from Sergeant Marlin. The sergeant, having carried the flag for more than a year, "had become so attached to it that he would have carried it into the jaws of death rather than part with it." Marlin

155th Infantry

the 155th marched north to Washington, took part in the Grand Review, and was mustered out of service on June 2. Sergeant Marlin carried the remnant of the state color during the 1866 parade in Philadelphia. The veteran sergeant became a doctor after the war and eventually migrated to Missouri, where in 1905 he passed away.[9]

Regimental Color

This flag was acquired at some point during the regiment's term of service and carried later in the conflict. It was apparently not carried at Fredericksburg.[10] Prior to the engagement at Five Forks, Corporal Thomas McCush (Company I) carried this banner. At this latter battle, McCush acted as one of Marlin's color-guards and fell dead, shot through the head. He was only eighteen years old.[11]

Colonel Alfred L. Pearson

Regimental Color
Maker: EH
1985.280

curtly refused Pearson's demand, telling his commander: "Tell me where you wish the flag to be carried, Colonel, and I'll take it there." Pearson wrenched the flag from Marlin's grasp and shouted, "Follow me, men, or lose your colors." He rode ahead of the battleline and found some enemy soldiers concealed behind a sawdust pile. The 155th quickly sprang forward and seized the Rebel position. For his gallant act, Pearson was breveted brigadier-general and in 1897 received a Medal of Honor.[8]

After fighting at Five Forks on April 1, the regiment participated in the pursuit of Lee's army to Appomattox. Following the end of hostilities in Virginia,

Presented Flag

On September 3, 1862, the ladies of Pittsburgh's Second Ward presented a flag to Colonel Allen. No other documentation concerning this flag appears in the written record.[12]

Notes

1 *Maltese Cross*, pp. 78, 600, indicates that Colonel J. H. Puleston presented the flag on October 17. A colored, cardboard stock illustrating the flag and its history can be found in RG 25. This card indicates that Colonel Samuel B. Thomas presented the banner on September 28. The actual presentation more likely occurred on October 17, during Colonel Thomas's visit to the Army of the Potomac to present colors to all the new Pennsylvania regiments.

2 *Maltese Cross*, pp. 101, 600.

3 *Ibid.*, pp. 101, 600, 602; "The Flag of Col. Allen's Regiment," *Pittsburgh Evening Chronicle*, February 18, 1863; "The Flag of the 155th Regiment," *Pittsburgh Gazette*, February 18, 1863.

4 *Maltese Cross*, pp. 192-93, 195, 602, 604.

5 *Ibid.*, 604.

6 *Ibid.*, pp. 298, 416, 604.

7 *Ibid.*, pp. 321, 604; "Letter from the 155th Regiment," *Pittsburgh Evening Chronicle*, October 15, 1864.

460

Advance the Colors!

8 Bates 4: 805; *Maltese Cross* pp. 343-44, 604.

9 *Maltese Cross*, pp. 604-5, 607.

10 General Andrew A. Humphreys to General Darius N. Couch, February 10, 1863, copy in RG 25 from original in Humphreys Papers, Historical Society of Pennsylvania. In this letter, Humphreys listed how many flags each of his eight regiments was carrying.

11 *Maltese Cross*, pp. 492, 501.

12. *Ibid.*, pp. 558-59.

Bibliography

Allen, David. "Execution of Deserters." *NT*, November 30, 1905.

____. "An Incident of Chancellorsville." *NT*, October 14, 1886.

____. "Just Before the Break Up. Where Part of the Fifth Corps was March 25, 1865." *NT*, May 26, 1904.

____. "Recollections of Gettysburg." *NT*, January 6, 1927.

Brown, William J. "Picketing on the Rappahannock." *NT*, September 15, 1921.

Clowes, H. R. "Collection of War Relics." *NT*, June 21, 1906.

1862. 1896. Fifth Reunion of the One Hundred and Fifty-fifth Regiment Pennsylvania Volunteers, Held at Normal Hall, Clarion, Pennsylvania, July 29th and 30th, 1896. Pittsburgh: Rawsthorne Engraving and Printing Company, 1896.

"First and Last Shots. Remarkable Experience of Major Laughlin, 155th Pa." *NT*, March 11, 1909.

Fitch, George W. "The Last Wounded." *NT*, April 8, 1915.

Hays, John A. "The 155th Pa. at Appomattox." *NT*, June 21, 1923.

Hill, J. H. "Armstrong's Mills." *NT*, August 25, 1892.

Hill, S. W. "Allabach's Brigade. It Went as Near as Any Others to the Deadly Stonewall at Fredericksburg." *NT*, April 16, 1908.

____. "Sergeant Secrist's Death." *NT*, May 13, 1915.

Kerr, John. "Oration Delivered at the First Reunion of the One Hundred and Fifty-fifth Regiment, Penn'a. Veteran Volunteers at Lafayette Hall, Pittsburgh, Friday Evening, September 17, 1875." Pittsburgh: Samuel F. Kerr, Printer, 1875.

Kitchin, E. C. "Appomattox Apple Tree." *NT*, February 25, 1897.

Lee, F. M. "Last Charge on Lee." *NT*, May 19, 1904.

McClintock, Charles A. (editor). "Memories at Appomattox, by George McCully Laughlin." *Western Pennsylvania Historical Magazine* 42 (1959): 259-63.

McDowell, J. A. "The Petersburg Mine." *NT*, August 22, 1929.

Marshall, D. Porter. *Company "K," 155th Pa. Volunteer Zouaves, A Detailed History of Its Organization and Service to the Country During the Civil War, From 1862 Until the Collapse of the Rebellion, Together With Many Incidents and Reminiscences of the Camp, the March and the Battle Field, Also Much of the History of the Grand Old 155th.* N.p., 1888?

Meyers, Herman. 1864 Diary. Western Reserve Historical Society.

Morgan, George F. "A Cool Hand. A Little Story of Bravery Under Trying Circumstances." *NT*, September 19, 1895.

Paup, Mary E. "Ran Away to Enlist." *NT*, November 3, 1927.

Rial, John. "Sergeant Secrist's Death." *NT*, April 22, 1915.

Sager, Harrison. 1864 Diary. Soldiers & Sailors Memorial Hall.

Taylor, Thomas. "Little Round Top Saved by the 155th Pa." *NT*, April 28, 1892.

Under the Maltese Cross, Antietam to Appomattox, The Loyal Uprising in Western Pennsylvania, 1861-1865, Campaigns 155th Pennsylvania Regiment Narrated by The Rank and File. Akron: Werner Company, 1910.

Williamson, R. L. "At Gettysburg." *NT*, September 1, 1892.

Winger, Joseph G. "At Gettysburg." *NT*, August 9, 1894.

157th Infantry

National Color

Organized initially in the fall of 1862, the 157th Pennsylvania never had enough recruits to form more than a four-company battalion. The unit was sent to Washington, remaining in the city's defenses until late May 1864. At this time, the 157th was sent to join the Army of the Potomac. It was assigned to the Fifth Corps when it arrived at the front on June 2. Thereafter, the battalion participated in the fighting at Cold Harbor, in the Petersburg assaults later that month, at the Weldon Railroad (August 18-21), Poplar Spring Church (September 30), Boydton Plank Road (October 27), and Hatcher's Run (February 5-7, 1865). During this last-named engagement, Corporal William H. Howard of Company A was cited for "gallantly pressing forward with the regimental colors, inciting the men to rally around him."[1] On March 21, the survivors of the battalion were consolidated with the 191st Pennsylvania. The battered national color was given to the Commonwealth after the close of the war.

National Color
1985.281

State Color *1985.282*
Maker: HB

State Color

Major Edmund T. Tiers wrote to Adjutant-General Russell on March 21, 1865, asking for a state color. The major reminded Russell that his command had never obtained a flag from the state.[2] Since the battalion was broken up that same day, the 157th never saw its flag, which was forwarded to the State Agency and was still there in February 1866. This color evidently was installed in the original flag room, but was stolen at some point and not returned for many years. On January 31, 1900, the director of the Harrisburg city dump found the flag in a pile of rubbish. It was retrieved and sent to the Flag Room.[3]

Notes

1 "A Roll of Honor," *Philadelphia Inquirer*, March 23, 1865. In addition to Howard, Sergeant Francis A. Olmstead carried the flag at some unspecified period. He is identified as a color-bearer in *Memorial Record of Wilde Post 25, Grand Army of the Republic, Chester, Pennsylvania*, p. 73, original book in Delaware County Historical Society.

2 Tiers to Russell, March 21, 1865, RG 25.

3 "Found a State Flag," *Harrisburg Telegraph*, February 1, 1900.

Bibliography

Other than Bates and Taylor, no other secondary studies seem to exist.

The author has not located any letter or diary collections.

14th Cavalry (159th Regiment)

First State Standard

This cavalry regiment was recruited during the months of August through November 1862, the men rendezvousing at a camp near Pittsburgh. Most of the troopers came from Allegheny, Fayette, Armstrong, and Erie counties, with a single company from Philadelphia. The new command first went to Harper's Ferry in December, where it was deployed in guarding the approaches to that military base. A Horstmann-made state standard was sent to the State Agency in early May 1863, then forwarded to the regiment at some unspecified date.

In May 1863, the 14th Cavalry moved westward along the Baltimore & Ohio Railroad and was attached to Brigadier-General William W. Averell's brigade. The unit engaged enemy troops at Beverly, West Virginia, in early July, then cooperated with the Army of the Potomac in harassing Lee's troops as his defeated army crossed the Potomac River.

Following this service, the regiment took part in Averell's Rocky Gap Raid that occupied most of August. The raid culminated in a battle at White Sulphur Spring (August 26-27), where the 14th lost 102 troopers. In November, Averell launched another raid from Beverly, West Virginia, that was highlighted by a combat at Droop Mountain (November 6). In December, Averell led a raid against the Virginia and Tennessee Railroad. The path of the raiders started at New Creek, West Virginia, and ended at Beverly. In between, the brigade marched four hundred miles through a desolate, mountainous region of the state, suffering few casualties but enduring great hardships. Thereafter, the regiment went into winter camp near Martinsburg, West Virginia.

When the regiment broke winter camp in April 1864, it first participated in an expedition against some Confederate saltworks in southwestern Virginia. The raid failed largely because of a superior enemy defense, which actually moved to attack the Yankees at Cove Gap (May 10). The expedition pushed on to Lewisburg, where it remained until early June. At this time, the command joined Major-General David Hunter's Lynchburg Expedition. This column of troops marched south through the Shenandoah Valley to Lynchburg, where enemy reinforcements from Lee's army forced Hunter to retreat. His troops retired across the mountains to Parkersburg, West Virginia, the 14th Cavalry acting as part of the rearguard.

Hunter was relieved from command and his troops joined the new Army of the Shenandoah, fighting at Winchester (July 24-25 and September 19), Fisher's Hill (September 21-22), and Cedar Creek (October 19). The regiment sustained few losses in these major engagements. Thereafter, the regiment performed picket duty in the Valley, remaining in this duty until the end of hostilities.

Second State Standard

Evans & Hassall sent a replacement standard to the State Agency in January 1865. It was apparently forwarded to the regiment at some unspecified point. When the war ended in Virginia, the 14th Cavalry went to Washington, encamping near the city for two months. It was then sent to Fort Leavenworth, Kansas. The troopers remained on this tour of duty until Au-

Second State Standard
Maker: EH
Size: 41 1/4 x 45 3/4
1985.284

gust, when most of them were mustered out of service. Company A finally returned to the Commonwealth in November. The replacement standard was officially given to state care in 1866. The disposition of the original standard remains a mystery. Colonel John M. Schoonmaker queried Adjutant-General Russell about the fate of the first standard in February 1866.[1] He later discovered that other officers believed it has been sent to Harrisburg, but it was never discovered.[2]

Notes

[1] Schoonmaker to Russell, February 15, 1866, Regimental Papers, RG 19.

[2] Schoonmaker to Russell, June 7, 1866, RG 19.

Bibliography

Abraham, William. Letters, January 1863-August 1864. Historical Society of Pennsylvania.
Byers, C. G. "The Newmarket Race." *NT*, December 6, 1906.
Davis, William A. R. "At Rocky Gap, W.V." *NT*, November 3, 1910.
Felt, John. "Battle of Piedmont." *NT*, March 21, 1895.
Fisher, Jesse. "The Newmarket Races." *NT*, February 28, 1907.
____. "The Salem Raid." *NT*, March 7, 1912.
Frazier, J. J. "Sheridan's Famous Ride." *NT*, November 2, 1905
____. "What the 14th Pa. Cav. Did. An Answer to a Query Regarding Them at Cedar Creek." *NT*, February 10, 1898.
Fry, David. "Pennsylvanians were with Sheridan." *NT*, June 7, 1906.
"General James M. Schoonmaker." *NT*, April 17, 1913.
Groft, Joshua. "Averell's Queer Skirmish at Rocky Gap." *NT*, Spetember 27, 1883.
Hays, James F. "Averell's Raid. A Long, Hard March Over the Mountains to Wytheville." *NT*, May 9, 1918.
____. "Battle of Droop Mountain." *NT*, September 9, 1915.
____. "Battle of the Opequon." *NT*, October 24, 1918.
____. "Enlisted Brothers." *NT*, April 1, 1909.
____. "Fighting Mosby's Guerrillas." *NT*, December 16, 1909.
____. "The 14th Pa. Cavalry. A Harvest of Prisoners of War by a Cavalry Division." *NT*, November 21, 1907.
____. "Hanged by Gen. Hunter." *NT*, May 25, 1905.
____. "Last Year of the War." *NT*, September 28, 1905.
____. "The Lynchburg Raid." *NT*, May 8, 1913.
____. "Shell Fire 45 Years Ago." *NT*, November 30, 1905. (Dry Creek, WV)
Hertzog, A. J. "Milroy at Close Range." *NT*, March 31, 1910.
Jacobs, Rozel. "Cold in the East." *NT*, October 13, 1910.
McJ, Co.C. "From the Ranks. Here's a Comrade Who Won't Whitewash Col. Blakely." *NT*, December 27, 1894.
Mestrezat, Walter A. Papers. West Virginia University.
Mowrer, Geroge H. *History of the Organization and Service, During the War of the Rebellion, of Co. A, 14th Pennsylvania Cavalry*. N.p., 189-.
Osborn, A. L. "An Incident of the Hunter Raid." *NT*, July 6, 1905.
Poundstone, H. W. "Veteran Recalls Sheridan's Ride." *NT*, April 15, 1937.
Reges, Francis A. D. Letters, December 1862-May 1865. USAMHI, CWMisc Collection.
Slease, William D. *The Fourteenth Pennsylvania Cavalry in the Civil War, A History of the Fourteenth Pennsylvania Volunteer Cavalry From Its Organization Until the Close of the Civil War, 1861-1865*. Pittsburgh: Art Engraving & Printing Company, 1915.
Willcox, M. B. "Severity was Necessary." *NT*, August 26, 1909.
Woods, David L. "Civil War Synopsis." Crawford County Historical Society.

15th Cavalry (160th Regiment)

State Standard

Colonel William J. Palmer began recruiting troopers for this regiment in August 1862, on authority from the War Department. Palmer had been captain of the Anderson Troop, a company of Pennsylvanians that had been organized to serve as a bodyguard for Brigadier-General Robert Anderson, the hero of Fort Sumter. After Anderson retired, the troop served as guards for the headquarters of the Army of the Cumberland. Palmer's recruits rendezvoused at Carlisle Barracks. Some of the recruits served as scouts during the 1862 Maryland Campaign; Palmer himself was captured while in disguise behind Rebel lines.

After Palmer's capture, the recruits were forwarded to Nashville. Here, because of Palmer's absence, a proper regimental organization with proper officers was not fully implemented. Because of the dissatisfaction in the new regiment, several hundred soldiers refused to enter active duty when the army marched out of Nashville in late December 1862. Part of the regiment acted with the army's cavalry and suffered heavy losses fighting enemy infantry just prior to the battle at Murfreesboro. Those who did not go with their comrades were arrested. When Palmer finally returned from his captivity in early February, he immediately reorganized the 15th Cavalry. Although the regiment performed creditably throughout the war, the mutiny of half of the unit left a stain on the regiment's record.

By this time, a state standard had been sent to the regiment through a captain in the 77th Pennsylvania who was home on leave. During the campaigns of 1863, the 15th Cavalry acted as an independent organization at army headquarters. In early April, the regiment scouted toward Woodbury and McMinnville, skirmishing with enemy cavalry. During the Tullahoma Campaign (June-July), the regiment engaged the enemy at Rover (June 24) and near Tullahoma (June 29). At Chickamauga (September 19-20), the regiment at first guarded the army's right flank, then helped cover the withdrawal of Rosecrans's defeated troops to Chattanooga.

Thereafter, the regiment marched to Knoxville with the troops assigned to relieve General Burnside's besieged defenders. The regiment was engaged with the enemy in East Tennessee until mid-February 1864, when it returned to Chattanooga. During this period, Palmer's command fought in several engagements with Rebel cavalry, most notably at Dandridge (December 24), Mossy Creek (December 29), and at Schultz's Mill on Cosby Creek (January 14, 1864).

When the regiment returned to Chattanooga, it was broken down and exhausted by its service in the mountains. In early May 1864, the 15th was sent to Nashville to refit. It remained here until early August, then started south. The regiment halted at Chattanooga to act as scouts against a Rebel Cavalry raid and followed part of the raiding force into East Tennessee. Palmer's regiment then moved to join a raid into southwestern Virginia, fighting at Jonesboro (October 3), McKinney's Ford on the Holston River (Oc-

State Standard
Maker: HB
1985.285

tober 7), as well as several smaller combats. The regiment then returned to Chattanooga, moving immediately to Decatur, Alabama. Throughout the last week of December, the regiment participated in the pursuit of Hood's retreating army, then attacked Brigadier-General Hylan B. Lyon's Confederate brigade at Red Hill, Alabama (January 15, 1865).

Then, the regiment broke up Colonel L. G. Mead's guerrilla band in the Cumberland Mountains. In the spring of 1865, the 15th was attached to Major-General George Stoneman's command. This column of troops crossed the mountains into North Carolina, destroying the Virginia and Tennessee Railroad, capturing Salisbury (April 12), and in general spreading havoc in the western part of the state. Upon the war's end, the regiment returned to Nashville and was disbanded on June 21. The standard was apparently turned in by 1866, although it does not appear on any of the early flag lists.

Presented Flag

On April 27, 1864, Colonel P. S. White, acting on behalf of seven young Philadelphia ladies, presented a "beautiful and costly flag" to the regiment. Captain George S. Clark of Company E accepted the flag for the regiment. The presentation took place in front of the Church of the Evangelist on Catharine Street. No further information has been located about this flag.[1]

Company Guidons

On December 7, 1861, Horstmann Brothers completed a company guidon for the orginal Anderson Troop, from which many of the officers of the 15th Cavalry were promoted. The use and disposition of this guidon is not documented in the written record. In July 1920, a guidon carried by Company L was sent to the state adjutant-general by a descendant of one of the regiment's veterans. The flag was sent to the vault of the State Arsenal and has since disappeared.[2]

Color-Bearers

Names of two bearers have been located. Sergeant G. P. Davis, listed as a color-bearer of Company M, was promoted to captain of Company B, 183rd Infantry. However, his name does not appear in Bates's rosters of either unit.[3] Sergeant George W. Spencer of Company D was appointed color-bearer on August 16, 1864.[4]

Notes

1 "Flag Presentation," *Philadelphia Inquirer*, April 27, 1864.

2 John H. Scheide to Adjutant-General Frank D. Beary, July 15, 1920, and Captain L. A. Luttringer to Colonel Jere M. Leaman, November 18, 1920, both letters in RG 19.

3 "Promotion," *Philadelphia Inquirer*, January 9, 1864.

4 "George Willig Spencer" obituary, Military Order of the Loyal Legion of the United States, California Commandery, 1908, Whole #902, in Special Collections, Pattee Library, Penn State University.

Bibliography

Betts, Charles M. "Stoneman's Great Raid in 1865." *NT*, December 9, 1926.

____. Papers. Historical Society of Pennsylvania.

Carraway, William E. "The Mutiny of the 15th Pennsylvania Volunteer Cavalry." *Denver Westerners Monthly Roundup* 17 (November 1961): 5-15.

Colton, Jessie S. (editor). *The Civil War Journal and Correspondence of Matthias Baldwin Colton*. Philadelphia: MacRae-Smith Company, 1931.

Company M. "Chasing Hood." *NT*, October 7, 1886.

Conaway, John. "Colonel Cabana's Mistake. Mistook Some Yankee Raiders for a Detachment of Lyon's Forces." *NT*, June 4, 1925.

Frankenberry, Allen D. Diary. West Virginia University.

Fulton, Louis B. Diary, August 13, 1862-November 4, 1863. University of Michigan.

Gass, Samuel W. Diary, September 10, 1862-March 11, 1863. Washington County Historical Society.

Granger, Arthur O. "A Witness to History." *Civil War Times Illustrated* 24 (April 1985): 40-41.

Hersh, Paul. Letters, October 12, 1862-May 25, 1865. USAMHI, CWMisc Collection.

Holt, William S. "Capturing a Flag." *NT*, December 26, 1912.

Kirk, Charles H. "Arthur P. Lyon. Death of the Bravest Soldier in the 15th Pennsylvania Cavalry." *NT*, November 21, 1889.

____. *History of the Fifteenth Pennsylvania Volunteer Cavalry, Which was Recruited and Known as the Anderson Cavalry in the Rebellion of 1861-1865*. Philadelphia, 1906.

Lane, Nelson L. "Nashville." *NT*, September 6, 1894.

Neil, George. "After General Lyon." *NT*, July 12, 19, 1900.

Overhalt, John. Diary. Westmoreland-Fayette Historical Society.

Palmer, William J. *Letters, 1853-1868, Gen'l. Wm. J. Palmer. Compiled by Isaac H. Clothier*. Philadelphia: Ketterlinus, 1906.

Pontiers, Joseph. "Sojourn in Dixie. Attempt to Conquer a Rebel Division Got a Yankee Regiment in Trouble." *NT*, January 2, 1896. (Dandridge, TN)

Reppert, W. E. "Rosecrans—A Great General." *NT*, May 19, 1910.

Shaw, Milton. Letters, March 1863-May 1864. USAMHI, CWTI Collection, George A. Breckenridge.

Storey, Brit A. *The Mutiny of the Fifteenth Pennsylvania Cavalry, 1862-1863*. Alamosa, CA: Adams State College, 1973.

To the Members of the Society of the 15th Pennsylvania Volunteer Cavalry, A Short Account of the Annual Banquet Held at Philadelphia . . . . Philadelphia, 1884-1927. (Annual pamphlets published separately.)

Weller, Charles. Letters, July 1862-September 1865. USAMHI, CWTI Collection.

Williams, John A. B. *In Commemoration of the Eleventh Annual Reunion of the Anderson Cavalry, December 5, 1883*. N.p., n.d.

____. *Leaves from a Trooper's Diary*. Philadelphia: Bell, Printer, 1869.

Wilson, Selden L. *Recollections and Experiences During the Civil War, 1861-1865, in the 15th Penna. Vol. Cavalry, Better Known as the Anderson Cavalry*. Washington, 1913.

Wilson, Suzanne C. *Column South, With the Fifteenth Pennsylvania Cavalry from Antietam to the Capture of Jefferson Davis*. Flagstaff, AZ: J. F. Colton & Company, 1960.

16th Cavalry (161st Regiment)

State Standard

Comprised of troopers recruited in more than seventeen counties across the state, the 16th Cavalry was organized at Harrisburg in November 1862. Soon thereafter, the new regiment went to Washington, then on to join the Army of the Potomac. The regiment's first duty was to patrol the army's right flank for a distance of nearly eight miles that winter. Its first engagement with the enemy was at Kelly's Ford on March 17, 1863. During the Chancellorsville Campaign, the regiment was engaged in skirmishing in the Brandy Station-Culpeper area. It was not engaged in the cavalry action at Brandy Station (June 9), but fought at Middleburg (June 18-19) and Gettysburg (July 3), suffering few casualties. During the pursuit of Lee's army, the 16th was engaged at Shepherdstown on July 16. Following this campaign, the regiment took part in the Bristoe Station and Mine Run campaigns before erecting winter quarters near Bealton Station.

A Horstmann-made state standard was sent to the State Agency in January 1863. However, the regiment failed to receive the standard. Colonel John Irvin Gregg complained that his letters to the agency went unanswered. Finally, Major William H. Fry acknowledged receipt of the standard on December 14, 1863.[1]

The regiment participated in several small cavalry raids throughout the winter and early spring of 1863-64. During Grant's 1864 Virginia Campaign, the 16th, a part of the Second Division, Cavalry Corps, Army of the Potomac, rode in most of the significant cavalry actions with the main army. After skirmishing in the Wilderness (May 6-7), the regiment went with Sheridan on his Richmond Raid (May 9-24), then fought at Haw's Shop (May 28), suffering thirty-five casualties in this latter engagement. In June, the regiment fought at Trevilian Station (June 11-12), Saint Mary's Church (June 24), and in several minor skirmishes.

During the operations around Petersburg, the Second Cavalry Division remained with the army after Sheridan took the other two divisions to the Shenandoah Valley in August. The 16th took part in both expeditions to Deep Bottom (July and August). It then fought at Reams' Station (August 23-25). The regiment engaged the enemy at Poplar Spring Church (September 15 and September 30-October 1) with few casualties. Fighting dismounted at the Boydton Plank Road (October 27), the 16th lost thirty-two officers and men. After some December raids on railroads, the regiment went into winter camp.

During the 1865 fighting, the 16th fought at Hatcher's Run (February 6-7), White Oak Road (March 31), Five Forks (April 1), and Farmville (April 7). Following Lee's surrender, the regiment was sent to Lynchburg on garrison duty, remaining there until it went to Richmond, where it was mustered out of service on August 7. The remnant of the state standard was offically returned on July 4, 1866.

State Standard
Maker: HB
1985.286

Regimental Officers, Fall 1863
State Standard Pinned Against Tent

Notes

1 For the correspondence regarding the state standard, see the following: J. I. Gregg to Adjutant-General Russell, December 4, 1862; A. L. Russell to Gregg, March 3, 1863; Gregg to Russell, August 24, 1863, all in Regimental Letter Indorsement, Journal, and Miscellaneous Book, RG 94; and W. H. Fry to A. L. Russell, December 14, 1863, RG 25.

Bibliography

Ball, Norman. Diaries, 1863-64. Connecticut Historical Society.
Billings, J. W. "How He Reported." *NT*, March 7, 1912.
Boyle, J. W. "Recalling War Memories." *NT*, May 27, 1909.
Brace, J. A. "The Last War Horse." *NT*, June 26, 1902.
Crawford, James. Letters, April 1864-June 1865. Erie County Historical Society.
____. "General Gregg's Capture." *NT*, September 19, 1912.
Davis, Luke. 1864 Diary. Pennsylvania State Universtiy.
Dick, Henry. "A Good Day's Work." *NT*, January 27, 1910.
____. "Punishing Swipers." *NT*, June 29, 1911.
Follmer, John D. Diaries, 1862-65. University of Michigan.
Hasson, James. "Chased by Cavalry." *NT*, April 6, 1911.

Henderson, John W. Diary, 1864-65. Kansas State Historical Society.
History of the 16th Regiment, Pennsylvania Cavalry, for the Year Ending October 31st, 1863. Philadelphia: King & Baird, Printers, 1864.
Hotchkiss, B. D. "The 16th Pa. Cav. at Hatcher's Run." *NT*, April 18, 1907.
McWilliams, B. C. "An Old Prisoner." *NT*, April 11, 1901.
Mohr, James C. (editor). *The Cormany Diaries: A Northern Family in the Civil War*. Pittsburgh: University of Pittsburgh Press, 1982.
Reeves, Lemuel C. "Remembers Lincoln." *NT*, December 26, 1912.
____. "Who's Your Nigger Now?" *NT*, December 21, 1911.
Ressler, Isaac H. Diaries, 1862-65. USAMHI, CWTI Collection.
Yoder, Jonah. 1863 Diary. USAMHI.

17th Cavalry (162nd Regiment)

First State Standard

Another of the state's three-year cavalry regiments recruited in the fall of 1862, the 17th's troopers came from fourteen counties. Except for Beaver County (Company A), the remaining eleven companies were from central and eastern Pennsylvania, from Franklin to Bradford and Philadelphia. The regiment assembled at Harrisburg's Camp Simmons, then moved to Washington in late November. After a month near the city, the regiment marched south and performed duty in the Occoquan area, remaining here until early January 1863, when the 17th was assigned to the First Division, Cavalry Corps, Army of the Potomac. A Horstmann-made standard was sent to the State Agency in January and forwarded to the regiment at some unspecified date.

During the Chancellorsville Campaign, the 17th Cavalry was one of the few cavalry regiments that remained with the army instead of joining the raid against Lee's supply lines. On the evening of May 2, as Jackson's Confederates crushed the Eleventh Corps and threatened the entire army's safety, the 17th was placed in position at Hazel Grove to support some artillery. It successfully helped rally some other troops to defend the guns and stop a further enemy breakthrough. Following this campaign, the regiment fought at Brandy Station (June 9), Upperville (June 21), and at Gettysburg on July 1. It then participated in the pursuit of Lee's army back to Virginia. During the fall 1863 campaigns, the regiment fought primarily in the October activities of Bristoe Station and the November operations along Mine Run. The regiment then erected winter quarters near Culpeper.

In 1864, the regiment participated in Judson Kilpatrick's February-March raid on Richmond, then fought in the Wilderness (May 6-7) and at Spotsylvania (May 8) before embarking on Sheridan's Richmond Raid (May 9-24). Upon returning from this operation, the regiment skirmished along the North Anna River, then moved on to Bethesda Church and Cold Harbor (May 30-June 1). On June 11-12, the regiment engaged enemy horsemen at Trevilian Station as Sheridan attempted to interdict one of the railroads supplying Lee's soldiers. Thereafter, the 17th was engaged in several skirmishes on the Peninsula, covering the army's crossing of the James River. In July, the regiment participated in the operations at Deep Bottom (July 27-29).

In early August, the First and Third Divisions of the Cavalry Corps were sent to the Shenandoah Valley as part of the forces gathered by Sheridan to expel Jubal Early's Confederate army. During the ensuing campaign, the 17th fought at Newtown (August 11), Front Royal (August 16), and Kearneysville (August 25), as well as many other lesser skirmishes during the campaign's opening stage. The regiment then fought at Winchester on September 19. After this battle, the regiment was detached to help guard against guerrilla attacks on the Union supply base that was established in Winchester.

First State Standard
Maker: HB
1985.288

The regiment rejoined the division in late October. After engaging enemy cavalry near Gordonsville in late December, the regiment returned to Winchester and went into winter quarters. In February 1865, Sheridan's cavalry raided south to the James River Canal, eventually moving east to join Grant at Petersburg in time to fight at the White Oak Road and Five Forks (March 31-April 1). The regiment was also engaged at Saylor's Creek on April 6. After Lee's surrender at Appomattox, the regiment moved to Washington and was mustered out of service on June 16. The remnant of the state standard was officially returned in 1866.

Second State Standard

This flag was completed by Horstmann Brothers in late April 1865. It was sent to Adjutant-General Russell's office in Harrisburg. There seems to be no documentation to indicate if the flag was then forwarded to the 17th Cavalry prior to muster out. This standard was also included in the 1866 ceremony.

Second State Standard
Maker: HB
1985.287

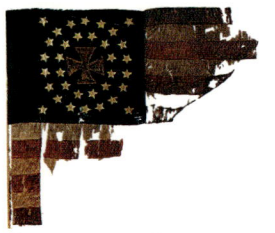

Company Guidon

Company Guidons

During the confusion of the May 2, 1863, fighting at Chancellorsville, the regiment lost at least three of its company guidons. Colonel Josiah Kellogg reduced to the ranks three sergeants of Companies D, F, and I for their bad conduct at this battle.[1] The federal-style guidon of one of the regiment's companies can be seen at Motts Military Museum in Groveport, Ohio. During the Gettysburg Campaign, Companies D and H were detached as Fifth Corps headquarters guards. The guidon illustrated here was found on the battlefield by a civilian and remained in a local family until the 1960s, when it was sold at auction. The Ohio museum purchased the flag in 1985. It is adorned with a Fifth Corps maltese cross.

Notes

1 On the Chancellorsville reductions, see Orders #15, May 9, 1863; Orders #22, May 31, 1863; and Orders #23, June 1, 1863, all in the Regimental Letter and Order Book, RG 94.

Bibliography

Bean, Theodore W. *The Roll of Honor of the Seventeenth Pennsylvania Cavalry; Or, One Hundred and Sixty-second of the Line, Pennsylvania Volunteers.* Philadelphia: James S. Claxton, 1865.

____. "The Sevententh Pennsylvania Cavalry, 162d P.V., in the Gettysburg Campaign, July 1-3, 1863." *Philadelphia Weekly Press*, January 27, 1886.

____. "Who Fired the Opening Shots?" *Philadelphia Weekly Times*, February 2, 1878. (Gettysburg)

Bloss Family Papers. Pennsylvania State Archives.

Clark, James A. "The Making of a Volunteer Cavalryman." Military Order of the Loyal Legion of the United States, District of Columbia Commandery, Paper Number 70, 1907.

DeWitt, J. Wilson. "Some Grand and Some Horrible Sights in the Chancellorsville Campaign." *Grand Army Scout and Soldiers Mail*, December 6, 1884.

Fox, John J. "Cavalry at Gettysburg." *NT*, March 5, 1914.

McCabe, J. E. "The First Shot at Gettysburg." *NT*, August 28, 1913.

____. "Scouting Under Sheridan." *Philadelphia Weekly Times*, July 28, 1883.

____. Papers. University of Virginia.

Moore, James B. *Two Years in the Service.* N.p., n.d.

Morley, John W. "Rode with Sheridan." *NT*, January 26, 1911.

Moyer, Henry P. *History of the Seventeenth Regiment Pennsylvania Volunteer Cavalry; Or, One Hundred and Sixty-second in the Line of Pennsylvania Volunteer Regiments, War to Suppress the Rebellion, 1861-1865.* Lebanon: Sowers Printing Company, 1911.

Mullihan, G. D. "They Rode with Sheridan." *NT*, February 22, 1906.

Spera, W. H. "Sheridan's Ride." *NT*, May 17, 1906.

18th Cavalry (163rd Regiment)

State Standard

Another three-year cavalry regiment recruited during the fall of 1862, the 18th Cavalry's troopers came from more than thirteen counties spread across the breadth of the Commonwealth. After organizing at Camp Curtin, the regiment moved to Washington in December 1862. In early January 1863, the 18th marched south into Virginia to reinforce the garrison troops watching the southern approaches to the city's defenses. At some point that month, a Horstmann-made state standard was sent to the regiment from the State Agency building in Washington.

State Standard
Maker: HB
1985.28

The regiment joined the Army of the Potomac in late June 1863, as part of the Third Division, Cavalry Corps. On June 30, the division tangled with Confederate cavalry led by Jeb Stuart in and around Hanover, Pennsylvania. At Gettysburg, the regiment was in action on the army's left flank, skirmishing with Southern infantry south of the Devil's Den area. During the pursuit of Lee's army, the 18th fought primarily at Hagerstown, Maryland, on July 6. Since joining the army, the regiment had suffered almost two hundred casualties in a week of hard fighting and riding.

During the fall of 1863, the regiment was actively engaged in many skirmishes with enemy horsemen, including near Culpeper (September 18), Brandy Station (October 11), and Auburn (October 13). On November 18, while most of the regiment was employed on picket duty, a force of enemy cavalry attacked and overwhelmed the regiment's camp near Germanna Ford on the Rapidan River. Among the trophies carried off was the state standard. In April 1865, Colonel Loomis L. Langdon, an artillery officer, found the flag in Richmond and appropriated it as a souvenir. By 1884, the standard was on display in a museum on Governor's Island, New York, owned by the Military Service Institution of the United States. It was there in 1909 when the 18th's history was published. It was returned to the state sometime between 1909 and 1914.[1]

Unidentified Standard

Available sources do not indicate what type of replacement standard the regiment used throughout the remainder of its term of service. Following the disaster at Germanna Ford, the regiment went into winter quarters, then participated in Judson Kilpatrick's February-March 1864 attempt to free Union prisoners in Richmond.

During the 1864 Virginia Campaign, the 18th fought in the Wilderness (May 5-6), Spotsylvania (May 8), Sheridan's Richmond Raid (May 9-24), Cold Harbor (May 31-June 1), and Saint Mary's Church (June 15), as well as numerous smaller actions. During the Petersburg operations, the regiment was initially detached from the Third Division and helped guard the army's left flank, fighting at Yellow House on the Weldon Raid on June 23.

In August, the 18th moved with its division to the Shenandoah Valley. Here, the unit fought at Winchester (September 19), Brock's Gap (October 6), Cedar Creek (October 19), and many other cavalry skirmishes in the Valley. After some November operations near Cedar Creek, the regiment marched north to Harper's Ferry for the winter. It fought at Waynesboro (March 2, 1865), then returned to Winchester. While stationed here, Sergeants Alder Smith (Company I) and Charles Beck (both of Company I) acted as color-bearers.[2] In early May, the regiment moved north to Cumberland, Maryland, where it was disbanded on June 24.

Notes

1 Regimental history, pp. 19-20, 99. See also Military Service Institution of the United States, *The Catalogue of the Museum, 1884* (New York: G. P. Putnam's Sons, 1884), 9.

2 Special Orders #28, March 28, 1865; and Special Orders #54, June 20, 1865, both in Regimental Letter, Indorsement and Order Book RG 94.

Bibliography

Athearn, Robert G. (editor). "The Civil War Diary of John Wilson Phillips." *Virginia Magazine of History and Biography* 62 (1954): 95-123.

History of the Eighteenth Regiment of Cavalry Pennsylvania Volunteers (163rd Regiment of the Line). Compiled and Edited by the Publication Committee of the Regimental Association. New York: Wynkoop Hallenbeck Crawford Company, 1909.

Howard, David. Papers. Pennsylvania State Archives.

Lowry, Titus. Andersonville Letters. Crawford County Historical Society.

Phillips, John W. "Experiences in Libby Prison." Military Order of the Loyal Legion of the United States, Missouri Commandery, *War Papers and Personal Reminiscences 1861-1865*, 1: 54-73. St. Louis: Becktold & Company, 1892.

____. "Amid Bullet and Shell. The 18th Pa. Cav. had Lively Work in the Mine Run Fight." *NT,* May 27, 1897.

____. "Cavalry's Bold Move. More About the Dash Sheridan Made at Richmond." *NT,* May 6, 1897.

Potter, Henry C. Memoirs. Gettysburg National Park Library.

Pownall, Isaac. "A Sawed-off Runaway." *NT,* September 9, 1915.

Rodgers, W. A. "Cavalry's Bold Move. Story of the Dash Sheridan Made at Richmond." *NT,* April 15, 1897.

Seal, William P. "Battle of Cedar Creek." *NT,* July 7, 1921.

____. "Kilpatrick's Cavalry. The Great Charge on the Right the Third Day." *NT,* October 12, 1916. (Gettysburg).

____. "Story of a Boy Who Served Throughout Civil War Without Being Enlisted." *NT,* February 11, 1932.

"Sheridan and Custer at Cedar Creek." *NT,* August 6, 1885.

St. Clair, Samuel. "Colonel Dahlgren's Wound." *NT,* March 12, 1896

Webster, C. T. "Cedar Creek." *NT,* September 9, 1909.

1862-63 Drafted Militia
(158th, 165th-179th Infantry)

On August 4, 1862, President Lincoln requested 300,000 militia volunteers to serve for nine months unless sooner discharged. For those states that could not meet their assigned quotas, the federal government was prepared to enforce a draft. In preparation for the draft, federal marshals were appointed to update the defective militia rosters of most of the Commonwealth's counties. When the state failed to meet its quota, the actual draft began in mid-October. Rendezvous camps were established at Harrisburg, Pittsburgh, Philadelphia, Chambersburg, Gettysburg, York, and Reading. By early December, fifteen regiments totalling about 15,000 men had been formed and mustered into federal service. Of the fifteen regiments formed, ten (158th, 165th, 166th, 167th, 168th, 171st, 174th, 175th, 176th, 177th) were initially sent to Suffolk to strengthen the garrison there. Four regiments (169th, 172nd, 178th, 179th) went to join the Yorktown area defenses, while the 173rd joined the garrison at Norfolk. The 170th was never formed.

State Color, 165th Infantry
Maker: HB
1985.290

State Color, 158th Infantry
Maker: HB
1985.283

State Color, 166th Infantry
Maker: HB
1985.291

Regimental Color, 167th Infantry
Maker: EH
1985.292

State Color, 167th Infantry
Maker: HB
1985.294

Thereafter, most of these regiments spent their terms of service in their initial assignment areas. Six regiments (158th, 168th, 171st, 174th, 175th, 176th) moved to North Carolina and reinforced the garrisons at New Bern and Washington for several months. The 177th Infantry later joined the 173rd in Norfolk. By June 1863, thirteen of the regiments were concentrated in the Yorktown area as part of Major-General John A. Dix's command. The remaining two units—the 174th and 176th—went to Hilton Head, South Carolina, for garrison duty. During the final stages of the Gettysburg Campaign, four of these drafted units (158th, 168th, 171st, 175th) moved to Harper's Ferry, while five others (167th, 169th, 172nd, 173rd, 177th) joined the Army of the Potomac for a brief time. All fifteen regiments were mustered out of service by mid-August 1863. Few saw any combat action. Losses for the drafted units totalled nine battle deaths and more than three hundred by disease. Hundreds more deserted when given the chance.

Documentation for these regiments is sadly lacking and thus it is difficult to ascertain how and when colors were obtained for these units. A color for the 158th was ordered from Horstmann Brothers on August 30, 1862, then returned to the company for altering in January 1863.[1] Adjutant-General Russell ordered colors for the 165th-169th regiments from Horstmann Brothers on December 9, 1862. Russell ad-

National Color, 167th Infantry
1985.293

State Color, 168th Infantry
Maker: HB
1985.295

474

Advance the Colors!

State Color, 169th Infantry
Maker: HB
1985.296

National Color, 171st Infantry
1985.298

vised the company that the flags should be lettered "Penna. Regiment" rather than "P.V.," as these troops were not volunteers. On the same day, Russell sought colors for the 170th-178th regiments from Evans & Hassall.[2] A color for the 179th Infantry was ordered from Evans & Hassall on March 6, 1863.[3] The remaining colors under the two December 1862 contracts were forwarded to the State Agency in January 1863, according to the extant bills in the State Archives.

Thereafter, it appears that many of these state colors were never obtained by the regiments for which they were intended. On May 26, 1863, Adjutant Frank Reeder of the 174th Infantry acknowledged that he had obtained a state color from the State Agency.[4] Otherwise, the extant sources are silent on the acquisition of state colors by the other drafted units. Twice, in September 1863 and October 1864, the State Agency listed colors that had not been picked up.[5] On both these lists, colors for the 166th, 167th, 168th, 169th, 175th, 176th, and 177th appear as being unclaimed. In February 1866, Frank Jordan reported that colors for the 166th, 167th, 173rd, 176th, and 177th were among the flags at the Agency.[6] Given this information, it is quite apparent that many of the drafted units never bothered to claim their state colors.

State Color, 171st Infantry
Maker: EH
1985.297

Regimental Color, 171st Infantry
1985.299

1862-63 Drafted Militia

475

State Color, 172nd Infantry
Maker: EH
1985.300

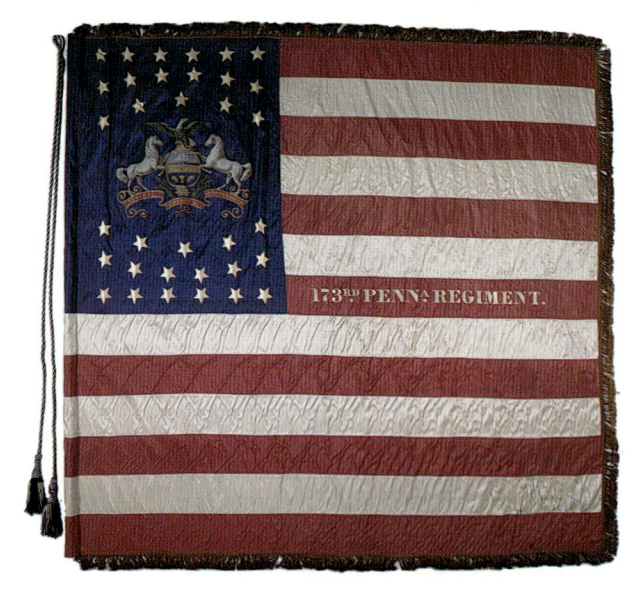

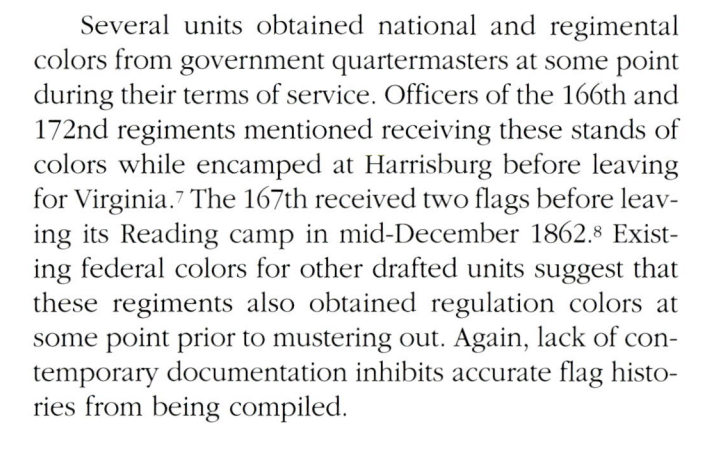

State Color, 173rd Infantry
Maker: EH
1985.302

Several units obtained national and regimental colors from government quartermasters at some point during their terms of service. Officers of the 166th and 172nd regiments mentioned receiving these stands of colors while encamped at Harrisburg before leaving for Virginia.[7] The 167th received two flags before leaving its Reading camp in mid-December 1862.[8] Existing federal colors for other drafted units suggest that these regiments also obtained regulation colors at some point prior to mustering out. Again, lack of contemporary documentation inhibits accurate flag histories from being compiled.

From existing evidence, it seems that the state colors were all carried in the 1866 parade and officially returned to the state at that time. The state color for the 174th Infantry is missing, apparently never returned by the unit after receiving it in May 1863.

Notes

1 Russell to Horstmann Brothers & Company, August 30, 1862; Russell to Horstmann, January 10, 1863, both in Adjutant-General's Letter Book, 1861-63, RG 19.

2 Russell to Horstmann, December 9, 1862; Russell to Evans & Hassall, December 9, 1862, both in Letter Book, RG 19.

Regimental Color, 173rd Infantry
Maker: W. F. Scheible
1985.301

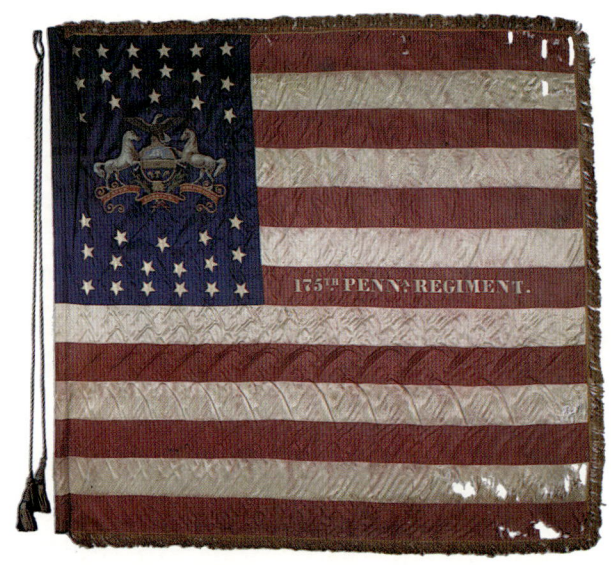

State Color, 175th Infantry
Maker: EH
1985.303

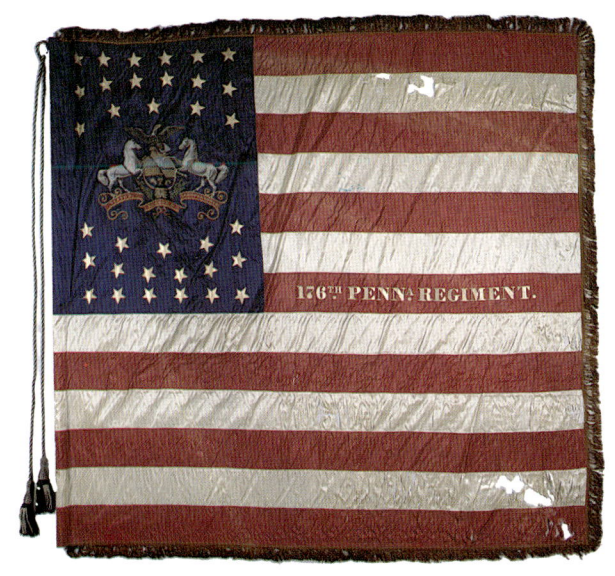

State Color, 176th Infantry
Maker: EH
1985.304

Regimental Color, 177th Infantry
Maker: HB
1985.306

3 Russell to Evans & Hassall, March 6, 1863, Letter Book, RG 19
4 Frank Reeder to A. L. Russell, May 26, 1863, RG 25.
5 Major James Gilleland to Russell, September 29, 1863, RG 25; Colonel Frank Jordan to Commander, 206th Pennsylvania, October 7, 1864, 206th Pennsylvania Regimental Descriptive, Letter, Order, and Index Book, RG 94.
6 Jordan to J. L. Reynolds, February 10, 1866, RG 25.
7 Lieutenant William E. Patterson to Russell, March 20, 1863, in 166th Pennsylvania Regimental Correspondence, RG 19; Colonel Charles Kleckner to Russell, March 19, 1863, in 172nd Pennsylvania Regimental Correspondence, RG 19.
8 *Norristown Herald*, December 16, 1862.

Bibliography

158th Infantry
Swinn, Clarence M., Jr. (editor). *Letters to Lannah: A Series of Civil War Letters Written by Samuel Ensminger, A Drafted Union Soldier*. N.p., 1986.

167th Infantry
Melefsky, A. (editor). "A Quaker Goes to War." *Historical Review of Berks County* 33 (Spring 1968): 46-47, 60-61. (James Meredith)

169th Infantry
McClintock, D. N. "Driving Lee Out of Maryland." *NT*, November 10, 1910.
_____. "A Pennsylvania Regiment. Reminiscences of Some of the Service of the 168th." *NT*, June 21, 1900. (The use of 168th is apparently a mistake, since Bates has McClintock listed in Company A, 169th.)

State Color, 177th Infantry
Maker: EH
1985.305

National Color, 177th Infantry
1985.307

1862-63 Drafted Militia

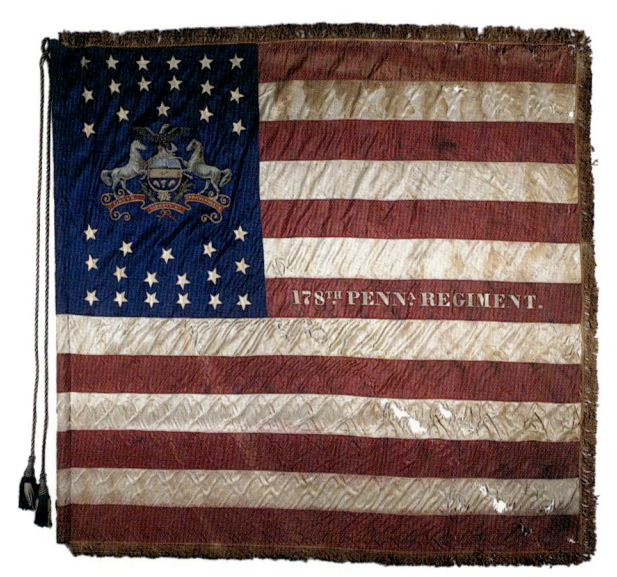

State Color, 178th Infantry
Maker: EH
1985.308

State Color, 179th Infantry
Maker: EH
1985.309

Nelson, J. W. "The 169th Pa. A Splendid Record Made By This Command." *NT*, May 16, 1901.

171st Infantry
Cox, Robert C. *Memories of the War.* Wellsboro: Agitator Book Print, 1893.
Moist, R. S. "That Maryland Spy." *NT*, July 4, 1918.

173rd Infantry
Lingle, John B. Letters. In Boyer Family Collection. USAMHI, HbCWRT Collection.

174th Infantry
Wood, Joseph. Letters. USAMHI, HbCWRT Collection.

176th Infantry
Brown, James P. Diary. Monroe County Historical Society.

177th Infantry
Parliman, A. C. "Suffolk." *NT*, January 29, 1885.

178th Infantry
Stahl, William H. Memoir. USAMHI, CWMisc Collection.

179th Infantry
"Daily Duties of the 179th Regt. Pa. Yorktown, Va." In Charles Oellig Collection, USAMHI.
Gamer, R. A. "A Wake in Camp." *NT*, June 9, 1892.

19th, 20th, 21st Cavalry (180th-182nd Regiment)

None of these three cavalry regiments ever received any state-issued standards. Documentation is lacking on any flags carried during these units' terms of service. The following brief descriptions summarize their wartime experiences and include the scant information on their flags that has been discovered.

19th Cavalry

Recruited in Philadelphia, Blair, and Huntingdon counties, this unit is perhaps one of Pennsylvania's most-forgotten fighting units. Upon organization in early November 1863, the regiment started for Washington. It was soon ordered to Columbus, Kentucky, for duty. Upon arrival there, the 19th moved into Tennessee as part of a flanking column supporting General Sherman's Meridian Expedition. The regiment fought in several skirmishes, notably at Egypt, Mississippi (February 19, 1864) and Joy Farm (February 22). After participating in scouting expeditions around Memphis, the regiment fought at Brice's Crossroads (June 10). In July and August, the regiment took part in two expeditions into Mississippi, again engaging the enemy in some minor skirmishing. That fall, part of the regiment was sent to Missouri to aid in repelling Sterling Price's great raid across the state. In December, the regiment moved to Nashville and took part in the battle there (December 15-16) and in the pursuit of Hood's battered Confederates. In 1865, the regiment was sent to Louisiana and performed garrison duty in that state and eastern Texas until mustered out of service in May 1866.

The regiment probably carried a national standard during its term of service. On May 17, 1864, Sergeant John Ery of Company I was appointed color-bearer.[1] The Company L guidon in the state collection was sent to the adjutant-general in 1897 by Norman M. Smith, formerly adjutant of the regiment. In his letter accompanying the banner, Smith pointed out several visible bullet holes in the guidon.[2]

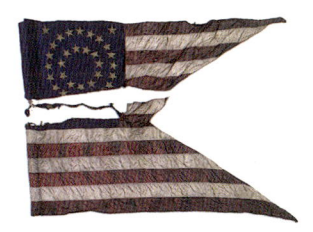

Company L Guidon, 19th Cavalry
Size: 24 3/8 x 40
1985.310

Notes

1 Special Orders #23, May 17, 1864, Regimental Descriptive, Letter and Order Book, RG 94.

2 Smith to Adjutant-General Thomas J. Stewart, June 16, 1897, RG 25.

Bibliography

Hemler, Mahlon R. "Sturgis at Guntown." *NT*, November 10, 1927.
Mullihan, J. D. "Sheridan's Ride." *NT*, July 11, 1907.
Wenrick, James E. Diary, April-October 1864. Historical Society of Pennsylvania.

20th Cavalry

Originally recruited for a six-month term of service during the summer of 1863, the 20th Cavalry was reorganized for three years in early 1864. In May, the regiment was assigned to the Union troops operating in the Shenandoah Valley. The regiment was engaged at New Market (May 15) and in the June operations that resulted in the retreat from Lynchburg. Thereafter, the 20th fought at Winchester (July 24), then was sent to perform garrison duty near Harper's Ferry. It rejoined Sheridan's cavalry in time to move to Petersburg, fighting at the White Oak Road and Five Forks (March 31-April 1, 1865). Following Lee's surrender at Appomattox, the regiment was consolidated with the 2nd Cavalry as the 1st Provisional Cavalry, then was mustered out of service in July.

This regiment also likely carried a national standard. On February 3, 1864, Sergeant William R. Barnes was appointed color-bearer.[1]

Notes

1 Special Orders #9, February 3, 1864, Regimental Descriptive, Letter and Order Book, RG 94.

Bibliography

Baker, G. F. "It was Only a Stampede." *NT*, March 5, 1891. (Incident at Bath, VA)
Ely, Albert S. Papers, 1863-65. Bucks County Historical Society.
Ely, Samuel S. 1864 Diary. Bucks County Historical Society.
Kirk, John. "Company F, 20th Pa. Cavalry." *NT*, January 29, 1914.

Landis, William J. Diary, July 1863-October 1865. USAMHI, CWMisc Collection.
Morrow, Joseph. 1865 Letters. USAMHI, HbCWRT Collection.
Smith, David H. "One of the Rescued." *NT*, October 29, 1891.
Woods, J. W. Diary, 1864-65. Historical Society of Montgomery County.

21st Cavalry

This regiment was originally recruited for a six-month term of service during the second half of 1863. In February 1864, the regiment was reorganized for three years. Its troopers came from more than ten counties, with the largest number from Franklin and Dauphin. The regiment formed in a camp near Chambersburg. On March 31, a deputation of Philadelphia ladies arrived to present a "beautiful standard" to the regiment. Colonel Alexander K. McClure, a prominent Philadelphia editor, gave the presentation address. The ceremony was followed by an evening ball at Franklin Hall in the city.[1]

National Standard, 21st Cavalry
1985.311

In mid-May, the regiment moved to Washington, where, owing to a shortage of horses, it was equipped as infantry and sent to join the Fifth Corps, Army of the Potomac. The 21st fought as foot soldiers at Cold Harbor (June 2-3), Petersburg (June 18 and 22), Weldon Railroad (August 18-22), and Poplar Spring Church (September 30-October 1), suffering a total loss of about two hundred in these engagements. Finally, just after the Poplar Spring Church battle, the regiment was mounted and assigned to the Second Division of the army's Cavalry Corps. Serving as mounted troops, the regiment engaged enemy horsemen at the Boydton Plank Road (October 27), then participated in two December raids to Stony Creek Station and Belfield.

During the 1865 operations, the regiment fought at Hatcher's Run (February 5-7), Quaker Road (March 29), Paine's Crossroads (April 5), Saylor's Creek (April 6), Farmville (April 7), and Appomattox (April 9). Following Lee's surrender, the regiment was sent to Lynchburg on provost guard duty, then on to Danville. The regiment was mustered out of service at Lynchburg on July 8. The federal standard in the collection was turned over to the state in August 1865. No documentation seems to exist which can verify this flag's wartime use. One of its bearers may have been Israel B. Bair of Company I.[2]

Notes

1 "From Co. F, 21st Pa. Cavalry," *Cambria Tribune*, April 15, 1864; "Flag Presentation and Ball," *Chambersburg Valley Spirit and Times*, April 6, 1864. B. F. Sterner, in his *NT* article of April 15, 1909, wrote that the flag came from the ladies of Chambersburg, who also gave the regiment twelve company guidons.

2 Bair obituary in *NT*, August 24, 1922.

Bibliography

Annual Report of the 21st Penn'a. Vol. Cavalry Asso'n . . . 1891-1908. 16 different pamphlets with slightly differing titles.

Brenizer, Lafayette. "On the Nottoway." *NT*, October 19, 1905.
Charles, Henry F. Reminiscences. USAMHI, Boyer Collection.

Glass, Samuel P. Papers. Pennsylvania State Archives.
Gracey, Daniel. "The Falling Flag." *NT*, December 22, 1904.
Hassler, C. C. "The Flat-footed Cavalry." *NT*, May 8, 1890.
Kendig, Jacob H. Letters, February-June 1864. Historical Society of Pennsylvania.

Sterner, B. F. "The 21st Pa. Cav. A Memorable Charge at Poplar Spring Church." *NT*, June 17, 1920.
"21st Pa. Cavalry." *Maine Bugle*, July 1897: 284-92.

183rd Infantry

Union League Colors

This regiment was recruited in Philadelphia throughout the fall of 1863 to early spring of 1864. The Union League of Philadelphia assisted in the organization and equipping of this unit, hence its nickname "4th Union League Regiment." On February 22, 1864, the League presented a "set of colors" to the regiment.[1] Shortly thereafter, the regiment left the city for Virginia, where it was assigned to the First Division, Second Corps, Army of the Potomac.

During Grant's 1864 Virginia Campaign, the 183rd was engaged in most of the important battles. It suffered no loss during the two-day fighting in the Wilderness (May 5-6), but lost 161 officers and men at Spotsylvania (May 8-18), including combat at Laurel Hill, along the Po River, and in the epic May 12 Second Corps assault. After action along Totopotomoy Creek (May 30), the regiment fought at Cold Harbor (June 3). Then followed the initial fighting at Petersburg (June 16-18 and 22). During the ensuing siege operations around Petersburg, the regiment participated in the two Deep Bottom expeditions of the Second Corps (July-August), then fought at Reams's Station on the Weldon Railroad (August 25).

National Color
1985.313

By this time, the regiment was much reduced in numbers and was sent to guard a portion of the military railroad leading to the supply base at City Point. In late September, the regiment rejoined the Second Corps in the siege lines, remaining on this duty throughout the fall and winter. It engaged the enemy on March 25, 1865, in the picket line fighting following the action at Fort Stedman. The 183rd was present on the field of Five Forks (April 1), then was under fire at Sutherland's Station (April 2). Following Lee's surrender, the regiment moved to Washington, took part in the Grand Review (May 23), and was mustered out of service on July 13. Both Union League presentations were left at Camp Cadwalader in Philadelphia, then sent to Harrisburg.

State Color

This flag was completed by Horstmann Brothers in late November 1864, then forwarded to the regiment

Regimental Color
1985.312

at some unspecified date. It was apparently carried by the regiment until disbanded. It was officially returned to state care in 1866.

Company G Flag

On February 4, 1864, a "beautiful flag" was presented to Company G by Mr. William Hunter, chairman of a committee of coal operators who had helped recruit the men. No additional information about this flag has been found.[2]

Color-Bearer

During the course of a May 1884 reunion, "color-bearer Richardson spoke of a time when a rebel soldier had hold of one end of the flag and he had hold of the other, but he kept the colors."[3] The article contains no additional information. The only Richardson in Bates is William Richardson of Company G.

State Color
Maker: HB
1985.314

Notes

1 "Flag Presentations," *Philadelphia Public Ledger*, February 23, 1864.

2 "Sword and Flag Presentations," *Philadelphia Daily Evening Bulletin*, February 5, 1864.

3 "Reunions. The 183rd Penna. Vols.," *Grand Army Scout and Soldiers Mail*, May 17, 1884.

Bibliography

Cox, William H. Letters. USAMHI, CWMisc Collection.

184th Infantry

State Color
Regimental Color

Recruited primarily in eleven central-south central counties, the 184th Infantry was formed at Camp Curtin in May 1864. Before its organization was complete, it was dispatched to the Army of the Potomac's Second Corps, joining it on May 28 in time to fight along the Totopotomoy Creek. It then fought at Cold Harbor, suffering more than a hundred casualties. During the ensuing attacks on Petersburg, the regiment was engaged on June 16-18 and 22, losing more than two hundred soldiers, most of them captured on June 22 when the regiment was outflanked.

During the siege operations around Petersburg, the 184th took part in both Deep Bottom operations (July and August), then fought in the August 25 engagement at Reams's Station. The remnant of the command then fought in the Boydton Plank Road fight (October 27). During the final operations in 1865, the unit fought at Hatcher's Run (February 5-6) and was present in many of the engagements leading to Lee's surrender at Appomattox. The regiment took part in the Grand Review (May 23) and was mustered out of service on July 14.

Both flags in the state collection were received in Harrisburg in August 1865. The state color was completed by Horstmann Brothers in early July 1864 and forwarded to the State Agency for distribution. It was apparently carried by the regiment after this period and officially returned to state care in 1866.

Bibliography

Ammerman, Robert B. "The 184th Pa." *NT,* January 3, 1907.
Metzger, Henry C. Letters. USAMHI, HbCWRT Collection.
Young, Joseph H. Papers. Southern Historical Collection.

State Color
Maker: HB
1985.316

Regimental Color
1985.315

Advance the Colors!

22nd Cavalry (185th Regiment)

Unidentified Standard

This regiment was formed in February 1864 from two separate units. Five companies were composed of re-enlisted troopers from a six-month cavalry battalion formed during the Gettysburg Campaign. The other seven companies comprised a battalion known as the Ringgold Cavalry, originally seven independent companies recruited in Washington County in 1861-62.

When the 22nd Cavalry was formed, it was divided for a time. One battalion, composed primarily of the new men, moved to Pleasant Valley, Maryland, then to a training camp near Washington. In June, the battalion moved to Martinsburg, West Virginia, and participated in several small actions in the Harper's Ferry area. Thereafter, this battalion moved into the Loudoun Valley, again fighting enemy cavalry and guerrillas in several skirmishes. In August, the battalion was engaged at Kernstown (August 21), Clarkstown (August 25), and several smaller engagements.

The other battalion participated in the May 1864 Shenandoah Valley operations, primarily General David Hunter's Lynchburg Expedition (June) and the fight near Winchester (July 25). The regiment was finally reunited at Hagerstown, Maryland. Throughout late August and most of September, the regiment engaged enemy horsemen in several actions in the northern Shenandoah Valley. In the subsequent Valley operations led by Phil Sheridan, the 22nd Cavalry fought at Winchester (September 19), Fisher's Hill (September 22), and Cedar Creek (October 19).

After this last battle, the regiment escorted a wagon train to Martinsburg, where it went into camp until late December. Over the winter of 1864-65, the regiment was transferred to New Creek, West Virginia, where it performed guard duty in several counties. Part of the regiment was mustered out of service in April 1865; the remainder of the regiment was consolidated with the 18th Cavalry as the 3rd Provisional Cavalry. This command guarded the peace in West Virginia until disbanded on October 31, 1865.

Color-Sergeant Michael H. Core

No description of the standard carried by the 22nd Cavalry seems to exist. This flag was placed in the care of one of the veterans. After his death, it was turned over to GAR Post 120 in Washington, Pennsylvania. The veterans of the 22nd Cavalry at one time looked into the possibility of securing their old banner so they could send it to Harrisburg, but nothing seems to have come of this effort. The present location of this flag, if it yet remains, is unknown.[1]

National Flag

The 22nd Cavalry never received a state-issued flag. In 1897, the veterans of the regiment began a quest to rectify this oversight. The regimental association appointed a three-man committee to confer with the Legislature. On April 28, 1899, the governor signed Act Sixty into law. This bill provided the sum of one hundred dollars to cover the cost of a national flag to be inscribed with the battles in which the 22nd Cavalry had fought. Adjutant-General Thomas J. Stewart met the veterans at their twenty-sixth annual reunion at Monongahela, Pennsylvania, to present the flag on August 16, 1899. Thereafter, the veterans appointed a delegation to take the flag back to Harrisburg so it could be placed in the state collection.[2]

National Flag
Maker: J. H. Wilson
1985.317

Notes

1 Ringgold Cavalry Minute Book, Twenty-seventh Annual Reunion, August 16, 1900, West Brownsville, p. 43.

2 *Laws of the General Assembly of the Commonwealth of Pennsylvania, Passed at the Session of 1899 . . .* (Harrisburg: William S. Ray, State Printer, 1899), pp. 66-67; Ringgold Minute Book, pp. 34-35 (Twenty-fourth Annual Reunion, August 19-20, 1897), 37-38 (Twenty-fifth Annual Reunion, August 19, 1898), 39 (Twenty-sixth Annual Reunion, August 16-17, 1899).

Bibliography

Cru, A. H. "Sheridan's Famous Ride." *NT*, November 30, 1905.

Elwood, John W. *Elwood's Stories of the Old Ringgold Cavalry, 1847-1865, The First Three Year Cavalry of the Civil War.* Coal Center: The author, 1914.

Farrar, Samuel C. *The Twenty-second Pennsylvania Cavalry and the Ringgold Battalion 1861-1865.* Pittsburgh: New Werner Company, 1911.

Haas, Ralph (editor). *The Ringgold Cavalry—The Rest of the Story.* Apollo, PA: Closson Press, 1988.

Harrison, J. F. "At Libby Prison." *NT*, December 5, 1912.

Hasson, Benjamin F. *Escape from the Confederacy, Overpowering the Guards, Midnight Leap from a Moving Train, Through Swamps and Forest, Blood Hounds, Thrilling Events.* Bryant, OH, 1900.

____. "The 22nd Pa. Cav." *NT*, December 12, 1907.

____. *War Memories.* Washington: Herbert A. Eby, Printer, n.d.

McClelland, Russ. "We were Enemies: Pennsylvanians and Virginia Guerrillas." *Civil War Times Illustrated* 22 (December 1983): 40-45.

Miller, W. A. "A Great March." *NT*, July 22, 1915. (Lynchburg)

Ringgold Cavalry Minute Book, 1897-1933. Washington County Historical Society.

Shallenberger, J. S. "A Close Squeeze." *NT*, May 14, 1896. (Lynchburg)

____. "A Gallant Charge. How 45 Cavalrymen Tried to Take a Battery." *NT*, April 28, 1887. (Winchester 7/64)

Sharrer, W. F. "Let Us Have Peace. The Controversy Over Cedar Creek and Fisher's Hill." *NT*, April 14, 1887.

Weight, W. H. "Getting Relief." *NT*, July 5, 1923.

Weiser, John S. Letters. USAMHI, CWMisc Collection.

Weiser Family Collection. Pennsylvania State Archives.

Wickersham, A. "McCausland's Retreat from Chambersburg." *NT*, February 28, 1907.

186th Infantry

National and Regimental Colors

This regiment was recruited in Philadelphia during the winter and spring of 1864. Upon organization, it was assigned to provost duty in the city, remaining in this service until mustered out on August 15, 1865. Although Captain John H. Jack sought a state color for the 186th, the regiment never received one.[1]

The two flags in the collection were probably obtained via requisition from the Philadelphia quartermaster depot. On May 9, 1865, the regimental council of administration approved the expenditure of $3.75 to letter the regimental colors. Since the national color does not appear to have ever been painted, this money must have gone to letter the blue regimental color.[2]

Sergeant Charles M. Koons of Company H was appointed color-bearer on October 24, 1864, a duty he apparently held until ordered back to his company in January 1865.[3]

Both colors were left with Major Lane's office when the 186th went home and were still there in April 1866 when the major tallied the flags under his control.

Notes

1 Captain Jack to Adjutant-General A. L. Russell, April 9, 1865, in Regimental Letter, Indorsement, Order, and Miscellaneous Book, RG 94.

2 May 11, 1865, report of Council of Administration meeting for May 9, Ibid.

3 Special Orders #70, October 24, 1864; and Special Orders #16, January 18, 1865, both in Ibid.

Bibliography

Ryan, William. Letters. USAMHI.

National Color
1985.318

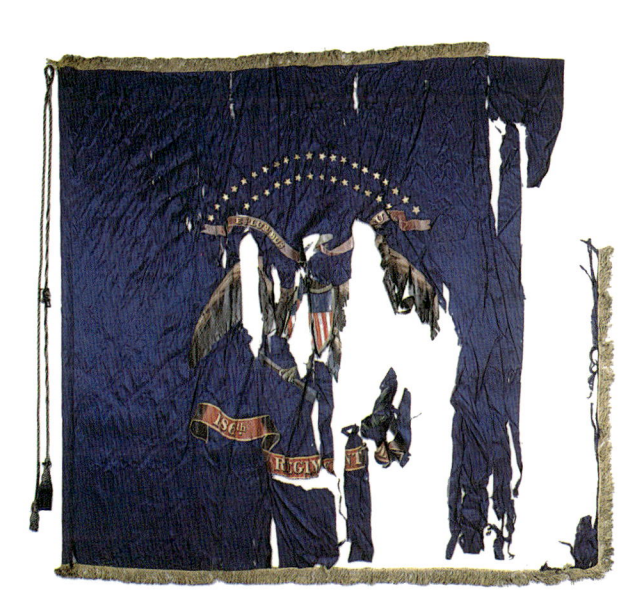

Regimental Color
1985.319

187th Infantry

State Color

This regiment was recruited chiefly from soldiers who reenlisted from a battalion raised for six-months' service during the Gettysburg Campaign. A full regiment was organized from these troops during the spring of 1864. The new unit was at first stationed at various provost-marshals across the state to help enforce the draft. In mid-May, the regiment reassembled at Harrisburg and was then sent to Washington. The 187th escorted supply trains from Port Royal, Virginia, to join the Army of the Potomac at Cold Harbor. Here, the 187th was assigned to the First Division of the Fifth Corps. Its first engagement with the enemy occurred on June 18, as it attacked the Petersburg defenses. Losses totalled 189 officers and men. After participating in the four-day engagement at the Weldon Railroad (August 18-21), the regiment returned to active duty in the trenches near Petersburg.

In late September, the 187th was sent back to Pennsylvania for duty. It was initially stationed at Camp Cadwalader outside Philadelphia, from whence detachments of the regiment escorted recruits and draftees to City Point, Virginia. Other detachments served as honor guards at funerals of military officers and part of the regiment helped escort President Lincoln's funeral procession through Philadelphia. In May 1865, the regiment was distributed at several locales statewide for provost guard duty. By late July, the regiment had assembled at Camp Curtin where it was mustered out of service on August 3.

A state color for the 187th was sent to the State Agency in late September 1864. By this time, the regiment had already returned to Pennsylvania, and the date on which the 187th received this color is unknown. On December 10, Sergeant John S. Ware of Company C was appointed color-bearer.[1] The flag was returned when the regiment disbanded in 1865 and was present in the 1866 parade.

State Color
Maker: EH
1985.320

Notes

1 Special Orders #30, December 10, 1864, in Regimental Letter, Indorsement, Order, and Miscellaneous Book, RG 94.

Bibliography

Baldwin, George H. Diary. Susquehanna County Historical Society.
Gibbs, James M. *History of the First Battalion Pennsylvania Six Months Volunteers and 187th Regiment Pennsylvania Volunteer Infantry, Six Months and Three Years Service, Civil War, 1861-1865.* Harrisburg: Central Printing and Publishing House, 1905.
Ployer, Fred K. 1864 Letters. USAMHI, HbCWRT Collection.
Stone, William A. *The Tale of a Plain Man.* N.p., n.d.

188th Infantry

State Color

By the beginning of 1864, the ranks of the 3rd Pennsylvania Heavy Artillery, part of the Fort Monroe garrison, had swelled to hundreds more than required by regulations. In April, a call was made for volunteers from this unit to form a new regiment of infantry, to be numbered the 188th. This regiment was formed later that month. On the first of May, Lieutenant-Colonel George K. Bowen notified Governor Curtin that the 188th was formed and requested a state color for the unit.[1] By late June, the 188th still had not obtained a flag, causing Bowen to query the state military department for a banner. In reply, Adjutant-General Russell noted that the Horstmann-made flag had already been sent to the State Agency in Washington.[2] Apparently, Colonel Frank Jordan had not yet forwarded it to the regiment.

Once organized, the 188th was assigned to the First Division, Eighteenth Corps, Army of the James. The regiment participated with this army in the engagements culminating in the defeat at Drewry's Bluff (May 16) as Major-General Benjamin Butler's troops were stymied in an attempt to attack Richmond. After occupying earthworks on the Bermuda Hundred line, the division was part of the force detached and sent to join the Army of the Potomac at Cold Harbor. Here, in fighting on June 1 and 3, the 188th sustained 171 casualties. Following the initial operations at Petersburg, the 188th manned a portion of the siege line on the army's right for about two months, then was transferred to Bermuda Hundred.

In late September, the corps vacated its section of the line and was part of the force assigned to attack the Confederate fortifications at Chaffin's Farm, north of the James River. The division to which the 188th was attached assaulted Fort Harrison. The advancing troops had to pass over almost a mile of open ground, exposed to cannon and musketry fire as they came closer and closer. There was a brief pause when the attackers reached a shallow ravine less than fifty yards from their goal. After closing the gaps and catching their breaths, the troops bounded toward Fort Harrison. Color-Sergeant William Sipes (Company I) was

State Color
Maker: HB
1985.321

shot dead as the 188th reached the fort's ten-foot-deep dry moat. Corporal William L. Graul, a member of the color guard, instantly threw down his rifle and grabbed the fallen banner. The eighteen-year-old then climbed up the sod wall of the fort and planted the stars and stripes on the parapet. He then cheered his comrades on as more and more bluecoats surged over the walls to capture the fort. Later that day, the regiment advanced on Fort Hoke and was repulsed. As the division retired that evening, Graul retrieved the 4th New Hampshire's fallen color. In 1865, Graul was awarded a Medal of Honor for his gallantry at Fort Harrison.[3]

The action at Fort Harrison was the last major engagement for the 188th. It remained in the area to guard part of the entrenchments north of the James. In late 1864, the white troops in the Army of the James were consolidated into the Twenty-fourth Corps, the 188th being assigned to the Third Division. The winter of 1864-65 passed quietly for most of the troops north of the James. In March 1865, the 188th's brigade went on an expedition to Fredericksburg to destroy military supplies collected for Lee's army. Following Lee's surrender, the regiment moved to Lynchburg and Danville for provost guard duty. The regiment was assembled at City Point and mustered out of service on December 14. The state color was returned to state care on July 4, 1866.

Regimental Color

This flag was carried alongside the state color by the 188th. During the assault on Fort Harrison, the bearer of this flag was apparently shot near the moat. Private William Bourke of the 58th Pennsylvania Infantry retrieved the fallen flag. At this time, both regiments, part of the same brigade, seem to have become mixed together as the Yankees congregated in the moat around the fort. No sooner had Bourke taken the flag than a rifle bullet grazed his forehead, knocking the soldier against Captain Cecil Clay, then commanding the 58th regiment.

The bullet wound sent a sizeable amount of blood flowing, temporarily blinding Bourke. Clay quickly took stock of the situation, then decided to try to climb the wall into the fort. He grabbed a sword from another officer and jabbed it into the sod bank. Clay then took the flag from Bourke, and using the sword as footing, sprang up to the parapet. As he did, Clay noticed two other soldiers reach the top; one was killed and the other wounded. It took but a moment for a wave of Union soldiers to enter the fort, whose occupants either surrendered or retreated. As Clay cheered his comrades, he was hit in the right arm by two bullets. He no sooner switched the flag to his left hand than a third musket ball crashed into that hand. The twenty-two-year-old captain leaned the flag against the ramparts until someone from the 188th claimed it. Clay's wounds soon led to the amputation of his right arm. For his bravery, Clay later was awarded a Medal of Honor.[4]

This blue color, together with the state color, was left in Philadelphia when the regiment returned home in late 1865. It has remained in state care since that time.[5]

Captain Cecil Clay, 58th Infantry

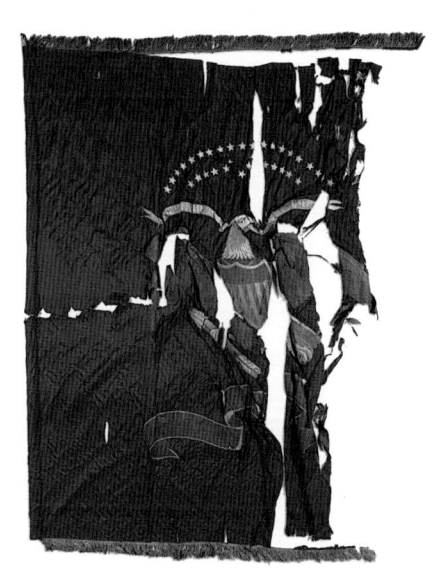

Regimental Color
Maker: EH
1985.322

Notes

1 Bowen to Curtin, May 1, 1864, RG 25.

2 Bowen to Adjutant-General A. L. Russell, June 20, 1864, Regimental Papers, RG 19. A pencilled note on his letter indicates that the flag was sent to Washington. The bills for state flags in RG 25 include two for the 188th, one dated June 6 and one dated July 27. The note attached to Bowen's June 20 letter seems to indicate that the flag had already been finished and sent to the State Agency. Therefore, the July 27 bill remains a mystery. There is no documentation to indicate that the 188th lost a flag in battle.

3 Mulholland, p. 514; Beyer-Keydel, pp. 435-36. Graul's medal citation reads as follows: "First to plant the colors of his State on the fortifications." In addition to Graul and Captain Clay, a third man was awarded a medal for gallantry at Fort Harrison. Corporal Charles Blucher of Company H was awarded a medal with the citation: "Planted first national colors on the fortifications." (*Medal of Honor Recipients 1863-1978*. Washington: Government Printing Office, 1979, pp. 34, 99.) From the descriptions in the literature, it is apparent that Graul carried the state color and Clay a blue regimental. Blucher's actions are not described in detail

in any existing documentation known to the author. Thus, the identification of this flag must remain a mystery.

4 Mulholland, pp. 508-11; Beyer-Keydel, pp. 431-33. In his recollection of the day's events, Clay described the flag he carried as the "blue State flag of the 188th Penna." The regimental color in the collection is not painted with a regimental designation. This, and evidence from other regiments that blue regimental colors were not referred to as state flags unless painted with the regimental designation, leads the author to question whether the flag in the state collection is the same one carried at Fort Harrison.

5 Lieutenant-Colonel S. Irvin Givin to Adjutant-General A. L. Russell, June 21, 1866, RG 19.

Bibliography

Depew, A. R. "The Capture of Fort Harrison." *NT*, October 28, 1886.
Hinds, S. J. "Fort Harrison Again." *NT*, June 21, 1888.
Sheet, Isaac. "Entrance into Richmond." *NT*, October 12, 1911.
____. "First into Richmond." *NT*, March 14, 1912.
Walters, W. H. "Last Call Man." *NT*, October 8, 1891.

190th & 191st Infantry
(1st & 2nd Veteran Reserves)

Presented Color

When the regiments of the Pennsylvania Reserve Volunteer Corps began mustering out in the spring of 1864, those veterans who had re-enlisted, together with all the new recruits, were retained in service. In late May, these survivors were formed as the 190th and 191st Pennsylvania regiments. The flag presented to the original Bucktails (13th Reserves) by the 149th Pennsylvania in 1863 was retained for use by the 190th Pennsylvania. When formed, these two regiments engaged the enemy at Cold Harbor, then at White Oak Swamp (June 13) and the initial operations at Petersburg (June 17-18). During the engagement at the Weldon Railroad (August 19), most of the soldiers in both regiments were employed as skirmishers. The bulk of both units was captured when the enemy suddenly outflanked the skirmish line. The flag was also captured and was returned in 1905 by the War Department. (See Volume One, pages 113-14, for more details on this flag.)

State Color, 190th Infantry
Maker: EH
1985.323

State Colors

After the capture of over six hundred officers and men, the survivors were reorganized and participated in the fighting at Poplar Spring Church on October 1. Over the winter, the regiments took part in a raid to tear up the Weldon Railroad some thirty miles south of Petersburg (December 8-9). In January 1865, Evans & Hassall completed new state colors for both units. These flags were carried in the February 5-7 action at Hatcher's Run, then in the series of combats known as Quaker Road, White Oak Road, and Five Forks (March 29-April 1). Following Lee's surrender at Appomattox, the regiments moved to Washington, took part in the Grand Review, and were mustered out of service on June 28. Both state colors were included in the 1866 proceedings.[1]

State Color, 191st Infantry
Maker: EH
1985.324

Notes

1 McBride, *In the Ranks*, p. 205, writes that a Sergeant Huck of the 191st Regiment was the first to plant a color on the Confederate earthworks at Five Forks. However, Sergeant Huck's name does not appear in Bates's roster for the 191st.

Bibliography

Cook, W. I. "Prison and Escape." *NT*, July 6, 1905.
Crocker, Silas W. "Dread Days in Dixie." *NT*, August 9, 16, 23, 30, September 6, 13, 20, 1900.
Elmendorf, N. W. "An Ex-Prisoner of War." *NT*, January 1, 1903.
Green, Harrison. "He Fired 'de Last Shot'." *NT*, September 4, 1913.
McBride, Robert E. "At Appomattox." *NT*, May 30, 1895.
____. "At White Oak Road." *NT*, March 12, 1896.
____. "Battle of Five Forks." *NT*, July 22, 1920.
____. "Battle of White Oak Road." *NT*, February 16, 1922.
____. "Bucktails. Some Notes in the History of a Gallant Band." *NT*, February 12, 1885.
____. "Five Forks." *NT*, August 16, 1923.
____. *In the Ranks, From the Wilderness to Appomattox Court-house, The War as Seen and Experienced by a Private Soldier in the Army of the Potomac.* Cincinnati: Walden & Stowe, 1881.
____. "Killed at Appomattox." *NT*, June 1, 1899.
____. "Last Man Killed at Appomattox." *NT*, December 19, 1912.
____. "Pennsylvania Reserves. Career of Those Veterans from Cold Harbor to Appomattox." *NT*, November 10, 1898.
____. "Sheridan was Slow. Warren's Not the Blunder at Five Forks Fight." *NT*, February 13, 1896.
____. "Survivor of Gravelly Run Battle Describes Hard Fought Engagement." *NT*, October 28, 1937.
____. "Truth About Warren." *NT*, December 3, 1925.
____. "White Oak Road." *NT*, July 11, 1895.
____. "Writer Declares Fifth Corps Did Not Get Proper Credit in History." *NT*, December 7, 1933.
McLaughlin, Florence C. (editor). "Diary of Sailsbury [sic] Prison by James W. Eberhart." *Western Pennsylvania Historical Magazine* 56 (1973): 211-51.
Moore, Wallace M. "A Pennsylvania Reserve." *NT*, July 1, 1920.
Springer, Thomas W. Diary, August 18-November 29, 1864. University of Virginia.
Thompson, James B. Memoir. USAMHI.
Yerger, William H. "The Battle of the Weldon Railroad. Capture of the Remnants of the Pennsylvania Reserve Corps. Life in Saulsbury [sic] Prison." *Grand Army Scout and Soldiers Mail*, May 17, 1884.

1864 One Hundred Days Troops (192nd-197th Regiments)

On July 6, 1864, President Lincoln called on the states for short-term militia to help repel a Confederate invasion of Maryland. Pennsylvania supplied six infantry regiments, an independent company, five cavalry companies, one artillery battery, and an artillery battalion, for a service period of one hundred days. The six infantry regiments were sent outside the state for active service, but none of these units engaged the enemy during the one hundred days. All six units were mustered out of service by mid-November.

Horstmann Brothers supplied state colors for the 193rd, 194th, and 195th Infantry. The flags were completed in mid-August and sent to Baltimore for distribution. The 192nd did not receive a flag at this time. However, when that regiment reorganized in 1865, Horstmann supplied a state color in late April. The 196th Infantry was recruited by the Union League of Philadelphia, which furnished that regiment with a color. The 197th Infantry also did not receive a state color, and documentation on any presentations is lacking.

Regimental Color, 192nd Infantry
1985.325

The 192nd Infantry was recruited in the Philadelphia area for one hundred days' service. It was initially sent to Baltimore for guard duty, then transferred at first to Johnson's Island Prison Camp, and finally to the supply depot at Gallipolis, Ohio, opposite the mouth of the Kanawha River. Most of the 192nd remained on duty here. A battalion was detached and sent to Weston, West Virginia. Both detachments were relieved from duty and sent to Philadelphia, where muster out occurred on November 11, 1864. One company re-enlisted for a year's service. In the spring of 1865, the regiment was rebuilt with nine new companies. The state and regimental colors in the state collection both date from this second organization. The regiment spent its term of service on duty in the Shenandoah Valley, and was mustered out of service on August 24. The state color was included in the 1866 ceremony.

Most of the 193rd Infantry was recruited in the Pittsburgh area. Upon organization, the regiment was

State Color, 192nd Infantry
Maker: HB
1985.326

sent to Baltimore, where it remained throughout its term of service. Several companies were detached and sent for duty to Wilmington, Delaware. The regiment returned to Pittsburgh and was disbanded on November 9. Colonel John B. Clark retained the state color, but brought it to Philadelphia in time to be included in the 1866 ceremony.[1] On July 28, 1864, Company I received a silk flag from the Huff Family of Wilkinsburg. The subsequent use and disposition of this company flag is undocumented.[2]

Soldiers for the 194th Infantry were recruited in nine counties, spread from Cambria in the west to Luzerne in the northeast. The regiment formed at Camp Curtin, then was sent to Baltimore. The regiment spent its entire term of service on guard duty in and around the city. It was mustered out of service at Harrisburg on November 6. The state color was present for the 1866 ceremony, when it was carried by Sergeant Henry Walbridge of Company C.[3]

The 195th Infantry was recruited in Lancaster, Berks, Union, Mifflin, and Cumberland counties. After organizing at Camp Curtin, the regiment at first was stationed at Monocacy Junction as railroad guards, then moved to Berkley County, West Virginia, to patrol the Baltimore & Ohio Railroad. It remained on this duty until mustered out of service on November 4. While at Monocacy, a state color was unfurled for the first time on August 26, when the unit formed for evening dress parade. A soldier present noted that nothing was done in the way of speeches. The flag was simply unfurled in the breeze, "and each man felt that was his to defend and preserve, and that under it, if need be, he would die."[4] The bearer apparently

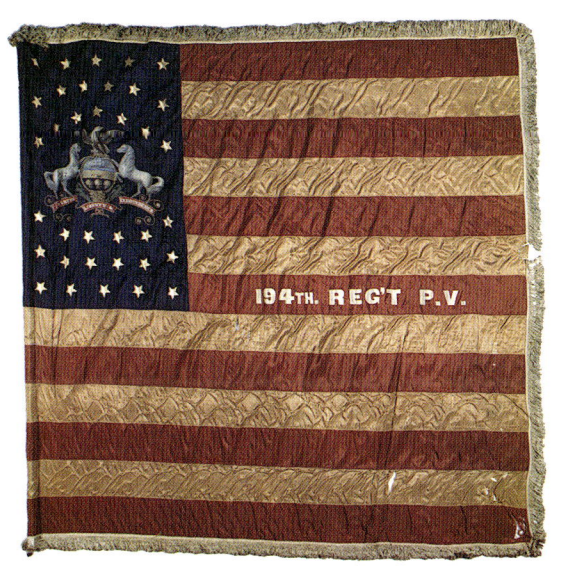

State Color, 194th Infantry
Maker: HB
1985.328

State Color, 193rd Infantry
Maker: HB
1985.327

was Sergeant Thomas E. Allen of Company F, who also carried the flag during the 1866 ceremony.[5]

When the 195th went home, three companies of its men re-enlisted for a one-year term of service. Seven new companies were added in February 1865 to rebuild the regiment to full strength. On March 15, Adjutant-General Russell ordered the state's quartermaster department to send the 195th's color to the new organization.[6] The 195th was formed at Martinsburg, West Virginia. It remained on guard duty in the Shenandoah Valley until June, when it was transferred to Washington, where it performed similar duty until mustered out of service on January 31, 1866. Sergeant Christian Hanlin of Company F was apparently the regiment's first color-bearer, appointed as such on March 28, 1865. He remained as bearer until superseded by Sergeant Israel Bair (Company F) on May 8.[7]

Organized in the Philadelphia area by the Union League, the 196th Infantry was also known as the 5th Union League Regiment. This unit received a stand of colors from the League. The presentation ceremony took place on July 28, 1864.[8] The 196th then moved to Baltimore for two weeks and then went by rail to Chicago. Here, it spent its time guarding Camp Douglass, a prison camp. One company was detached for provost duty in Springfield, Illinois. The regiment returned to Philadelphia and was mustered out of service on November 17. The Union League colors apparently have not survived.

The 197th regiment was recruited in the Philadelphia area by the Coal Exchange, hence its nickname "3rd Coal Exchange." After spending two weeks in Baltimore, the 197th moved to Rock Island, Illinois, to guard the prison camp at that place. It returned to

1864 One Hundred Days Troops

State Color, 195th Infantry
Maker: HB
1985.329

Regimental Color, 197th Infantry

Philadelphia and was mustered out on November 11. A blue regimental color for the 197th is owned by a private collector. This seems to be the only flag in existence, and its history remains undocumented.

Notes

1 Clark to Adjutant-General Russell, June 9, 1866, RG 19.
2 Untitled story in *Erie Observer*, August 18, 1864.
3 Walbridge's name appears on the 1866 checklist in RG 25.
4 "From the One Hundred Days' Boys," *Huntingdon Globe*, September 7, 1864.
5 Allen's name appears on the 1866 checklist in RG 25. His name also appears in the Company F roster for the one hundred days' regiment in Bates 5: 412.
6 Russell to Quartermaster-General J. L. Reynolds, March 15, 1865, RG 25.
7 Special Orders 3, March 28, 1865, and Special Orders 14, May 8, 1865, both in Regimental Descriptive and Order Book, RG 94.
8 Scharf-Westcott, p. 817, notes that a "stand of colors" was presented. The story "Off for the Seat of War," *Philadelphia Public Ledger*, July 29, 1864, indicates that "flags" were presented to the regiment.

Bibliography

192nd Regiment
Myers, John C. *A Daily Journal of the 192d Reg't. Penn'a. Volunteers, Commanded by Colonel William B. Thomas, in the Service of the United States for One Hundred Days*. Philadelphia: Crissy & Markley, Printers, 1864.
Miles, William H. Letters. USAMHI, CWMisc Collection.

193rd Regiment
Donaghy, John. *Army Experience of Captain John Donaghy, 193d Penna. Vols. 1861-1864*. Deland, FL: E. O. Painter Company, 1926.

195th Regiment
Gauchnauer, Jacob. 1865 Letter. USAMHI, HbCWRT Collection.
Kutz, Bently. Letters. USAMHI, HbCWRT Collection
Walters, Edgar. Diary. Cumberland County Historical Society.
____. 1864 Memoir. USAMHI, HbCWRT Collection.

196th Regiment
Burrill, John C. Journal. Bucks County Historical Society.
Greble, Edwin. In Greble Family Papers. Library of Congress.

198th Infantry

Union League Colors

Recruited under the auspices of the Union League, the 198th Infantry contained fourteen companies from Bradford in the north to Philadelphia in the south. The regiment was organized in early September 1864 to serve for one year. On September 18, as the regiment marched through the city to take a train for Virginia, it stopped at the Union League headquarters at Thirteenth and Chestnut streets. Here, in a brief ceremony, the League presented the 198th with four "beautiful flags."[1]

The regiment moved to Virginia and joined the Fifth Corps, Army of the Potomac, in time to participate in combat at Poplar Spring Church (September 30 - October 2). Following this action, the regiment engaged the enemy at the Boydton Plank Road (October 27-28). Thereafter, the 198th erected winter quarters and remained in camp throughout the winter of 1864-65.

In the 1865 engagements, the regiment first took part in the fighting at Hatcher's Run (February 5-6). Then followed the climactic series of battles that culminated in the victory at Five Forks (April 1). The 198th suffered heavy losses in the fighting on March 29 and 31 (Quaker Road and White Oak Road). On April 1, Major Edwin A. Glenn, then in command of the regiment, was mortally wounded as his troops surged forward to break the Confederate line.

Second National Color
1985.331

First National Color
1985.330

Regimental Color
Maker: HB
1985.332

198th Infantry

497

Brigadier-General Joshua L. Chamberlain, watching his brigade steadily advance on the enemy, later noted that the 198th's flag went down three times, "but rises ever again passing from hand to hand of dauntless young heroes. Then bullet-torn and blood-blazoned it hovers for a moment above a breastwork, while the regiment goes over like a wave."[2]

After taking part in the Appomattox surrender proceedings, the regiment eventually marched back to Washington, took part in the Grand Review (May 23), then was disbanded on June 3. Of the three flags in the state collection, one appears on Major Lane's April 1866 list. The other two—a national and the regimental color—were sent to Harrisburg by the Union League in late July 1866. These colors originally had been deposited with the League, but Colonel Horatio G. Sickel and his command wished them to be sent to Harrisburg as a record of the service of the 198th regiment. They were received by Adjutant-General Russell's office on July 21.[3]

Notes

1 "Departure of a Regiment—The 6th Union League," *Philadelphia Inquirer*, September 19, 1864. Bates 5: 464, has September 19 as the presentation date.

2 Joshua L. Chamberlain, *The Passing of the Armies* (New York: G. P. Putnam's Sons, 1915), p. 138.

3 James H. Orne to Russell, July 19, 1866, RG 25. Since the two Union League flags were the only two sent to Harrisburg in 1866, it is probable that the reference to the presentation of four flags refers to these two colors plus two flank markers; the latter guidons apparently have not survived.

Bibliography

Burnett, John W. "Closing War Days. Fifth Corps Comrade's Reminiscenes after the Fall of Petersburg." *NT*, May 20, 1897.

____. "Hatcher's Run #2." *NT*, July 7, 1892.

Shuman, Josiah. Diary, August 30, 1864-June 13, 1865. USAMHI, CWMisc Collection.

Williams, Hiram. Letters. USAMHI, HbCWRT Collection.

Woodward, Evan M. *History of the One Hundred and Ninety-eighth Pennsylvania Volunteers, Being a Complete Record of the Regiment, With Its Camps, Marches and Battles, Together with the Personal Record of Every Officer and Man During His Term of Service*. Trenton, NJ: MacCrellish & Quigley, Printers, 1884.

199th Infantry

National Colors
Regimental Colors

Recruited during the fall of 1864 by Philadelphia's Commercial Exchange, the 199th Infantry included soldiers from at least nine counties spread across the state. The new regiment was assigned to the First Division, Twenty-fourth Corps, Army of the James. During the winter of 1864-65, the 199th was stationed north of the James River, where it helped guard a part of the Federal entrenchments.

The regiment moved south of the river and took part in the final operations around Petersburg. Its primary combat occurred on April 2, 1865, as the regiment assaulted Fort Gregg, suffering about a hundred casualties.[1] Thereafter, the 199th skirmished with the retreating Confederates at Rice's Station (April 6) and Appomattox (April 9). The regiment then moved to Richmond, remaining there on guard duty until it was discharged from service in late June.

Little is known about the 199th's colors. The regiment did not receive a state color. Instead, it carried regulation national and regimental flags. The two in the state collection were left in Philadelphia when the regiment returned home. The national color was apparently the only color used in the 1866 parade. In 1977, the State Museum received a second pair (national and regimental) from the Union League of Philadelphia when that institution donated its collection to the Commonwealth.

Regimental Color
1985.334

National Color
1985.333

Regimental Color

199th Infantry

499

Notes

1 In his *NT* article, W. J. Britton wrote that Colonel James C. Briscoe was wounded in the assault on Fort Gregg as he planted the colors on the fort's ramparts. However, in his official report (*O.R.* 46.1, p. 1190) Briscoe wrote that he was slightly wounded as the 199th advanced toward the fort. The report clearly indicates that he was not bearing one of the colors.

Bibliography

Britton, W. J. "Fort Gregg—First Colors Up." *NT*, April 21, 1904.
Cornett, Joseph P. Letters, 1864-65. Historical Society of Pennsylvania.
Dunn, Michael. "Fort Gregg Again." *NT*, July 16, 1891.
McAlliston, R. A. "The McLean House." *NT*, October 5, 1916.
Snyder, Samuel W. "The Assault on Fort Gregg." *NT*, February 5, 1903.
Spire, Charles W. April 1865 letters. USAMHI, HbCWRT Collection.

200th Infantry

State Color

Most of the soldiers who enlisted for a one-year term of service in this regiment came from south-central Pennsylvania, primarily the counties of Dauphin, Cumberland, York, Lebanon, and Lancaster. Upon organization at Camp Curtin in early September 1864, the regiment was sent to the Army of the James in Virginia. The 200th was initially posted near Dutch Gap to guard a portion of the trench line in that vicinity. The state color was apparently received sometime after the regiment arrived in Virginia. Horstmann Brothers altered a color originally ordered for the 71st Infantry for use by the new 200th Infantry. It was at the State Agency as late as October 7.[1]

In late November, the regiment was transferred to the Army of the Potomac and assigned to the new Third Division, Ninth Corps, composed of the 200th, 205th, 207th, 208th, 209th, and 211th Pennsylvania infantry regiments. This division was posted as a reserve force behind the main line. Throughout the winter, the new units drilled and prepared for the coming spring campaign.

On March 25, 1865, Confederate forces launched a surprise dawn attack on the Union entrenchments, capturing Fort Stedman and the surrounding trenches. Brigadier-General John F. Hartranft, commanding the division, was instructed to place his troops to prevent a further breakthrough. Hartranft did so, then received permission to attempt to recapture the fort. The 200th advanced twice to the brow of a hill and was repulsed. By the time it was ready for a third try, the division was formed and advanced. As the line dashed forward, the color-bearer fell. Lieutenant-Colonel William H. H. McCall then seized the fallen banner and urged his troops forward, also calling upon someone else to take the flag. Private Levi A. Smith (Company E) sprang forward, took the flag, and carried it throughout the engagement. Later, soldiers counted nineteen bullet holes through the silk.[2]

Following the recapture of Fort Stedman, the regiment took part in the successful but bloody assault of April 2 on the Petersburg defenses. The division was among the first Union troops to enter the city, where the 200th's flag was displayed from the courthouse.[3] Thereafter, the regiment was stationed at Nottoway Court House for a short time, then was sent to Alexandria, where it took part in the Grand Review (May 23). It was mustered out of service a week later. The damaged state color was officially returned in 1866.

State Color
Maker: HB
1985.335

Notes

1 Frank Jordan to Commander, 206th Pennsylvania, October 7, 1864, in 206th Pennsylvania Regimental Descriptive, Letter, Order and Index Book, RG 94.

2 *O.R.* 46.1, p. 352; William F. Winkleman to parents, March 27, 1865; Bates 5: 521.

3 *Proceedings of the Reunion of the Third Division, Ninth Corps, Army of the Potomac, Held at York, Pa., March 25, 1891* (Harrisburg Publishing Company, 1892), p. 78.

Bibliography

Jones, A. Stokes. 1864 Letters. USAMHI, HbCWRT Collection.
Kerr, Jonathan W. Diary, 1864-65. Pennsylvania State Archives.
Smith, James A. "Getting into Petersburg." *NT*, May 12, 1887.
Winkleman, William F. Collection. USAMHI.

201st Infantry

State Color

The soldiers of this regiment were recruited in eight south-central counties, primarily those of Dauphin, Cumberland, and Franklin. Upon organization at Camp Curtin in late August 1864, the regiment was dispatched to Chambersburg. In mid-September, four companies were detached and sent to various sections of the Commonwealth on provost guard duty. The remainder of the 201st moved south into Virginia to patrol a section of the Manassas Gap Railroad. In November, the regiment was transferred to Alexandria, remaining here until sent to Fort Delaware in late May 1865. The regiment then reassembled at Harrisburg and was disbanded on June 21. The state color, delivered to the regiment by Horstmann Brothers sometime after September 21, 1864, was delivered to the state by Colonel F. Asbury Awl in time for the 1866 ceremony.[1]

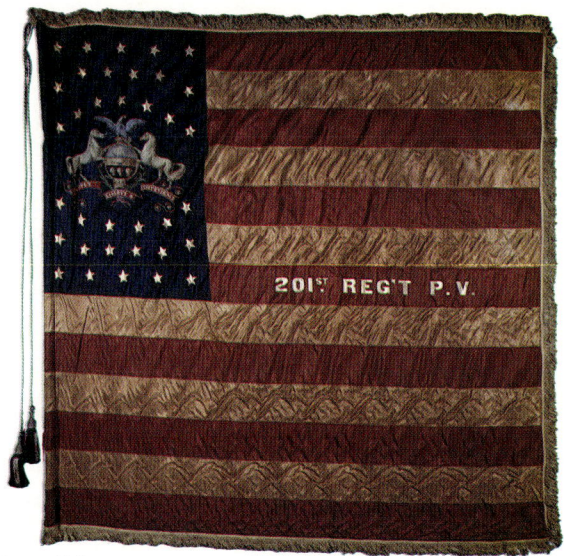

State Color
Maker: HB
1985.336

Regimental Color

The regiment received this color on September 13, 1864. A Private Smith of Company B was appointed color-bearer. The company muster roll in RG 94 has three Smiths listed. Without further information, it is impossible to discern which of the three was bearer.[2] This color was turned in to the state when the regiment went home. Over the years, the flag's identity was lost. Either of the two unidentified regimental colors (1985.173 and 1985.174) may be that carried by the 201st.

Notes

1 Awl to Adjutant-General A. L. Russell, June 2, 1866, RG 19.
2 "From the 201st Regiment," *Pennsylvania Daily Telegraph*, September 14, 1864.

Bibliography

Ashenfelter, Benjamin. Letters. USAMHI, HbCWRT Collection.
[Baum, Adam H.]. Series of letters in the *Pennsylvania Daily Telegraph*, September 3, 1864-February 15, 1865. Most of these letters are initialled "A.H.B., Company I."

Wagenseller, B. Meade. "Dr. Benjamin Franklin Wagenseller, Surgeon in the War." *Snyder County Historical Society Bulletin*, pages 835-39 of volume two reprint.

202nd Infantry

This one-year regiment was composed of soldiers from more than fourteen counties in the central and eastern portions of the state. After being organized at Camp Curtin on September 3, 1864, the 202nd was sent to Chambersburg. In late September, the regiment moved to Virginia and was assigned to guard a section of the Manassas Gap Railroad. The regiment performed this duty until the conclusion of Sheridan's Valley Campaign. During this time, several companies skirmished with Confederate guerrillas. The 202nd then was transferred to patrol a section of the Orange & Alexandria Railroad, remaining on this duty until May 1865. The regiment then returned to Pennsylvania, where its men were employed as guards in the anthracite coal region in the northeast. It was mustered out of service on August 3. The state color, finished by Horstmann Brothers in September 1864, was sent to the State Agency, where it yet remained in December.[1] The set of national and regimental colors remains undocumented.

State Color
Maker: HB
1985.337

National Color
1985.338

Regimental Color
Maker W. F. Scheible
1985.339

Notes

1 Colonel Frank Jordan to Commander, 202nd Pennsylvania, December 1, 1864, in Regimental Descriptive, Letter and Order Book RG 94.

Bibliography

Barton, Michael. " 'The Brave Two Hundred and Second': A Pennsylvania Sergeant's Poem on Mosby and the Railroads." *Pennsylvania History* 43 (1976): 139-45

Shedd, Nancy (editor). *Civil War Sketchbook by Henry Hudson, Civil War Diary by Philip Bolinger*. Latrobe: Foothills Lithograph Company for the Huntingdon County Historical Society, 1988.

203rd Infantry

State Color
National Color

Although composed of soldiers recruited in more than ten counties, the majority of this one-year regiment was from the counties of Lancaster and Luzerne. The 203rd was organized at Camp Cadwalader, near Philadelphia, in September 1864. It moved to Petersburg later that month and was assigned to the Second Division, Tenth Corps, Army of the James. A Horstmann-made state color was sent to the State Agency in early October and forwarded to the 203rd at an unspecified date. This flag does not seem to have survived, making further documentation impossible. The regiment apparently obtained the national color present in the collection at an early date in its history. Its battle damage attests to hard use.

At first, the 203rd was given the less-than-glamorous tasks of provost guard duty, picket duty, and escorting Rebel prisoners to the rear. Its first combat action occurred on October 27-28, when the corps skirmished with the enemy along the Darbytown Road outside the Richmond defenses. The regiment escaped with only eight men wounded. In the army reorganization of early December, the 203rd became a part of the new Twenty-fourth Corps.

Later in December, the regiment was part of the force sent to capture Fort Fisher, the principal fortification guarding the entrance to the port of Wilmington, North Carolina. The first attack was bungled by the Federal high command but in mid-January 1865 a second expedition was dispatched to attack the fort.

The 203rd also participated in this second expedition. It was in the assaulting column when the army attacked the fort on January 15. Led by Colonel John W. Moore, the 203rd rushed forward. Together with Colonel Galusha Pennypacker's 97th Pennsylvania, the 203rd was one of the first units to breach Fisher's sand walls. As the regiment struggled forward and captured the second traverse forming part of the fort's defenses, Private George Deitrich of Company F, carrying the "regimental flag," was shot down. Colonel Moore then seized the flag and led his men forward, only to fall dead, pierced by more than a dozen lead balls.[1]

Of the 525 officers and men in action at Fort Fisher, 40 were killed, 146 wounded, and one missing, for a total of 187, about thirty-five percent of the number engaged. Sergeant Joseph Potts of Company K wrote soon after the end of the fighting that "our colors were about one-fourth blown off by a piece of shell, and I counted twenty-eight bullet holes through the remainder."[2] Another account stated that more than sixty bullets and shell fragments perforated the flag.[3] More than twenty years after the war, Corporal William L. Parker recalled that he carried one of the flags after its bearer was shot down, and that over ninety bullets struck the flag and staff during the January 15 battle.[4] Since the state color is missing, the above accounts cannot be ascribed with accuracy to either flag.

After the capture of Fort Fisher, the 203rd took part in the brief campaign that resulted in the occupation of Wilmington on February 22. The regiment then participated in the victorious advance of the army into North Carolina until the war effectively

National Color
1985.341

Regimental Color
1985.340

closed in April. The 203rd was stationed in Raleigh on provost guard duty until it was mustered out of service on June 22.

Regimental Color

This color does not appear to contain any battle damage, so it must have been carried at some point after the Fort Fisher assault. This flag, together with the national color, was left in Major Lane's Philadelphia office when the regiment returned to Pennsylvania. There is no surviving evidence that either flag was included in the 1866 ceremony.

Color-Bearer

Sergeant John Lee of Company B was color-sergeant until detailed as orderly sergeant of Company D on October 12, 1864.[5]

Notes

1 Turner *NT* article, July 1, 1915.
2 "From the 203d Pennsylvania," *Lancaster Daily Evening Express*, January 30, 1865.
3 "The 203rd Pa. Regt.," *Philadelphia Inquirer*, February 7, 1865.
4 William L. Parker biography in *Pennsylvania Grit* (Williamsport), February 11, 1888.
5 General Orders #5, October 12, 1864, in Regimental Descriptive, Letter, Order and Index Book, RG 94.

Bibliography

Breneman, Amos. Letters, October 1864-April 1865. USAMHI, CWMisc Collection
Gingrich, David. Letters, January-June 1865. USAMHI, CWMisc Collection.
Lamoreux, Philip. "Opening the Gate at Fort Fisher." *NT*, March 25, 1915.
Noble, W. R. Papers. USAMHI.
Recollections in the Army of Virginia and North Carolina, by "Hermit" of the 203rd Pennsylvania Volunteers.... Wilkes-Barre: Printed on the Record of the Times Press, 1865.

Sourbeer, Franklin. "At Fort Fisher." *NT*, June 24, 1915.
____. "Fort Fisher." *NT*, April 3, 1890.
Stevens, Horace. Letters. Susquehanna County Historical Society.
Turner, William C. "Fort Fisher." *NT*, July 1, 1915.

5th Heavy Artillery (204th Regiment)

State Standard
Regimental Color

This artillery regiment was recruited primarily in southwestern Pennsylvania during the late summer of 1864. Upon organization at Pittsburgh, the regiment moved to Washington and was placed on garrison duty in some of the forts north of the Potomac River. Soon afterward, the 5th Artillery moved out to guard the Manassas Gap Railroad, and was engaged on several instances with Major John S. Mosby's southerners. In late October, the command returned to the Washington area and was stationed south of the Potomac for the remainder of its term of service. The regiment returned to Pittsburgh and was disbanded on June 30, 1865.

Little is known about the two flags in the state collection. The Evans & Hassall standard was sent to the

Regimental Color
Maker: HB
1985.343

State Standard
Maker: EH
1985.342

State Agency on October 5, 1864. Both flags were left in Pittsburgh when the regiment went home in 1865. The standard was present in the 1866 ceremony. At this time, Sergeants John W. Williams and Richard H. Jones of Company C acted as bearers.[1] Williams was still alive in 1914 and carried the regimental color during this ceremony.[2]

Notes

1 Colonel George S. Gallupe letter, July ?, 1866, RG 25.
2 Corporal James C. Hunter of Company C wrote his name on the staff label of the standard in 1914, so Williams carried the second flag.

Bibliography

Keill, Morris. Letters. USAMHI, CWMisc Collection.

Spher, Daniel. Letters. USAMHI, CWMisc Collection.

205th Infantry

State Color

Composed of troops recruited in Berks, Mifflin, Huntingdon, and Blair counties, the 205th Infantry was organized at Camp Curtin in early September 1864. The new command was sent to Washington, then on to City Point, the main supply base for the Federal armies operating in the Richmond-Petersburg area. After spending some time on guard duty here, the regiment was assigned to the Army of the James, performing twenty days of picket duty. At this time, the regiment was transferred to the Army of the Potomac and joined the new Third Division, Ninth Corps, consisting of six new Pennsylvania regiments. On October 23, Colonel Joseph A. Mathews presented a new state color to his command.[1]

Throughout the fall and winter, the division remained behind the lines at Petersburg as a reserve. Its first combat action occurred on March 25, 1865. When a Confederate sortie captured Fort Stedman, Brigadier-General John F. Hartranft led his division to plug the temporary gap in the line, then sent his troops surging forward to reclaim the fort. During this action, the 205th was kept as a reserve for most of the fighting and suffered few casualties. However, it lost 126 officers and men during the April 2 assault on the Petersburg defenses. Private Henry Naber of Company C, the color-bearer, fell wounded after planting the state color on the enemy's parapets.[2] Following Lee's surrender, the regiment moved north to Alexandria, took part in the Grand Review, and was mustered out of service on June 2. The state color was officially returned in 1866.

State Color
Maker: EH
1985.344

Notes

1 "Flag Presentation," *Huntingdon Globe*, November 16, 1864.
2 *O.R.* 46.1, p. 1038.

Bibliography

McClintick, D. R. "Fort Steadman, Va." *NT*, September 10, 1885.
Ross, George W. "The Nottaway Expedition." *NT*, February 9, 1911.
Whitaker, H. "Battle of Fort Stedman." *NT*, August 31, 1922.
_____. "The 207th Pa. at Stedman." *NT*, September 13, 1923.
Wolf, John G. "Captured Fort Mahone." *NT*, October 29, 1925.

206th Infantry

State Color
National Color

This regiment was recruited primarily in the counties of Indiana, Westmoreland, and Jefferson to serve for one year. The regiment formed near Pittsburgh in early September 1864, then moved directly to join the Army of the James near Richmond. Its eventual assignment was to the Twenty-fourth Corps. The 206th remained with this organization north of the James River, garrisoning a part of the siege line. During the final operations that led to the Confederate evacuation of Richmond and Petersburg, the 206th remained behind as a guard force, much to the disappointment of the officers and men. The regiment marched unopposed into Richmond, then moved to Lynchburg on guard duty for two weeks before returning to Richmond. It remained in this city until mustered out of service on June 26, 1865.

The Evans & Hassall State Color was sent to the State Agency, which forwarded the flag to the regiment on October 8, 1864.[1] Both flags were returned to Harrisburg in August 1865. The state color was present in the 1866 ceremony.

State Color
Maker: EH
1985.345

National Color
1985.346

Notes

1 Colonel Frank Jordan to Commander, 206th Pennsylvania, October 8, 1864, in Regimental Descriptive, Letter, Order, and Index Book, RG 94.

Bibliography

Fair, Daniel M. "Fall of Richmond." *NT*, April 8, 1920.
Ferguson, J. B. "Dealing With Bounty-jumpers and Deserters." *NT*, January 15, 1903.
____. "General Robert E. Lee's Parting With His Staff." *NT*, February 6, 1902.
Haddon, W.A. "First in Richmond." *NT*, October 24, 1912.
Keihl, Jacob. "First in Richmond." *NT*, January 2, 1913.
Work John S. Letter, November 17, 1864. Western Reserve Historical Society.

207th Infantry

State Color

Recruited primarily in eight north-central and south-central counties, the 207th Infantry was formed at Camp Curtin in early September 1864. It moved to City Point, Virginia, and was assigned initially to the Army of the James. Its first engagement with Rebel troops occurred on the evening of November 16, when a Southern foray attacked the picket line on the Bermuda Hundred front. By this time, the state color finished by Horstmann Brothers in late September seems to have been delivered to the regiment.

In late November, the regiment was transferred to the Army of the Potomac and placed in the Third Division, Ninth Corps, composed of six new Keystone regiments. The division remained in reserve until the February 1865 movement to Hatcher's Run. Although present on the field, Brigadier-General John F. Hartranft's troops were not engaged. On March 25, Confederate troops assaulted Fort Stedman just before daylight, seizing the fort and threatening to break through the Union line. Hartranft placed his troops in position to block further penetration, then pushed them forward to recapture the fort. According to one report, the colors of the 207th were the first to be placed on the fort. Five bullet holes were later counted in the silk banner.[1]

On April 2, the division attacked the enemy works opposite Fort Sedgwick. In this bloody assault, Color-Sergeant George T. Horning fell, pierced with seven lead bullets. When the flag fell, Sergeant Charles H. Ilgenfritz of Company E seized the banner and led the 207th over the enemy parapets. For his bravery this day, Ilgenfritz later received a Medal of Honor.[2] The loss in the regiment amounted to 185 officers and men.

Following the capture of Petersburg, the regiment eventually returned to Washington and was mustered out of service on May 13. The state color was officially returned in 1866.

State Color
Maker: EH
1985.347

Notes

1 "From the 207th Pa. Regiment," *Wellsboro Agitator*, April 5, 1865.
2 Bates 5: 672-73. Sergeant Horning was appointed color-bearer on January 26, 1865; see Special Orders #3, January 26, 1865, in Regimental Letter and Order Book, RG 94.

Bibliography

Brion, Daniel. Diary, September 8, 1864-June 6, 1865. USAMHI, CWTI Collection.
Cox, Robert C. *Memories of the War*. Wellsboro: Agitator Book Print, 1893.
Linck, J. H. "Death of Gen. Hill." *NT*, April 5, 1906.
Moore, A. J. "Fort Steadman." *NT*, April 9, 1885.
Riley, Lawrence. "Executions at Petersburg." *NT*, December 22, 1910.
Reynolds, W. B. "Raw Keystone Boys Took Fort Stedman." *NT*, June 2, 1904.
Smith, F. M. "Holding Line at Petersburg." *NT*, January 26, 1928.
_____. "Recapture of Fort Stedman." *NT*, March 25, 1920.
_____. "Thought Six-Shooters There. How Some Green Troops Acted at the Battle of Fort Stedman." *NT*, September 6, 1928.

208th Infantry

State Color
Regimental Color

Recruited in a range of counties from Bedford in the west to Union and Northumberland in the east, the 208th Infantry organized at Camp Curtin in mid-September 1864. The new unit was sent to Virginia and was at first assigned to the Army of the James before it was transferred to the new Third Division, Ninth Corps, Army of the Potomac.

The regiment first engaged the enemy at Fort Stedman on March 25, 1865, as Lee's troops attempted to break the Union siege of Petersburg. Then, on April 2, the 208th formed part of the assaulting column on the Confederate works at Petersburg. Here, the regiment suffered a loss of 47 soldiers. Following Lee's surrender, the regiment moved north to Alexandria, took part in the Grand Review (May 23), and was mustered out of service on June 1.

Evans & Hassall sent the 208th's state color to the State Agency in Washington in late September 1864. This flag, together with the blue infantry regimental color in the collection, were both sent to Harrisburg in June 1865. The state color was used in the 1866 ceremony.

On March 1865, Sergeant Joshua Heck of Company C was appointed color-bearer.[1] Another bearer, Corporal Jeremiah Long of Company D, was mortally wounded during the April 2 attack. According to a post-war account, Long fell just outside the enemy works. Major Alexander Bobb found him dying, with the shattered staff across his body. The dying Long asked the major not to let the flag die with him. Bobb had barely raised and planted the flag when a shell exploded in its folds, "broke the remnant of the staff into splinters and tore the flag into shreds."[2] This story, however, is not supported by the present condition of either flag.

State Color
Maker: EH
1985.349

Regimental Color
Maker: W. F. Scheible
1985.348

Notes

1 Special Orders #9, March 18, 1865, in Regimental Descriptive and Order Book, RG 94.

2 *Proceedings of the Reunion of the Third Division, Ninth Corps, Army of the Potomac, Held at York, Pa., March 25, 1891.* (Harrisburg: Harrisburg Publishing Company, 1892), pp. 105-6.

208th Infantry   511

Bibliography

Bessor, Phil. "He Delivered the Order to Col. Heintzelman." *NT,* August 12, 1886.

Billow, J. J. "Executions Before Petersburg." *NT,* January 16, 1916.

____. "In Front of Petersburg." *NT,* September 7, 1916.

____. "The 208th Pa. A Brief Sketch of Its History." *NT,* July 8, 1886.

Eckard, W. S. "The Petersburg Executions." *NT,* December 30, 1915.

Feeher, Joseph H. "Band of the 208th Regiment, P.V.I." *Snyder County Historical Society Bulletin*, pages 209-11 of volume one reprint.

Hoffman, J. F. "Waiting 41 Years to Find Out to Which Side the Scout Belonged." *NT,* July 12, 1906.

Huyette, M. C. "Capturing a Flag." *NT,* December 30, 1915.

____. "Fight at Fort Stedman." *NT,* February 29, 1912.

Inch, William. 1864-65 Diary. USAMHI, Save the Flags Collection.

McKeehan, F. M. "Death of Gen. Hill." *NT,* June 21, 1888.

209th Infantry

State Color
Regimental Color

This regiment was organized at Camp Curtin in mid-September 1864. The soldiers comprising the 209th were recruited in the counties of Cumberland, Adams, York, Franklin, Lebanon, Cambria, Huntingdon, Columbia, and Lehigh. Upon organization, the regiment was assigned to the Army of the James. The 209th remained with this army until mid-November, when it was assigned to the Ninth Corps, Army of the Potomac. A Horstmann-made state color was forwarded to the State Agency in early October. The regiment obtained the flag at some unspecified date later that fall.

During its stay with the Army of the James, the 209th was constantly engaged on the picket line. Its first major combat occurred on March 25, 1865, when the Third Division of the Ninth Corps was instrumental in the recapture of Fort Stedman. Here, the regiment sustained a loss of fifty-five officers and men.

On April 2, the 209th took part in the Ninth Corps assault on the Confederate works at Petersburg, suffering an additional sixty-two casualties. Following Lee's surrender, the regiment returned to Washington, marched in the Grand Review (May 23), then was mustered out of service on May 31.

The state color, together with the blue infantry regimental color, was turned over to the state when the 209th disbanded. Apparently, both were carried side by side in combat. Sergeants Edward J. Humphreys and Elbridge Stiles (both of Company C) were the color-bearers at the Fort Stedman fight.[1] The regimental color has the name of Thomas C. Culbertson (Company G) pencilled on the red scroll. The state color was present in the 1866 parade. A national color without a staff was also given to the state. Later annotations on the 1865 flag list indicate that this flag was placed on a staff in May 1866. It appears on lists as late as that compiled for the old flag room, then disappears.

State Color
Maker: HB
1985.351

Regimental Color
1985.350

Notes

1 *O.R.* 46.1, p. 349.

Bibliography

Caba, G. Craig (editor). "Incidents of the Grand Review at Washington." *Lincoln Herald* 82 (Spring 1980): 337-40.

Hunter, S. S. "The 209th Pa. at Fort Stedman." *NT*, August 23, 1923.

Jamison, I. J. "Fort Stedman." *NT*, September 26, 1912.

Wert, J. Howard. Manuscript Regimental History. Muhlenberg College.

210th Infantry

State Color
National Color

Composed of recruits from more than sixteen central Pennsylvania counties, the 210th Infantry was organized at Camp Curtin in late September 1864. Soon thereafter, the regiment was assigned to the Third Brigade, Second Division, Fifth Corps, Army of the Potomac. A Horstmann-made state color was sent to the State Agency in Washington on October 3. It was forwarded to the regiment at some unspecified date.

The 210th was under fire at the Boydton Plank Road (October 27-28) but suffered negligible losses. In early December, it participated in the Fifth Corps raid south along the Weldon Railroad. Its first significant battle action occurred on February 5-6, 1865, at Hatcher's Run, also known as Dabney's Mills. The regiment suffered heavy casualties on March 31 during the fighting on the White Oak Road (also known as Gravelly Run). It also fought at Five Forks on April 1.

National Color
1985.352

State Color
Maker: HB
1985.353

Following Lee's surrender, the regiment moved to Washington, took part in the Grand Review (May 23), then was mustered out of service on May 30. Both flags were sent to Harrisburg; the state color was included in the 1866 parade.

Sergeant Manaris Humelstine of Company D was a color-bearer until relieved of this duty on April 18, 1865. The sergeant had straggled during recent marches. He was replaced by Sergeant Josiah Kissinger of Company H.[1]

When the flags were moved in 1914, one of the spearpoints was inadvertently mislaid and was not found until 1930. At that time, the adjutant-general's office sent the relic to the Secretary of Property and Supplies, with the understanding that the finial would be rethreaded and placed on the flag when Property and Supplies would open Case #5.[2] Both flags of the 210th have finials. That attached to the staff of the national color has a longer thread and is probably the mislaid spearpoint that was attached sometime after March 1930.

Notes

1 Regimental Order #31, April 18, 1865, in Regimental Descriptive, Letter and Order Book, RG 94.

2 See the following letters, all in the Pennsylvania State Archives, RG 20, Deputy Secretary, Property and Supplies, Historical File. Beary's letter is also in RG 19, General Correspondence File of the Adjutant-General's Office: F. D. Beary to B. E. Taylor, February 26, 1930; George R. Hoyer to George P. DeHaven, February 28, 1930; and B. E. Taylor to F. D. Beary, March 1, 1930.

Bibliography

Hudson, Hosea. "Saw Differently." *NT*, June 27, 1895. (Hatcher's Run)
Mellan, J. E. "Very Youthful Warrior." *NT*, February 4, 1904.

211th Infantry

State Color

Comprised of recruits from more than ten western counties, the 211th Infantry was formed at Camp Reynolds near Pittsburgh in mid-September 1864. Four days after being formed, the regiment arrived at Bermuda Hundred and was assigned to the Army of the James. The regiment remained on picket duty here until late November, when it was transferred to the Army of the Potomac. During this time period, a Horstmann-made state color was sent to the State Agency and forwarded to the regiment at some unspecified date.

When the 211th joined the Army of the Potomac, it was assigned to the new Third Division, Ninth Corps, composed of six Pennsylvania regiments led by Brigadier-General John F. Hartranft. Throughout the winter of 1864-65, this division remained in reserve behind the trench lines. The unit participated in the February 1865 movement to Hatcher's Run but was not engaged in combat.

On March 25, Confederate troops attacked and captured Fort Stedman. Hartranft's division was encamped nearby and quickly moved to halt a further breakthrough. When the general had his troops arrayed for a counterattack, he sent his largely untried recruits forward. Hartranft used the 211th to draw initial enemy fire as the other five regiments massed for the attack. Fortunately, the regiment suffered slight loss during the charge. Color-Sergeant William R. Moore of Company D carried the state color during this and all subsequent engagements.[1]

During the April 2 assault on the Petersburg fortifications, the 211th suffered 135 casualties. Sergeant Moore was cited in the official reports for his gallantry that day. He was the second color-bearer to unfurl his flag in Petersburg.[2] Following the capture of Petersburg and Lee's subsequent surrender a week later, the 211th returned to Washington, took part in the Grand Review (May 23) and was mustered out of service on June 2. The state color was returned in 1866.

State Color
Maker: HB
1985.354

Notes

1 *Proceedings of the Reunion of the Third Division, Ninth Corps, Army of the Potomac, Held at York, Pa., March 25, 1891* (Harrisburg: Harrisburg Publishing Company, 1892), p. 133.

2 O.R. 46.1, p. 1038.

Bibliography

Anderson, L. M. Papers. Pennsylvania State Archives.
Baldridge, David. Letters. Pennsylvania State University.
Beam, Abram. "The 211th Pa. Heard From." *NT*, July 21, 1887.
"Dad." "The Charge at Fort Steadman." *NT*, October 6, 1910.
Holden, A. M. "Lincoln at Petersburg." *NT*, February 7, 1924.
____. "President Lincoln Acted as Guide for Recruit in Capitol." *NT*, February 1, 1940.
____. "Saw Lincoln." *NT*, August 10, 1916.
Miller, Samuel K. Letters. Crawford County Historical Society.
Weimer, Thomas W. Typescript diary. In Regimental Papers, RG 19.

6th Heavy Artillery (212th Regiment)

State Standard
Regimental Color

This heavy artillery regiment was organized in mid-September 1864, and consisted of soldiers from a dozen western counties. Upon formation, the regiment moved to Washington for about two weeks. Then it was assigned to patrol duty along the Orange & Alexandria Railroad between Alexandria and Manassas. The 6th Artillery remained on this duty until mid-November, when it returned to the Washington defenses. It was stationed at several forts south of the Potomac River until mustered out of service on June 17, 1865.

Regimental Color
1985.35

State Standard
Maker: EH
Size: 39 1/2 x 39 3/4
1985.356

The regiment carried at least three flags during its term of service. The state standard was sent to the State Agency in Washington on October 5, 1864, and forwarded to the regiment at an unspecified date. When the unit disbanded, it also turned over to the state a set of national and regimental colors. The regimental color has survived but the national color seems to have disappeared, although it may be one of the unidentified colors in the collection. The standard was present in the 1866 ceremony.

Bibliography

"Captain Daniel Gravatt's Company D, 6th Regiment, Heavy Artillery." *Tarentum Times* 5 (September 1976): 77-79
Milligan G. K. "Draped for Lincoln." *NT*, February 20, 1913.

"Sixth Pa. Heavy Artillery." *NT*, October 28, 1915.
Sober, Daniel. Diary, September 3, 1864-January 8, 1865. USAMHI, CWMisc Collection.

213th - 215th Infantry

These three regiments, all raised under the auspices of the Union League of Philadelphia, were the last regiments recruited in the Commonwealth. The 213th and 214th were formed in March 1865, while the 215th was not organized until April 21. None of these units saw any combat. The 213th was stationed at Frederick and Annapolis, Maryland, on guard duty for a month, then was concentrated in the Washington defenses, where it remained until mustered out of service on November 18. The 214th was at first sent to the Shenandoah Valley for similar duty, then was transferred to Washington and Annapolis. The regiment was mustered out on March 21, 1866. The 215th went to Dover, Delaware, and performed duty throughout this state and the eastern shore of Maryland until discharged on July 31, 1865.

Because of these regiments' limited service, documentation on their flags is equally limited. The 213th apparently never obtained its state color, which was still in the State Agency in February 1866. It was included in the 1866 parade. The national and regimental colors were left at Camp Cadwalader outside Philadelphia when the regiment was mustered out of service.

The 214th's state color was also sent to the State Agency. Colonel David B. McKibbin recalled that his command did not obtain the flag until late in its term

National Color, 213th Infantry
1985.358

State Color, 213th Infantry
Maker: EH
1985.357

Regimental Color, 213th Infantry
1985.359

213th-215th Infantry 519

State Color, 214th Infantry
Maker: EH
1985.360

National Color, 214th Infantry
1985.362

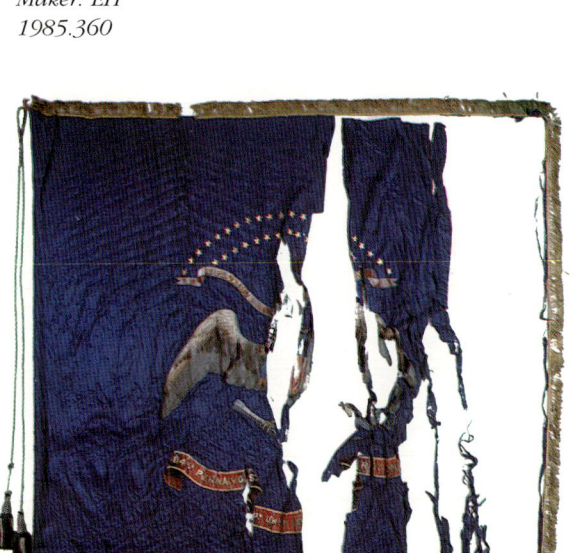

Regimental Color, 214th Infantry
1985.361

Regimental Color, 215th Infantry
1985.363

of service. Lieutenant-Colonel William H. Harrison apparently took this flag along with him, but Colonel McKibbin took possession of it in time for the 1866 ceremony.[1] The national and regimental colors are possibly those presented by the Union League on April 8, 1865.[2] During the regiment's service, Sergeant Gabriel L. Todd of Company C was the 214th's primary color-sergeant. He was appointed on April 28, 1865, and apparently served as such until mustered out of service.[3] On September 4, 1865, Sergeant Joshua W. Knight, also of Company C, was appointed another bearer.[4] This latter appointment may indicate that the Union League presented a single flag, with the second being obtained in September 1865.

The 215th Infantry was not issued a state color. The regimental color in the collection, together with two guidons, was left at Camp Cadwalader when the regiment went home. The regimental color was included in the 1866 parade. Sergeant John H. Engle of Company B was appointed color-bearer on May 19, 1865.[5]

Notes

1 D. B. McKibbin to Adjutant-General A. L. Russell, June 3, 1866, RG 19.

2 "Departure of the 8th Union League Regiment," *Philadelphia Public Ledger*, April 10, 1865.

3 Todd's name appears as color-bearer in Special Order #7, April 28, 1865; and in Special Order #56, September 4, 1865, both in Regimental Letter, Indorsement, Furlough, and Order Book, RG 94.

4 Special Order #56 quoted above in Note 3.

5 Special Order #4, May 19, 1865, in Regimental Consolidated Morning Report, Letter, Order, and Miscellaneous Book, RG 94.

Bibliography

No letter or diary collections for any of these regiments have come to the author's attention, nor are there any published materials.

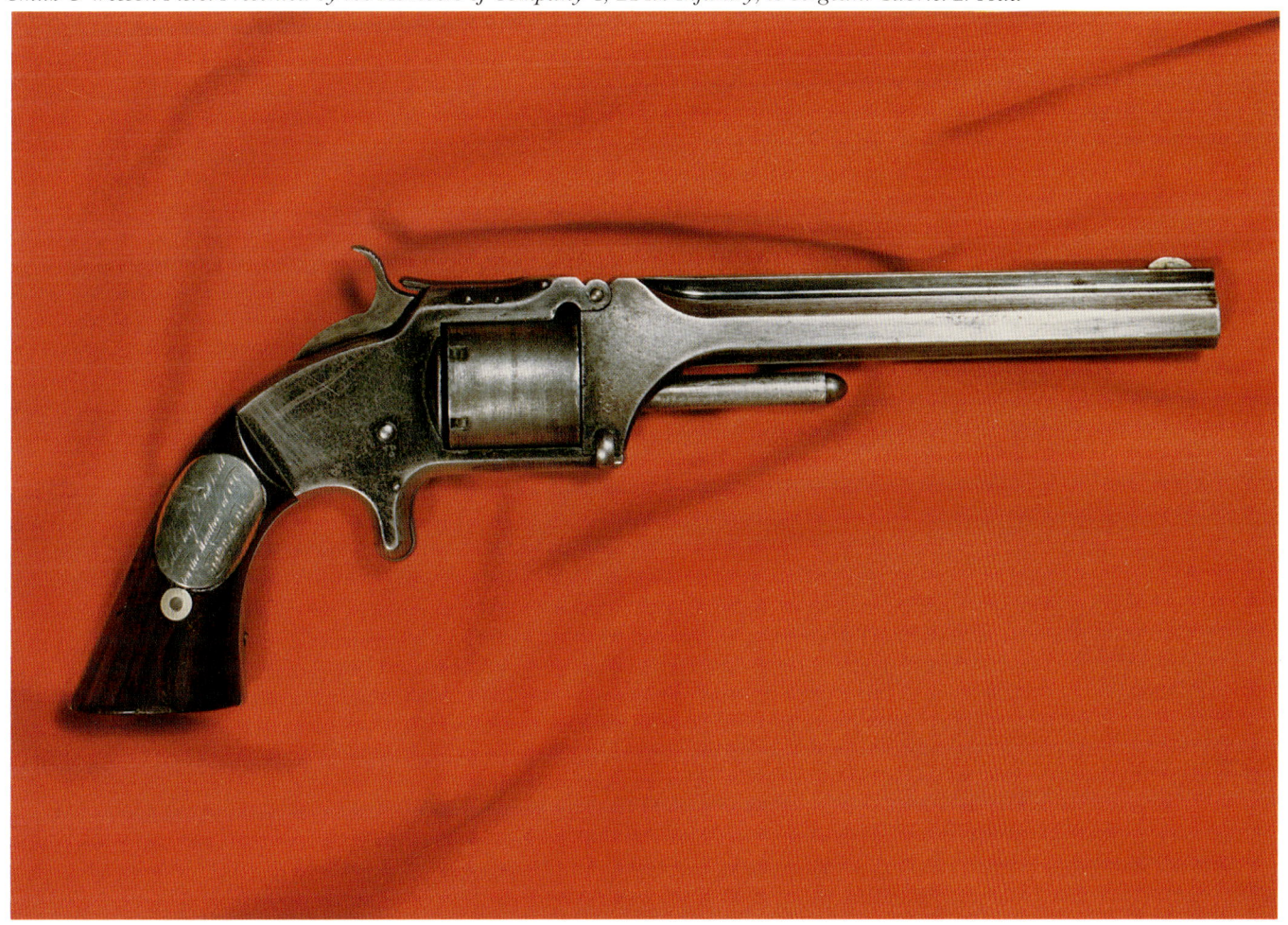

Smith & Wesson Pistol Presented by the Members of Company C, 214th Infantry, to Sergeant Gabriel L. Todd

Independent Batteries

In addition to the six artillery regiments recruited throughout the Commonwealth, Pennsylvania raised ten independent batteries. Nine were lettered "A" through "I" while the tenth was known as the "Keystone Battery." Batteries A through F served from 1861 to 1865, Batteries G and H from 1862 to 1865, while Battery I served during the final two years of the conflict. The Keystone Battery had two terms of service; the first from August 1862 to August 1863, the second for the hundred days' service in the summer and fall of 1864.

The state did not provide battery guidons for any of these independent units. Such flags as were carried were obtained either through local presentation or by federal requisition. Few guidons survive. A federal guidon for Independent Battery F (Robert Hampton's from Pittsburgh) is illustrated on page 24 of Volume One. The War Library in Philadelphia owns a guidon used by Independent Battery I (John I. Nevin's from Philadelphia). Finally, a collector owns a guidon of the Keystone Battery. It is not known in which enlistment this flag was used. There seems to be no surviving documentation for any of these guidons.

Keystone Battery Guidon

Battery D Guidon

Independent Battery D, captained by George W. Durell, contained recruits from Berks and Bucks counties. The battery was originally intended as an integral part of the 104th Infantry, but was soon detached and served its term of enlistment as one of the batteries attached to the Ninth Corps. This battery was presented with three guidons during its service. The first, pictured in the battery history, was presented by the citizens of Reading sometime in late 1861. A replacement, the gift of a number of Bucks County ladies, was presented to the battery on November 23, 1863, while the unit was stationed at Covington, Kentucky.[1] A third guidon was sent to the battery in December 1864 by Anthony B. Bitting.[2] None of these guidons seems to have survived to the present.

Captain James M. Knap commanded Independent Battery E, recruited in Pittsburgh and Philadelphia. This battery also received at least one guidon through local presentation. Captain Knap resigned in May 1863. When the re-enlisted veterans of his old battery came home on furlough in early 1864, he presented them with a new guidon. The February 24 ceremony took place at Pittsburgh's Washington Hall on Reuben Street. The guidon was some type of national flag, with "Knap's Pa. Battery, Presented by Citizens of Allegheny, February, 1864," painted in gold on the stripes. Names of ten battles also decked the flag. A streamer painted with "God and Liberty" and a silver bugle, was attached to the staff. This guidon was carried until late 1864. The batterymen had promised to return the banner when the storm of battle rendered it unfit for use. On November 22, 1864, the *Philadelphia Inquirer* reported: "The condition has now been fulfilled." The guidon's present location is not known.[3]

Notes

1 Cuffel, pp. 164-66.
2 Letter in *Bucks County Intelligencer*, December 20, 1864.
3 "An Elegant Flag," *Pittsburgh Gazette*, February 13, 1864; "A Series of Presentations," *Ibid.*, February 25, 1864; "Knap's Battery," *Pittsburgh Evening Chronicle*, February 25, 1864; "A Tattered Relic of Battle," *Philadelphia Inquirer*, November 22, 1864.

Bibliography

Independent Battery D

Cuffel, Charles A. *Durell's Battery in the Civil War (Independent Battery D, Pennsylvania Volunteer Artillery),* . . . . Philadelphia: Craig, Finley & Company, 1900, 1903.

Ganster, W. A. "With Durell's Battery in Front of Petersburg." *Grand Army Scout and Soldiers Mail*, November 24, 1883.

Rhoads, Samuel H. *Oration Delivered by Samuel H. Rhoads, Late Captain Commanding Battery "D" Pennsylvania Volunteer Artillery, from October 4, 1864, to June 13, 1865, at the Dedication of the Monument Erected by the State of Pennsylvania on the Battle Field of Antietam, to Commemorate the Battle Record and Services of Durell's Battery "D" Pennsylvania Volunteer Artillery, from September 24th, 1861, to June 13th, 1865.* Philadelphia, 1904.

Independent Battery E

Atwell, Henry. "Peachtree Creek." *NT*, November 4, 1926.
Christy, Washington. "Peach Tree Creek." *NT*, May 12, 1887.
Cochran, James H. "Wauhatchie." *NT*, March 28, 1907.
McCluskey, Sylvester W. "Borrowing Horses. Some Experiences in Georgia by a Lieutenant in Knap's Battery." *NT*, August 5, 1909.
____. "Knap's Battery Too." *NT*, May 13, 1909. (Kolb's Farm, GA)
McGowan, John C. Letters. USAMHI, CWMisc Collection.
Nichol, David. Papers. USAMHI, HbCWRT Collection.
Sims, Daniel. "Could Not Have Been. A Knap's Batteryman Explains About Peach Tree Creek." *NT*, January 27, 1898.
____. "Killing of Gen. Polk." *NT*, April 23, 1903.
____. "Saw Polk Killed." *NT*, December 17, 1903.

Independent Battery F

Clark, William. *History of Hampton Battery F Independent Pennsylvania Light Artillery, Organized at Pittsburgh, Pa., October 8, 1861, Mustered Out in Pittsburgh, June 26, 1865.* Akron: Werner Company, 1909.
Creese, S. J. "Gettysburg." *NT*, February 5, 1891.
____. "That Abandoned Battery Again." *NT*, July 10, 1890. (Winchester, July 24, 1864).
Marshall, George V. "Hampton's Battery." *NT*, July 18, 1901.
Workmaster, Wallace F. (editor). "The Frank H. Shiras Letters, 1862-1865." *Western Pennsylvania Historical Magazine* 40 (1957): 163-90.

Independent Battery G

Sanderlin, Walter S. (editor). "Corporal Crumrine Goes to War." *Topic: A Review of the Liberal Arts* 2 (Fall 1961): 48-64.
Wilson, W. Emerson (editor). *Fort Delaware Journal: The Diary of a Yankee Private, Alexander J. Hamilton, 1862-1865.* Wilmington, DE: Fort Delaware Society, 1981.

Independent Battery H

Friley, T. M. "Battery H." *NT*, April 29, 1915.

1863 Militia Colors

During the emergency occasioned by General Lee's invasion of south-central Pennsylvania, the Commonwealth raised and equipped 36 regiments, 5 battalions, and 12 companies of infantry, 2 battalions and 16 companies of cavalry, and 10 batteries of artillery. It is probable that most of these units received flags, either by presentation or by government requisition. Only one identified militia color seems to have survived, a regulation blue infantry regimental color utilized by the 51st Militia (also known as the 2nd Coal Trade Regiment). Here follows a list of presented flags as identified in contemporary sources.

Regimental Color, 51st Militia

20th Militia

On July 26, Governor Curtin presented a "stand of regimental colors" to this unit, which was then stationed at Fort Washington, across the Susquehanna River from Harrisburg.[1]

32nd & 33rd Militias

These two units, known respectively as the "Grey Reserves" and "Blue Reserves," returned to Philadelphia on the afternoon of July 27. Both regiments marched to Independence Square, where, in consecutive ceremonies, each unit received a set of national and regimental flags. The national colors contained the inscriptions "Carlisle" and "Hagerstown," while the regimental colors had "The City of Philadelphia to the Blue [Grey] Reserves."[2] On August 3, friends presented the men of Company D, 32nd Militia, with a "handsome flag."[3]

34th Militia

This regiment received a "splendid regimental flag" from the ladies of the Nineteenth Ward in Philadelphia. The presentation took place on July 23.[4]

45th Militia

Mr. J. R. Fry presented this Philadelphia regiment with a "beautiful stand of colors" on July 7. Mr. Fry acted on behalf of the Union League, which sponsored the mustering of this unit.[5]

46th Militia

A deputation of Huntingdon ladies presented a national flag to this unit, recruited primarily in Blair and Huntingdon counties. The July 23 presentation took place at the regiment's Philadelphia camp.[6]

59th Militia

Another Union League regiment, the 59th received a "silk flag" from the ladies of Philadelphia's Eighteenth Ward. The ceremony took place in front of the League's headquarters on August 25.[7]

Dana Cavalry Troop

On July 23, this cavalry company received a "beautiful guidon" from Mrs. General Napoleon J. T. Dana.[8]

Guss's Battery

Known as the "Chester County Artillery," this artillery unit received a flag from a group of West Chester ladies. Upon disbanding, the batterymen donated the guidon to Lieutenant William E. Moore.[9]

Notes

1 "Gov. Curtin and the Militia of the State," *Philadelphia Inquirer*, July 28, 1863.

2 "Return of 'Emergency' Regiments," *Philadelphia Daily Evening Bulletin*, July 28, 1863.

3 "Flag Presentation," *Ibid.*, August 4, 1863.

4 Letter in July 28, 1862, edition of the *Norristown Herald*.

5 "Military Matters," *Philadelphia Daily Evening Bulletin*, July 7, 1863.

6 "Flag Presentation," *Huntingdon Journal and American*, August 5, 1863; "Flag Presentation in the City of Philadelphia," *Huntingdon Globe*, August 5, 1863.

7 Captain C. H. Carson to officers of Union League, August 24, 1863, in "Flag Presentations" folder in Archives of the Union League.

8 "Presentation of a Flag to the Dana Troop," *Philadelphia Inquirer*, July 24, 1863.

9 "Flag Presentation," *West Chester Village Record*, August 29, 1863.

Bibliography

Beck, Harry R. (editor). "Some Leaves from a Civil War Diary." *Western Pennsylvania Historical Magazine* 42 (1959): 363-82. (51st regiment)

Blackmar, H. C. "Reminded of Morgan's Raid." *NT*, August 21, 1924. (58th regiment)

Gotwald, W. H. "Checked Early's March." *NT*, March 28, 1918. (26th regiment)

Graham, D. F. "Pennsylvania Emergency Men." *NT*, April 25, 1907. (26th regiment)

Hall, C. R. "Services Not Recognized." *NT*, August 2, 1923. (57th regiment)

Lower, J. P. S. "The Tablet at Oyster Point." *NT*, November 13, 1913. (Spencer Miller's battery)

Vaughn, R. B. "The Pennsylvania Militia." *NT*, April 1, 1915. (28th regiment)

Wallace, William W. "War Reminiscences of a Presbyterian Elder." *The Presbyterian*, June 14, 21, 1911. (Huntingdon County)

Miscellaneous Flags

When the flags were collected at the end of the war, the identities of a few were lost. Two state colors were marked as "unidentified." One (1985.175) has "E&H" engraved on the finial base. The only missing Evans & Hassall-made state color in the collection is that of the 174th Infantry. The single unknown national color was heavily souvenired. It is missing both the canton and

Unidentified State Color
1985.177

Unidentified Regimental Color
Maker: EH
1985.174

Unidentified National Color
1985.176

the regimental number on the center red stripe. Three blue infantry regimental colors without regimental numbers were turned over to the state. Based upon archival evidence, one was identified as belonging to the 81st Infantry and is included in Volume One with that regiment. Of the remaining two, 1985.173 is pictured in the first volume, while the second (1985.174) appears here. One of these two flags was probably used by the 201st Infantry. This unit turned in a regimental color that was apparently unmarked and its identity soon was lost.

Since the inception of the flag program, two additional blue regimental colors have been added to the collection. The first, donated by Dennis Kelly, came from the Zook GAR Post in Norristown. The second was donated by the Ezra S. Griffin Camp #8, Sons of Union Veterans, Scranton. Both colors cannot be ascribed to any units.

In 1922, Northumberland resident Milton MacPherson sent a flag to the state adjutant-general's office. MacPherson was a veteran who served in Company B, 5th Reserves, then in Company C of the 191st Infantry (2nd Veteran Reserves). The flag was the triangular brigade headquarters standard of the Third Brigade, Second Division, Fifth Army Corps. The flag was installed in Case #3 in the Rotunda sometime afterward.

Unidentified Regimental Color
1986.001

Unidentified Regimental Color
1988.002

Unidentified State Color
1985.175

Designating Flag of 3rd Brigade, 2nd Division, 5th Corps
Maker: EH
Size: 71 1/2 x 88
1985.179

Miscellaneous Flags

PART III

Chapter V
Corrections to Volume One

Listed below are several errors in volume one. Some are typographical, while others are factual. In attempting to condense regimental histories, I followed Bates much of the way, and it appears that I repeated some of Bates's mistakes. I am grateful to astute readers kind enough to share with me such inconsistencies they noticed.

Page	Column	Line	Correction
xii	2	25-26	Jackson's rank should be Lieutenant-General.
20	1	22	Gibbon's rank should be Major-General.
35	2	4	Read "Company C" for "Company A."
45	1	35	Ord's column actually attacked the Chaffin's Farm-Chaffin's bluff area of the Southern line. The 6th USCT was attached to Birney's column for this operation.
46	2	43	Date is September 29, 1864.
48	1	20	The Confederate general's name is spelled Finegan.
48	1	18-19	Read "Seymour's" for "Truman's."
64	1	Bibliography	Delete the Cruishank entry.
82	1	15-16	Porter's rank was Brigadier-General.
88	2	36	Read "unsuccessful" for "unsucessful."
117	2	9-10	The fight at Middleburg occurred on June 19. Aldie took place on June 21; the 1st Cavalry covered the Union withdrawl on June 22.
118	1	16	There seems to have been no fighting at Reams' Station on July 12—Bates is apparently in error.
129	1	37-38	Read "Totopotomoy Creek" for "Totopotomy River."
130	1	flag photo	Maker is EH.
136	2	32-33	Read "Department of *the* Ohio" for "Department of Ohio."
154	1	7	Read "Chaffin's Bluff" for "Chapin's Bluff."
159-60		flag photos	The images of the First State Color and Second State Color were reversed. The photo on page 159 is that of the Second Color, while the first appears on page 160.
163	1	1	Bates was apparently in error about the action at Spring Hill on December 8; there seems to have been no fighting there on that day.
166	1	31-32	Kelly's Ford took place on March 17, 1863.
166-67		flag photos	The images of the First and Second State Standards are reversed. The First appears on page 167; the Second is that on page 166.
169-70		flag photos	The First State Color appears on page 170, while the Second appears on page 169. Again, the images are reversed.
170	1	20	The bulk of the Sixth Corps protected the army's *left* flank at Gettysburg.
177	1	19	Read "Oak Grove" for "Seven Oaks."
180	2	17-18	Middleburg was fought on June 19.
182	1	21	Wade Hampton's cavalry did not make this attack. It was the Holcombe Legion, Colonel W. P. Shingler commanding.
191	1	19	Read "May 27" for "May 25."
205	2	29-30	Read "Richmond and Petersburg Railroad" for "Petersburg and Weldon Railroad."
209	2	13	The correct date is November 30.
231	2	14	Read "extensive" for "extensived."
236	1	21	Milroy's rank was Brigadier-General.

Corrections to Volume One 531

Chapter VI
Addenda to Volume One

Pre-Civil War Pennsylvania Military Flags

Since the publication of Volume One, additional pre-war militia flags have come to light. In 1988, the Ezra S. Griffin Camp #8, Sons of Union Veterans, Scranton, donated three flags to the Capitol Preservation Committee. Among these is a state militia regimental color. This flag consists of a blue field with a centered state arms. In the upper left corner is a circle of twenty-four six-pointed stars surrounding a cartouche inscribed with the word "Pennsylvania." The number of stars date this flag from 1822-1836. According to a Scranton newspaper article, this militia color was used by a local company that helped quell an 1851 railroad riot near Scranton.[1]

Pennsylvania Militia Color, 109th Infantry 1985.199

Pre-War Pennsylvania Militia Color, 1822-36 Period 1988.001

A second militia color was found wrapped around one of the two flagstaffs labelled as 109th Infantry. This is a national color. The canton contains a circle of stars that originally contained twenty-one six-pointed stars, which would date the flag 1819-1820. The cartouche within the star formation is inscribed "109th Regt. Pennsylvania." The 109th Militia was a Montgomery County unit. There is no further information available about this flag. It was apparently included in the 1866 return list. The author of this book finds it hard to believe that a Philadelphia Civil War regiment would carry an old militia color during its term of service. Thus, this flag must remain a mystery unless some new information can be located to ascertain its history.

Finally, when the War Department returned the captured flags in 1905, it sent to Pennsylvania a thirty-two star national color. The canton included an eagle crouching on a shield, together with a scroll inscribed "Logan Guards." The War Department, which numbered this flag "108," listed it as "U.S. Flag. Probably belongs to the State of Illinois, Inscribed 'Logan Guards,' no history."[2] However, the War Department assumed that the Logan Guards flag belonged to

National Color Inscribed "Logan Guards" 1985.008

532   *Advance the Colors!*

Pennsylvania because Company A, 46th Pennsylvania, was the old Logan Guards. Adjutant-General Thomas J. Stewart sent a letter of inquiry about this flag to the First Defenders Association. In reply, H. A. Eisenbise remarked that the Logan survivors could not recall ever having this national flag. The writer suggested that this flag was inscribed in honor of Major-General John A. Logan of Illinois. Nothing seems to have been done to follow up this letter. The flag remained in state custody and was carried by a Logan survivor in the 1914 parade. To this day its history remains suspect.[3]

Three-Month Regiments

On April 20, 1861, the Excelsior Band of Huntingdon presented a "beautiful flag" to the men of Company D, 5th Pennsylvania.[4] On the afternoon of May 18, the citizens of Philadelphia's Fourteenth Ward presented a "handsome silk flag" to the 20th Regiment.[5] No further information has been located about either flag.

23rd Infantry

(page 65): At Fair Oaks, Lieutenant Henry A. Marchant of Company F was the man who retrieved the fallen color after Sergeant Bolton was shot down.[6]

Corporal Charles J. Barger, Co.B, 26th Infantry
His Discharge Certificate Indicates He was a Color-Bearer

Remnant of Regimental Color, 29th Infantry
Maker: HB

(page 66): The flag purchased with funds raised from the December 1863 ball was presented to the regiment on January 29, 1864. Former Governor James Pollock made the presentation, which took place in Philadelphia.[7]

According to the August 23, 1861, edition of the *Philadelphia Daily Evening Bulletin*, friends of Colonel Birney presented a "set of regimental colors" to the 23rd on August 21.

27th Infantry

On June 11, 1861, Mr. Moses A. Dropsie presented "state and national flags" to the regiment. The ceremony took place at Franklin Square in Philadelphia.[8]

28th Infantry

(page 72): At Antietam, Private Gustavus Hoffman (Company P) was one of the bearers slain that day.[9]

(page 74): On July 22, 1861, a group of friends arrived at the 28th's camp in Oxford Park to present a "beautiful silk flag, with staff and eagle."[10]

29th Infantry

(page 78): After the war, Colonel William Rickards left Philadelphia and moved to Franklin, Venango

County. The colonel toted along with him the remnant of one of the 29th's colors. It is a blue infantry regimental color, with enough of it left to identify Horstmann Brothers as the maker. The remnant of the red scroll indicates that this color was the gift of a group of Philadelphia ladies. It is quite probable that this is the flag presented to the regiment on June 4, 1863. In 1915, George Rickards, one of the colonel's sons, had the flag framed and donated it to the Oil City Armory, where it remains today.[11]

30th Infantry (1st Reserves)

According to the September 30, 1862, edition of the *West Chester Village Record*, William H. Bradley of Company G was a color-bearer earlier that year. Bradley was captured at some point during the Seven Day's Battles. Bates (1: 567) does not indicate when he was taken prisoner.

31st Infantry (2nd Reserves)

(page 89): The May 29, 1861, presentation is described as a "silk national color."[12]

Sergeant William Derr, 2nd Reserves, Inscribed His Name on This U.S. Belt Buckle

32nd Infantry (3rd Reserves)

Private David Jones (Company K) retrieved the fallen colors of the regiment at New Market Cross Roads (June 30, 1862). Jones recorded that this act was the most important of his army career. In his brief recount of his service record, Jones wrote "Fland's Farm"; the interpretation as Frayser's Farm (New Market Cross Roads) is the author's.[13]

At Second Manassas, Color-Sergeant William F. Roberts of Company C was wounded on August 30, 1862.[14]

33rd Infantry (4th Reserves)

(page 93): Color-Sergeant Jacob Wheeler of Company C carried the flag at Antietam. He was badly

Corporal A. J. Bisset and the First State Color of the 8th Reserves

bruised when the staff was shot in two by a cannon projectile. The damage to the staff, illustrated here, thus happened at Antietam.[15]

34th Infantry (5th Reserves)

(page 95): In a short autobiographical sketch, Captain Thomas Chamberlin described the action at New Market Cross Roads as follows:

"Mine was the 'color' company, and three color-bearers (Serg't. Michael Leary, Corporal Joseph C. Carson and another corporal, whose name has escaped me) were shot down in quick succession. As all of the color-bearers were gone, I took the colors myself and bore them some distance; but being badly 'winded' by the long charge over loose earth, I was compelled to put them in the hands of a private soldier."[16]

37th Infantry (8th Reserves)

(page 102): During the fighting at Antietam, Corporal George Horton of Company F was the color-bearer. A rifle bullet broke his ankle, but Horton did not relinquish the colors until killed by a bullet in his head. Lieutenant Lewis B. Waltz of Company F rescued the fallen banner as the regiment fell back.[17]

38th Infantry (9th Reserves)

In May 1861, a group of Meadville ladies made a silk flag for the men of Company F, the "Meadville Volunteers." Mr. James E. McFarland was to journey to Camp Wilkins (near Pittsburgh) to make the formal presentation.[18]

39th Infantry (10th Reserves)

Sometime in May 1861, the ladies of Canonsburg presented a silk flag, "their own proud gift and handiwork," to Company D, the "Jefferson Light Guards."[19]

41st Infantry (12th Reserves)

When the "Easton Guards" departed for the war on May 6, 1861, a group of ladies presented the company with a silk flag. This unit became Company E of the 12th Reserves.[20]

1st Cavalry (44th Regiment)

In September 1861, Company B, the "Lower Merion Troop" from Montgomery County, received a "beautiful national flag" from the ladies of that township. This flag was sent to the regiment's camp near Washington.[21]

Colonel Frank Jordan of the State Agency
Photographed by Charles Cohill's "Root Gallery" in Philadelphia

During the fighting on April 5, 1865, Sergeant Antoine Wolf of Company M carried the regimental standard.[22]

48th Infantry

(pages 128-29): The photograph on page 128 is the First State Color, not the Second. The replacement color, altered from the 146th Infantry by Horstmann Brothers, was found mislabelled as belonging to the 148th Infantry. There is no question that the staff label is wrong; the center stripe clearly shows the "48th Regt. P.V." painted over the earlier 146th designation. The First Color was manufactured by Evans & Hassall.

Second State Color, 48th Infantry
Maker: HB
1985.269

52nd Infantry

This regiment must have carried a second color of some type. It was taken home and displayed at several postwar reunions. It apparently failed to survive until the present time.[23]

53rd Infantry

(page 148): During the fighting at Fair Oaks, Corporal Joseph Black of Company H was killed while carrying the state color.[24]

54th Infantry

(page 152): During the April 2, 1865, assault on Fort Gregg, Color-Corporal James P. Ryan (Company D) was killed as the regiment rushed toward the fort. When Ryan fell, Private Michael Lohr (Company C) seized the flag, sprang into the ditch, planted the flag on the parapet, and remained there until the regiment climbed into the fort, when he carried the silk banner forward.[25]

Addenda to Volume One

Major Henry J. Biddle, Who Advocated that State Flags be Issued

56th Infantry

(page 157): The 56th's Second State Color was still in the State Agency Building as late as October 7, 1864. It is not known when the regiment finally obtained this flag.[26]

57th Infantry

(page 160): According to a biography in the November 3, 1883, issue of the *Greenville Advance-Argus*, Corporal Robert G. Madge (Company C) was the soldier carrying the flag at Cold Harbor when a bullet hit the staff six inches above his head.

58th Infantry

Sergeant A. H. Baumgartner of Company B is listed as a color-bearer in "58th Regt. Re-union," *Tunkhannock Republican*, October 10, 1890.

61st Infantry

(page 172): The flag obtained by a group of Philadelphia citizens was furnished by Evans & Hassall. It was still on display at their establishment as late as March 2, 1865.[27]

62nd Infantry

(page 175): At Malvern Hill, Sergeant Jefferson Truitt of Company D was the color-bearer who saved the flag as described in Note 3. Bates used "Smith" rather than "Truitt."[28]

(page 175): Apparently, it was Corporal Johnson C. Gardner of Company C who rescued the state color when its bearer, Jacob Funk, was shot. When the regiment became mixed with Confederates in the Wheatfield, Funk saw a captured Rebel pick up a gun and spy the state color. The enemy soldier poked the gun at Funk and ordered him to surrender. Funk stared at his assailant, then pointed behind the Reb, calling on some of his comrades to rescue him. As the Rebel looked around only to see no other Yankees behind him, Funk took off at a run. However, as he reached the stone wall at the edge of the field, he was hit near the right shoulder by a musket ball. As he fell, he called out for someone to save the flag. Gardner was the man who rescued the flag, then carried it until the regiment went home in July 1864.[29]

Company M Flag

In 1861, the young women of Hollidaysburg, Blair County, held a fair to raise money for the local soldiers. The ladies used part of the proceeds to purchase a national flag. During a ball to honor those who were about to enter the military, a spokeswoman announced that the flag would be given to the soldier who promised to take good care of it and bring it back after the war. Jack Mufty stepped forward and said he was the man. He was given the flag and soon enlisted in Company M, 62nd Pennsylvania.

The flag survived the war. Mufty gave the flag to the editor of the *Hollidaysburg Standard*, where it remained until his death in 1896. The editor's widow

National Flag of Company M, 62nd Infantry

returned the banner to Mufty, who had it encased in glass to better preserve the relic. For many years, the flag hung in the borough building. The last survivor of Company M asked that the banner be placed in a fireproof building. In 1938, his request was honored when the flag was given to Hollidaysburg High School, where it can still be viewed.[30]

63rd Infantry

(page 178): The second state color was unfurled by the regiment at dress parade on December 13, 1863.[31]

(page 178): After Sergeant House was wounded on May 5, 1864, Private Joseph P. Rankin of Company G became bearer.[32]

4th Cavalry (64th Regiment)

On September 14, 1861, Mrs. Parker of Oil City presented a "handsome flag" to the men of the Oil City cavalry company.[33]

Color-Sergeant Amos Bolton, 4th Cavalry

68th Infantry

According to Charles H. Haber of Company B, Sergeant James McFaren was shot in the head at Mine Run. When the color fell, Haber picked it up and carried it until the end of the war. He was promoted to color-sergeant by age sixteen, then carried the flag in the 1866 parade.[34]

69th Infantry

Further research indicates that the two Irish flags presented to this regiment contained different designs. The March 22, 1862, edition of the New York *Irish American* contained a story about the first color presented to the 69th. The obverse of the flag was painted with an Irish harp, together with "Presented to the 69th Pennsylvania Regiment by their friends." The reverse depicted the state coat-of-arms.

The design of the second Irish flag was three Irish symbols—wolfhound, sunburst, and round tower—on one side, with the state arms on the other.

78th Infantry

Corporal Abraham W. Rudisill of the replacement Company D was one of the regiment's color-bearers.[35]

79th Infantry

Colonel David Miles identified the following soldiers as color-bearers during the war: Sergeants John Beichler [Jacob H. Beichler, Company A?], John Dean (Company A), Henry Reed (Company H), and Corporals William Powell (Company H), H. B. Vondersmith (Company K), George L. Danner (Company B), and Andrew J. Huffnagle (Company A).[36]

82nd Infantry

(page 224): The February 5, 1864, presentation seems to have included a national color with the battle honors inscribed on the stripes as well as a pair of guidons.[37]

(page 225): Sergeant William P. Beale of Company D is mentioned as a color-bearer in the May 16, 1863, edition of the *Philadelphia Daily Evening Bulletin*.

85th Infantry

(page 234): Some new evidence about the Uniontown flag has been supplied by the Mason-Dixon Civil War Roundtable of Uniontown. A scrapbook of newspaper clippings indicates that the spearpoint of the second state color was hit by a bullet at Deep Bottom. When the regiment went home, the men wished to keep this memento, so they exchanged flagstaffs. Thus, the second state color's flagstaff went home to Uniontown, while the staff of the Uniontown flag was deposited in Harrisburg as part of the state color. This new information allows the reader to make more sense of the flag history booklet cited in the bibliography. Color-bearers for the Uniontown flag were Reager (November 1861-April 27, 1862), Deffenbaugh (through sometime in 1863), Moore (October 1863-November 1864), and Walter C. Craven, Company C (temporarily in August 1864 when Moore was suffering from sunstroke). The bearers of the state colors were probably Lincoln (wounded at Fair Oaks), Orbin (July 1862-September 1863), and Ross (May through November 1864).

Notes

1 "Three Great Relics," *Scranton Republican*, May 26, 1902.

2 Entry in Captured Flags Document.

3 *Annual Report of the Adjutant-General of Pennsylvania, 1905*, pp. 13-14. Copeland, in his *Logan Guards*, p. 63, noted that this flag was carried in the 1914 parade by Frank B. Wentz. "This was not, of course, the original flag; but a national flag bearing the name of the Logan Guards." Copeland thus failed to note the significance of this mystery flag.

4 *Huntingdon Journal and American*, April 24, 1861.

5 *Philadelphia Daily Evening Bulletin*, May 20, 1861.

6 "Promotions and Resignations, *Philadelphia Daily Evening Bulletin*, January 24, 1863.

7 "Flag Presentation," *Ibid.*, January 30, 1864.

8 "Parade of Col. Einstein's Regiment and Flag Presentation," *Philadelphia Public Ledger*, June 12, 1861.

9 J. R. Hoffman, "Killed at Antietam," *NT*, November 23, 1905.

10 *Philadelphia Daily Evening Bulletin*, July 23, 1861.

11 Carollee Michener, "Album Highlight: Civil War Flag," *Franklin News-Herald*, February 17, 1990.

12 "Departure of Col. Mann's Regiment—Flag Presentation—Interesting Ceremonies," *Philadelphia Daily Evening Bulletin*, May 29, 1861.

13 *Personal War Sketches Presented to Anna M. Ross Post 94, Philadelphia, by Mrs. W. H. Kemble* (Philadelphia, 1897), 2: 6. This GAR post book can be found in the GAR Museum, Philadelphia.

14 "The Third Reserves," *Doylestown Democrat*, September 9, 1862.

15 "Partial Roster of Line Officers, 4th Regt., Pa. Res. Vols.," John M. Gould Papers, microfilm copy in Antietam National Battlefield Park Library.

16 From Thomas Chamberlin, "Short Personal History," copy in USAMHI.

17 Frank Holsinger, "Antietam," *NT*, April 9, 1908.

18 "Beautiful Flag," *Crawford Journal*, May 14, 1861.

19 "Meeting of the Jefferson Guards," *Washington Reporter and Tribune*, May 9, 1861.

20 "Departure of Capt. Baldy's Company," *Easton Argus*, May 9, 1861.

21 Untitled story in *Norristown Herald*, September 17, 1861.

22 H. S. Thomas, *Some Personal Reminiscences*, p. 25.

23 See the following stories for mention of this flag: "Re-union of the 52d P.V.," *Tunkhannock Republican*, October 4, 1889; reunion notice in the *NT*, November 25, 1897; and "Reunion of the 52d Pa.," *NT*, December 24, 1903.

24 James M. Linn, "The Ninth Army Corps," *Lewisburg Chronicle*, February 8, 1896.

25 O.R. 46.1, p. 1219 (Report of Colonel W. B. Curtis, brigade commander); A. I. Ellis, "The First Colors on Fort Gregg," *NT*, January 8, 1903.

26 Frank Jordan to Commander, 206th Pennsylvania, October 7, 1864, in 206th PA Regimental Descriptive, Letter, Order, and Index Book, RG 94.

27 "Handsome Compliment to the Pa. 61st," *Philadelphia Daily Evening Bulletin*, March 2, 1865.

28 George W. Swetnam, " 'Never-Say-Die' 62nd," *Pittsburgh Press*, January 28, 1962.

29 Jacob Funk undated letter about Gettysburg, in John S. Patton Papers, Historical Society of Western Pennsylvania; J. C. Gardner, "Medal of Honor," *NT*, March 29, 1917.

30 Information supplied by Lucy Wolf, in editorials in the *Altoona Mirror*.

31 Daniel Dougherty Diary, entry for December 13, 1863, Historical Society of Pennsylvania.

32 Rankin obituary in *NT*, May 1, 1919.

33 "Flag Presentation and Supper at Oil City," *Pittsburgh Gazette*, September 20, 1861.

34 Haber to Assistant Adjutant-General Samuel P. Town, March 8, 1926, in George G. Meade Commission Papers, RG 25.

35 Rudisill to Adjutant-General A. L. Russell, June 26, 1866, RG 25.

36 Undated letter from Miles regarding the 1866 ceremony, RG 25.

37 "Flag Presentation," *Philadelphia Daily Evening Bulletin*, February 6, 1864.

Chapter VII
Appendix II Additions

Since the publication of Volume One, ongoing research has uncovered many additional company names as well as a few corrections to the published county rosters. Most of the additional company names were culled from Record Group 19 in the State Archives. While searching one regiment's files, the author delved into the Returns of Commissioned Officers file and discovered that the printed forms for the original company officers of the 1861 and early 1862 units included a column for the original company names. Any names listed in this addition supersede such names printed in Volume One when the names conflict.

11th	H	Rosecrans Rangers)	*Doylestown Democrat*, 11/5/61.
24th	B	(National Guards)	*Philadelphia Saturday Bulletin*, 5/4/61.
28th	B	(Jackson Guard)	*Philadelphia Daily Evening Bulletin*, 6/28/61.
	I	(Gorgas Light Guard)	*PPL*, 6/29/61 (probable).
	K	(Rover Guards)	*PDEB*, 7/18/61.
32nd	C		As Newtown Rifles in *Doylestown Democrat*, 7/16/61.
	H		As Applebachville Artillerists in *DD*, 7/16/61.
33rd	K	(Exton Guards)	*Montgomery Ledger*, 7/2/61 (NOT Enton Guards).
45th	B	(Donegal Infantry)	All Companies from Returns of
	D	(Linn Rifles)	Commissioned Officers, 10/19/61,
	F	(Wayne County Volunteers)	RG 19.
	H	(Girard Guards)	
	K	Shawnee Rifles)	
47th	A	(Easton Rifle Company)	*Easton Journal*, 9/12/61 (article states that this company was formerly the Easton Jaegers [G, 9th Inf]).
	A	(Easton Rifles)	All companies from Returns of
	B	(Allen Rifles)	Commissioned Officers, 9/24/61,
	D	(Woodruff Rifles)	RG 19.
	E	(Easton Fencibles)	
	F	(Catasauqua Rifles)	
	G	(Allen Infantry)	
	H	(Elliottsburg Light Artillery)	
	I	(Allen Zouaves)	
	K	(Lehigh German Infantry)	
48th	E	(Wynkoop Artillery)	All companies from Returns of
	G	(Washington Artillery)	Commissioned Officers, 9/20/61,
	H	(Scott Infantry)	RG 19.
	I	(Anthracite Infantry)	
49th	D	(Standing Stone Guards #2)	*Huntingdon Journal & American*, 8/27/61.
	A	(Russel Rifles)	All companies from Returns of
	D	(Parker Light Infantry)	Commissioned Officers, 10/23/61,
	F	(West Chester Rifles)	RG 19.
	H	(Potts Guards)	

49th (Continued)	I	(Juniata Rifles)	
	K	(Governor's Guards)	
50th	C	(Scott Artillerists)	All companies from Returns of
	F	(Steuben Guards)	Commissioned Officers, 9/30/61,
	I	(Meylart Light Infantry)	RG 19.
	K	(Wilmot Guards)	
52nd	A	(Mayer Rifles)	All Companies from Returns of
	B	(Wyoming Rangers)	Commissioned Officers, 11/4/61,
	C	(Mackey Guards)	RG 19.
	E	(Mountain Lake Rangers)	
	G	(Keystone Sharpshooters)	
	K	(Fellows Guards)	
53rd	A	(Madison Guards)	All companies from Returns of Commissioned Officers, 11/5/61, RG 19. Company A as Summer Rifles in *Montgomery Ledger*, 7/1/62.
	B	(Downingtown Guards)	Recruited primarily in Chester County.
	C	(James Creek Guards)	
	D	(McCann Rifles)	
	E	(Rooke Guards)	
	H	(Lawson Guards)	
	I	(Union Guards)	
54th	B	(Stoystown Zouaves)	All companies from Returns of
	C	(Somerset Rifles)	Commissioned Officers, 2/26/62,
	D	(Johnstown Infantry)	RG 19.
	E	(Union Cadets)	
	F	(Marion Rifles)	
	G	(Berlin Infantry)	
	H	(Maxwell Guards)	
	K	(Allentown Guards)	
55th	A	(Washington Rifles)	Companies from Returns of Commissioned
	C	(Montgomery Rifles)	Officers, 11/18/61, RG 19.
	D	(Bedford Rifles)	
	H	(Black Plumed Rifles	
	B		As Womelsdorf Infantry in *Berks & Schuylkill Journal*, 12/14/61.
57th	G	(Culp Guards)	Returns of Commissioned Officers, 12/13/61, RG 19.
59th	A	Bucks County	*Doylestown Democrat*, 12/3/61.
60th	D	(McClellan Rangers)	Returns of Commissioned Officers, 12 23/61, RG 19.
61st	A	(Mahoning Rifle Guards)	All Companies from Returns of
	C	(Richard Guards)	Commissioned Officers, 3/18/62, RG 19.
	D	(Emley Zouaves)	
	E	(Simpson Light Infantry)	
	G	(Holt Guards)	
	H	(Independent Greys)	
	K	(1st Pennsylvania Zouaves)	
62nd	F	(Eighth Ward Guards, Company A)	All companies from Returns of
	K	(Eighth Ward Guards, Company B)	Commissioned Officers, 11/12/61, RG 19.
63rd	B	(Harmer Guards)	All companies from Returns of
	E	(Etna Infantry)	Commissioned Officers, 10/9/61,
	F	(Clarion County Cadets)	RG 19.
	I	(McKeesport Rifle Greys)	
67th	D	(Monroe Guards)	Stroudsburg *Jeffersonian*, 10/10/61.
71st	C	(Pennsylvania Guards)	*PDEB*, 5/20/61.
	F	(Spring Garden Minie Rifles)	*PDEB*, 5/23/61.
	R	(Washington City Zouaves)	Recruited in District of Columbia; see *National Tribune* article by W. H. Cullimore, 3/15/06.

72nd	E	(Ellsworth Zouaves)	*PDEB*, 8/31/61. Regiment consolidated 11/14/62.
76th	A	(Lawrence Zouaves)	All companies from Returns of Commissioned Officers, 1/6/62, RG 19.
	B	(Sharon Zouaves)	
	C	(Iron Heads Zouaves)	
	D	(Union Guards)	
	E	("Bowman Boys")	
	F	(Altoona Guards)	
	G	(Conemaugh Rangers)	
	H	(Curtin Zouaves)	
	I	(National Guards)	
	K	(Hampton Guards)	
78th	A	(Union Guards)	*Indiana Weekley Register*, 5/24/61.
79th	B	(Lancaster City Rangers)	All companies from Returns of Commissioned Officers, 12/6/61, RG 19.
	C	(Greble Guards)	
	F	(Hambright Guards)	
	G	(Independent Greys)	
	H	(National Guards)	
	I	(Lyon Guards	
	K	(Conestoga Rifles)	
88th	F	(Montgomery Guards)	Returns of Commissioned Officers, 11/25/61, RG 19.
89th	M	Bucks County	*Doylestown Democrat*, 10/8/61.
95th	B	New Jersey	Bates 3: 335.
96th	G	(Hamburg Light Infantry)	*Berks & Schuylkill Journal*, 11/30/61.
97th	E	(Mulligan Invincibles)	Returns of Commissioned Officers, 11/16/61, RG 19.
99th	I	(Jackson Zouaves)	*PDEB*, 12/23/61.
100th	B	(Lawrence Rifles)	All companies from Returns of Commissioned Officers, undated 1862 date, RG 19.
	C	(Zeigler Guards)	
	D	(Darlington Independent Blues)	
	E	(Washington Guards)	
	F	(Lawrence Greys)	
	H	(Lawrence Guards)	
	I	(Lawrence Guards	
	K	(Leasure Guards)	
	M	(Cowan Guards)	
104th	D	(Davis Guards)	Returns of Commissioned Officers, 11/5/61, RG 19.
	E	(Doylestown Guards)	
105th	B	(Dowling Invincibles)	All companies from Returns of Commissioned Officers, 10/7/61, RG 19.
	C	(Craig Guards)	
	G	(Ringgold Riflemen)	
	H	(McKnight Guards)	
	I	(Jefferson Phalanx)	
	K	(Altman Guards)	
109th	D	Recruited in Lawrence County	Individual muster rolls, RG 19.
110th	D	(Hart's Log Infantry)	NOT Hart's Loq Infantry. All companies from Returns of Commissioned Officers, 12/28/61, RG 19.
	B	(Mount Union Guards)	
	C	(Woodberry Infantry)	
	D	(Juniata Infantry)	
	G	(Lubis Guards)	
	H	(Fritz's Guards)	
	I	(Crowther Guards)	
113th	D	(Northampton Light Cavalry)	*Easton Journal*, 9/26/61.
119th	H	Bucks County	Bucks County Historical Society, Bucks County Militia Collection, Folder Nine.

Appendix II Additions

122nd	E	(Wickersham Guards)	*Doylestown Democrat*, 9/2/62.
128th	D	(Allen Rifles)	Article by C. J. Mattern in *Pennsylvania Folklife* 36 (Autumn 1986): 3.
129th	I	(Wetherill Blues)	Norristown *Herald & Free Press*, 8/12/62.
161st	I	(Russell Troop)	*PDEB*, 9/19/62.
162nd	G	(Waynesboro Cavalry)	Moyer, *17th PA Cavalry*, 155.
	M	(Wayne County Cavalry)	*Ibid.*, 90.
192nd	N	Chester & Delaware counties	*WCVR*, 7/26/64.
198th	M	Monroe County	Stroudsburg *Jeffersonian*, 6/15/65.

Chapter VIII
Saving the Flags: The Conservation Procedure

It was evident from the onset that a conservation/preservation project for the large collection of Civil War battle flags would be a very major undertaking. Long-term vertical display of the flags rolled on their staffs contributed greatly to an accelerated deterioration rate. The preliminary examinations of selected flags indicated that they were in fragile condition and would require delicate handling. In addition to powdered and fragmented silks, the distorted painted and gilded areas required serious attention. With the support of the Capitol Preservation Committee and full legislative backing, the project proceeded with the unrolling, extensive documentation, minor treatment, and proper storage of the collection. Specific objectives and long-term goals were developed to provide the project with a definite direction.

In addition to the publishing of this two-volume history of the Pennsylvania Civil War flags, the goals of the project have been to document, stabilize, and preserve the collection. The flag collection belongs to the people of the Commonwealth. Hence, a major objective was the establishment of a study/storage facility to provide for long-term preservation of the flags as well as public accessibility.

The first step in initiating this long-term project was the development of a textile conservation laboratory. Due to the individual and collective size of the flags, a large work space was required. The second floor of the old Publications Building in Harrisburg was renovated to create a fully-equipped conservation laboratory. The workroom accommodates six 8x8-foot temporary storage racks, a custom-made photographic station, several work tables, and enough space to safely move the flags on large panels. A separate room furnished with a large wash table and a deionized water system was constructed to facilitate wet cleaning of other objects in future projects. A chemical room incorporates a fume hood, chemical storage cabinets, and standard laboratory equipment.

The conservation process was divided into three separate phases. The first phase involved the physical removal and transfer of the flags from the display cases in the Capitol Rotunda to the conservation site for preliminary documentation and photography.

The five cases were emptied on separate occasions between June 1985 and April 1989. This required a cooperative effort between the project staff and Capitol personnel. There was no easy access to the material in the cases. The convex glass was carefully released to allow for the removal of the flags, after which the glass was replaced.

In 1914, the ferrules of the flag staffs were plastered into metal cups, which in turn were plastered into holes in the tiered marble floor of the cases. The plaster had to be softened with the use of warm water and thin metal spatulas. Various other tools were used to pry up the display cups, most of which remained adhered to the ferrules. The flags were then removed from the cases and carefully wrapped with acid free tissue to contain any loose fragments and to protect the flags during the transfer. The wrapped flags were laid into a layer of polyethylene foam which fit into cradles of specially designed wood pallets. The foam acted as a cushion against mechanical shock and provided partial insulation against rapid environmental changes during the move. Each pallet carried four flags and was clearly labelled. The flag removal process for each display case was carried out over four days. The pallets were then transported by truck to the conservation site. The flags remained in their respective pallets until they were to be handled for documentation and preservation.

At the laboratory site, the flags were assigned registration numbers. The military historian identified each flag as the project continued and assigned historical names. Documentation worksheets were developed to record various aspects of the conservation process for the flags and their associated artifacts. Sections include checklists and logs for treatment and photography as well as diagrams and condition comments. Design and construction elements are subjects for potential study.

Preliminary written and photographic documentation could then begin with the unfurling process. All materials removed from the flags throughout the treatment procedure have been retained in polyethylene sample bags. Photographs were taken to document the associated artifacts that had to be removed. The ribbons, streamers, and cord and tassels remain with the flags. The streamers and ribbons were tied around the top of the flag staff, at the finial base. The finial device, and sometimes the finial base, had to be temporarily unscrewed to accommodate the staff removal. This also allowed the associated artifacts to be slipped off over the end of the finial base, thereby limiting excess handling of the extremely fragile silk ribbons used for streamer attachments. The cardboard label printed with the regimental designation was also removed at this time. A chiffon sleeve encased the rolled flag and offered a limited degree of protection from the dust in the cases. The sleeve also served to contain any loose fragments of silk. The chiffon was weakened and very soiled. The chiffon sleeves (added in 1914) were attached with ties at the upper and lower ends. For removal, the ties were unknotted and the chiffon cut along the seam. The sleeve and label were kept together in a sample bag.

Before each flag could be unrolled, tacking stitches spaced in several locations along the fly edge of the flag had to be clipped and removed. Often the tight stitching thread had cut the silk and caused further damage. Condition details such as this were recorded during and after unrolling. These details also may have included damaged or shattered silk caused by binding cords or long-term vertical display. Knotted silk and stress-causing repairs or alterations were photographed and stabilized. Sound historic repairs were noted and left in place. Each flag was unrolled on a nylon or polyester gossamer sheet on large movable table tops. Throughout the conservation process, this inert, non-acidic support fabric was used to handle the flag without exposing the fragile silk to undue stress. It remains with the flag in final storage. The portable table tops were used for transfer and handling of flags between locations.

Based on logistics and the fragile state of the silk flags, a decision was made to remove the staffs and store them separately. The staff attachments were photographed prior to removal. In most instances the staff attachments consisted of several small tacks or nails through a narrow glazed cloth strip located at the upper and lower pole sleeve edges. Generally, these tacks could be gently pried up with a small screwdriver. Another common example of staff attachment was the use of a leather tab with a buttonhole that slips over a screw on the staff. This arrangement held the pole sleeve taut against the staff.

Removal of Flag from Rotunda Case and Preparation for Transport

Unrolling a Flag

The most difficult situations involved removal of wood splint repairs that were nailed through the pole sleeves. Concommitant damage to pole sleeves and staffs was photographed.

Staffs were described, measured, and documented on the worksheets. The excess plaster on the display cups was scraped and wiped off with water and ethanol. The wood staffs, finial devices, finial bases, and ferrules were then labelled with their respective registration numbers. Random wood identification testing verified that the majority of the staffs are made of ash. Staffs which differed visually were tested as part of the documentation process. Other examples found in the collection include walnut or butternut, chestnut, and cherry. The flag staffs have been stored vertically in pull-out, permanent storage units of stainless steel construction. This custom-made system allows for easy viewing as well as protection from light and dust.

Once unrolled and the staff removed, each flag was surface-cleaned through polyethylene screening using a modified vacuum. Using short, light strokes, the powdered silk and abrasive particulate matter were removed. These particles were collected by a paper filter during vacuuming and retained for potential analysis.

Next, the flag was placed beneath an eight-foot-high photographic station for full-view photography. Large-format photographs of both the obverse and reverse were taken in black and white for documenta-

Staff Storage Unit

tion and color for publication. To turn the flag over, it was sandwiched between gossamer sheets and rolled using a heavy-gauge mylar tube.

The unrolled flags were stored flat and fully supported on temporary racks. The stable environmental conditions of the workroom allowed the previously rolled flags to relax until the second phase of treatment was undertaken.

Phase Two entailed the balance of the documen-

Saving the Flags: The Conservation Procedure

Textile Conservator Surface-Cleaning a Flag

tation of each flag. Detailed information was recorded on the documentation worksheets. This includes design, construction and condition comments, detail and overall measurements, diagrams, and detail photography of all aspects of the flags and associated artifacts. Some categories were not completed at this time, but may be added as the collection is utilized by the public, students, and researchers. For example, seam construction could be surveyed and studied more extensively. Information recorded on the worksheets was entered into a computer file to supplement the written documentation.

The paint on some flags was physically distorted. This condition increased the risk of fracturing the designs and splitting along the paint/fabric interfaces. Distortions also obscured the inscriptions necessary for accurate identification. This problem required a unique solution. After consultation with several conservators actively involved with humidifying paintings on canvas, a humidification system was developed to relax the distorted flags.

The basic components of the humidification chamber are a wash table and an acrylic dome. The wash table holds photographic trays of saturated salt solutions. A perforated panel is placed across the top of the table to support the flag on its gossamer sheet. With the aid of a hydraulic crane, the dome is lowered over the table, enclosing the entire flag in the chamber.

Various situations and methods of introducing humidity were tested. The use of saturated salt solutions proved to be the most practical source of humidity

Photographic Stantion in Use

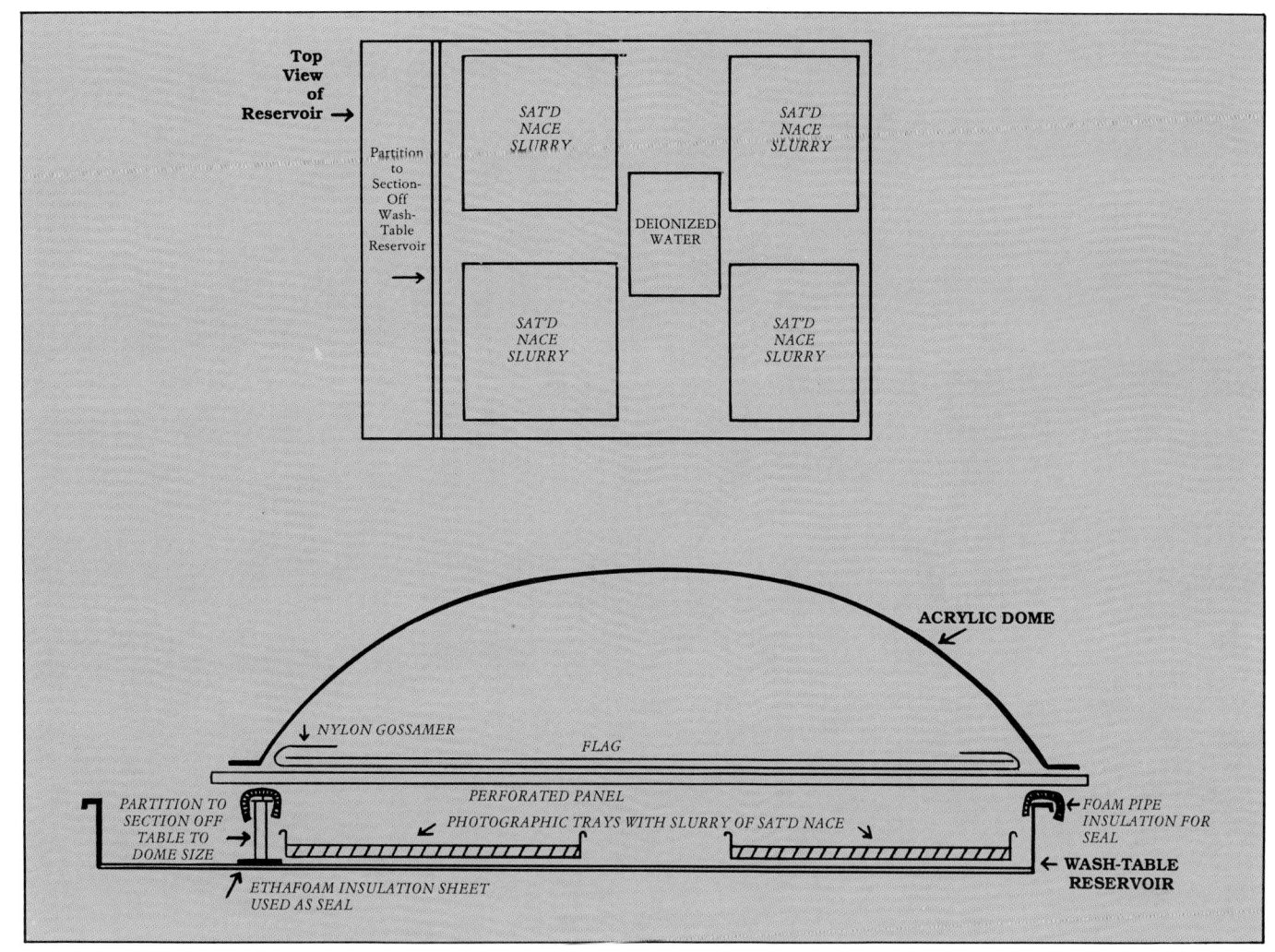

Diagrams of the Humidification Chamber

control. Sodium chloride (NaCl) holds humidity levels at approximately 75% relative humidity at approximately 70° F. By adding a small tray of deionized water to the chamber reservoir, the humidity can be increased to approximately 80%, at which point the paint becomes more pliable. Caution was exercised due to the fragility of the silks, the soils present, and mold/mildew potential. The relative humidity was carefully controlled and the length of time at high humidity minimized.

A flag was placed in the chamber to acclimatize for approximately twenty-four hours. The dome was then lifted and the fragments were manipulated and gently persuaded with varying weights of glass plates. The process was repeated as necessary depending upon the condition of the flag. The treatment was very successful with some dramatic improvements in paint condition. The average treatment time was three days, with the most severely distorted flags requiring up to nine days.

Phase Two also involved further detail photography. The fringe was straightened and debris such as leaf fragments, burrs, and twigs was removed. The flags and all detachable parts were labelled with their respective registration numbers.

Phase Three entailed the final preparation and implementation of the storage system. Guidelines for use of the final storage/study facility were established. A large room at the conservation site was renovated to serve as the storage/study facility. An environmen-

Flag in the Humidification Chamber

Saving the Flags: The Conservation Procedure

First State Standard of the 1st Cavalry, Shown Before (left) and After (right) Humidification

tal control system was installed to maintain the conditions at constant levels of 70-74° F and 45-50% relative humidity. These are the recommended levels for storage of historic textiles. The most important factor in preserving the fragile silks is to avoid rapid environmental fluctuations, especially in humidity. A leak detection system will alert the staff to potential moisture or water problems within the room. A dry chemical fire extinguishing system for the storage/study room requires further consideration.

To provide flat storage of the flags, custom-designed racks and panels were purchased. The flags have been fully supported on 7x7-foot acid-free honeycomb panels. Each panel is covered with muslin to provide additional protection. The panels are placed on stainless steel racks each of which has twenty-two flags. A shelf holds one large flag or up to four smaller flags. A nylon cover with zippered front and back openings placed over each rack unit provides for light and dust protection. For viewing, a specific flag is easily pulled out on its individual panel. The flag locations are referenced by rack and shelf number in the documentation packet and on the computer.

A file packet was compiled for each flag. It contains the documentation worksheets as well as an abridged version of the design, condition, and treatment reports. Also included are black and white photographic proof sheets, sample bags, and the vacuum sample. Basic sortable data was entered into a data management system to aid visitors and researchers to identify flags exhibiting similar characteristics.

The study/storage facility is open to the public for viewing and research purposes. Visitors may have access to the information in the packets and in the computer. Compiling additional information as the collection is used and studied more thoroughly will increase its usefulness as a public resource. Only those flags which are in stable condition will be considered for

Individual Shelf on Flag Storage Rack

individual, short-term display in the Capitol building.

The flags unquestionably have benefitted from this project. Relieving the stress of vertical display has improved the condition of the flags and diminished their rapid degradation. In addition to deterioration of the silk, other typical damage includes dye bleed, fading, and discoloration of the white silk — often to an ivory or gold color. The flags exhibit various types of soils and stains. Some examples are presumed to be mildew, gunpowder, and blood. The paint on some flags is cockled, brittle, and fractured as well as suffering from bloom, a whitish appearance of the paint caused by a breakdown or fracturing of the paint components.

The priority of the project has been to preserve the flags by physically stabilizing the component materials and placing them in a proper environment. Limited treatment is generally considered the best conservation approach for a large collection such as this. It is a valuable historical resource for a variety of fields, having been well documented since the end of the Civil War and virtually undisturbed since 1914.

A better understanding of the materials used in manufacturing the flags will ultimately aid in their preservation. Many questions have been raised and briefly studied. An initial survey of the pigments used in the painted arms designs was conducted by Nancy Pollak, a Winterthur conservation intern. While not all results were conclusive, the survey provides some answers to the general palettes used by the flag manufacturers of the time. Analysis by McCrone Research Institute determined the gilt to be composed of genuine gold. Fragmented silks, most noticeable in white silks, have been a concern of curators and conservators of museum collections. Samples were sent to the Conservation Analytical Laboratory of the Smithsonian Institution to test the theory that metallic salts used to weight silk may have accelerated the aging process. Mary Ballard, Ron Koestler, and Norman Indictor determined that inorganic salts are not present in the silks. It is more likely that the dyes and/or processing treatments account for the degradation. The dyes present in the samples tested were identified as cochineal (reds) and Prussian Blue.[1]

The Pennsylvania Civil War flag collection may be used as an interdisciplinary research tool. It provides a basis for answers to historical, textile, pigment, method, and fabric treatment questions. Hopefully this preservation will be beneficial to many more disciplines than presently foreseen.

Notes

1 M. Ballard, R. J. Koestler, and N. Indictor, "Historic Silk Flags from Harrisburg", in S. Haig Zeronian and Howard L. Needles (eds.), *Historic Textile and Paper Materials II: Conservation and Characterization* (Washington: American Chemical Society, 1989) pp. 134-42.

Chapter IX
Conclusions

Having examined the flags carried by Pennsylvania commands, including state issue, local presentation, and federal government requisition, there are several conclusions about Civil War-period flags that can be adduced from both the written record and physical evidence. This chapter surveys the state flags, provides an overview of federal government contracts and types of flags, and highlights problems encountered during the course of research. A more complete analysis, as well as more definitive answers, can be had only when other states follow Pennsylvania's lead by examining their own collections.

State Colors and Standards

In general, the flags produced for the Commonwealth by Horstmann Brothers & Company and Evans & Hassall followed Army Regulations. Both companies used silk exclusively, painting the state arms, stars, and unit designations on each flag. Each company pieced together each stripe, canton, and polesleeve to make the infantry colors. Both companies hand-sewed the majority of their flags, even though Horstmann Brothers, the largest military goods dealer in the country, had the latest machines that could have performed such labor.[1] Apparently, the workers took pride in assembling the flags by hand rather than by machine. A few colors exhibit a mixture of hand- and machine-sewing along the stripes.

The only major consistent difference between the two companies is in the width of the canton. Horstmann tended to use a rectangular canton generally measuring 38-39 inches in length by 24-25 inches in width. An Evans & Hassall canton tended to be 38-39 inches in length, but 29-30 inches wide. Otherwise, the physical construction of the flags is remarkably similar.

The painting on each flag tends to be greatly varied in nature. Judging from the appearance of the flags themselves, the artist used a stencil outline to position the stars and coat-of-arms. Once the outline was in place, the artist then filled in the details. Thus, very few arms are exactly alike. Horses appear as gray, white, brown, or a combination of these three colors.

The shield outline differs from flag to flag. The eagle surmounting the shield was painted facing either the fly edge or polesleeve of the flag. The position of the bird's talons and nails varies greatly. The cornstalks behind each horse differ from artist to artist. Even the red bow tying the cornstalks together can be very different from flag to flag.

It is within the shield that the greatest variety in style is found. Sometimes the ship is very detailed, complete with rigging and pennants; other ships are very stylized and plain. Steven Pomeroy, an intern from Penn State, spent several months examining and typifying the coats-of-arms. Of the seventy arms examined, he found that there are nineteen different sail patterns easily visible on the flags. The sea appears calm or white-capped (or a combination thereof), depending on the artist's outlook. Sky appears blue, red, or gray. In classifying the plough, which occupies the center of the shield, Steven sketched a remarkable twenty-three different coupling devices used to attach the horses to the plough. He also noted fourteen different patterns in the positioning of the wheat sheaves. The shading of colors within each coat-of-arms also varies greatly, again depending on the artist's interpretation of the state arms.[2]

Although these flags can be grouped according to general artistic style, it is almost impossible to match them with any particular artist. Few of the flags are signed by the artist. The most frequent signature is by an artist who signed a white "M" on Horstmann-supplied flags for the 44th, 52nd, 70th, 76th, 83rd, 102nd, 139th, 143rd, 209th, 210th, and 211th regiments. All of these flags were finished after October 1864. If one examines these arms very closely, it is quite apparent that even a single artist varied his work, for these arms are not identical.

There are a few other signed flags in the collection. One of the standards for the 4th Cavalry (64th Regiment) is signed "BB." C. F. Berger signed his full name to the fancy state and national arms he painted on a blue color for the 82nd Infantry. A blue regimental color of the 183rd Infantry is inscribed with "Heiss." This man may be Emanuel Heiss, an artist lo-

1.

2.

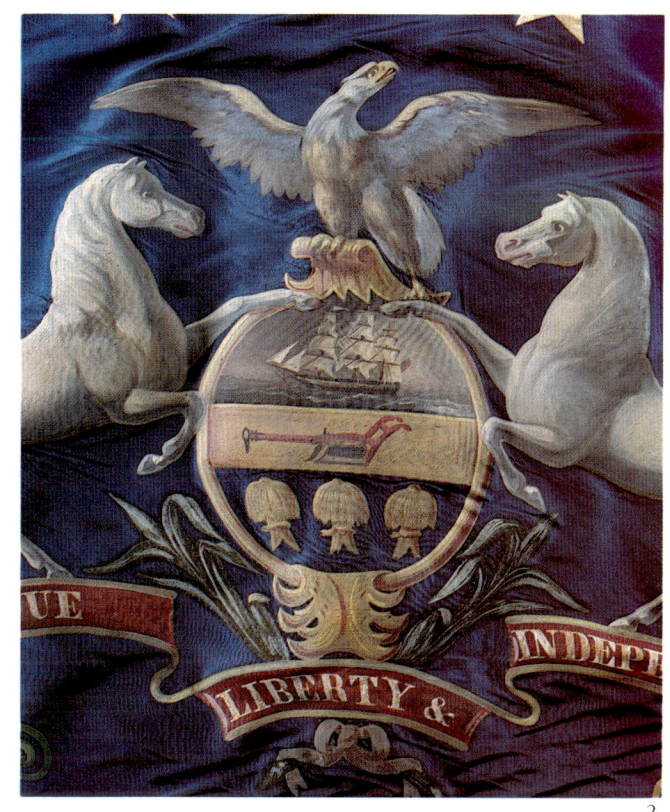

Three Views of the State Coat-of-Arms, Illustrating Some of the Variations

3.

Signature of Artist "M" on the Third State Color of the 76th Infantry

cated at 1316 Brandywine Street, according to the 1863 Philadelphia City Directory.

Since the company records of the flag makers no longer exist, we can only speculate about their man-ufacturing process. It is quite possible that both companies subcontracted the painting to qualified artists residing in the Philadelphia area. Prior to the Civil War, the Regular Army's Office of Clothing and

Conclusions

551

Equipage, working through its Philadelphia Depot, followed this process when contracting for colors for the regulars. The Depot acquired the silk, cut it to regulation size, then sent the material to local artist Samuel Brewer for painting and final assembly.[3] There is no reason to suppose that Horstmann and Evans & Hassall did not follow this type of production. Without further documentation, we can never know the answer.

Neither company followed regular canton patterns throughout the war. Both companies centered the state arms, then painted the stars in six gentle arcs, three above and three beneath the arms. Both manufacturers used gold stars, generally measuring about two and a half inches in width, although some colors have smaller stars.

In its initial contract of September 6, 1861, Horstmann followed a pattern of 5-6-7-arms-5-6-5, for a total of thirty-four stars. The company then changed to a 5-6-6-arms-6-6-5 pattern until September 1862, when it reverted to its September 1861 arrangement, which lasted for all other 34-star colors furnished to the state. Thereafter, Horstmann supplied two different patterns. The initial 35-star arrangement appeared as 5-6-6-arms-6-6-6, followed in mid-1864 by a 5-6-7-arms-6-6-5 style. This arrangement was used through the May 1865 contract.

However, Horstmann supplied 36-star flags before it was proper to do so. Nevada entered the Union in late 1864 but was not eligible to appear as a star on the national flag until July 4, 1865. In its contracts of February 6 and April 26, 1865, Horstmann's artists painted thirty-six stars. The two flags finished on February 6 and the colors for the 52nd and 83rd Regiments in the April contract portrayed a pattern of 5-6-7-arms-7-6-5. The colors for the 157th and 192nd Regiments delivered in April contained an unusual star grouping. A row of seven stars is found on each side of the canton. The remainder of the pattern consists of a 3-4-5-arms-3-4-3 arrangement.

All of the other Horstmann-supplied colors at the end of the war contained thirty-five stars in the patterns listed above. However, the three final colors completed at various times in July 1865 (for the 53rd, 76th, and 81st Regiments) contained a very unusual star pattern. Above the arms, the three rows were arranged 6-4-6, with the third row much arced. Between the second and third rows were two single stars, one on each side of the arc. Beneath the arms were three rows of 5-6-6, with the first two rows somewhat irregularly arranged. Even the regimental designations on the center red stripe were not uniform. Horstmann's initial contracts used a REG^T P.V. This was one of the more common versions of the designation. Two others appeared as REG: P.V. and REG'T P.V. For the drafted militia regiments, Horstmann used PENN^A REG^T on the red stripe.

Evans & Hassall seemed to follow a more uniform painting style. Even this firm's coats-of-arms usually seem to be more uniform (and artistically more basic) than the Horstmann arms. All of Evans & Hassall's 34-star state colors contain a 6-6-5-arms-5-6-6 star pattern with one exception. But even these flags are slightly varied. Some colors in the company's initial contract of September 14, 1861, contain tight arcs of stars (47th, 52nd, 56th Regiments), while other patterns are more evenly distributed across the canton (45th, 51st, 54th).

The exception to this arrangement is the color provided to the 46th Infantry. When Evans & Hassall first expressed an interest in obtaining a state contract, the company supplied a blueprint showing the proposed canton arrangement. This version, illustrated here, depicts a widely dispersed star arrangement. However, the company seems to have followed its initial design proposal only with the color for the 46th Infantry. The canton of this flag, captured in 1863 and returned in 1905, has been humidified and flattened since the publication of Volume One. This allows a reconstruction of the star pattern. It seems to show rows of six stars at the top and bottom of the canton, with six stars painted along each side between the top and bottom rows. The remaining ten stars are scattered around the edge of the state arms.

Evans & Hassall used two star patterns for their 35-star colors. They appear as either a 6-6-5-arms-6-6-6 version or a 5-6-6-arms-6-6-6 arrangement. The

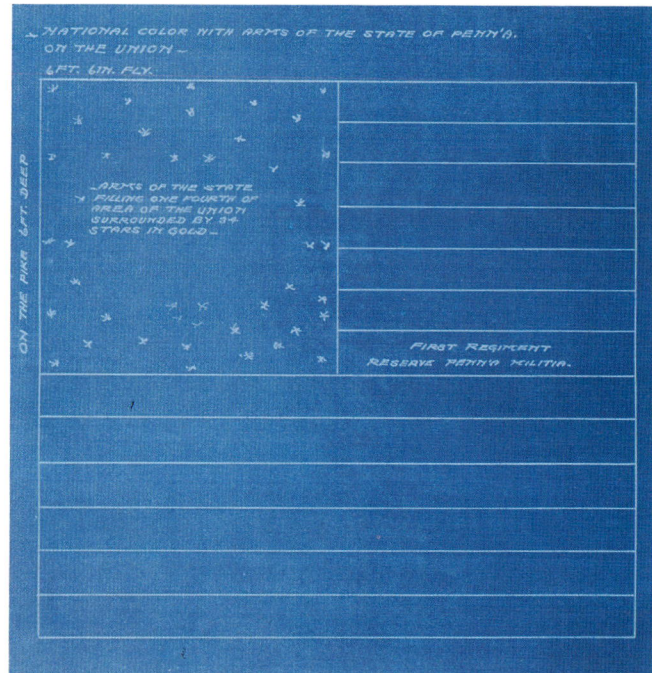

Evans & Hassall Blueprint for State Color

552

Advance the Colors!

company's regimental designations also varied. The common REG:T P.V. appears, as does REG: P.V., REG:T PENN:A VOL:S, REG: PENNA: VOLS:, and REG'T P.V., along with some other minor inconsistencies. Both companies painted a few of their colors with a P.V.V. marking (Veteran Volunteers), but this designation was not used for all the units that veteranized.

Horstmann's cavalry standards followed a common pattern, with two exceptions. The "normal" pattern contains a centered arms. Above is a dark blue scroll with the line number of the regiment. Below is a red scroll with the cavalry designation. Thus, the 4th Cavalry's standard reads "64th REG:T P.V." above and "4th REG:T PENN:A CAV." below. Replacement standards for the 7th and 9th Regiments furnished in May and June 1864 contained a different version of the state arms with both versions of the regimental designation painted on a single red scroll beneath the arms. A circle of thirty-five gold stars surrounds the central motif.

Evans & Hassall did not follow regulations when furnishing their standards. The company supplied three standards for the 3rd, 8th, and 14th Regiments. Only one, that for the 14th Cavalry, survives intact. The 3rd Cavalry's standard is only polesleeve and fringe, while the 8th's is missing from the collection. The surviving standards are much larger than the regulation size of 27 x 29 inches. That for the 3rd Cavalry measures 38 x 45 inches, while the 14th Cavalry's standard is 44 x 41 inches. The design is a centered coat-of-arms with red scrolls both above and below. The higher scroll is inscribed with the line number of the regiment, while the branch number (cavalry) is located on the lower scroll.

Both companies shared the colors and standards contracted by the state for the six artillery regiments. Horstmann supplied state colors for the 1st, 2nd, and 3rd Artillery regiments. These colors are identical to the infantry colors. In May 1865, Horstmann furnished an artillery standard for the 2nd Artillery. This banner matches the standards issued to the cavalry units. Evans & Hassall furnished standards for the 4th, 5th, and 6th Artillery. These flags match the larger-scale cavalry standards manufactured by this company.

Other aspects of the flags and associated items also vary from company to company as well as flag to flag. Both companies furnished a complete flag. The gold fringe is usually two inches in width. Most of it is knotted, although some flags have unknotted fringe. Cords and tassels of the infantry colors varied a bit in exact design, as illustrated by the accompanying photograph. Both companies used the standard spearpoint finial; finials for the infantry and artillery colors are slightly larger than those used for the cav-

The Four Major Patterns of the Cord and Tassels Arrangement for Infantry Colors

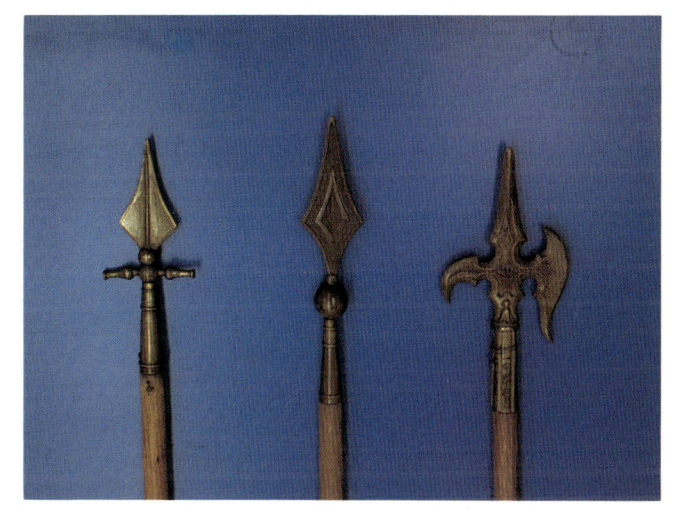

Examples of Finials that Could be Obtained from Flag Manufacturers

alry and artillery standards. Most of the staffs are ash, but there are other woods as well, primarily butternut and walnut.[4]

Both companies were called upon to alter earlier work on flags originally painted for regiments which failed to organize. During the course of the conflict, Horstmann made colors for the 144th, 146th, 154th, and 156th Regiments, none of which were organized. Later, Horstmann altered these colors by simply painting over the gold number designation with red paint, then adding the new number on the overpainting. The company also altered flags originally designed for the 48th and 71st Infantry. A color intended for the 157th was altered for use by the 83rd Infantry. The 157th was at battalion strength and was not authorized to carry a color, although Horstmann supplied this unit with a state color in April 1865. The company provided a standard for the 10th Cavalry (94th Regiment), which was never formed. There is no surviving record to indicate whether this standard was altered for reuse.

Horstmann also repainted the color intended for the 158th Infantry. This unit was one of the 1862-63 drafted militia regiments. Its color was originally included on Horstmann's November 22, 1862, bill, inscribed as a volunteer regiment. The flag was sent back to Horstmann for repainting. Horstmann sent the color back to the state under its bill dated May 16, 1863. Owing to a probable bookkeeping error, the state paid twice for this flag. This seems to be the only instance in which an altered color was bought twice.

Evans & Hassall altered two colors. They were intended for the 120th and 170th Infantry, two more units that failed to organize. The company altered them for use by the 205th and 206th Infantry. The original center red stripe with the unit designation seems to have been unstitched and replaced by a stripe bearing the correct designation. The original colors contained thirty-four stars in the canton; Evans & Hassall did nothing to add a thirty-fifth star to update the flag to the correct number.

There are a few bill discrepancies with the flags. The State Archives has an extensive file of the bills presented by Horstmann and Evans & Hassall to the Commonwealth for payment. This file seems to be complete, but some of the bills do not match the surviving flags. There are three bills for colors of the 81st Infantry. The bills are dated December 9, 1861, January 10, 1865, and July 11, 1865. Horstmann delivered the first and third flags, while Evans & Hassall completed the second color. The collection includes the final two colors delivered in January and July 1865. The first is missing. A pencilled note on the Horstmann list in Record Group 25 notes that a replacement color was ordered on January 20, 1864. This flag also is not identified, and there seems to be no surviving bill that specifies a delivery date.

There are three bills for colors of the 85th Infantry. Two are from Evans & Hassall, dated November 9, 1861, and December 3, 1863. A July 2, 1864, Horstmann bill is also extant. When the state military department was accounting for all the state-issued flags at war's end, an officer of the regiment informed Adjutant-General Russell that the unit had received only two colors from the state.[5] Both colors clearly show a wide canton, indicating Evans & Hassall as the maker. Thus, it appears that the Horstmann bill is in error. This bill quite possibly is the color intended for the 81st Infantry and may simply be a clerical mistake. Since the flag in question is missing from the collection, we can never be sure.

Finally, there are two bills, dated June 6 and July 27, 1864, for Horstmann-supplied colors for the 188th Infantry. Surviving documentation indicates that the June 6 bill is correct, since a color had already been sent to the State Agency when the lieutenant-colonel queried the state for this flag.[6] Without further information, the July 27 bill must remain a mystery. There is no evidence that the regiment lost its state color to the enemy.

The state did not issue flags to every active regiment recruited during the war. Four cavalry regiments—19th, 20th 21st, 22nd (180th, 181st, 182nd, 185th Regiments)—failed to received a state standard. The 154th Infantry, a three-company battalion that perfomed provost duty in Philadelphia for less than a year before discharged, was not given a state color. Other infantry units that did not obtain state colors were the 196th, 197th, 198th, 199th, and 215th. There is no surviving documentation to indicate why these regiments were passed over by the state government in regard to flags.

Federal Government Flags

The colors and standards obtained from the federal government are much more difficult to document than the state-issued flags. It appears that volunteer regiments were not automatically issued regulation flags. If a colonel wanted either or both, he had to requisition them. Therein lies the problem of documenting the field use of these flags. Many of the infantry national and regimental colors in the collection do not seem to have suffered damage from extensive use. Most of the fabric and paint damage seems to have been caused by aging rather than enemy bullets. This suggests that many of the veteran regiments obtained their colors to carry alongside the battle-damaged flags during the Grand Review. The author has read through all existing regimental-level order and letter books in the National Archives for Pennsylvania commands. There are no entries to indicate how any of the regimental commanders obtained such colors. Did they go through the brigade quartermaster, who in turn sent the request on through division, corps, and army, which in turn contacted one of the government depots run by the Office of Clothing and Equipage? Until more research is done, or someone turns up some key information buried in an archive, this question must remain unanswered.

As mentioned previously, the federal government obtained flags for the Regular Army through the Office of Clothing and Equipage, which contracted for the flags through its Philadelphia Depot, centered at the Schuylkill Arsenal. During the opening months of the Civil War, the government did nothing to obtain flags for volunteer units. In early 1862, Washington shouldered the responsibility of equipping the volunteer regiments, assuming this job from the state governments. On February 11, the government, working through the New York Depot, let a contract to a local supplier for national and regimental colors. Six days later, Horstmann received a similar contract. The government expanded its flag suppliers in October by starting contracts issued through the Cincinnati Depot.[7]

These three depots accounted for all of the federal government's flag purchases during the course of the war. According to a summary drawn up in 1865, flag purchases totalled as follows:

Depot	National Colors	Regimental Colors	Standards	Guidons	Camp Colors
Cincinnati	500	564	700	1476	3000
Philadelphia	890	765	286	4189	1000
New York	917	1021	225	4551	7550

However, extant contracts reveal the following totals:

Depot	National Colors	Regimental Colors	Standards	Guidons	Camp Colors
Cincinnati	475	592	700	2470	1502
Philadelphia	597	471	220	2336	1819
New York	827	846	175	3050	7800

The differences between the actual contracts and total purchases may be accounted for by the government's practice of "open market" purchases."[8]

Each of the three depots that issued flag contracts used several different suppliers. The Philadelphia Depot, for example, in addition to Horstmann Brothers and Evans & Hassall, awarded contracts to other suppliers. William F. Scheible was one of the most frequent contractors. The 1862 Philadelphia City Directory lists this man as a stencil cutter, with a flag business located at 49 South Third Street. New York artist Albert T. Ertle received contracts to furnish regimental colors to the Philadelphia Depot. Another New Yorker, James Toft, received a March 1862 contract to deliver twenty cavalry standards to the Philadelphia Depot. Finally, a local sailmaker, J. C. McCormick, received an October 1863 contract for three hundred guidons. Together, these manufacturers furnished the Philadelphia Depot with the number of flags listed above.[9]

Because Civil War vexillology is still a relatively unstudied field, it is difficult to determine how contracts were awarded, how the flags were supplied, and how the designs differed from depot to depot. Howard Madaus, in conjunction with Steven Hill, has studied many, many flags and has arrived at some tentative conclusions based upon the surviving physical evidence. Army Regulations provided general descriptions of how the regulation flags were to appear. However, the Regulations did not give exact sizes for the eagle on the blue regimental color, cannon on the yellow color, star pattern on the national colors, and other details connected with the flags.

Based upon Madaus's and Hill's observations of government contract flags in several state collections, it appears that each of the three depots had its own version of how the contractors were to manufacture the flags. Because documentation is sadly lacking, there are numerous questions involved that have yet to be answered. For example, did each depot have a specific stencil pattern the contractors were to use, or did the depot send an actual sample flag to be copied by the contractor? As with the Pennsylvania state flags, were minor variations the result of artistic license?[10]

National colors furnished through the New York Depot contained a square canton with five horizontal rows of stars, numbering either 7-7-6-7-7 or 7-7-7-7-7. New York-style blue regimental colors portray a "relatively unrealistic eagle." The double row of stars (18 over 16 or 17) extend beyond the tips of the red scroll inscribed with the motto "E Pluribus Unum." The red scroll beneath the eagle has its center section raised, while gold flourishes adorn the ends of the scroll, like the pre-war Regular Army colors. In most, if not all instances, the scrolls were prepainted with REGIMENT INFANTRY on the center and right sections. For an example, see the 106th Infantry's regimental color pictured on page 355. Yellow artillery regimental colors contained a rather large version of the crossed cannon, with a similar red scroll beneath, prepainted with REGIMENT ARTILLERY.[11]

National colors issued through the Cincinnati Depot contained rectangular cantons with the stars arranged in horizontal rows of 5-5-5-5-5-5-4 or 5-5-5-5-5-5-5. The blue regimental colors portrayed a smaller, more realistic eagle of two types. One type, tentatively identified to Cincinnati flag maker Schilleto, bears an artistically well-developed eagle. The bird's head is usually surmounted by a double arc of stars in a 20-15 arrangement, slightly overlapping the ends of the "E Pluribus Unum" scroll. See page 212 for an example of the regimental color carried by the 78th Infantry. The second type, definitely identified to Cincinnati maker Longley & Brother, bears a poorly-rendered eagle, usually with a black eye within a very white feathery head. The double arc of stars above the "E Pluribus Unum" scroll were arranged in a 21-13 or 21-14 pattern. The arc pattern did not extend beyond the tips of this scroll. See the 83rd Infantry's color as an example (page 228). In both patterns, the red scroll beneath the eagle contains a lowered center section, with no prepainted inscriptions. Artillery regimental colors likewise contained a smaller pair of crossed cannon than the New York design.[12]

National colors provided for the Philadelphia Depot contained a unique oval pattern. These colors had a rectangular canton, with a star painted in each corner. Then followed two ovals. On flags delivered by Horstmann and Evans & Hassall, the outer ring bore twenty stars, the inner ring bore nine or ten, depend-

Conclusions

ing on the entire star count. Finally, a single star was painted within the inner oval. Thus, the star pattern can be classed as 4-20-9-1 or 4-20-10-1. On flags made by Scheible, the outer ring contained twenty-one stars and the inner ring ten; there was no center star. Blue regimental colors contained a small, elegantly executed eagle. The double arc of stars was similar to the Longley & Brother Cincinnati pattern, 21-13 or 21-14, not extending beyond the tips of the "E Pluribus Unum" scroll. Beneath the eagle, the red scroll seems to have varied with the supplier. Some have a raised center portion, while it is more common to see a lowered center portion. No inscription was prepainted on this scroll. Yellow artillery colors contained a small cannon pattern and a raised center section of the red scroll beneath the cannon.[13]

The Pennsylvania flag collection contains a mixture of federal contract flags. Exclusive of known local presentations, there are forty-one national colors in the collection. Of these, seventeen are too fragmented to indicate exact star patterns. Of the remaining twenty-four, there are only three New York pattern colors. Two of these are marked "A. Brandon Manufr. N.Y." on the polesleeve. The third is not, but is remarkably similar to the Brandon colors. The firm of Alexander Brandon, located at 4 Tryon Row, was a contractor through the New York Depot. The two marked flags also contain the name of J. W. Duncan, a federal inspector who certified the flags as acceptable under the provisions of the contracts.[14]

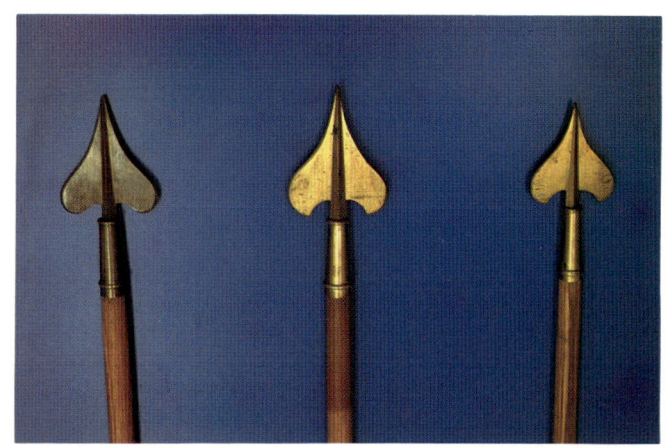

Three Regulation Finials
The Two on the Left are for Infantry Colors While that on the Right is for a Cavalry Standard

Alexander Brandon Imprint on National Color of the 57th Infantry

All remaining identifiable national colors contain the Philadelphia oval pattern. Fourteen have thirty-four stars arranged as 4-20-9-1, while the six 35-star colors have a 4-20-10-1 star pattern. One color has a pattern of 4-17-12-1. Two of these flags, for the 105th and 214th regiments, have "E&H" engraved on the finial base, indicating an Evans & Hassall product. None of the other oval patterns have any manufacturer's marks that have been located. Horstmann, Evans & Hassall, and William F. Scheible were the only three suppliers of national colors to the Philadelphia Depot. Further inductive research, such as star width and exact measurement of the oval pattern, may yield subtle differences that could identify the suppliers.

Again excluding known local presentations, there are fifty-five blue infantry regimental colors in the collection. Sixteen are too fragmentary to draw a clear picture of their exact design. The remaining colors identify manufacturers that supplied both Philadelphia and Cincinnati Depots with such colors. Most identifications are painted along the edges of the red scroll beneath the eagle. There are no New York pattern regimental colors in the collection.

Horstman Brothers is identified as the maker of four colors (for the 50th, 84th, 177th, and 198th Infantry). The major variation easily visible in these four flags is in the red scroll. Two have raised center sections, while that inscribed for the 50th Infantry has a lowered center portion. Since Horstmann supplied regimental colors to both the Philadelphia and Cincinnati Depots, the variance can possibly be ascribed to the different depot patterns. Also, depending on how the flags were stenciled, it is possible that the stenciller simply positioned the stencil the wrong way.

Evans & Hassall is so marked on ten intact or near-intact regimental colors. Seven have lowered center sections of the red scroll while the remaining two have raised center sections. Extant contracts reveal that Evans & Hassall delivered all of its contract colors to the Philadelphia depot. Therefore, this major difference is hard to explain.

William F. Scheible's imprint appears on the intact regimental color for the 173rd Infantry and on the remaining fragment of the 148th Infantry's color. The staffs of the blue colors of the 202nd and 208th Infantry have "W. R. Scheible" branded into the wood. A cursory examination reveals that Scheible's painting style and appearance is very similar to the Evans & Hassall colors. This suggests that each depot did indeed insist on a specific flag pattern.

The remaining regimental colors are unmarked. Nine of these colors exhibit a similar appearance. The eagle has a very white head and the red scroll contains matching shaded areas. Madaus has observed that these flags were probably manufactured by the Cincinnati firm of Longley & Brother. All are 35-star colors. Longley had contracts with the Cincinnati Depot in October 1862 and August 1863 for a total of thirty-five colors, but then received a two-hundred-flag order in October 1864. If these are Longley colors, they all date from this last contract.

There are four yellow artillery regimental colors in the collection. One, for the 112th Regiment, is fragmentary but the tip of the red scroll indicates that the flag was made in Philadelphia. Of the remaining three colors (152nd, 204th, and 212th Regiments), Horstmann is inscribed on the flags of the 152nd and 204th Regiments. All three intact colors are similar, with a raised center section of the scroll beneath the crossed cannon. These scrolls are adorned with flourishes at each end and on the lower edge of the center section. On the color for the 212th, the center section of the top scroll in repainted with "U.S." Otherwise, it appears identical to the marked Horstmann colors. It is interesting to note that there are no surviving Horstmann contracts to deliver artillery colors to any of the federal depots. Therefore, their supply dates and depot of origin must remain unknown.

Much preliminary works remains to be done regarding Civil War cavalry flags. There are only two intact federal standards in the collection, for the 12th and 21st Cavalry (112th and 182nd Regiments). Both seem identical in appearance. The red scroll beneath the eagle contains a raised center portion of each flag. Both scrolls end with gold flourishes. Neither is marked with any discernible manufacturer's imprint.

This is where current research stands. Madaus's regionalization hypothesis seems to make sense when applied to the Pennsylvania collection, then compared to documented flags from other collections. It does appear that each of the three depots had its own version of Army Regulations that it required contractors to follow to some degree. The several minor variations in some of the flags are probably due to artistic license. The contract flags in the state collection primarily represent the Philadelphia depot patterns, with several from Cincinnati evident as well. Until more nationwide research is done, several questions pertaining to this theory must remain unanswered.

Problems

There are several problems associated with documenting the flag collection. Chief among these is the terminology inconsistencies so prevalent during the Civil War. The state-issued infantry flags were called "state colors" by the state military department and by many of the soldiers. However, these flags were also termed "national colors" by other soldiers and writers. The term "colors" itself could refer to one or more flags, depending on how the user defined this term. The term "stand of colors" could also represent one or more flags, again depending on the user's definition and frame of reference. While researching the histories of the flags, the author had to be extremely careful not to draw too many conclusions based upon such inconsistent period terminology. In many instances, descriptions of battle damage ascribed to flags in the state collection could not be corroborated by the banners themselves.

During the course of research, the author began to note a pattern that was repeated by many written documents. At the beginning of this program, when reading the term "blue state color," the author imagined this type of flag to be a blue regimental color painted with the state coat-of-arms. However, it seems that this is not what contemporary writers had in mind. Blue colors with the state arms are few in number. Those that survive are all the products of local presentations. The state did not issue any such flags.

The key was provided by the regimental color of the 96th Infantry. This flag was sent to the Commonwealth in early 1914 by the veterans of the regiment who had originally entrusted the color to the care of the Historical Society of Schuylkill County. Adjutant-General Stewart acknowledged receipt of the "Blue Standard or State Flag" of the 96th Infantry when thanking the veterans for sending it to Harrisburg.[15] The surviving fragments of this color clearly indicate that the flag was painted with a national eagle, not the state arms.

Likewise, when examining the much-tangled history of the 149th's colors at Gettysburg, the author was able to reconcile the written evidence with the physical evidence only by assuming that Captain Bassler, when writing "national color," referred to the state-issued stars and stripes with the state arms in the canton. When mentioning the "state color," Bassler must have meant a blue regimental color with the national eagle. This is the only way to reconcile the capture information printed on the state color with Bassler's account of the loss of the flags.

Frederick L. Hitchcock, adjutant and major of the 132nd Infantry, wrote about his experiences with this unit in his *War from the Inside*. Hitchcock wrote the following description of part of a grand review of the Army of the Potomac in early 1863: "Each of the regiments displayed its two stands of silk colors, one the blue flag representing the State from which it came, the other the national colors."[16] Although this description is very general, it points out the tendency of contemporary writers to refer to the blue regimental flags as "state colors." By doing so, contemporaries such as Hitchcock seem to have called "state colors" those blue colors that included an inscribed red scroll beneath the eagle.

In addition to the written evidence from the 96th, 132nd, and 149th Regiments, similar documentation from the 88th, 118th, and 188th Regiments confirms the above descriptions. Thus, anyone researching the histories of Pennsylvania's flags must be extremely careful to detail when comparing the written record with the physical evidence. This is a task easier said than done.

A second major problem is determining when each regiment actually carried its flags and how many flags were carried. Army Regulations specified that each artillery and infantry regiment should carry two flags—national and regimental. However, regulations were not always followed in a volunteer army. Clearly, many Pennsylvania regiments carried only the state color in lieu of the national color. Such regiments included most of the Reserve Corps regiments, 53rd, 58th, and 150th Regiments. Some regiments carried two colors in a variety of combinations. For example, the 85th Infantry carried the state color alongside a locally-presented national color. The 69th Infantry carried its state color together with a green Irish flag. The 107th Infantry apparently carried its state color and a blue regimental color, as did the 110th, 188th, and 201st Regiments. A very few units seem to have carried three large colors. The 51st Infantry carried its state color as well as a set of local presentations that included national and regimental colors. During the Atlanta Campaign, the 111th Infantry carried three flags—state, national, and regimental.

Many Pennsylvania regiments received local presentation flags during the war. Since the collection has so few, and because many have not survived, it is hard to document their use. Clearly, most units did carry their local flags into combat. At times, these local flags supplanted the state-issued flags. The 23rd Infantry retired its state color in January 1863 and carried local presentations thereafter. The 84th retired its state color in November 1862, the 88th in December 1863, the 105th in April 1864, and the 138th in December 1864. In one of the few documented cases of a regiment not carrying its state color into battle, the 72nd Infantry kept its state color out of action at Gettysburg. It carried a local presentation instead.

In addition to the above regiments retiring their state colors, some units that lost their colors in battle failed to ask for replacements from the state. The 56th, 149th, and 150th Regiments all simply obtained colors from other sources. In the case of the 56th Infantry, the officers pooled some money to buy a "state color" from Evans & Hassall, judging from the width of the canton. Other regiments substitued local presentations for captured state flags. The Bucktails (13th Reserves) used a national color presented to Company K in lieu of their state color lost on the Peninsula.

Some regiments obviously failed to carry their presented flags into battle. A prime example is the blue regimental color presented to the 82nd Infantry in October 1861. The physical evidence clearly shows that the regiment did not use this color in battle. The Cooper Shop Refreshment Saloon color presented to the 2nd Reserves in March 1864 also lacks identifiable battle damage.

Many companies also received locally-presented flags to carry. This entire class of flags is hard to document. Although Army Regulations were not always enforced, it is readily apparent that the company flags, most of which were much smaller than the regulation-size flags, were not carried in battle. There were exceptions. For example, the flag presented to Company K of the 42nd Infantry (13th Reserves, or Bucktails) was used as the regimental color after the state color was captured during the Seven Days' Battles. This flag was used until May 1863, when the regiment received a national color from the 149th Infantry.

More than forty regiments had companies which received flags. Many of these banners have not survived the ravages of time. Most of the newspaper accounts of the presentations do not provide specific information as to size or appearance. There is a prevalent myth that local women sewed the flags for their local soldiers, but the surviving evidence does not support this myth. Most citizens, when they wished to present flags either to an entire regiment or a single company, pooled their money and had the flags done by a professional. Few surviving flags attest to strictly local workmanship. The flag most documented as to its origin is that presented by the ladies of Martinsburg to the 11th Infantry. The women of Uniontown seem to have personally sewn the national color presented to the 85th Infantry.

The majority of the company flags that have survived do not contain evidence of battle damage. Since regulations would not have permitted the field use of company flags, most were probably relegated to use as the company commander's flag in the company street of the campsites. Some were sent home. For example, the St. Clair Guards, which became Company H, 62nd Infantry, purchased a small silk national flag in 1860. When the regiment left Pittsburgh for Harrisburg, the men took this flag with them. However, the flag was not allowed to be used and the soldiers sent it back home. Company K, 1st Cavalry, likewise returned their presented flag when the regiment received its state standard.

Some officers also received personal flags to carry off to war. One example that has survived was presented to Lieutenant George W. Eyre, quatermaster of the 91st Infantry. According to his notes, the lieutenant used this flag as his headquarters tent flag while on campaign with the regiment. The flag was never used in battle.

Lieutenant George W. Eyre's Personal Flag Used During the War

The problem of documenting a unit's colors is further compounded by the knowledge that not all flags have survived, either in the extant written records or as relics in public or private collections. Thus, the complete story will never be known. Some examples illustrate this problem. Colonel Joseph B. Kiddoo of the 137th Infantry wrote that his unit received flags when it left Harrisburg in the fall of 1862. Since the regiment's state color apparently was not delivered until May 1863, Kiddoo referred to other colors, presumably a pair of national and regimental colors. These flags were not turned over to state care and have not survived to the present.[17]

The colonels of two of the drafted militia regiments commented on the flags they received. Colonel William Brisbane of the 166th Infantry recalled that while encamped at York the regiment obtained through a quartermaster a set of national and regimental colors. When informed that the state color was at the agency building in Washington, Brisbane wrote to General Russell and informed him that these colors could be turned over to any army quartermaster when the state color arrived. Likewise, Colonel Charles Kleckner of the 172nd Infantry obtained not only the regulation pair of colors but a set of guidons while in Harrisburg.[18] None of these federal colors were given to the state; their eventual disposition is unknown.

Finally, in regard to a unit's flags, many Pennsylvania regiments also obtained flank markers and camp colors for use. The flank guidons (variously

Flank Marker of 91st Infantry
Size: 19 x 23

termed "flank markers," "general guide markers," "markers," or "guidons") were not used as regulation flags by the Regular Army until 1885. Any such flags used by volunteer units largely came via local presentation. Thus, these flags were of varying size, shape, and composition. Several have survived, some in the state collection, many others in public and private collections. Some regiments, judging from photographic and physical evidence, seem to have requisitioned generic cavalry company guidons to use as flank markers.

Many regiments obtained the regulation camp colors, bunting flags eighteen inches square. They were authorized for infantry and artillery regiments. In January 1862, the War Department changed the design to

Camp Color of the 83rd Infantry
Size: 18 x 18
1985.364

Conclusions

a small national flag. These flags were originally intended to mark the limits of a regimental camp, but many commanders seem to have used them as flank markers as well. In essence, the volunteer service during the Civil War generally regarded flank markers and camp colors as roughly for the same purpose. Thus, it appears that these small flags were interchangeably used for a variety of purposes, but primarily for use by the general guides to mark the ends of the regimental line of battle. Usage also seemed to depend on which tactical manual was used by a particular regiment. William Gilham's manual defined expanded uses for the guide markers while Silas Casey's tactics did not. At present, these small flags remain a little-studied aspect of Civil War vexillology.[19]

Battle honors painted on the flags and attached streamers pose another, though lesser, problem, in documenting the flags. Forty-four flags in the collection have battle honors painted on them, while thirty-eight flags have streamers attached. Judging from the newspaper descriptions, the streamers seem to have been specially made for use in the 1866 Philadelphia ceremony. Some news stories even listed the names of the battles visible on some of the streamers.

The honors painted on the flags themselves pose more of a problem. Many are hard to date. Only a few can be accurately dated to actual wartime conditions. Governor Curtin, to honor the Reserve Corps regiments involved in the Dranesville action in December 1861, had the colors of the five regiments engaged taken to Horstmann Brothers to inscribe the battle on each flag. The 29th Infantry had its flag sent back to Evans & Hassall to have its Shenandoah Valley campaign inscribed on its state color. The 51st Infantry inscribed its honors on the state color as the war progressed. In late March 1862, Captain James M. Linn recorded that Fred Ervine painted the engagements of Roanoke Island and New Bern on the unit's flag.[20] A photograph of this flag (see page 140) clearly shows different painting styles as names were added to this banner.

Other colors had battles added by the time they were turned over to state care. The July 1865 photographs of the 50th Infantry encamped at Gettysburg show that this unit's blue regimental color had been suitably inscribed by that time. By May 31, 1866, when the adjutant-general's office was collecting flags for the upcoming ceremony, a list was annotated with "battles show" for colors of the 51st, 58th, 73rd, 77th, 85th, 98th, 100th, 103rd, and 104th Regiments. Of these, the 73rd's must have been painted when the flag was delivered by Evans & Hassall, for the artist inscribed the regimental designation on the top stripe,

Officers of 50th Infantry at Gettysburg in July 1865 The Regimental Color with Battle Honors Can Be Seen as a Blurred Outline in the Center of the Photograph

then listed the battles in chronological order on successive stripes.

Some commanders sought custody of their flags prior to the 1866 ceremony so they could have the battles inscribed. For example, Colonel Robert L. Orr of the 61st Infantry requested his flag in mid-June.[21] On June 26, the adjutant-general's office gave the 151st Infantry state color to Colonel George F. McFarland.[22] Although neither letter specifically mentions the painting of honors, it is probable that this is why these officers, as well as others, asked for their flags for a few days.

Many of the local presentations, especially later in the war, contained painted honors as an integral part of the flag. Presented colors in the collection so painted include the national colors given to the 31st, 42nd, 51st, and 88th Regiments. The remnants of blue regimental colors for the 48th and 96th Regiments also portray battle honors. Several flags in other collections also illustrate prepainted honors, such as those presented to the 44th, 93rd, 109th, 138th, and 150th Regiments.

If battle honors are hard to document exactly, one sure way of dating the field use of a flag is by the remnants of black crepe attached to staffs or sewn on some of the flags. On April 16, 1865, the War Department announced to the armed forces the death of President Abraham Lincoln. The following statement was included with General Orders #66: "The officers of the Armies of the United States will wear the badge of mourning on the left arm and on their swords, and the colors of their commands and regiments will be put in mourning for the period of six months."[23] The mourning consisted of using black crepe to drape the flags. Several dozen flagstaffs still have pieces of crepe tied around the finial bases. A few regiments, including the 11th Infantry and 5th Heavy Artillery, sewed the black crepe directly to their silk colors. Flags thus marked undoubtedly were carried from April 1865 until the regiments were disbanded.

Finally, there are some problems associated with the postwar history of the flag collection. There are a few surviving requests from veterans asking for the loan of their battle-scarred flags so they could be displayed at reunions. However, it seems the adjutant-general was reluctant to allow the flags to be loaned. The one exception was for the funeral procession of General Meade in 1872. Colonel Horatio G. Sickel received permission to borrow the colors of the Reserves, which were proudly a center of attention of the long procession.[24] Otherwise, the government rejected loan requests.

The exact locations and conditions of the flag collection throughout the period before 1914 is somewhat of a mystery. It is not known exactly how they were stored in the State Arsenal prior to the opening of the Flag Room in 1873. The present paper labels on the staffs were adhered at some now-unknown time. At times, flags were added to the collection. A survey reveals that several additions have not survived. For example, in 1871 the Quartermaster-General of the Army, Montgomery C. Meigs, authorized the return of some Pennsylvania flags then stored in the Schuylkill Arsenal. The flags in question appear to have been ten guidons of the 6th Pennsylvania Cavalry.[25]

When removing the staff of the national color of the 78th Infantry, a label was found with the following inscription: "Guidon—6th Regt. Penna. Cavalry. Received from Lt. J. Allison, RQM." Handwritten over this label is the following: "Taken for purpose of displaying flag of 78' Regt. P. V. Infty. Dec 2/85." One of the regimental colors of the 78th also has similar labels attached. The blue regimental color attributed to the 76th Infantry has a printed label with "....Regt. Penna. Cavalry. Guidon. Company _D_." Thus, at least these three flagstaffs once contained cavalry guidons that were removed so the infantry colors could be displayed. Why this was done in lieu of placing the infantry colors on new staffs is a mystery.

According to Army Regulations, the staffs were supposed to measure an even nine feet in length for cavalry flags and nine feet, ten inches for infantry colors. The existing staffs are all at least a foot shorter. In 1896, a veteran of the 52nd Infantry brought with him to the annual reunion the lower end of one of the staffs of the 52nd, "which had to be sawed off in order to get the flag into the glass case at Harrisburg."[26] Thus, when the flags were moved from the Capitol into the Library in 1893, they must have been made to fit into existing glass cases rather than have special cases designed to hold the flag collection.

The labelling of the collection also had to be carefully documented as the project unfolded. Each of the flags mounted on staffs prior to 1914 had labels printed with the regimental number attached to the staff. At some point, someone using a red pen inked the type of flag beneath the regimental number, i.e. "State," "U.S.," "U.S.R.," or "Presented by friends." These labels probably date from the 1873 Flag Room, since flags added in the 1880s and later have handwritten labels attached to their staffs. Only four incorrect labels have been noticed. The 48th Infantry's second state color was marked as belonging to the 148th, the 2nd Cavalry's original standard was labelled in 1914 as that of the 2nd Provisional Cavalry, an unmarked national color with a penciled "148th P.V." on a white stripe was identified as a color of the 118th,

Conclusions

and the camp color of the 83rd Infantry was marked "Sheridan Troop" on its staff. Otherwise, the flags seem to match what is written on their staffs.

Some flags once turned over to state care were either loaned out and never returned or were not sent to Harrisburg. When Major Lane compiled a list of flags remaining in his Philadelphia office in April 1866, he included national colors for the 114th, 119th, and 152nd Regiments that are not present in the state collection. Three colors for the 90th Infantry were given to Colonel Peter Lyle. The 209th Infantry turned in a national flag without a staff. This color was placed on a staff in May 1866, then marked "out" on the list. The 6th Heavy Artillery turned in a national color in bad condition. This flag has apparently not survived, unless it is one of the unidentified colors.

This, in brief, is an analysis of the state-issued flags, government-contract flags, and the problems associated with the documentation of the state Civil War flag collection. Much work remains to be done. The artwork on the flags needs more detailed studies, as does the differences between government contractors and their products. More research in manuscript collections and newpapers may well fill in some of the gaps that exist at present. In sum, the Pennsylvania collection beckons to art historians, painting and silk textile conservators, ballistics experts, vexillologists, and others to continue work on this fascinating aspect of American material culture.

Notes

1 Some of the few surviving Horstmann Papers can be found in the Lippincott Papers, Historical Society of Pennsylvania. This collection includes a Horstmann Machine Record Book from the late 1850s.

2 Pomeroy's full report can be found in the files at the conservation laboratory. He was able to inspect the flags published in Volume One as well as the additional flags that had been placed in the new storage room by late summer 1989. Half the collection remains to be studied.

3 Howard Madaus, "The Conservation of Civil War Flags: The Military Historian's Perspective," p. 74. In Pennsylvania Capitol Preservation Committee, *Flag Symposium, Papers Presented at the Symposium, Harrisburg, PA, October 29-30, 1987* (Harrisburg: Department of General Services, 1988).

4 Nancy R. Pollak, "Identification of Woods Used in Staffs," Summer 1989 Intern Project, conservation laboratory files.

5 Lieutenant-Colonel Edward Campbell to A. L. Russell, May 31, 1866, RG 19.

6 Lieutenant-Colonel George K. Bowen to A. L. Russell, June 20, 1864, Regimental Papers, RG 19.

7 Madaus, "Historian's Perspective," p. 75.

8 *Ibid.*, p. 90.

9 Bruce S. Bazelon and William F. McGuinn, *A Directory of American Military Goods Dealers & Makers 1785-1885* (Manassas, VA: REF Typesetting & Publishing, Inc., 1987), p. 73; Madaus, pp. 76-77.

10 Madaus, p. 80.

11 *Ibid.*, pp. 79-81.

12 *Ibid.*, pp. 82-85.

13 *Ibid.*, pp. 81-82.

14 Bazelon & McGuinn, p. 9.

15 Adjutant-General Thomas J. Stewart to Baird Halberstadt, January 28, 1914, RG 25.

16 Hitchcock, *War from the Inside*, p. 193.

17 Colonel Joseph B. Kiddoo to A. L. Russell, May 10, 1863, RG 25.

18 Lieutenant William E. Patterson to A. L. Russell, March 20, 1863; Colonel Charles Kleckner to A. L. Russell, March 19, 1863, both in RG 19.

19 I am indebted to Howard Madaus for information on these small flags. Madaus has written an article on camp colors and guide markers that he is in the process of revising for publication.

20 James M. Linn, "The Burnside Expedition," *Lewisburg Chronicle*, August 11, 1894.

21 Colonel Robert L. Orr to A. L. Russell, June 21, 1866, RG 19.

22 Pencilled notation on May 31, 1866, list of flags, RG 25.

23 *O.R.* 46.3, p. 788.

24 Sickel to "Dear Major," November 12, 1872, Sickel Letters in Claude W. Unger Collection, Historical Society of Pennsylvania.

25 Meigs to Adjutant-General of Pennsylvania, February 13, 1871, RG 25. In January 1871, the Schuylkill Arsenal received several boxes of flags to store at the arsenal. The list and accompanying letter can be found in the National Archives, RG 92, Records of the Office of the Quartermaster-General.

26 Untitled story about the 52nd's reunion in *NT*, October 15, 1896.

Chapter X
Epilogue

Once the war ended, most of the boys in blue shed their uniforms and returned to civilian life. The hundreds of Pennsylvanians who carried the colors of their regiments quickly passed into the obscurity of history as they coped with daily problems. Some became prominent in local politics and government, others used their talents to help their state and federal governments. Some moved west in search of better opportunities; many more returned home to their old jobs. What follows are brief biographical sketches of selected color-bearers to illustrate that their lives did not come to a halt once the shooting stopped.

James Robinson Balsley of the 142nd Infantry was wounded in both thighs at Gettysburg and left behind on the battlefield as the regiment fell back. The crippled soldier was rescued and carried to the field hospital set up in the Catholic Church. He remained here until July 17, then was transferred to the Cotton Factory Hospital in Harrisburg. When released in December, Balsley was not able to walk normally. Instead of receiving a medical discharge, he was transferred to Company A, 7th Veteran Reserve Corps. He performed duty with this unit until January 1865. By this time, he had become ill with fever and doctors recommended a discharge.

Balsley returned home to Connellsville. He had been a shoemaker before the war, but he now turned to work with the Baltimore & Ohio Railroad. He soon transferred to Calhoun & Company, a local lumber mill, as a superintendent of their planing mill. In the early 1880s, he purchased an old lumber plant and established the Youghiogheny Lumber Yard, which he owned and operated until 1892, when he retired.

The veteran married in 1867 and sired four children. Balsley was an active member of both the local Odd Fellows Lodge and Post 104, Grand Army of the Republic. However, as he grew older, his wounds contributed to his suffering. By the time he died on September 21, 1924, Balsley had become an invalid and was confined to a bed in his son Charles's home. Increasing senility also plagued the old soldier. A sore on the side of his face speeded his death as well. He was not quite eighty-one years old when he died. Balsley was buried in the Chestnut Hill Cemetery in Connellsville.

John B. Cooke of the 95th Infantry was wounded while carrying a flag at Saylor's Creek. The ankle wound was Cooke's second, the first having occurred at Spotsylvania. After he was discharged, the twenty-two-year-old at first went home, then entered Bucknell University, graduating in 1873. He then attended the Crozer Theological Seminary in Chester, graduating in 1877. For the next nine years, Cooke was an active Baptist minister, at first in Lima, Ohio, then in Greeley, Colorado. Ill health forced him to step down from the pulpit. He then became a school superintendent in Weld County, Colorado. In 1901, Cooke was appointed clerk of the Colorado Supreme Court and was admitted to law practice. He returned to Philadelphia in 1904, where he acted as an elder of St. Paul's Presbyterian Church for fifteen years until advancing years forced him to retire. He died in 1939.

William Coon of Company D, 61st Infantry was hit in the left knee just as the regiment started its charge on April 2, 1865. When Coon fell, another soldier seized the color and advanced. In the end, three men were awarded Medals of Honor for their bravery in carrying the colors that day. Coon was not so fortunate. He was sent to a Washington hospital, then transferred to Chestnut Hill Hospital in Philadelphia. He was still there when the regiment was mustered out in late June 1865.

After his discharge, Coon went home to Miners Mills, Luzerne County. He married Maria Smith in October of that year. Coon went to work for a flour mill near home. His war wound continued to plague him. Chronic rheumatism, the apparent result of his exposure to the elements during the Peninsula Campaign, caused almost daily pain as he grew older. He also complained of occasional fits of dizziness, caused, he maintained, by a wound to his left temple that he received at Fair Oaks. In 1875, while unloading heavy boxes from a freight car, Coon slipped and fell, straining his back. This injury also caused prolonged suffering. Friends who provided affadavits for his continued requests for an increase in his pension wrote that Coon should not have continued work at the mill, but the charitable owners refused to discharge him. Finally, in the winter of 1898, during a spell of dizziness, Coon fell into the machinery he was operating. Before he was pulled free, he lost one finger and had a second badly mangled. Coon passed away on March 7, 1900. Cause of death was listed as acute hepatitis and general debility. Gastritis also contributed to his demise. At the time, Coon was receiving eight dollars a month in pension benefits from the federal government. His widow survived until 1924.

Carbondale native Patrick DeLacy returned home after his distinguished service record with the 143rd Infantry. His bravery at the Wilderness, where he shot a Rebel color-bearer and seized the man's flag, earned him a Medal of Honor in 1894. When the shooting stopped, DeLacy settled in Scranton and resumed his living as foreman of a tannery. In 1867, he was appointed a deputy federal marshal in Scranton. Four years later, DeLacy successfully ran for the state House of Representatives. He remained in the House until he ran for a Senate seat in 1874. He was defeated in his bid and returned to the leather business.

John C. Delaney

Thereafter, DeLacy held a variety of civil posts in Scranton. In succession, he was deputy sheriff of Lackawanna County (1876), county auditor (1877-79), Scranton Chief of Police (1879-85), Assistant Postmaster (1885), and a Seventh Ward Alderman from 1889 until his death in April 1915. In addition, DeLacy was an active member of the GAR, serving his local post as commander for five terms. He was the most influential member of the 143rd Regimental Association; his comrades elected him president for almost fifty straight years. A son and daughter survived Scranton's "grand old man."

Irish-born John Carroll Delaney enlisted in Company I, 107th Infantry, while he was not yet fourteen years old. His entire army career was filled with danger and excitement. Six times he claimed to have been captured by the enemy but escaped in each instance. He helped rescue the 107th's colors at Antietam, barely escaping in a hail of lead bullets. At Gettysburg, Delaney was wounded in the right leg, then captured by advancing Confederates.

However, he was left behind when the Southerners retreated and managed to obtain treatment at a Union field hospital. At Petersburg on June 18, 1864,

Patrick DeLacy, Shown Here as Sergeant-Major

Delaney helped carry his wounded company captain off the field. That October, the plucky lad was promoted to sergeant. During the fighting at Hatcher's Run (February 6, 1865) small brush fires threatened many of the wounded Federals left between the lines after an unsuccessful charge. Delaney asked for volunteers to save the helpless men from burning to death; when everyone else declined, Delanely sprang over the line of breastworks and carried a man back to safety, braving enemy rifle bullets fired at him. Others saw Delaney's heroic efforts and helped their commander bring several men to safety, earning cheers by the grayclad spectators. For his bravery, Delaney received a Medal of Honor in 1894. By the time of his discharge in May 1865, Delaney was a lieutenant in command of Company I.

Scantly educated, Delaney learned during the war, with help from his commanding officers. On returning to Luzerne County, Delaney attended Kingston Academy and then joined the Lehigh Valley Engineer Corps. In 1873, Governor John F. Hartranft appointed the veteran his personal messenger. He was appointed Senate Librarian seven years later. While living in Harrisburg, Delaney married a local woman and fathered three children. In 1890, President Benjamin Harrison appointed him Receiver of Public Monies for the Oklahoma Territory.

Delaney returned to Harrisburg in 1894. A year later, Governor Daniel Hastings employed him as Superintendent of Public Grounds and Buildings, a post he retained until 1899. For the fiscal year ending June 1896, Delaney instituted a price scale based on feet and pounds for supplies purchased by the Commonwealth. Unless rigorously enforced, this vaguely-worded statement easily could be subject to abuse. Indeed it soon was, for his friend John Sanderson was one of the prime suppliers of furnishings to the new state capitol that was completed in 1906. The resulting Capitol Graft Scandal ruined Sanderson and many others involved in this complex affair. Delaney escaped any blame, but his career was hurt. Governor Samuel W. Pennypacker appointed him chief State Factory Inspector in 1903, a position he retained until 1913. At that time, Delaney announced that he had a confession from Sanderson, now dead. The new governor, John K. Tener, removed Delaney from office for his remarks. Delaney's wife later maintained that her husband's failing health became steadily worse after his removal from state employment. Delaney died on April 14, 1915, and was buried in Arlington Cemetery.

Fergus Elliott was discharged in 1865 when the 111th Infantry, with which the 109th had been merged in March, was disbanded. He returned to Philadelphia. By 1871, Elliott was serving on the city's police force. From 1887 to 1890, he was House Sergeant of the Chestnut Hill Station, then returned to patrol duty when the station closed. A year later, Elliott was House Sergeant at the Olney Station, where he remained until 1902. At that time, he was assigned to the Germantown Station, followed in succession by transfers to Olney and Chestnut Hill. He retired from the force in 1917, looked upon as the dean of Philadelphia's police sergeants. Death from myocarditis came in December 1923 at his beach bungalow in Bradley Beach, New Jersey. He and his wife (who died in 1917) are buried in Saint Luke's Cemetery, Germantown.

Colonel Jacob G. Frick was discharged in May 1863 when his 129th Infantry went home, but his Civil War service was not yet complete. A scant five weeks later, Frick was commissioned colonel of the new 27th Pennsylvania Emergency Militia, one of the regiments organized to oppose General Lee's invasion of the Commonwealth. Frick was dispatched to guard the bridge over the Susquehanna at Wrightsville. Supplemented by convalescent soldiers from the York Hospital, a portion of the 20th Militia, the Philadelphia City Troop, and four independent companies (including one composed of free blacks from Lancaster County), Frick had about 1,500 men to oppose the enemy. On the evening of June 28, a brigade of Jubal Early's Division approached Frick's defensive line and began probing the position. Lacking any artillery, Frick's green troops were eventually forced to retire towards the bridge. When it became apparent that he could not hold the line, Frick sent his troops across the span and then burned the structure to prevent the Rebels from seizing this crossing point. Frick was subsequently placed in command of a militia brigade until discharged on July 31.

Frick then returned home to Pottsville. He entered the screen business, building a shop at the corner of Railroad and East Norwegian Streets. He was married twice, fathering three sons and a daughter. The colonel was an active member of the First Presbyterian Church and the local GAR Post. He died on March 5, 1902, of heart disease and dropsy.

William L. Graul served out his time in the 188th Infantry, then returned home to Reading. A Democrat in politics, he was active in local affairs. At one time he was alderman for the city's Eighth Ward. Graul opened a hotel in nearby Temple. This facility became known as one of the best roadhouses in eastern Pennsylvania, "its cuisine being noted far and wide." Its proprietor was described as "genial and wholesouled . . . and a good conversationalist." He was one of the most esteemed members of Elks Lodge 115. In 1909,

William L. Graul

Graul bought one of the new "horseless carriages." Accompanied by his wife and Dr. and Mrs. Samuel E. Slegel, Graul drove off for a five-day trip to Delaware Water Gap. On the return journey, they entered Douglassville and approached the Pennsylvania Railroad crossing. Here, the track curved behind the station. Although a warning bell announced an approaching train, the engine noise apparently drowned out the warning signal. The locomotive crashed into Graul's automobile, hurling it down an embankment. As the collision took place, the auto's gas tank exploded. Graul, his wife, and Mrs. Slegel all were killed. The doctor was in bad shape but survived the ordeal.

Coatesville native Walter W. Greenland helped save the color of his 125th Infantry at Antietam. Once his military service was over, Greenland began to study civil engineering. Sometime after the war, he moved to Clarion where he became involved in the oil business. He also served as county prothonotary. In 1886 he joined the 16th Regiment, National Guard of Pennsylvania. Greenland was rapidly promoted and in 1891 he was appointed quatermaster-general. A year later, Governor Robert E. Pattison appointed him Adjutant-General. Greenland died on March 23, 1895, of complications resulting from a cold that infected his lungs and heart.

German-born John Hirschling survived his service in the 98th Infantry. After he was mustered out of service, he returned to Philadelphia and resumed his job as a machinist. In addition to recurring problems because of the slight wound to his right wrist, Hirschling suffered from other army-related maladies such as chronic rheumatism. In 1882, during a bout of typhoid fever, he mistook a window for a door and fell through it, breaking his left leg. This accident forced him to leave his job and depend on his family for sustenance. Hirschling lingered on and died in February 1913.

Lieutenant Frederick L. Hitchcock of the 132nd Infantry went home to Scranton briefly after the regiment was mustered out of service. He sought a higher rank and decided to enter the Free Military School in Philadelphia. This school educated soldiers seeking commissions in the United States Colored Troops. Hitchcock passed the examination and was commissioned lieutenant-colonel of the 43rd USCT. He was promoted to colonel in mid-1864, commanding this regiment until it was disbanded in December 1865.

Hitchcock went to Scranton on furlough in January 1865 so he could wed Caroline Kingsbury. After the war, Hitchcock again settled in Scranton and returned to his law practice. He devoted much of his time to public service. Hitchcock acted as Director of Public Safety for the city, served a term as City Treasurer, was a member of the Chamber of Commerce, and initiated much historical research on Scranton's growth. He was also commander of the 13th Regiment, Pennsylvania National Guard, from its organization until 1888. His literary efforts included *War from the Inside* (a personal account of his service with the 132nd), *The History of Scranton and Its People*, a regimental history of the 13th National Guard published in 1924, as well as numerous contributions to local newspapers. In September 1924, Hitchcock tripped over a rug and fell, injuring his hip. His health was improving when he suffered a heart attack and died on October 9. A local reporter wrote that "his death is Scranton's loss, robbing the city of the services of one of its most illustrious men whose life was a story of brilliant achievements in war and peace."

One of fourteen black soldiers awarded a Medal of Honor for heroism at Chapin's Farm and New Market Heights, Alexander Kelley of the 6th USCT went home to Coultersville, located near Pittsburgh. The

horses and mules. The soldiers formed a defensive position as the Indians kept them under fire, slowly whittling away their numbers and threatening the men with eventual starvation from lack of food and water.

Rankin was one of four volunteers who left the soldiers in an attempt to reach help. He proved to be the only man who got through. He eluded the Utes and rode 165 miles to the town of Rawlins, where a telegraph operator sent word to the army for help. Colonel Wesley Merritt and the "buffalo soldiers" of the 9th United States Cavalry, guided to the scene by Rankin, reached the trapped force and rescued the survivors, who had spent a week under constant Indian fire. In 1890, Rankin was appointed federal marshal for part of the Wyoming Territory. A much-respected citizen, Rankin died in his sleep at his San Diego home on March 9, 1919, aged 74 years.

When Reuben Schell was captured in the Wilderness along with most of the 7th Reserves, he wept

Alexander Kelley Lies Beneath an Almost Illegible Tombstone

veteran apparently resumed his occupation as a coal miner. On July 30, 1866, Kelley was married in the Baptist Church at Hollidaysburg, Blair County. The couple remained childless but did adopt some children who were grown when Mrs. Kelley died in 1898. By that time Kelley had relocated to Pittsburgh, where he worked as a night watchman at a livery stable. Sergeant Kelley passed away on June 19, 1907. He and his wife are buried side by side in East Liberty's St. Peter's Cemetery. However, time and acid rain have almost erased the tombstone inscriptions.

Private Joseph Rankin of the 63rd Infantry carried the flag from the Wilderness to Appomattox. After the war, Rankin migrated westward to the Colorado Territory. In 1879, he performed the greatest feat of his life. After being mistreated by the local Indian agent, the Ute tribe rebelled and killed the man and his family. Major Thomas T. Thornburgh led a force of cavalry to round up the hostiles, with Rankin serving as a civilian scout to guide the troopers. The Utes ambushed the column, killing the major and most of the

Reuben Schell, Photographed in Lock Haven

Epilogue

when he was forced to relinquish the new stand of colors to the 61st Georgia. Upon capture, Schell and his comrades were sent to the infamous Andersonville prison. After about five months in Georgia, Schell was transferred to the prison at Florence, South Carolina. As the war progressed, Reuben was sent to other prisons, then finally paroled at Wilmington, North Carolina, in March 1865. After a hospital stay here, Schell went north to another facility on Long Island. He then was assigned to the 190th Infantry as a lieutenant in Company H. He was discharged with the regiment in July 1865.

Schell, worse the wear because of his incarceration, returned to Clinton County. Disease had robbed him of all but seven of his teeth and led to ulcers and recurring gum problems. Varicose veins had developed in his lower right leg, accompanied by the usual army-related illnesses like rheumatism. Once home, he discovered that his brother Benneville, who also surrendered at the Wilderness, had escaped from prison, was recaptured, and later died. Somehow, he managed to have a fellow prisoner deliver a hundred dollars to his family, in hopes that his brother's body could be retrieved and sent north for proper burial. However, their father used the money for whiskey to satisfy his addiction, dying of the disease eventually in 1881.

Reuben went to work as a filer in a saw mill. In 1870 he married and moved to Lock Haven a year later. By the early 1880s, Reuben's physical disabilities prohibited him from pursuing manual labor, so his employer at the West Branch Tannery transferred him to the bookkeeping department, of which he eventually became head. Schell was an active member of the local GAR Post, St. John's Lutheran Church, and was a member of the city council. He died in April 1909.

James M. Seitzinger was only eighteen years old when the 116th Infantry was disbanded in 1865. After carrying the colors at Cold Harbor, Seitzinger was wounded at Reams's Station in August and ranked as a sergeant when the shooting stopped. Young Seitzinger returned home to the small town of Gordon in Schuylkill County. He married in 1867, fathering five children by 1881. After his first wife passed away in 1898, he married a second time in 1903. Seitzinger was employed by the Pennsylvania & Reading Railroad as an engineer for more than fifty years. He expired on January 14, 1924.

Henry H. Spayd of the 149th Infantry survived the Civil War and went home to Myerstown, a small village in Lebanon County. He married a local woman, Sara Donaberger, then moved to Philadelphia and went into the mercantile business. Spayd returned to Lebanon County to take a position as a schoolteacher. In 1871, the Spayds moved to Minersville so Henry could accept the position as principal of the local grammar school. Thereafter, Spayd devoted forty years of his life to the school, where he was promoted to superintendent in 1883. He was a life member of the State Teachers Association, a member of the National Education Association and American Institute of Civics, as well as many other professional societies. He was also a charter member of the Historical Society of Schuylkill County.

Spayd was interested in the community and helped organize the Union National Bank of Minersville. Once he retired from teaching, he worked as a clerk in that bank. In 1910, he entered into partnership in a local dry goods establishment. He was an active member of both the Baptist Church and the Odd Fellows.

Because of his veteran status, Spayd was also energetic in local GAR affairs. He carried a flag of the 149th in both the 1866 and 1914 ceremonies. When the Commonwealth dedicated a memorial to General George G. Meade in Washington, Spayd was chosen as the principal speaker. The date was October 19, 1927, a rainy, chilly day in the nation's capitol. After remarks by Governor John S. Fisher and President Calvin Coolidge, Spayd went to the podium and began to deliver his speech. "He began in a vigorous fashion, and his fine, full voice could be distinctly heard at the farthest edge of the crowd. Then it began to get weaker and weaker, and finally he could not speak at all." The proud veteran's voice began to weaken at the point in his speech when he began to reminisce about his heroic actions at Gettysburg. One of the president's aides finally prevailed upon Comrade Spayd to stop his talk. When Spayd sat down, he collapsed. In an unconscious condition, Spayd was rushed to a nearby hospital and died the next day.

When Gariel L. Todd enlisted in the 214th Infantry in March 1865, it was his second tour of duty. His first was in the 3rd Reserves, where he served as a sergeant in Company I, Philadelphia's Ontario Infantry. When he joined the 214th, he was assigned the honorable position of color-sergeant. At the time, Todd was described as a 34-year-old carpenter from Somerville, New Jersey. After leaving the army, Todd returned home and married in 1868. Five years later, the veteran died of consumption, a disease contracted while in the service of his country.

Charles T. Vansant saved the colors of the 71st Infantry at Ball's Bluff. Afterward, he served honorably for three years and went home to his small farm near Cornwell Station in Bucks County. His fortunes must have gone downhill for the veteran became addicted to alcohol. One night in November 1882, Vansant was seen standing on the railroad tracks near the station. A few minutes later, the station master heard a startled cry. Other men came running as well, to find that Vansant had been sliced in two by a train that had backed up the tracks. The fifty-year-old soldier left behind a wife and several children.

Chapter XI
The Flag Sponsorship Program

To help enlist public support for the conservation program, in 1983 the Capitol Preservation Committee began its "Save the Flags" project. This widely-advertised program sought public financial help for the conservation program by establishing a sponosrship agreement. Under the terms of this contract, individuals or groups could sponsor the conservation care of one or more flags at the cost of $1,000 per flag. Each sponsor received a number of benefits, including the award of a Commonwealth Citation and a copy of the conservation report and photograph of the sponsored flag. The Committee also accepts donations of less than a thousand dollars. To date (November 1991), 107 flags have been fully sponsored. A list of sponsors follows. A complete roster of all contributors can be found in the files of the Capitol Preservation Committee.

Regiment Number	Sponsor
87th	Company C, 87th Pennsylvania Volunteer Infantry
69th	Honorable Matthew J. Ryan
11th	Westmoreland County Historical Society
29th	Richard & Camille Yeager
71st	Honorable John B. Hannum
31st (2nd Reserves)	Smithkline Beckman Corporation
69th	First Pennsylvania Bank
97th	Sun Company, Inc.
122nd	Educators Mutual Life Insurance Company
30th (1st Reserves)	Camp & Auxiliary 50, Carlisle
90th	Pennsylvania Credit Union League
143rd	Pennsylvania Credit Union League Services, Inc.
104th	Pennwood Middle School Students
55th	Chambers Hill Lions Club
76th	Michael Helfrich
95th	Edward A. Town
152nd (3rd Artillery)	Pennsylvania Builders Association
83rd	Pennsylvania Association of Realtors
38th (9th Reserves)	W. I. Patterson Charitable Fund
101st	Stambaugh's Air Service
110th	Stambaugh's Air Service
201st	Stambaugh's Air Service
46th (2 flags)	Dalmatia Elementary School, 5th Grade Class
107th	Harrisburg Civil War Round Table
150th (2 flags)	Crawford County Historical Society
163rd (18th Cavalry)	Pennsylvania Department, Sons of Union Veterans
42nd (13th Reserves)	Pennsylvania Bankers Association
11th (2 flags)	Westmoreland County Historical Society; Westmoreland Civil War Round Table; Company D, 11th Pennsylvania Skirmish Group
30th (1st Reserves)	Biglerville High School
53rd	Company C, 53rd Pennsylvania Volunteer Infantry
130th	Post 130, National Sojourners
55th	Neal J. Hinton
83rd	Sergeant Ralph Davis
119th	Rittenhouse Foundation, Arthur Klein
51st	Harcum Junior College, Arthur Klein
128th	VFW Post 8344, Schnecksville, PA
99th	Scott Paper Company, Clemens S. Andes, Jr.
50th	Meridian Bancorp, Inc., Reading
124th	Bell of Pennsylvania
114th	Charles Klein
110th	Historical Military Impressions
110th	Commandery of Pennsylvania, Military Order of the Loyal Legion of the United States
36th (7th Reserves)	Company H, 36th Pennsylvania Volunteer Infantry
117th (13th Cavalry)	Irish Society
72nd	Suns Refining and Marketing Company
48th	Third grade class of the John S. Clarke Elementary Center; Pottsville Joint Veterans Council
47th	Civil War Round Table of Eastern Pennsylvania
45th	Historical Times Inc.
34th (5th Reserves)	Alliance of Bikers Aimed Toward Education (ABATE)
42nd (13th Reserves)	Perry County Council of Republican Women
49th	Colonel James D. Campbell (AUS, Retired)
79th	Lancaster Fencibles

Advance the Colors!

Regiment	Sponsor
149th	Pennsylvania Council of Republican Women
143rd	First Eastern Bank of Wilkes-Barre
78th	Kittanning Elks Lodge
207th	Gregory K. Bailey & Boy Scout Troop #160, Lititz
151st	Juniata County Council of Republican Women; Juniata County Republican Council
126th	Greencastle-Antrim Civil War Round Table
153rd	Northampton County Historical & Genealogical Society
88th	Exeter Township School District; Key Club of Exeter Township Senior High School; Washington Camp #230, Patriotic Order Sons of America
203rd (2 flags)	Student Council of the Lampeter-Strasburg High School
35th (6th Reserves)	Craig Truax Family
107th	Craig Truax Family
129th	Civil War Round Table of Eastern Pennsylvania; New York Life Insurance Company
153rd	Exchange Club of Easton, PA, Inc.
131st	Governor William W. Scranton and Family in Honor of Craig Truax
51st	House Republican Members in Honor of Craig Truax
148th (2 flags)	Friends of Craig Truax
41st (12th Reserves)	National Association of Retired Federal Employees
80th (7th Cavalry)	National Association of Retired Federal Employees
188th	Pennsylvania State Grange
80th (7th Cavalry)	Pennsylvania State Grange
104th	Pennridge School District
121st	Venango County Historical Society
51st	Susquehanna Civil War Round Table
209th	Northern York County Historical & Preservation Society; South Mountain VFW Post 6771
51st	Republican Women of the Main Line
97th	Unionville High School Student Council
108th (11th Cavalry)	Southern Chester County Republican Women's Council
61st	AFSCME, Council 13
77th	AFSCME, Locals 1981, 2245, 2456, 2608
84th	AFSCME, Locals 1022, 1523, 1534, 2545
54th	Grand Lodge Knights of Pythias—Domain of Pennsylvania
79th	Citizens of the 99th Legislative District, 1987
162nd (17th Cavalry)	Citizens of the 99th Legislative District, 1987
92nd (9th Cavalry)	Knights of Pythias, Buehler Lodge 269, Marysville
161st (16th Cavalry)	Ray E. Keifer Family, Scottdale
127th	Derry Township Council of Republican Women
141st	Susquehanna County Federated Women's Clubs
46th	Dalmatia Elementary School, Fifth Grade Class
141st (2 flags)	Bradford County Council of Republican Women
47th	Emmaus Flag Day Association
162nd (17th Cavalry)	Citizens of the 99th Legislative District, 1988
40th (11th Reserves)	Pomona Grange #58, Indiana County
148th	Central Pennsylvania Civil War Round Table
28th	Mr. Lloyd D. VanBlargan
33rd (4th Reserves)	Honorable Philip Price, Jr.
58th	Pennsylvania Questers
112th (2nd Artillery)	Pennsylvania Questers
159th (14th Cavalry)	Pennsylvania Questers
182nd (21st Cavalry)	IBM

Appendix

Appendix III
Pennsylvania Civil War Color-Bearers

This appendix lists all known color-bearers included in both volumes. A few are marked with asterisks (*); these men are not mentioned in the regimental sketches since their names were found after the manuscript was completed. Some of these men carried flags in 1866 and were listed as previous bearers without elaboration. Names include rank, company, and fate, including dates bearing flag. Regiments are listed in numerical order.

Abbreviations: Pvt. = Private; Cpl. = Corporal; Sgt. = Sergeant; Lieut. = Lieutenant; Col. = Colonel.

11th Infantry
Sgt. Charles H. Foulke, Co.A	11/20/61-8/11/62
Sgt. Robert H. Knox, Co.C	severely wounded 8/30/62
Sgt. Samuel S. Bierer, Co.C	wounded 8/30/62
Lieut. Absalom Schall, Co.C	wounded 8/30/62
Sgt. Samuel S. Bierer, Co.C	took flag 8/30/62
Pvt. Daniel Mathews, Co.C	wounded 9/17/62
Pvt. William Welty, Co.C	killed 9/17/62
Cpl. Frederick Welty, Co.C	severely wounded 9/17/62
Lieut. Edward H. Gay, Co.F	twice wounded, 9/17/62
Sgt. Henry Bitner, Co.E	took flag 9/17/62
Cpl. John V. Kuhns, Co.C	thrice wounded 12/13/62
Pvt. Cyrus W. Chambers, Co.C	killed 12/13/62
Cpl. John W. Thomas, Co.C	severely wounded 12/13/62
Capt. Benjamin F. Haines, Co.B	took flag 12/13/62
Cpl. John H. McKalip, Co.C	wounded 7/1/63
Pvt. Michael Kepler, Co.C	7/1/63-4/64
Cpl. Jacob J. Lehman, Co.D	4/64-killed 5/8/64
*Lieut. Samuel McCutchen, Co.F [unidentified]	took flag 5/8/64 wounded 5/12/64
Cpl. William Mathews, Co.C	5/12/64-12/3/64
Sgt. Albert Carter, Co.A	12/3/64-5/28/65
Sgt. J. C. Scheurman, Co.A	5/28/65-7/1/65
*Sgt. John P. Shaeffer, Co.B	1/17-29/62, Martinsburg flag
Sgt. William Feightner, Co.I	1/29/62-wounded & captured 8/30/62, with Martinsburg flag
Cpl. Henry B. Temple, Co.K	designating flag 7/8/62-?
Pvt. William H. West, Co.K	designating flag bearer 8/30/62

23rd Infantry
Sgt. Samuel F. Bolton, Co.H	killed 5/31/62
Lieut. Henry A. Marchant, Co.	rescued flag 5/31/62
*Sgt. Isaac S. Williams, Co.I	prior to 1/63
Sgt. Francis M. Worth, Co.H	wounded 6/1/64

26th Infantry
Sgt. William S. Small, Co.I	1/17/62-?
Sgt. George W. Roosevelt, Co.K	rescued flag 8/29/62
Cpl. Charles J. Barger, Co.B	prior to muster-out

27th Infantry
Sgt. Henry E. Rosengarten, Co.K	wounded at Chancellorsville
*Sgt. John W. Detjen, Co.G	killed 5/2/63

28th Infantry
Sgt. George Grady, Co.G	7/10/62-?
Pvt. Gustavus Hoffman, Co.P	killed 9/17/62
Sgt. Charles P. Kennedy, Co.I	1/23/63-?
Sgt. Jacob G. Orth, Co.D	4/16/63-?

29th Infantry
Sgt. William Betzold, Co.H	9/5/63-?
Cpl. Charles H. Martin, Co.F	presented color, 11/24/63

30th Infantry (1st Reserves)
Pvt. William H. Bradley, Co.G	bearer in 1862
Pvt. Thomas McNamee, Co.C	9/14/62
Sgt. Bertoless Slott, Co.G	wounded 7/2/63
Cpl. George K. Swope, Co.B	7/2/63-?

31st Infantry (2nd Reserves)
Sgt. William J. Fulton, Co.H	wounded 9/17/62
Sgt. William Derr, Co.C	mortally wounded 12/13/62
Sgt. James Toomey, Co.D	wounded 7/2/63
Sgt. Joseph F. Sweeton, Co.K	presented flag 3/16/64-?

32nd Infantry (3rd Reserves)
Pvt. David Jones, Co.K	rescued flag 6/30/62
Sgt. William F. Roberts, Co.C	wounded 8/30/62
Sgt. T. Watson Bewley, Co.C	last bearer, 1864

33rd Infantry (4th Reserves)
Cpl. M. H. Vanscoten, Co.H	9/10/61-?
Sgt. Jacob Wheeler, Co.C	9/17/62
Sgt. C. W. Whiteman, Co.G	killed 5/9/64

34th Infantry (5th Reserves)
Sgt. Michael Leary	6/30/62
Cpl. Joseph C. Carson, Co.B	wounded 6/30/62
Capt. Thomas Chamberlin, Co.D	6/30/62
Cpl. James C. Voris, Co.B	killed 12/13/62
Cpl. William Kohler, Co.H	listed as bearer, 1866

35th Infantry (6th Reserves)
Sgt. George W. Deen, Co.E	mentioned for 1/13/63
*Sgt. William E. Ackey, Co.E	listed as bearer, 1866

36th Infantry (7th Reserves)
Pvt. Adam Wray, Co.F	9/10/61-wounded 6/62
Sgt. Reuben W. Schell, Co.D	8/62-captured 5/5/64
Pvt. Henry Dilman, Co.C	killed 12/13/62 after he took flag from Schell

37th Infantry (8th Reserves)
Cpl. George Horton, Co.F	killed 9/17/62
Lieut. Lewis B. Waltz, Co.F	took flag 9/17/62
Cpl. John M. Oliver, Co.K	listed as bearer, 1866
Cpl. A. J. Bisset, Co.I	photographed with flag

38th Infantry (9th Reserves)
Sgt. Henry W. Blanchard, Co.H	wounded 6/30/62 & 9/17/62
Pvt. Walter Beatty, Co.I	killed 9/17/62
Pvt. Robert Lemmon, Co.I	killed 9/17/62
Pvt. Edward Dorien, Co.H	9/17/62-?
*Cpl. William Altsman, Co.G	listed as bearer, 1866

39th Infantry (10th Reserves)
*Sgt. John C. Gaither, Co.A	1861-6/27/62
*Sgt. N. B. McWilliams, Co.E	listed as bearer, 1866

40th Infantry (11th Reserves)
Sgt. James L. Hazlett, Co.E	wounded 8/30/62
Pvt. James J. Fritz, Co.E	12/13/62

41st Infantry (12th Reserves)
Lieut. Edward Kelly, Co.E	took flag 8/30/62
Pvt. David H. Graham, Co.E	killed 9/17/62
Sgt. William H. Weaver, Co.D	wounded 5/10/64
Sgt. James Johnson, Co.E	took flag 5/10/64

42nd Infantry (13th Reserves)
Cpl. John Looney, Co.G	mortally wounded 12/13/62

43rd Regiment (1st Artillery)

44th Regiment (1st Cavalry)
*Cpl. Isaac Kennedy, Co.G	5/64
Sgt. Antoine Wolf, Co.M	4/5/65

45th Infantry
Sgt. Joseph Reigle, Co.E	state color 10/22/61-2/64; national color 2/64-wounded 6/3/64; 6/19/64-captured 9/30/64
Cpl. Justus D. Strait, Co.I	6/3-19/64
Cpl. John Kinsey, Co.B	rescued flag 5/18/64
Cpl. Thomas Evers, Co.D	wounded 6/18/64
Cpl. Charles T. Kelley, Co.G	6/18/64-captured 9/30/64
Sgt. Andrew J. Goodfellow, Co.A	4/2/65

46th Infantry
Sgt. James McQuillan, Co.D	wounded 5/25/62
Sgt. Charles A. Row, Co.E	11/62
Sgt. William Baron, Co.E	Atlanta Campaign

47th Infantry
Sgt. Benjamin F. Walls, Co.C	wounded 4/9/64
Sgt. William Pyer, Co.C	wounded 4/9/64

48th Infantry
Sgt. John Roarty, Co.C	to 10/2/64
Sgt. Samuel A. Beddall, Co.E	10/2/64-7/20/65
Sgt. John Taylor, Co.A	4/2/65
*Sgt. Arthur P. Hatch, Co.C	listed as bearer, 1866
*Sgt. Edward Flanagan, Co.G	listed as bearer, 1866

49th Infantry
Sgt. Theodore D. Hoffman, Co.D	to 8/30/61
Sgt. John M. Thompson, Co.I	9/3/62-10/24/62
Sgt. John J. Hight, Co.D	3/7/64-10/19/64
Sgt. Henry Entriken, Co.F	9/64-?
Cpl. Theodore H. McFarland, Co.D	10/26/64-?
Sgt. Samuel H. Irvin, Co.C	sometime in 1864

50th Infantry

51st Infantry
Cpl. George W. Foote, Co.E	3/14/62
*Sgt. Patrick Kevin, Co.C	killed 5/6/64
Sgt. Nathan H. Ramsey, Co.C	wounded 5/12/64
Cpl. James Cameron, Co.I	captured 5/12/64
*Sgt. Isaac E. Filman, Co.A	listed as bearer, 1866

52nd Infantry
Sgt. Henry A. Mott, Co.K	mentioned 10/11/62
Sgt. Niram A. Fuller, Co.F	1/27/64-4/1/65
Cpl. Philip G. Killian, Co.A	mentioned 7/5/64
*Cpl. Samuel Williams, Co.I	listed as bearer, 1866

53rd Infantry
Sgt. Dewalt S. Fouse, Co.C	original bearer 1861-?
Cpl. Joseph Black, Co.H	killed 6/1/62
Sgt. John M. Harvey, Co.K	wounded 12/13/62
*Sgt. David B. Rothrock, Co.C	listed as bearer, 1866

54th Infantry
Cpl. James P. Ryan, Co.D	killed 4/2/65
Pvt. Michael Lohr, Co.C	4/2/65-?

55th Infantry
Sgt. James Miller, Co.E	died 7/15/63
Sgt. Michael Murray, Co.E	wounded 6/3/64
Sgt. Augustin Flanagan, Co.A	wounded 9/29/64
Sgt. Hezekiah Hammer, Co.K	took flag 9/29/64
*Pvt. Alexander Ow, Co.F	listed as bearer, 1866

56th Infantry
Sgt. Archibald C. Bruce, Co.B	3/7/62-died 3/20/62
Sgt. Josiah Yohe, Co.C	7/19/62-8/29/62
Sgt. Wallace Early, Co.A	11/15/62-?
Sgt. Henry Eby, Co.H	wounded 7/1/63
Cpl. Patrick Burns, Co.D	wounded 7/2/63
Cpl. Ira Knapp, Co.A	after Gettysburg
Cpl. Winfield S. Carr, Co.I	after Gettysburg
Sgt. John Y. Earhart, Co.B	6/24/65-?
Sgt. Hugh Logue, Co.I	6/24/65-?

57th Infantry
Sgt. Edgar Williams, Co.E	prior to 1864
Sgt. Cyrus P. Slaven, Co.I	4/23/64-wounded 5/6/64
*Sgt. Thomas P. Hamilton, Co.F	10/17/64-?
Cpl. Robert G. Madge, Co.C	6/64

58th Infantry
Sgt. Charles Harman, Co.A	mentioned 9/25/63
Sgt. John Hoffa, Co.K	4/14/64-?
*Sgt. Hans Hanson, Co.K	9/16/64-?
Sgt. A. H. Baumgartner, Co.B	mentioned in postwar article

59th Regiment (2nd Cavalry)

60th Regiment (3rd Cavalry)

61st Infantry
Sgt. William H. Ronntree, Co.D	killed 5/31/62
*Cpl. James Mulligan, Co.F	saved flag 5/31/62
Sgt. David H. Ford, Co.K	wounded 5/3/63
Pvt. James Robb, Co.H	took flag 5/3/63
Cpl. William Taylor, Co.[G]	took flag 5/3/63

Sgt. Hugh Gorman, Co.C	killed 5/6/64
Sgt. William Coon, Co.D	wounded 4/2/65
Sgt. Joseph Fisher, Co.C	wounded 4/2/65
Cpl. Joseph C. Matthews, Co.A	4/2/65
Major Robert L. Orr	4/2/65

62nd Infantry

Sgt. Jefferson Truitt, Co.D	saved flag 7/1/62
Sgt. Thomas H. Budlong, Co.I	killed 7/2/63
Sgt. Jacob B. Funk, Co.A	wounded 7/2/63
Cpl. Johnson C. Gardner, Co.E	saved flag 7/2/63

63rd Infantry

Sgt. William W. Weeks, Co.H	wounded 8/29/62
Cpl. John Hoffman, Co.I	wounded 8/29/62
Cpl. George Lang, Co.E	8/29/62
Sgt. George W. Fizgerald, Co.K	wounded 5/3/63
Sgt. George F. House, Co.B	5/3/63-wounded 5/5/64
Pvt. Joseph P. Rankin, Co.G	5/5/64-?

64th Regiment (4th Cavalry)

Sgt. Amos S. Bolton, Co.F	12/25/61-5/27/62
Sgt. William Hazlett, Co.G	5/27/62-?
Pvt. William McDowell, Co.D	8/14/63-?
*Pvt. John Boyce, Co.B	6/64
*Sgt. James Smith, Co.A	listed as bearer, 1866

65th Regiment (5th Cavalry)

67th Infantry

Sgt. William A. Rager, Co.E	3/25/65

68th Infantry

Cpl. James McLarnon, Co.K	7/2/63-6/9/65
Sgt. Charles H. Haber, Co.B	mentioned in regtl papers

69th Infantry

Sgt. John King, Co.A	prior to 5/22/62
Sgt. Patrick Murphy, Co.B	5/22/62-3/23/63
Sgt. Michael Dougherty, Co.C	3/23/63-?
Sgt. Michael Brady, Co.C	wounded at Gettysburg

70th Regiment (6th Cavalry)

71st Infantry

Sgt. Thomas Vansant	rescued flag 10/21/61

72nd Infantry

Sgt. Frederick Mannes, Co.B	prior to 7/63
Sgt. William Finacy, Co.H	killed 7/3/63
Cpl. Francis O'Donnell, Co.D	wounded 7/3/63
Sgt. Thomas Murphy, Co.G	7/3/63-?

73rd Infantry

Sgt. William Burkhardt, Co.A	wounded 8/30/62
Sgt. Henry Hess, Co.H	wounded 8/30/62
Sgt. Charles Wendler, Co.G	state color 11/25/63
Capt. John Kennedy, Co.E	saved color 11/25/63

74th Infantry

Sgt. George Ekert	5/63

75th Infantry

Sgt. Robert Jordan, Co.A	killed 8/30/62
Sgt. Charles Haserodt, Co.E	[wounded 8/30/62]
Sgt. John Emleben, Co.D	took flag 8/30/62

76th Infantry

Sgt. Solomon C. Miller, Co.H	7/22/64-? wounded 8/14/64
Cpl. Albert Sanders, Co.C	9/27/64-? wounded 1/15/65

77th Infantry

Sgt. Scott R. Crawford, Co.C	mortally wounded 12/30/62
Pvt. James A. Rodgers, Co.E	wounded 12/30/62
Lieut. John C. Shroad, Co.K	took flag 12/30/62
Cpl. W. H. H. Woolslair, Co.C	captured 9/19/63

78th Infantry

Sgt. George D. Hamm, Co.C	12/62
Sgt. J. Waream, Co.C	to 5/20/65
Sgt. Thomas Evans, Co.B	5/20/65-?
Cpl. Abraham W. Rudisill, Co.D	claimed to be bearer, 1866

79th Infantry

Cpl. William F. Dostman, Co.H	killed 9/19/63
Sgt. John Dean, Co.A	listed as bearer, 1866
Sgt. Henry Reed, Co.H	ibid
Cpl. William Powell, Co.H	ibid
Cpl. H. B. Vondersmith, Co.K	ibid
Cpl. George L. Danner, Co.B	ibid
Cpl. Andrew J. Huffnagle, Co.A	ibid
Sgt. Jacob H. Beichler, Co.A	ibid

80th Regiment (7th Cavalry)

Sgt. John Ennis, Co.A	1/11/64-mortally wounded 4/2/65
Sgt. Louis H. Bickel, Co.I	took standard 4/2/65

81st Infantry

Sgt. John B. Munyan, Co.A	wounded 12/13/62
Sgt. James B. McHale, Co.B	took flag 12/13/62; killed 7/2/63
Sgt. Ephraim Davis, Co.D	killed 1864
*Sgt. James Wirt, Co.K	died of wounds recd at Cold Harbor
Sgt. James B. Murray, Co.H	killed 8/25/64
Sgt. John Adams, Co.D	8/25/64-?
Sgt. Isaac McLean, Co.I	wounded 8/25/64
Sgt. John Hughs, Co.E	wounded 8/25/64; mentioned 10/31/64
Sgt. William D. Parkhill, Co.C	killed 4/7/65
Sgt. Andrew J. Shiner, Co.F	mortally wounded 4/7/65

82nd Infantry

Sgt. William H. Gibson, Co.C	wounded 5/31/62
Sgt. William P. Beale, Co.D	5/63
Sgt. George Waterhouse, Co.B	6/64
*Sgt. Francis A. Drumel, Co.B	listed as bearer, 1866

83rd Infantry

Cpl. Walter Ames, Co.K	killed 6/27/62
Sgt. Alexander Rogers, Co.H	killed 5/5/64
Cpl. M. Francis Vogus, Co.G	wounded 5/8/64
Cpl. Daniel Jones, Co.F	rescued flag 5/8/64

84th Infantry

Sgt. Edward Stokes, Co.B	original bearer
Sgt. Hugh Smith, Co.D	wounded 3/23/62
Sgt. Thomas Gouldsberry, Co.I	took flag 3/23/62
Sgt. Charles White, Co.K	wounded & captured 5/3/63

85th Infantry

Sgt. Joseph G. Reager, Co.B	11/18/61-4/27/62
Sgt. Jacob Deffenbaugh, Co.I	4/27/62-7/63
Pvt. George Orbin, Co.C	7/63-9/63
Cpl. Richard S. Lincoln, Co.I	wounded 5/31/62
Cpl. Alexander Ross, Co.A	5/1/64-11/64
Sgt. John Moore, Co.K	state color, 8/16/64

Appendix III

87th Infantry
*Cpl. William Brubaker, Co.A	6/63
Sgt. Jonathan J. Keesey, Co.C	wounded 9/19/64
Cpl. Daniel P. Reigle, Co.E	took flag 9/19/64; saved flag 10/19/64
*Cpl. Henry Shultz, Co.A	10/64

88th Infantry
Sgt. John B. Donohoe, Co.C	8/62-9/62
Cpl. Lewis W. Bonnin, Co.B	wounded 7/1/63
Cpl. Francis Charles, Co.C	12/29/63-?
Sgt. Thomas Hartman, Co.H	12/29/63-?
Cpl. Charles McKnight, Co.K	5/12/64
Sgt. John Ewing, Co.D	wounded 6/18/64
Sgt. John Devine, Co.K	6/64 and 2/65

89th Regiment (8th Cavalry)
Sgt. George Stephens, Co.H	1/18/65-?

90th Infantry
Cpl. Theodore Mason, Co.E	killed 9/17/62
Sgt. William H. Paul, Co.E	saved flag 9/17/62; wounded 7/1/63
Lieut. William H. Hewlings, Co.C	took flag 12/13/62
Sgt. Thomas E. Berger, Co.K	wounded unknown date
Sgt. Johnson Roney, Co.G	wounded unknown date

91st Infantry
Sgt. Robert Chism, Co.K	mortally hurt 5/7/64
Sgt. Archibald Nimmo, Co.C	wounded 6/18/64
Cpl. Edward Gamble, Co.B	wounded 6/18/64
Pvt. James C. Sweeney, Co.D	mortally wounded 6/18/64
Sgt. Franklin C. Wolfong, Co.H	took flag 6/18/64
Cpl. Thomas C. Deveraux, Co.C	2/6/65
Sgt. William H. Geary, Co.D	on 1914 list as previous bearer

92nd Regiment (9th Cavalry)
Sgt. Jacob Wolfley, Co.C	1/7/65-?

93rd Infantry
Pvt. Henry Fittery, Co.A	11/8/61-mortally wounded 5/31/62
Sgt. John Hutchison, Co.E	wounded 5/5/62
Pvt. George K. Stoud, Co.C	12/62-7/63
Pvt. Gideon Mellin, Co.H	6/18/64
Sgt. William Risser, Co.C	wounded 9/19/64
Sgt. William H. Smith, Co.F	wounded 9/22/64
Cpl. Jacob Renkenberger, Co.A	took flag 9/22/64-?
Pvt. George Imboden, Co.A	wounded 10/19/64
Sgt. Charles Marquette, Co.F	wounded 4/2/65

95th Infantry
Sgt. William Byrnes, Co.F	wounded 6/27/62, 9/14/62, 10/19/64
Sgt. George W. Ulmer, Co.A	5/12/64
Sgt. Albert J. Bannon, Co.C	2/24/65-?
Pvt. John B. Cooke, Co.D	wounded 4/6/65

96th Infantry
Sgt. Joseph S. Johnson, Co.H	wounded 9/14/62
Cpl. William Ortner, Co.H	wounded 9/14/62
Sgt. Charles B. Zeigler, Co.H	killed 9/14/62
Sgt. Solomon M. McMinzie, Co.C	killed 9/14/62
Cpl. Thomas Oliver, Co.C	wounded 9/14/62
Pvt. Harry H. Hunsicker, Co.H	took flag 9/14/62
Sgt. J. W. Conrad	wounded 5/9/64

Cpl. George W. Foltz, Co.C	wounded 5/10/64
Sgt. Ezra Hendley, Co.D	wounded 5/64
*Sgt. William F. Lord, Co.A	killed 5/10/64

97th Infantry
Sgt. John D. Beaver, Co.C	11/61-?
Sgt. Samuel M. McBride, Co.D	5/19/64-wounded 5/20/64
Sgt. John A. Russell, Co.H	wounded 5/20/64
Capt. George A. Lemaistre, Co.H	wounded 5/20/64
Cpl. Thomas Forsythe, Co.E	took flag 5/20/64 & 9/1/64
Sgt. William McCarty, Co.D	wounded 1/15/65
Col. Gasusha Pennypacker	wounded 1/15/65

98th Infantry
Cpl. John V. Koch, Co.I	8/29/64-9/17/64
Sgt. John Hirschling, Co.I	9/26/64-5/1/65; wounded 10/19/64
Sgt. Jacob A. Schmid, Co.I	took flag 10/19/64
Sgt. Jacob Herrman, Co.C	5/1/65-?
Cpl. Henry Schlacter, Co.I	5/2/65-?

99th Infantry
Sgt. Samuel Hutton, Co.K	1/15/62-?
Sgt. Harvey M. Munsell, Co.A	8/8/62-?

100th Infantry
Sgt. Richard P. Craven, Co.K	wounded 9/14/62
Cpl. Richard Porter, Co.B	wounded 9/14/62
Sgt. Charles Oliver, Co.M	3/25/65
*Cpl. Alexander Boyd, Co.B	listed as bearer, 1866

101st Infantry

102nd Infantry
Cpl. Joseph Hucks, Co.M	mortally wounded 5/31/62
Sgt. George W. Workman, Co.K	mortally wounded 5/31/62
Sgt. Edwin Anderson, Co.B	5/31/62
Cpl. Charles L. Donohoe, Co.K	5/31/62
Cpl. William H. Cowan, Co.H	wounded 7/1/62
Sgt. John B. Devaux, Co.F	12/26/62-wounded 5/3/63
Cpl. John F. Brill, Co.L	5/3/63-?
Sgt. William G. Greenawalt, Co.A	9/64
Sgt. Lewis C. White, Co.H	wounded 10/19/64

103rd Infantry
Sgt. James H. Chambers, Co.C	original bearer
Sgt. William N. Barr, Co.C	5/31/62
Sgt. Anthony Spangler, Co.D	killed 12/14/62
Cpl. Robert J. Thompson, Co.E	captured 4/20/64

104th Pennsylvania
Sgt. John M. Laughlin, Co.A	10/31/61-5/12/62
Sgt. James L. Slack, Co.C	wounded 5/31/62
Sgt. Hiram W. Purcell, Co.G	wounded 5/31/62
*Cpl. Charles Michner, Co.C	took flag 5/31/62
*Sgt. Jacob Myers, Co.G	took flag 5/31/62

105th Infantry

106th Infantry
Sgt. Benjamin F. Slonaker, Co.C	10/6/61-9/17/62(?)
Sgt. Joseph N. Radcliff, Co.C	9/17/62-3/1/63
Sgt. Charles H. Hickok, Co.C	killed 5/6/64
Cpl. William C. Wagner, Co.A	wounded 5/12/64
Cpl. S. Macey Smith, Co.C	took flag 5/12/64
Cpl. John Houghton, Co.F	captured 6/22/64
Sgt. Rufus G. Brown, Co.C	listed as bearer, 1914

107th Infantry

Pvt. Thomas Kehoe, Co.C	mortally wounded 9/17/62
Sgt. Solomon R. Hough, Co.A	wounded 9/17/62
*Pvt. Russell Phillips, Co.A	9/62
Cpl. H. W. Smyser, Co.E	wounded 9/17/62
Pvt. Cornelius Regan, Co.A	killed 9/17/62
Capt. Henry J. Sheafer, Co.I	saved flag 9/17/62
Pvt. James Kennedy, Co.I	saved flag 9/17/62
Pvt. John C. Delaney, Co.I	saved flag 9/17/62
Cpl. Henry Sunniver, Co.B	12/13/62
Pvt. George Henthorne, Co.B	12/13/62
Cpl. George A. McConnelly, Co.H	killed 7/1/63
Cpl. Thomas Breash, Co.C	killed 7/1/63
Sgt. Francis J. Swoyer, Co.C	wounded 2/7/65
Cpl. John M. Hileman, Co.C	3-4/65

108th Regiment (11th Cavalry)

109th Infantry

Sgt. Lewis Shaw, Co.C	killed 8/9/62
Sgt. John Greenwood	killed 7/3/63
Sgt. William McNally	killed 7/3/63
Sgt. Fergus Elliott, Co.G	1864
Cpl. John M. Valleau, Co.C	1864-65
Sgt. Bernard J. Drury, Co.G	9/14/64-?

110th Infantry

Sgt. Davidson Martin, Co.E	original bearer
Sgt. William A. Norton, Co.I	8/30/62
Sgt. William H. Hill, Co.E	prior to 1/30/63
Cpl. Joseph White, Co.E	2/9/63-?
Sgt. Valentine Stewart, Co.B	killed 10/2/64
Sgt. Michael Feather, Co.H	2/65
Sgt. George G. Tate, Co.B	6/2/65-?

111th Infantry

Cpl. E. V. Sedgwick, Co.C	killed 8/9/62
Sgt. Alonzo Foust, Co.I	9/17/62-12/22/64
Cpl. Frank Guy, Co.E	12/63-12/22/64
Cpl. Calvin H. Blanchard, Co.D	3/23/64-12/22/64
Sgt. Alfred E. Harper, Co.E	12/22/64-?
Sgt. Myron P. Good, Co.C	12/22/64-?
Sgt. Lewis Minium, Co.G	12/22/64-?

112th Regiment (2nd Heavy Artillery)

Sgt. Stephen H. Witt, Co.F	6/5/63-?
Sgt. Charles Link, Co.G	6/5/63-?
Sgt. Henry F. Rutledge, Co.E	11/16/64-?
Sgt. James B. Furness, Co.M	11/16/64-?
Sgt. Lewis Wagner, Co.H	1/17/66-?
Sgt. Thomas Hackney, Co.C	1/17/66-?

113th Regiment (12th Cavalry)

114th Infantry

Sgt. Benjamin I. Baylitts, Co.C	5/63-?
Cpl. Michael Cannon, Co.C	wounded 7/2/63
Cpl. Harry Hall, Co.I	after 7/2/63
Sgt. Thomas Melsom	cited in 1866 article

115th Infantry

Sgt. Hugh Barr	8/62
Sgt. Benjamin Williams, Co.K	wounded 5/3/63
Cpl. Patrick Kenney, Co.E	took flag 5/3/63
Sgt. James Doyle, Co.B	2/13/64-?

116th Infantry

Sgt. William H. Tyrrell, Co.C	10/62-wounded 12/13/62
Lieut. Francis T. Quinlan, Co.H	took flag 12/13/62
Sgt. Abraham F. Detweiler, Co.C	12/14/62-11/63
Cpl. William Wertz, Co.H	killed 5/18/64
Sgt. Timothy A. Sloan, Co.E	wounded 6/3/64
Pvt. James M. Seitzinger, Co.G	took flag 6/3/64
Sgt. Peter Kelly, Co.D	6/64-wounded 4/2/65
Sgt. Edward S. Kline, Co.F	4/2/65
Sgt. Charles Maurer, Co.F	last bearer

117th Regiment (13th Cavalry)

118th Infantry

Pvt. William Hummel, Co.D	saved flag 9/20/62
Sgt. David L. Ware, Co.F	?-6/25/63
Sgt. John H. Williamson, Co.F	6/25/63-?
Cpl. William H. Wild, Co.C	mortally wounded 9/30/64
Capt. Isaac H. Seesholtz, Co.K	wounded 9/30/64
Pvt. Thomas Crealy, Co.C	took flag 9/30/64
Sgt. Samuel F. Delaney, Co.E	2/6/65

119th Infantry

Sgt. William M. Laughlin, Co.G	?-10/25/63
Sgt. George G. Lovett, Co.G	10/25/63-?

121st Infantry

Sgt. Erskine W. Hazard, Jr., Co.D	killed 12/13/62
Lieut. Joseph G. Rosengarten	took flag 12/13/62
Sgt. William G. Graham, Co.D	killed 5/5/64
Sgt. William Hardy, Co.B	killed 5/11/64
Sgt. Alfred Clymer, Co.I	mortally wounded 6/5/64
Sgt. James B. Graham, Co.D	6/5/64-3/65
Sgt. Louis Clapper, Co.C	3/65-end

122nd Infantry

Cpl. John S. Smith, Co.G	listed as bearer, 1866

123rd Infantry

Sgt. Samuel Caldwell, Co.E	12/13/62

124th Infantry

125th Infantry

Sgt. George A. Simpson, Co.C	killed 9/17/62
Pvt. Eugene Boblitz, Co.H	wounded 9/17/62
Pvt. Walter W. Greenland, Co.C	took flag 9/17/62
Sgt. L. Frank Wattson, Co.C	9/17/62-ca 2/7/63
Sgt. Charles E. Campbell, Co.C	listed as bearer on company memorial

126th Infantry

Cpl. Thomas Daily, Co.K	12/13/62
Cpl. Solomon B. Kauffman, Co.F	listed as bearer in regtl history

127th Infantry

128th Infantry

Sgt. Henry S. Lovett, Co.C	5/63

129th Infantry

Sgt. Lewis S. Boner, Co.E	5/3/63
Sgt. Peter M. Miller, Co.F	5/3/63
Col. Jacob G. Frick	rescued flags 12/13/62 & 5/3/63

130th Infantry

Col. Henry I. Zinn	killed 12/13/62
Sgt. Charles A. Smith, Co.A	listed as bearer, 1866

131st Infantry
Sgt. Henry H. McLaughlin, Co.D	listed in RG 19

132nd Infantry
Cpl. William Parks, Co.H	mortally wounded 12/13/62
Lieut. Henry H. Hoagland, Co.H	mortally wounded 12/13/62
Lieut. Charles M. McDougall, Co.C	took flag 12/13/62
Lieut. Frederick L. Hitchcock	wounded 12/13/62
*Cpl. P. P. Copeland, Co.K	listed as bearer, 1866

133rd Infantry

134th Infantry
Cpl. William E. Flugga, Co.E	listed as bearer, 1866

135th Infantry
Cpl. Samuel B. Harrison, Co.I	listed as bearer, 1866

136th Infantry
*Sgt. Joseph S. Durning, Co.E	9/8/62-?
Cpl. Philip Petty, Co.C	saved flag 12/13/62
Sgt. Jacob Johnston, Co.C	listed as bearer, 1866

137th Infantry
Cpl. William H. Chilson, Co.H	listed as bearer, 1866

138th Infantry
Cpl. John H. Ashenfelter, Co.K	killed 5/5/64
Sgt. John F. Biesecker, Co.B	mortally wounded 5/5/64

139th Infantry
Sgt. James S. Graham, Co.E	wounded 5/3/63
Major Robert Munroe	took flag 9/19/64
Sgt. David W. Young, Co.E	4/2/65

140th Infantry
Sgt. Robert Riddle, Co.F	wounded 7/2/63
Cpl. Jesse T. Power, Co.E	7/2/63-wounded 5/12/64
Sgt. A. G. Beeson, Co.E	wounded 5/12/64
Cpl. David Taggart, Co.G	took flag 5/12/64
*Sgt. Robert Dickey, Co.I	listed as bearer, 1866

141st Infantry
Sgt. George C. Beardsly, Co.C	mortally wounded 5/3/63
Capt. Abram J. Swart, Co.C	killed 5/3/63
Col. Henry J. Madill	took flag 5/3/63
Pvt. John J. Stockholm, Co.H	7/2/63
Cpl. Morton Berry, Co.D	mortally wounded 7/2/63
Pvt. Abner W. Forest, Co.K	mortally wounded 5/6/64
Sgt. John T. R. Seagraves, Co.G	5/6/64-1/65(?)
Sgt. Charles Scott, Co.C	5/12/64
Sgt. Stephen B. Canfield, Co.B	photographed with flags, 1865

142nd Infantry
Sgt. J. Robinson Balsley, Co.H	wounded 7/1/63
Sgt. Daniel Young, Co.C	10/18/64
Cpl. James X. Walter, Co.H	2/65-?

143rd Infantry
Sgt. Benjamin Crippen, Co.E	killed 7/1/63
Sgt. Owen Phillips, Co.B	7/1/63-mortally wounded 5/64
Cpl. Rogers W. Cox, Co.E	1865
Sgt. Patrick DeLacy, Co.A	rescued flag, 5/23/64
Pvt. Merritt Coughlin, Co.K	5/23/64
Sgt. W. H. Harden, Co.E	obituary as bearer
Sgt. Thomas Dakin, Co.C	listed as bearer, 1866

145th Infantry
*Cpl. Conrad Dippo, Co.K	fall 1862
Sgt. J. C. Veit, Co.B	6/64
Sgt. John P. Ferguson, Co.K	listed in county history

147th Infantry
Sgt. Samuel Henry, Co.C	killed 5/3/63
Sgt. Jesse K. Pryor, Co.C	listed as bearer, 1866

148th Infantry
Cpl. Hugh S. Neil, Co.K	killed 5/3/63
Sgt. John F. Benner, Co.C	7/2/63
Cpl. David H. Swyers, Co.B	wounded 5/10/64
Sgt. Robert A. Henry, Co.F	killed 5/10/64
Sgt. William Ward, Co.H	captured 6/16/64
Cpl. Joseph J. Shotstall, Co.E	killed 3/31/65
Cpl. Isaiah P. Leightley, Co.F	took flag 3/31/65

149th Infantry
Sgt. Henry G. Brehm, Co.C	mortally wounded 7/1/63
Cpl. Franklin W. Lehman, Co.C	wounded 7/1/63
Cpl. Henry H. Spayd, Co.C	wounded 7/1/63

150th Infantry
Sgt. Samuel Phifer, Co.I	killed 7/1/63
Cpl. Joseph S. Gutelius, Co.D	killed 7/1/63

151st Infantry
Sgt. Adam Heilman, Co.E	wounded 7/1/63

152nd Regiment (3rd Heavy Artillery)

153rd Infantry
Sgt. John Henning, Co.I	bearer of natl color

154th Infantry

155th Infantry
Sgt. Thomas Wiseman, Co.C	mortally wounded 12/13/62
Cpl. Charles Bardeen, Co.F	mortally wounded 12/13/62
Cpl. George W. Bratten, Co.E	mortally wounded 12/13/62
Sgt. Thomas C. Lawson, Co.H	12/13/62-7/63
Cpl. Matthew Bennett, Co.I	6/30/63-7/63 temp
Sgt. Thomas I. Marlin, Co.K	7/63-6/65, wounded 6/18/64
Cpl. Lemuel E. McPherson, Co.C	temp in 6/64
Sgt. Thomas C. Anderson, Co.I	9/30/64
Col. Alfred L. Pearson	3/29/65

157th Infantry
Cpl. William H. Howard, Co.A	2/5/65
Sgt. Francis A. Olmstead	listed as bearer, 1866

158th Infantry

159th Regiment (14th Cavalry)

160th Regiment (15th Cavalry)
Sgt. G. P. Davis, Co.M	?-1/9/64
Sgt. George W. Spencer, Co.D	8/16/64-?

161st Regiment (16th Cavalry)

162nd Regiment (17th Cavalry)

163rd Regiment (18th Cavalry)
Sgt. Alder Smith, Co.I	3/28/65-6/20/65
Sgt. Charles Beck, Co.I	6/20/65-?

165th Infantry

166th Infantry

167th Infantry

168th Infantry
169th Infantry
171st Infantry
172nd Infantry
173rd Infantry
*Sgt. Henry W. Cameron, Co.C   listed as bearer, 1866

174th Infantry
175th Infantry
*Sgt. Samuel O. Fernwalt

176th Infantry
177th Infantry
Sgt. Peter Franz, Co.C   listed as bearer, 1866

178th Infantry
179th Infantry
180th Regiment (19th Cavalry)
Sgt. John Ery, Co.I   5/17/64-?

181st Regiment (20th Cavalry)
Sgt. William R. Barnes, Co.E   2/3/64-?

182nd Regiment (21st Cavalry)
Sgt. Israel B. Bair, Co.I   obituary as bearer

183rd Infantry
184th Infantry
185th Regiment (22nd Cavalry)
Sgt. Michael H. Core, Co.A   photograph ID as bearer

186th Infantry
Sgt. Charles M. Koons, Co.H   10/24/64-?

187th Infantry
Sgt. John S. Ware, Co.C   12/10/64-?
*Cpl. John J. Hess, Co.B   listed as bearer, 1866

188th Infantry
Sgt. William Sipes, Co.I   killed 9/29/64
Cpl. William L. Graul, Co.I   9/29/64
Cpl. Charles Blucher, Co.H   9/29/64
Capt. Cecil Clay, 58th Infantry   wounded 9/29/64

189th Regiment (4th Heavy Artillery)
(2nd Provisional Heavy Artillery)
Sgt. John D. Wareing   wounded 6/18/64
Cpl. Minus Devins   mortally wounded 6/18/64

190th Infantry (1st Veteran Reserves)
*Sgt. Richard Looker, Co.G   listed as bearer, 1866

191st Infantry (2nd Veteran Reserves)
192nd Infantry
193rd Infantry
194th Infantry
Sgt. Henry Walbridge, Co.C   listed as bearer, 1866

195th Infantry
Sgt. Christian Hanlin, Co.F   3/28/65-?
Sgt. Israel Bair, Co.F   5/8/65-?
Sgt. Thomas E. Allen, Co.F   listed as bearer, 1866

196th Infantry
197th Infantry
198th Infantry
199th Infantry
200th Infantry
Pvt. Levi A. Smith, Co.E   3/25/65

201st Infantry
202nd Infantry
203rd Infantry
Sgt. John Lee, Co.B   ?-10/12/64
Pvt. George Deitrich, Co.F   wounded 1/15/65
Col. John W. Moore   killed 1/15/65
Cpl. William L. Parker, Co.I   1/15/65

204th Regiment (5th Heavy Artillery)
Sgt. John W. Williams, Co.C   listed as bearer, 1866

205th Infantry
Pvt. Henry Naber, Co.C   wounded 4/2/65

206th Infantry
207th Infantry
Sgt. George T. Horning, Co.E   wounded 4/2/65
Sgt. Charles H. Ilgenfritz, Co.E   4/2/65

208th Infantry
Sgt. Joshua Heck, Co.C   3/18/65-?
Cpl. Jeremiah Long, Co.D   mortally wounded 4/2/65

209th Infantry
Sgt. Edward J. Humphreys, Co.C   3/25/65
Sgt. Elbridge Stiles, Co.C   3/25/65

210th Infantry
Sgt. Manaris Humelstine, Co.D   ?-4/18/65
Cpl. Josiah Kissinger, Co.H   4/18/65-?

211th Infantry
Sgt. William R. Moore, Co.D   4/2/65

212th Regiment (6th Heavy Artillery)
213th Infantry
214th Infantry
Sgt. Gabriel L. Todd, Co.C   4/28/65-muster out

215th Infantry
Sgt. John H. Engle, Co.B   5/19/65-?

3rd United States Colored Troops
6th United States Colored Troops
Sgt. John D. West, Co.D   6/15/64
Lieut. Frederick Meyer, Co.B   killed 9/29/64
Lieut. Nathan H. Edgarton   wounded 9/29/64
Sgt. Alexander Kelley, Co.F   took flag 9/29/64
Sgt.-Major Thomas Hawkins   took flag 9/29/64

8th United States Colored Troops
Sgt. Samuel Waters, Co.C   mortally wounded 2/20/64
Sgt. Robert Brown, Co.F   6/13/64-?

22nd United States Colored Troops
Cpl. Nathan Stanton   10/27/64

Appendix III

24th United States Colored Troops
25th United States Colored Troops
Sgt. George W. Davis, Co.D   2/27/64-?
Sgt. William Lyons, Co.I   2/27/64-?
Sgt. Daniel Thompson, Co.A   7/30/65-?
Sgt. Henry Key, Co.H   11/23/65-?
32nd United States Colored Troops

41st United States Colored Troops
43rd United States Colored Troops
Sgt. William R. Butler, Co.F   5/16/64-?
45th United States Colored Troops
127th United States Colored Troops
Sgt. William Reynolds, Co.D   9/10/64-?

Index

Index

The index presented below includes both volumes. Not indexed is the material in the front matter, appendices, or most information in the Epilogue. The cities of Harrisburg, Philadelphia, Pittsburgh, and Washington are not included either. Names of counties are excluded as well. Readers wishing to know which units came from which counties should consult Appendix II in Volume One.

Abbreviations: Gen. = General; Col. = Colonel; LtCol. = Lieutenant Colonel; Capt. = Captain; Lieut. = Lieutenant; Sgt. = Sergeant; Cpl. =Corporal; Pvt. = Private; Rev. = Reverend; Rep. = Representative; Sen. = Senator; Gov. = Governor; n = note

Acheson, Mrs. A. W., 428
Adams, Sgt. John, 220
Adams Express Company, 18
Alabama, C.S.S., 69
Albright, LtCol. Charles, 412
Aldie, VA, 117, 164, 180, 191
Alexander, Mrs. Samuel, flag presented to 36th Infantry, 101
Alexandria, VA, 68, 73, 74, 78, 83, 91, 93, 96, 100, 103, 109, 122, 124, 125, 129, 149, 166, 169, 191, 198, 199, 238, 307, 313, 325, 349, 366, 379, 501, 502, 508, 511, 518
Allebaugh, Capt. William, 140, 141
Allegheny City, PA, 208, 211, 214; ladies of, flag presented to 7th Infantry, 12; to 12th Infantry, 12; to 46th Infantry, 125
Allegheny Greys, flag presented to 123rd Infantry, 397
Allegheny Light Guards, flag of, 12
Allen, Col. Edward J., 458, 460
Allen, Philip M., 355
Allen, Sgt. Thomas E., 495
Allentown, PA, ladies of, flag presented to 128th Infantry, 405
Amelia Springs, VA, 367
Ames, Col. John W., 46
Ames, Cpl. Walter, 227
Amwell Township, PA, ladies of, flag presented to 140th Infantry, 428
Anderson, Sgt. Edwin, 342
Anderson, Gen. Richard H., 343
Anderson, Gen. Robert, 465
Anderson, Sgt. Thomas C., 459
Anderson Cadets, flag of, 103

Anderson Guards, flag of, 69
Andersonville Prison Camp, GA, 34, 49, 198, 200, 209, 347, 444, 568
Annapolis, MD, 61, 85, 114, 121, 129, 137, 139, 140, 336, 519; ladies of, flag presented to 30th Infantry, 86
Antietam, MD, 62, 65, 72, 75, 82-83, 85, 88, 91, 93, 95, 97, 100, 103, 104-5, 106, 110, 113, 120, 123, 129, 133, 136, 140, 142, 148, 156, 169, 175, 180, 188, 191, 193, 195, 196, 220, 223, 227, 307, 309, 311, 312, 313, 318, 321, 325, 331, 336, 342, 354, 355, 357, 358, 363, 369, 375, 396, 398, 400, 402, 405, 406, 408-9, 410, 411, 414, 415, 419, 423, 439, 458, 533, 534, 564, 566
Appomattox Court House, VA, 57, 63, 135, 138, 149, 157, 172, 181, 183, 189, 192, 221, 228, 308, 310, 314, 335, 337, 344, 358, 361, 367, 387, 390, 393, 427, 432, 443, 454, 460, 470, 480, 484, 492, 498, 499, 567
Appomattox River, 45
Aquia Creek, VA, 82, 91, 120, 311, 336, 419
Ariel, U.S.S., 69
Arlington, VA, 226, 453
Armuchy Creek, GA, 218
Army of Northern Virginia, 110, 137, 384
Ashenfelter, Cpl. John H., 420
Ashland Station, VA, 360
Ashton, Mary, 36
Associator units, 3-4
Atlanta Campaign, 24, 71, 73, 75, 77, 124, 199, 209, 212, 215, 218, 363, 365, 370, 441
Atwater Kent Museum, 8
Auburn, VA, 471
Averasborough, NC, 317
Averell, Gen. W. W., 463
Awl, Col. F. Asbury, 502

Bachelor's Creek, NC, 162
Bailey, Mrs. Fannie, flag presented to 123rd Infantry, 397
Bailey, Capt. R. C., 48-49
Bair, Sgt. Israel B., 480
Bair, Sgt. Israel, 495
Baker, Col. Edward D., 71
Baldwin, FL, 349
Ball, Capt. John J., 404
Ball's Bluff, VA, 193, 194 n2, 354, 568

Index   585

Ballier, Col. John F., 331
Balsley, Sgt. John R., 433, 563
Baltimore, MD, 5, 8, 55, 88, 93, 114, 184, 236, 308, 311, 369, 384, 420, 426, 454, 494, 495
Banks, Gen. Nathaniel P., 72, 76, 112, 123, 126, 127, 363, 369, 377
Bannon, Sgt. Albert J., 323
Baran, Walter, 36
Barclay, Clement S., 167
Bardeen, Cpl. Charles, 459
Barger, Cpl. Charles J., 533
Barksdale, Gen. William, 429
Barnard, Capt. P. P. 42
Barnes, Sgt. William R., 480
Baron, Sgt. William, 124
Barr, Sgt. Hugh, 379
Barr, Sgt. William N., 346
Bass, Col. F. M., 45
Bassler, Capt. John C., 446, 447, 448, 557-58
Bates, Major James T., 56
Battle honors, on flags, 24-25, 73, 76, 78, 81, 89, 97, 104, 106, 110, 112, 1113, 115, 116, 120-21, 122, 127, 128, 130, 131, 138, 140, 141, 143, 149, 156, 157, 158, 162, 165, 171, 184, 199, 209, 215, 218, 230, 231, 234, 236, 307, 320, 326, 331, 334, 336, 337, 346, 348, 349, 364, 390, 404, 406, 421, 424, 437, 451, 453, 483, 486, 489, 515, 523, 524, 5376, 560-61
Battle streamers, attached to flags, 65, 68, 70, 77, 88, 91, 93, 149, 165, 167, 170, 189, 193, 203, 212, 223, 316, 317, 329, 346, 354, 379, 384, 387, 390, 454, 458, 465, 467, 483, 497, 499, 517, 533
Bauder, Pvt. Frederick, 338
Baumgartner, Sgt. A. H., 536
Bayard, Col. George D., 117
Baylitts, Sgt. Benjamin I., 378
Bayne, Col. Thomas M., 417
Beale, Sgt. William P., 537
Bealton Station, VA, 467
Beardsly, Sgt. George C., 429
Beary, Frank D., 337
Beatty, Pvt. Walter, 105
Beaufort, NC, 52, 349
Beaufort, SC, 120, 126, 136, 336
Beauregard, Gen. P. G. T., 153
Beaver, Sgt. John D., 328
Beaver Dam Church, VA, 360
Beck, Sgt. Charles, 471
Beddall, Sgt. Samuel A., 130
Beeson, Sgt. A. G., 427
Beichler, Sgt. Jacob H., 537
Belfield, VA, 480
Bell, LtCol. Thomas S., 139, 143
Belle Plain, VA, 392, 432

Belville, Rev. Jacob, 350
Benner, Sgt. John F., 443, 444
Bennett, Cpl. Matthew, 459
Bentonville, NC, 215
Berger, C. F., 550
Berger, Sgt. Thomas E., 312
Bermuda Hundred, VA, 205, 233, 328, 349, 372, 489, 510, 517
Berry, Cpl. Morton, 430, 431 n4
Berryville, VA, 171
Bertles, Capt. Jacob, 317
Bethesda Church, VA, 62, 83-84, 86, 89, 96, 98, 101, 107, 109, 111, 113, 129, 157, 188, 393, 459, 469
Bethlehem, PA, ladies of, flags presented to 1st Infantry, 11; to 9th Infantry, 12
Betzhold, Sgt. William, 78
Beverly, WV, 236, 463
Bewley, Sgt. T. Watson, 92
Bickel, Sgt. Louis H., 219
Biddle, Major Alexander, 392
Biddle, Col. Chapman, 392, 393
Biddle, Gen. Edward M., 14, 15, 17
Biddle, Henry J., 13, 536
Biddle, Nicholas, 8
Bierer, Sgt. Samuel S., 62
Biesecker, Sgt. John F., 420
Big Spring Adamantine Guards, guidon of, 167
Biles, Col. Edwin R., 335
Bird, Phineas, 338
Birmingham, Lieut. Thomas, 162
Birney, Gen. David B., 65, 533
Birney, Gen. William, 56
Bisset, Cpl. A. J., 103, 534
Bitner, Sgt. Henry, 62
Bitting, Anthony B., flag presented to Battery D, 522-23
Black, Cpl. Joseph, 535
Black, Col. Samuel W., 174, 175
Black Water River, VA, 162
Bladensburg, MD, 65
Blaines' Cross Roads, TN, 120
Blakely, LtCol. Archibald, 212
Blanchard, Cpl. Calvin H., 370, 371
Blanchard, Sgt. Henry W., 104-5
Bland, Surgeon D. W., 327
Blaney School, PA, girls of, flag presented to 103rd Infantry, 346-47
Blenker, Gen. Louis, 70
Blucher, Cpl. Charles, 490 n3
Blue Springs, TN, 120, 129
Bobb, Major Alexander, 511
Boblitz, Pvt. Eugene, 400
Bohlen, Mrs. Sophia, flag presented to 75th Infantry, 204

Boker, George H., 53, 157
Bolinger, Col. Henry C., 100
Bolton, Sgt. Amos S., 180, 537
Bolton, Levi, 142
Bolton, Sgt. Samuel F., 65, 533
Bolton, Col. William J., 11, 141, 142, 143
Boner, Sgt. Lewis S., 407
Bonnin, Cpl. Lewis W., 307
Bourke, Pvt. William, 490
Bowman, Capt. Francis L., 6
Bowman, Col. Samuel M., 230
Bowen, LtCol. George K., 489
Bowser, David B., 41-42, 44, 46, 49, 50, 51, 54, 55, 56, 57
Boyde, Harry J., 428
Boydton Plank Road, VA, 160, 164, 179, 181, 231, 310, 314, 335, 337, 352, 367, 384, 387, 393, 429, 432, 436, 448, 451, 462, 467, 480, 484, 497, 515
Boyer, Henry C., 326
Boyle, Rev. J. R., 34
Brabst, Nathan F., flag presented to 140th Infantry, 428
Bradley, Pvt. William H., 534
Brady, Sgt. Michael, 190
Brady Infantry, flag of, 428
Bragg, Gen. Braxton, 208, 209, 211, 214, 217
Brainerd, Lieut. Elisha B., 431
Brainerd, Rev. Thomas, 29
Brandon, Alexander, 160, 185, 444, 556
Brandy Station, VA; battle of, 23, 117, 180, 191, 467, 469, 471; camps near, 66, 83, 97, 107, 134, 159, 170, 178, 184, 186, 220, 223, 230, 318, 331, 334, 351, 354, 367, 380, 382, 386, 390, 420, 424, 427, 429, 432, 439, 467, 469, 471
Brandywine, battle of (1777), 4
Brannan, Gen. John M., 126
Bratten, Cpl. George W., 459
Braun, Capt. Gustavus L., 372
Brawner's Farm, VA, 155
Breash, Cpl. Thomas, 358
Brehm, Sgt. Henry G., 446, 447, 448
Bretz, Edward, 359 n4
Brewer, Samuel, 15, 552
Brice's Crossroads, MS, 479
Bridgeport, AL, 73, 76, 124, 203, 491
Bridgeville, PA, ladies of, flag presented to 1st Cavalry, 118
Brill, Cpl. John F., 343
Brisbane, Col. William, 559
Bristoe Station, VA, campaign of, 69, 83, 110, 117, 149, 156, 164, 166, 170, 175, 178, 184, 188, 191, 193, 195, 220, 223, 227, 236, 307, 309, 311, 313, 318, 321, 325, 331, 334, 343, 351, 354, 357, 367, 380, 382, 384, 386, 390, 392, 420, 424, 427, 429, 432, 434, 439, 443, 448, 451, 459, 467, 469; mentioned, 86, 88, 190, 110, 379
Brock's Grove, VA, 471
Brockenbrough, Col. J. M., 447
Brockway, Lieut. Charles B., 115
Brooke, Gen. John R., 28, 148, 149
Brown, Sgt. Robert, 49
Brown, Sgt. Rufus G., 355
Bruce, Sgt. Archibald C., 155
Bucks County, PA, women of, flag presented to 104th Infantry, 349-50; to Battery D, 522
Bucks County Historical Society, 350
Budlong, Sgt. Thomas H., 175
Buehler, Major C. H., flag presented to 87th Infantry, 238
Buell, Gen. Don Carlos, 208, 214
Buford, Gen. John, 497
Bull Run Mountains, VA, 61
Bundy, Capt. Henry, 364, 365
Burkesville, VA, 51, 149
Burkhardt, Sgt. William, 200
Burns, Cpl. Patrick, 157
Burnside, Gen. Ambrose E., 120, 128, 1229, 136, 137, 139, 140, 313, 321, 325, 336, 465
Buschbeck, Col. Adolph, 70, 71
Butler, Gen. Benjamin F., 42, 45, 153, 205, 328
Butler, Sgt. William R., 55
Butterfield, Gen. Daniel, 226
Buzzard's Roost, GA, 215
Byers, Capt. Nelson, 441
Byrnes, Sgt. William, 323

Cake, Col. Joseph W., flag presented to 25th Infantry, 13, 326
Caldwell, Sgt. Samuel, 396
Calhoun, KY, ladies of, flag presented to 9th Cavalry, 317
Camden, NJ, 379, 454
Cameron, Cpl. James, 143
Cameron, Sen. J. Donald, 141
Cameron, Simon, 80, 451
Camp Cadwalader, 27, 78, 157, 221, 376, 482, 488, 505, 519, 520
Camp Cameron, 174, 205, 217
Camp Campbell, 180
Camp Coleman, 318
Camp colors, 20, 156-57
Camp Copeland, 336, 338
Camp Curtin, 17, 27, 80, 110, 114, 120, 123, 126, 128, 133, 136, 137, 139, 142, 145, 148, 151, 153, 155, 159, 180, 181, 205, 230, 318, 340, 346, 366, 398, 400, 404, 405, 406, 408, 410, 414, 415, 416, 417, 420, 426, 429, 432, 441, 443, 446, 450, 453, 456,

Index 587

458, 471, 484, 488, 495, 502, 503, 508, 510, 511, 513, 515
Camp Dick Robinson, 136
Camp Douglas, 495
Camp Hamilton, 454
Camp Lookout, 51
Camp Nelson, 140
Camp Orr, 211, 346, 347
Camp Reynolds, 517
Camp Scott, 11
Camp Seward, 426
Camp Simmons, 409, 469
Camp Slifer, 12
Camp Wayne, 328
Camp Wilkins, 103, 106, 208, 214, 535
Camp William Penn, 40-41, 42, 44, 45, 46, 48, 50, 51, 54, 56, 57
Camp Wright, 102
Campbell, Charles E., 401
Campbell, Gen. Charles T., 28
Campbell, Col. David, 180
Campbell, LtCol. Edward, 233
Campbell, LtCol. H. S., 226
Campbell, Col. Jacob M., 151
Campbell, Rep. James H., 130
Campbell's Station, TN, 120, 129, 140, 336
Canfield, Sgt. Stephen B., 430
Cannon, Cpl. Michael, 378
Canonsburg, PA, ladies of, flag presented to 39th Infantry, 535
Canton High School, 355
Cape Hatteras, NC, 52
Captured flags, 32-33, 64, 71, 100-1, 108, 112, 114, 121, 124, 141, 143, 152, 155-56, 175, 179, 182, 183, 184, 192, 209, 215, 220, 337, 340, 343, 351, 443, 448, 451, 471, 492, 532
Carlisle, PA, 101
Carlisle Barracks, PA, 465
Carnegie, PA, 118, 175
Carolina Campaign (1865), 73, 78, 124, 199, 215, 317, 364, 370, 442
Carr, Cpl. Winfield S., 156
Carruthers, Lieut. H. W., 328
Carson, Cpl. Joseph C., 534
Carter, Sgt. Albert, 63
Casey, Sgt. Amos, 335
Casey, Gen. Silas, 19, 145, 340, 346, 348, 560
Cass Infantry, flag of, 397
Cassville, GA, 209
Castle Pinckney, SC, 147
Cedar Creek, Va, 127, 135, 152, 185, 237, 319, 320, 322, 323, 343, 344, 420, 425, 463, 471, 485
Cedar Mountain, VA, 61, 72, 113, 117, 118, 123, 230, 307, 311, 357, 363, 366, 369, 371

Cemetery Hill, VA, 328
Chaffin's Farm, VA, 54, 162, 372, 489
Chain, Benjamin E., 142
Chamberlain, Gen. Joshua L., 498
Chamberlin, Col. James, 18, 204
Chamberlin, Capt. Thomas, 534
Chambers, Pvt. Cyrus W., 62
Chambers, Sgt. James H., 346
Chambersburg, PA, 76, 473, ladies of, flags presented to 7th Infantry, 12; to 8th Infantry, 12
Chancellorsville, VA, 44, 62, 68, 70, 72-73, 75, 76, 113, 123-24, 133, 148, 156, 159, 164, 166, 175, 177-78, 180, 186, 188, 191, 193, 195, 196, 198, 201-2, 203, 220, 227, 231, 307, 309-10, 311, 313, 318, 321, 325, 331, 333, 342-43, 351, 354, 357, 363, 367, 369, 377, 379-80, 381, 386, 390, 392, 395, 396, 398, 401, 402, 404, 405, 406-7, 409, 410, 412, 414, 415, 416, 418, 419, 424, 426, 429, 432, 434, 439, 441, 443, 444, 446, 450, 453, 456-57, 459, 467, 469, 470
Chantilly, VA, 129, 136, 140, 159, 188, 333, 336
Chapin's Bluff, VA, 154
Charles, Cpl. Francis, 307
Charles City Cross Roads, VA, battle of (1864), 56, 164
Charleston, SC, 44, 54, 126, 127, 146-47, 153, 202, 205, 233, 328, 336, 349
Charleston, WV, 375
Charlestown, WV, 91, 94, 127
Charlottesville, VA, 361
Chattahoochie River, GA, 77
Chattanooga, TN, 71, 73, 76, 124, 198, 2203, 209, 211, 212, 214, 215, 217, 218, 316, 363, 369, 441, 465, 466. SEE ALSO Lookout Mountain, Missionary Ridge
Chester County Fair, 328
Chester County Historical Society, 118
Chicago, IL, 495
Chickahominy River, VA, 82, 93, 112, 148
Chickamauga, GA, 209, 211, 214, 215, 216, 218, 316, 465
Childsburg, VA, 117-18
Chilson, Cpl. William H., 419
Chism, Sgt. Robert, 314
Cincinnati, OH, 120
Citizens Artillery, flag of, 11
City Point, VA, 45, 55, 163, 372, 425, 482, 488, 490, 508, 510
Civil War flags; company flags, 558-59; local presentations, 558, 561; personal flags, 559; star patterns, 19; terminology problems with, 557-58; usage of, 558
—artillery flags, 23-24; types of, 23-24, 115-16
—cavalry flags, 21-23; guidons, 22; standards, 21-22; use of, 22-23
—infantry flags, 18-21; camp colors, 20, 156-57,

559-60; color-guard, 19; cord and tassel styles, 553; general guide markers, 20-21, 559, 560; importance to battleline of, 19-20; local presentations, 19; loss of colors, 20; national colors, 18; regimental colors, 18-19; types of flags, 18-19
Civil War Library and Museum, Philadelphia, 94, 118,156, 158, 167, 192, 311, 314, 355, 386, 421, 522 (called War Library throughout text)
Clapper, Sgt. Louis, 393, 394
Clark, Capt. George S., 466
Clark, Harrison G., 31
Clark, Col. John B., 396, 397, 495
Clarksburg, WV, 202, 236
Clarkstown, WV, 485
Clay, Capt. Cecil, 490
Clearfield, PA, 96
Cleburne, Gen. Patrick R., 71, 215
Cloud's Mills, VA, 74
Cloyd's Mountain, WV, 83, 91-92, 94
Clymer, Sgt. Alfred, 392-93
Clymer, Sen. Heister, 13
Coalfield, VA, 360
Cobb, Sgt. Henry Q., 386
Cobb, William S., flag presented to 99th Infantry, 335
Cobham, Col. George A., 370-71
Cold Harbor, VA, 62, 66, 114, 121, 129, 134, 138, 149, 153, 157, 160, 162, 170, 175, 178, 188, 191, 193, 195, 205, 220, 221, 224, 227, 231, 236, 308, 311, 318, 321, 325, 328, 331, 334, 337, 343, 351, 354, 357, 372, 373, 380, 382, 387, 390, 420, 424, 427, 429, 432, 436, 439, 443, 448, 451, 459, 462, 469, 471, 480, 482, 484, 488, 489, 492, 536, 568
Coleman, George Dawson, flags presented to 93rd Infantry, 319-20
Coleman, Pvt. Samuel, 64
Collier, Col. Frederick, 424
Collis, Col. Charles H. T., 377, 378
Columbia, KY, 336
Columbia, TN, 211, 214, 217, 218
Columbia Volunteer Battalion, flag of, 7
Columbus, GA, 218
Columbus, KY, 479
Conneautville (PA) Soldiers Aid Society, flag presented to 145th Infantry, 440
Conner, Cpl. Rodney, 452 n3
Conrad, Sgt. J. W., 327
Conyngham, LtCol. John B., 147
Cooke, Pvt. John B., 323, 563
Coon, Sgt. William, 171, 563-64
Cooper Shop Volunteer Refreshment Saloon (Philadelphia, PA), flag presented to 31st Infantry, 89; to 95th Infantry, 322
Coppee, Gen. Henry, 15
Core, Sgt. Michael H., 485

Core Creek, NC, 162
Corinth, MS, 208
Cosby Creek, VA, 465
Couch, Gen. Darius N., 65, 318, 342
Coughlin, Pvt. Merritt, 436
Coulter, Col. Henry, 61, 62
Coulter, Henry, Jr., 64
Cove Gap, VA, 463
Covington, KY, 120
Cowan, Sen. Edgar, flags presented by, 174, 226
Cowan, Cpl. William H., 342
Cox, Cpl. Rogers W., 437-38
Crab Orchard, KY, 140
Craig, Col. Calvin A., 351
Crater, VA, battle of the, 55, 121, 129,138, 141, 205, 328, 337, 338, 373
Craven, Lieut. Richard P., 336, 337
Craven, Walter C., 538
Crawford, Gen. Samuel W., 28, 62, 83, 85-86, 100, 357
Crawford, Sgt. Scott R., 208
Crealy, Pvt. Thomas, 388
Crippen, Sgt. Benjamin, 434, 435
Crook, Gen. George, 83, 91
Crosby, LtCol. John W., 171, 172
Cross, Capt. Murray S., 237
Cross Keys, Va, 70, 113, 198, 201, 203
Culbertson, Thomas C., 513
Culpeper, VA, 123, 155, 157, 191, 307, 311, 321, 392, 434, 448, 451, 467, 469, 471
Cumberland, MD, 95, 112, 151, 471
Cumberland Mountains, 466
Curry, LtCol. Wlliam L., 354
Curtin, Gov. Andrew G., 13, 14, 15, 16, 17, 24, 27, 28, 29-30, 40, 65, 72, 73, 163, 178, 326, 334, 373, 433, 489, 560; flags presented by, 61, 80-81, 88, 91, 93, 95, 97, 104, 106, 108, 112, 115, 117, 120, 123, 126, 128, 133, 136, 139, 145, 148, 151, 153, 155, 159, 162, 164, 180, 184, 191, 205, 208, 211, 214, 217, 223, 230, 233, 311, 313, 316, 318, 325, 328, 340, 346, 348, 357, 366, 369, 379, 453, 524
Curtin, Col. John I., 122
Curwensville, PA, 113
Cutler, Gen. Lysander, 156

Daily, Cpl. Thomas, 402
Dakin, Sgt. Thomas, 438
Dallas, GA, 71, 124, 209, 218, 370
Dalton, GA, 71
Dana, Col. Edmund L., 434, 437
Dana, Mrs. N. J. T., flag presented to Dana Troop, 524
Dandridge, TN, 316, 465
Danks, Major John A., 178
Danner, Cpl. George L., 537

Danville, PA, 99; ladies of, flag presentations to 11th Infantry, 12; to 93rd Infantry, 320
Danville, VA, 172, 332, 344, 390, 425, 480, 490
Danville Rifles, flag of, 12
Darbytown Road, VA, 49, 50, 54, 56, 163, 206, 234, 329, 360, 505
Davis, Lieut. A. B., 172
Davis, LtCol. Elisha W., 392
Davis, Sgt. Ephraim B., 222
Davis, Sgt. G. P., 466
Davis, Capt. G. W. P., 151
Davis, Sgt. George W., 53
Davis, Jefferson, 451
Davis, Sgt. John, 169
Davis, Gen. Joseph C., 447
Davis, Col. W. W. H., 348, 349, 350
Dean, Sgt. John, 537
Dean, Leonidas H., 143
Dechert, Henry M., flag presented by, 78
Deen, Sgt. George W., 98 n3
Decatur, AL, 466
Deep Bottom, VA, 160, 164, 191, 205-6, 220, 231, 234, 328, 334, 335, 351, 367, 382, 427, 429, 439, 443, 467, 469, 482, 484, 537
Deffenbaugh, Sgt. Jacob, 234, 538
Deitrich, Pvt. George, 505
DeLacy, Sgt. Patrick, 435-36, 564
Delaney, Pvt. John C., 358, 359 n4, 564-65
Delaney, Sgt. Samuel F., 388
Derr, Sgt. William, 88-89, 534
Deserted House, VA, 360
Designating flags, 64
Detweiler, Sgt. Abraham F., 382
Devaux, Sgt. John B., 343
Deveaux Neck, SC, 54
Deveraux, Cpl. Thomas C., 314
Devine, Sgt. John, 308
Devins, Cpl. Minus, 373
Dibrell, Gen. George G., 316
Dill, William, flag presented to 123rd Infantry, 397
Dillinger, Capt. J. P., 405
Dilman, Pvt. Henry, 100
Dix, Gen. John A., 474
Donaldson, Capt. Frank A., 386, 387, 388
Donaldson, Mrs. Sophia, flag presented to 118th Infantry, 386
Donohoe, Sgt. John B., 307
Donohue, Cpl. Charles L., 342
Dorien, Pvt. Edward, 105
Dostman, Cpl. William F., 215, 216
Doubleday, Gen. Abner, 155
Dougherty, Daniel, flag presented to 99th Infantry, 335
Dougherty, Sgt. Michael, 190

Dover, DE, 519
Doyle, Sgt. James, 380
Doylestown, PA, 348
Drewry's Bluff, VA, 153, 162, 205, 328, 489
Drainesville, VA, 81, 97, 104, 106, 110, 112, 117, 560
Droop Mountain, WV, 463
Dropsie, Moses A., flag presented to 27th Infantry, 533
Drury, Sgt. Bernard J., 364
Dug Gap, GA, 211
Duncan, J. W., 161, 556
Duncannon, PA. SEE Petersburg, PA
Dunne, Major John P., 380
Duquesne Greys, flag of, 12
Durell, Capt. George W., 522
Dutch Gap Canal, VA, 45, 501

Earhart, Sgt. John Y., 157
Early, Gen. Jubal A., 56, 135, 170, 237, 318, 322, 343, 375, 390, 420, 424, 469
Early, Sgt. Wallace, 156
East Baltimore, MD, ladies of, flag presented to 22nd Infantry, 12-13
Easton, PA, 80, 88, 91, 93, 220; ladies of, flags presented to 1st Infantry, 11; to 41st Infantry, 535
Easton Guards, flag of, 535
Easton Invincibles, flag of, 11
Easton Jaegers, flag of, 12
Eby, Sgt. Henry, 157
Eckman, Col. Charles W., 319, 320
Edisto Island, SC, 153
Edgerton, Lieut. Nathan H., 45-46
Edwards, Col. Oliver, 135
Egle, William H., 8
Egypt, MS, 479
1866 ceremonies, 28-31
Eisenbee, H. A., 533
Ekert, Sgt. George, 202
Elliott, Sgt. Fergus, 363, 365, 565
Ellmaker, Col. Peter C., 390
Elmira, NY, 448, 451
Ely, Lieut. Andrew F., 48-49
Ely, Col. John, 66
Emleben, Sgt. John, 204
Endicott, William C., 179
Engle, Sgt. John H., 520
Ennis, Sgt. John, 219
Entriken, Sgt. Henry, 134, 135
Erie, PA, 226, 227, 439; citizens of, flag presented to 145th Infantry, 440; ladies of, flag presented to 145th Infantry, 440
Erie County Library System, 175, 227, 228, 440
Ertle, Albert T., 555
Ery, Sgt. John, 479
Evans, Sgt. Thomas, 212

Evans & Hassall, 15, 16, 17, 68, 70, 72, 74, 76, 83, 130, 157, 163, 196, 212, 215, 233, 311, 337, 374, 382, 390, 392, 397, 416, 419, 421, 463, 475, 492, 507, 509, 511, 526, 535, 536, 550, 552, 553, 554, 555, 556, 557, 558, 560
Evers, Cpl. Thomas, 121
Ewell, Gen. Richard S., 84, 451
Ewing, Sgt. John, 308
Eyre, Lieut. George W., 559

Faller, Capt. John I., 101
Falling Waters, WV, 12, 63, 448
Falmouth, VA, 123, 148, 159, 166, 177, 186, 188, 191, 195, 203, 307, 331, 354, 357, 379, 381, 386, 390, 402, 406, 409, 410, 412, 414, 415, 418, 426, 429, 439, 443
Farmville, VA, 221, 427, 467, 480
Fayetteville, NC, 384
Feather, Sgt. Michael, 367
Federal government flags, depot involvement with, 554-55; Cincinnati depot, 555, 556, 557; New York depot, 555, 556; Philadelphia depot, 555-56, 557; purchases, 555; requisitioned, 554
Feightner, Sgt. William, 64
Ferguson, Sgt. John P., 440
Fernandina, FL, 328
Finacy, Sgt. William, 196
Finnegan, Gen. J. W., 48
First City Troop, flag of, 3; mentioned, 28; museum of, 192
First Defenders, flags of, 8-9, 532-33; mentioned, 28
First State Troop, flag of, 8
Fisher, Gov. John S., 35
Fisher, Sgt. Joseph, 171-72
Fisher, Col. Joseph, 83
Fisher's Hill, VA, 127, 152, 185, 237, 319, 322, 332, 343-44, 344, 420, 424, 463, 485
Fithean, Cpl. Joseph S., 344
Fittery, Pvt. Henry, 318, 319
Fitzgerald, Sgt. George W., 177
Five Forks, VA, 63, 149, 164, 167, 192, 228, 310, 314, 358, 361, 387, 432, 460, 467, 469, 480, 482, 492, 497-98, 515
Flanigan, Sgt. Augustin, 154
Flat Creek Bridge, VA, 360
Flat Rock, GA, 218
Florence, AL, 214
Florence, SC, 568
Flugga, Cpl. William E., 415
Flynn, Col. John, 73, 74
Folly Island, SC, 146, 233
Foltz, Sgt. George W., 327
Foote, Cpl. George W., 142
Ford, Sgt. David H., 170

Forest, Pvt. Abner W., 430-31
Forney, John W., 13, 42, 326
Forsythe, Cpl. Thomas, 328, 329
Fort Barrancas, 52
Fort Delaware, 372, 454, 502
Fort Fisher, 46, 206, 329-30, 505
Fort Gilmer, 49, 154, 329, 360, 372
Fort Gregg, 499, 535
Fort Harrison, 46, 162, 360, 489, 490
Fort Hoke, 489
Fort Jackson, 73
Fort Jefferson, 126
Fort Johnson, 146
Fort Leavenworth, 463
Fort McHenry, 5
Fort McRae, 388
Fort Mahone, 122
Fort Monroe, 23, 45, 120, 128, 129, 136, 153, 162, 193, 205, 318, 328, 360, 380, 454
Fort Pickens, 52
Fort Pitt Guards, flag of, 12
Fort Pulaski, 205, 328
Fort Ripley, 146
Fort Slocum, 377, 434
Fort Sedgwick, 510
Fort Stedman, 138, 337, 367, 390, 482, 501, 508, 510, 511, 513, 517
Fort Stevens, 343
Fort Sumter, 146
Fort Taylor, 126
Fort Tyler, 71
Fort Wagner, 44, 205, 233
Fort Washington, 524
Foster, Gen. John G., 340, 346
Foster's Place, VA, 328
Foulke, Sgt. Charles H., 61
Fouse, Sgt. Dewalt S., 148
Foust, Sgt. Alonzo, 369, 370, 371
Fowles, Sgt., 164, 165 n2
Frankfort, KY, 208, 316
Franklin, Benjamin, 3
Franklin, PA, 533
Franklin, TN, battle of, 204, 209-10, 212, 217; mentioned, 316
Franklin, VA, 201, 360
Frederick, MD, 519
Fredericksburg, VA, battle of, 62, 65, 68, 72, 83, 85, 88-89, 91, 93, 95-96, 97, 100, 103, 105, 106, 109, 110, 113, 117, 120, 123, 129, 133, 136, 140, 148, 155, 156, 159, 164, 166, 169, 170, 175, 177, 180, 186, 188, 190, 191, 193, 195, 203, 220, 223, 227, 231, 307, 309, 311, 313, 318, 321, 325, 331, 333, 336, 342, 351, 354, 357, 358, 363, 366, 369, 377, 379, 381, 386, 390, 392, 394, 395, 396, 401, 402, 404,

405, 406, 409, 410, 411-12, 414, 415, 417-18, 423, 429, 432, 439, 440, 458-59, 460; mentioned, 311, 366, 416, 441, 450, 456, 489
Free Military School, 41, 334
Freeman, Miss, 13
Freeman's Ford, VA, 201
Fremont, Gen. John C., 70
Fribley, Col. Charles W., 48
Frick, Col. Jacob G., 406, 407, 565
Friddell, Cpl. John, 447, 448
Frishmuth, Mrs. William, flag presented by, 376
Fritz, Pvt. James J., 109
Front Royal, VA, 72, 469
Fry, J. R., flag presented to 45th Militia, 524
Fry, Major William H., 467
Fuller, Sgt. Niram A., 146
Fulton, Sgt. William J., 88
Funk, Sgt. Jacob B., 175, 536
Furness, Sgt. James B., 373

Gaines' Mill, VA, 82, 85, 88, 91, 93, 95, 99, 102, 104, 106, 108, 110, 112, 175, 180, 191, 226-27, 321, 323, 325
Gallatin, TN, 214, 217
Gallipolis, OH, 494
Gallup, Mrs. George, flag presented to 37th Infantry, 103
Gambell, Cpl. Edward, 314
Gamble, Ralph E., 448
Ganoe, Rev. M. L., 34
Gap, PA, ladies of, flag presented to 1st Infantry, 11
Garlow, Sgt. Stephen E., 158
Gardner, Sgt. Johnson C., 536
Garnett's Hill, VA, 133
Gates, S. J., 143
Gay, Lieut. Edward H., 62
Geary, Gen. John W., 28, 30, 72, 73, 76, 78, 363, 364
Geary, Sgt. William H., 314
General guide markers, 20-21, 42, 66, 78, 89, 130, 131, 143, 158, 196, 200, 204, 215, 307, 314, 365, 388, 408, 421, 520, 537, 559-60
Georgia troops, 61st Infantry, 100, 568
Germantown, PA, 167; citizens, of, flag presented to 114th Infantry, 378; ladies of, flag presented to 6th Cavalry, 192
Gettys, Cpl. Sylvester G., 158
Gettysburg, PA, battle of, 32, 62, 66, 68-69, 70, 73, 76, 83, 85-86, 89, 96, 97, 105, 106-7, 109, 110, 113, 115-16, 117, 124, 133-34, 148-49, 156-57, 159, 164, 166, 170, 175, 178, 180, 186, 188, 190, 191, 193, 195, 198, 200, 202, 203, 220, 223, 227, 231, 307, 309, 311, 312, 313, 318, 321, 325, 331, 333-34, 343, 351, 352, 354, 357, 358, 360, 363, 367, 369, 377, 378, 380, 381-82, 386, 390, 392, 420, 424, 426-27, 429, 430, 432, 433, 434, 437, 439, 441, 443, 444, 446-48, 450-51, 453, 454, 457, 459, 467, 469, 470, 471, 474, 536, 564, 568; mentioned, 138, 473
Gettysburg National Military Park, 238, 352
Gibbon, Gen. John, 20, 62, 417
Gibbons, Charles, 57
Gibson, Col. Augustus A., 372, 373
Gibson, Sgt. William H., 225
Gilham, William, 20, 560
Gilmore, Cpl. Samuel, 452 n3
Giltinan, Capt. Henry J., 198
Givin, Lieut. James, 57
Glanz, Col. Charles, 456, 457
Glendale, VA, battle of (also known as New Market Cross Roads), 68, 82, 85, 88, 91, 93, 95, 99, 102, 104, 106, 108, 110, 112, 159, 177, 180, 188, 191, 193, 220, 325, 351, 354, 534
Glenn, Major Edward A., 497
Glenn, Col. John, 27, 66
Globe Tavern, VA, 62
Gloucester Point, VA, 349
Golding's Farm, VA, 133
Goldsboro, NC, 147, 233, 340
Good, Sgt. Myron P., 371
Goodfellow, Sgt. Andrew J., 122
Gordon, Gen. John B., 83, 100, 170
Gordonsville, VA, 469
Gorman, Sgt. Hugh, 170
Gosline, Col. John M., 321
Gosline, Mrs. Mary Ann, 322
Gouldsberry, Sgt. Thomas, 230
Governor's Island, NY, 471
Gowen, Col. George W., 129
Grady, Sgt. George, 75
Graham, Pvt. David H., 110
Graham, Sgt. James B., 393
Graham, Sgt. James S., 424
Graham, Sgt. William G., 393, 394
Gramlich, Lieut. C. F., 34
Grand Army of the Republic, 31, 33, 34, 47, 114; Maryland Post 1, 114; Post 1, 47, 158, 225; Post 2, 67, 78, 386, 391; Post 11, 94, 142, 526; Post 52, 421; Post 67, 228, 440; Post 84, 395; Post 120, 485; Post 153, 118, 175; Post 162, 33; Museum of, 66, 78, 124, 151, 172, 228, 322, 335 n10, 381
Grand Review, 122, 137, 138, 149, 161, 165, 215, 335, 337, 352, 358, 367, 370, 377, 382, 387, 391, 393, 427, 430, 433, 439, 442, 444, 460, 482, 484, 492, 498, 501, 508, 511, 515, 517, 554
Grant, Gen. Ulysses S., 20, 23, 42, 57, 62, 71, 83, 86, 100, 117, 120, 121, 137, 138, 140, 149, 153, 157, 160, 164, 167, 181, 184, 186, 192, 205, 208, 220, 227, 231, 336, 392, 425, 467, 469, 482; tomb of, 378
Graul, Cpl. William L., 489, 565-66

Gravel Hill, VA, 118
Great Falls, MD, 104
Green Plains, VA, 328
Green River, KY, 211, 214
Greenawalt, Sgt. William G., 343-44
Greene, Gen. George S., 72
Greenland, Walter W., 143, 400, 566
Greenwood, Sgt. John, 363
Gregg, Gen. David M., 28
Gregg, Col. John Irvin, 467
Gregg, LtCol. Theodore, 121
Gregory, Col. Edgar M., 314
Gressang, William, 407
Gries, Major John M., 348
Gries, Chaplain William R., 30
Griffin, Baldwin, 314
Griswold, GA, 317
Grover, Gen. Cuvier, 68
Greider, B. M., flag presented to 9th Cavalry, 317
Grow, Rep. Galusha A., 65, 81, 307
Guss, Col. Henry R., 328, 330
Gutelius, Cpl. Joseph S., 450-51
Guy, Cpl. Frank, 371

Haber, Sgt. Charles H., 187 n2, 537
Haberling, H. E., 338
Hackney, Sgt. Thomas, 373
Hagerstown, MD, 366, 419, 471, 485
Haines, Capt. Benjamin F., 62
Hall, Cpl. Harry, 378
Hambright, Col. Henry A., 214
Hamm, Sgt. George D., 211
Hammel, Cpl. John, 446, 447, 448
Hammer, Sgt. Hezekiah, 154
Hampton, Capt. Robert, 522
Hampton, Gen. Wade, 182
Hancock, MD, 230, 366
Hancock, Gen. Winfield S., 9, 28, 29, 30, 133, 149
Hanlin, Sgt. Christian, 495
Hanover, PA, 471
Hanover Court House, VA, 174-75, 191, 226, 360
Hanover Junction, VA, 331
Harden, Sgt. W. H., 438
Hardy, Sgt. William, 392, 393, 394
Harman, Sgt. Charles, 162
Harney, Lieut. F. M., 451
Harper, Sgt. Alfred E., 371
Harper's Ferry, WV, 72, 76, 88, 112, 123, 318, 331, 363, 369, 375, 381, 384, 398, 401, 405, 409, 417, 420, 424, 439, 440, 441, 463, 471, 474, 480, 485
Harrisburg, PA, ladies of, flag presented to 127th Infantry, 404
Harrisburg City Guards, flag of, 404
Harrisburg *Telegraph*, 34

Harrison, Cpl. Samuel B., 416
Harrison, LtCol. William H., 520
Harrison's Landing, VA, 82, 145, 223, 333
Harrisonburg, VA, 113
Hart's Island, NY, 187, 436-37
Hartman, Sgt. Thomas, 307
Hartranft, Gen. John F., 139, 140, 141, 501, 508, 510, 517
Hartshorne, Col. William R., 113-14
Harty, Capt. Edward S., 131
Harvey, Sgt. John M., 148
Haserodt, Sgt. Charles, 204
Hastings, Gen. Daniel H., 103, 156
Hatch, Gen. John P., 54
Hatcher's Run, VA, 20, 138, 141, 157, 160, 167, 181, 189, 220, 228, 308, 310, 313, 322, 357-58, 367, 382, 384, 387, 388, 390, 393, 427, 433, 436, 448, 451, 459, 462, 467, 480, 484, 492, 497, 510, 515, 517, 565
Hatteras Inlet, NC, 128, 139
Haw's Shop, VA, 118, 160, 164, 181, 384, 467
Hawkins, Sgt.Major Thomas, 46-47
Hawley, Col. Joseph W., 398
Hay, Col. George, 237
Hays, Gen. Alexander, 177
Hazard, Sgt. Erskine W., Jr., 392
Hazel River, VA, 325
Hazelton, PA, ladies of, flag presented to 28th Infantry, 75
Hazlett, Sgt. James L., 108
Hazlett, Sgt. William, 180
Hearns, George A., 41
Heck, Sgt. Joshua, 511
Heicchold, Surgeon A. P., 48
Heilman, Sgt. Adam, 453
Heintzelman, Gen. Samuel P., 68, 159
Heiss, Emanuel, 550-51
Henderson, LtCol. Robert M., 99, 100
Hendley, Sgt. Ezra, 327
Hennessy, Major John A., 146-47
Henning, Sgt. John, 456, 457
Henry, Mayor Alexander, 46; flag presented to 12th Cavalry, 376
Henry, Sgt. Robert A., 444
Henry, Sgt. Samuel, 441
Henry Guards, 28, 31
Henthorne, Pvt. George, 358
Herbert, Sgt. Richard, 136
Herbst, Sgt. William, 138 n1
Herring, Major Charles P., 388
Herrman, Sgt. Jacob, 332
Hershberger, Russell L., 36
Hess, Sgt. Henry, 200
Heth, Gen. Henry, 171

Index

593

Hewlings, Lieut. William H., 311
Hickok, Sgt. Charles, 355
Hiester, Mrs. Dr., flag presented to 5th Infantry, 12
High Bridge, VA, 152, 189
Hight, Sgt. John J., 134, 135
Hileman, Cpl. John M., 358
Hill, Gen. Ambrose P., 83, 375, 434
Hill, Pvt. Samuel W., 459
Hill, Steven, 555
Hill, Sgt. William H., 367, 368
Hilton Head, SC, 48, 54, 120, 126, 136, 153, 205, 233, 328, 336, 349, 474
Hirschling, Sgt. John I., 332, 566
Historical Society of Montgomery County, 142
Historical Society of Pennsylvania, 6, 167, 376
Historical Society of Schuylkill County, 7, 36, 129, 130, 131, 218, 326, 327, 557
Historical Society of York County, 12
Hitchcock, Col. Frederick L., 52-53, 411-12, 413, 558, 566
Hoagland, Lieut. Henry H., 411
Hoffa, Sgt. John, 162
Hoffman, Henry W., 452
Hoffman, Cpl. Frederick, 446, 447
Hoffman, Pvt. Gustavus, 533
Hoffman, Cpl. John, 177
Hoffman, Sgt. Theodore D., 133
Hofmann, Col. J. William, 155-56, 157
Hoke, Gen. Robert F., 346
Hollidaysburg, PA, ladies of, flag presented to 62nd Infantry, 536-37
Honey Hill, SC, 54
Honor, Sgt. William H., 392
Hood, Gen. John B., 73, 77, 209, 364, 370, 441, 442, 466, 479
Hooker, Gen. Joseph, 62, 70, 72, 76, 82, 85, 148, 203, 342, 357, 363
Hopkins Infantry, flag of, 103
Horning, Sgt. George T., 510
Horstmann Brothers & Company, 9, 12, 14-17, 22, 33, 42, 65, 77, 80, 83, 117, 118, 124, 127, 141, 147, 149, 154, 164, 166, 169, 171, 192, 195, 215, 220, 228, 233, 307, 309, 318, 331, 336, 340, 349, 354, 360, 372, 375, 377, 379, 380, 382, 384, 424, 425, 434, 437, 439, 441, 455, 463, 466, 467, 469, 470, 471, 474, 482, 484, 489, 494, 501, 502, 503, 505, 510, 513, 515, 517, 534, 535, 550, 552-57, 560
Horton, Cpl. George, 534
Hough, Sgt. Solomon R., 358
Houghton, Cpl. John, 354
House, Sgt. George F., 177-78, 537
Howard, Gen. Oliver O., 412
Howard, Cpl. William H., 462
Howe Engineers, flag of, 397

Howell, Col. Joshua B., 233
Hoy, Francis, 34
Hoyt, Col. Henry M., 146
Hubbert, Ruthann, 35
Hucks, Cpl. Joseph, 342
Huff Family, flag presented to 195th Infantry, 495
Huffnagle, Cpl. Andrew J., 537
Hughes, Major Chester K., 436
Hughs, Sgt. John, 220
Humelstine, Sgt. Manaris, 515
Hummel, Mr., flag presented to 127th Infantry, 404
Hummel, Pvt. William, 388
Humphreys, Gen. Andrew A., 396, 402, 406
Humphreys, Sgt. Edward J., 513
Hunsicker, Pvt. Harry H., 327
Hunter, Gen. David, 146, 463, 485
Hunter, Cpl. James C., 507 n2
Hunter, Mr. William, flag presented to 183rd Infantry, 484
Hunter's Chapel, VA, 201
Huntingdon, PA, 230, 366; Excelsior Band of, flag presented to 5th Infantry, 533; ladies of, flag presented to 46th Militia, 524
Huntingdon County Historical Society, 401
Huntsville, AL, 210, 218
Hustonville, KY, 120
Hutchison, Sgt. John, 320
Hutton, Sgt. Samuel, 333

Ilgenfritz, Sgt. Charles H., 510
Illinois troops, 92nd Infantry, 156
Imboden, Pvt. George, 320
Independence Hall, 27, 29-30, 189, 190, 204
Independence Hall National Historical Park, 4
Irish Infantry, flag of, 114
Iron City Guards, flag of, 105
Irvin, Sgt. Samuel H., 134, 135 n6
Irvin, Mrs. William, flag presented to 42nd Infantry, 113
Irvis, Rep. K. Leroy, 36
Irwin, Col. William H., 133
Iverson, Gen. Alfred, 62, 124

Jack, Capt. John H., 487
Jackson, Gen. Thomas J. (Stonewall), 61, 62, 63, 68, 70, 72, 76, 82, 85, 93, 105, 110, 113, 117, 123, 129, 155, 177, 198, 201, 203, 230, 309, 366, 379, 392, 417, 432, 456, 469
Jackson, MS, 120, 136, 140, 336
Jackson, VA, 360
Jackson Rifles, flag of, 11
Jackson Summit, PA, 418
Jacksonville, FL, 44, 48, 49, 126, 349
James Island, SC, 54

James River, VA, 45, 49, 50, 55, 66, 82, 118, 129, 145, 149, 153, 154, 160, 162, 175, 181, 195, 220, 236, 328, 360, 372, 387, 448, 469, 489, 499, 509
Jarrett's Station, VA, 360
Jefferson Light Guards, flag of, 535
Jefferson Riflemen, flag of, 103
Jennings, Col. William W., 404
Jensen, Les, 36
Jerusalem Plank Road, VA, 427, 443, 459
Johnson, Sgt. James, 110-11
Johnson, Sgt. Joseph S., 327
Johnson's Island, OH, 66, 223, 494
Johnston, Sgt. Jacob, 418
Johnston, Gen. Joseph E., 46, 65, 73, 78, 124, 348
Johnstown, PA, 151
Jones, Alfred T., 182
Jones, Cpl. Daniel, 227
Jones, Pvt. David, 534
Jones, Cpl. George E., 403 n4, 415
Jones, Mr. George F., flag presented to 26th Infantry, 69
Jones, Major George W., 451
Jones, Sgt. Richard H., 507
Jonesboro, VA, 465
Jordan, Col. Frank, 18, 27, 167, 425, 475, 489, 535
Jordan, Sgt. Robert, 204
Joy Farm, MS, 479
Judson, Capt. Amos, 227
Juniata Cavalry, flag of, 8

Kanawha River, WV, 91, 494
Kane, Col. Thomas L., 112-13
Kauffman, Cpl. Solomon B., 402
Kearneysville, VA, 469
Kearny, Gen. Philip, 333, 351
Keck, Sgt. Isaac, 227
Keesey, Sgt. Jonathan J., 237
Kehoe, Pvt. Thomas, 358
Keller, Keith, 35
Kelley, Sgt. Alexander, 45-46, 566-67
Kelley, Cpl. Charles T., 121
Kelley, Rep. William D., 307
Kellogg, Col. Joseph, 470
Kelly, Dennis, 324
Kelly, Lieut. Edward, 110
Kelly, Sgt. Peter, 382
Kelly's Ford, VA, 166, 180, 467
Kelso, Capt. James, 409
Kenesaw Mountain, GA, 73, 124, 199, 209, 212, 215, 441
Kennedy, Sgt. Charles P., 75
Kennedy, Pvt. James, 358, 359 n4
Kennedy, Capt. John, 198, 199
Kenney, Cpl. Patrick, 380

Kensington, PA, ladies of, flag presented to 26th Infantry, 69
Kentucky troops, 8th Infantry, 76
Kephart, Major Theophilus, 349
Kepler, Pvt. Michael, 62
Kernstown, VA, 230, 231, 485
Kershaw, Gen. Joseph B., 429
Key, Sgt. Henry, 53
Key West, FL, 126
Kiddoo, Col. Joseph B., 50, 419, 559
Kilby, Capt. R. L., 337
Killian, Cpl. Philip G., 146, 147 n3
Kilpatrick, Gen. Hugh J., 469, 471
King, Sgt. John, 190
King, Gen. Rufus, 155
Kinkead, LtCol. Joseph M., 342, 343
Kinsey, Cpl. John, 121
Kinston, NC, 233, 346
Kirk, Col. James T., 95
Kishacoquillas, PA, ladies of, flag presented to 1st Cavalry, 118
Kissinger, Sgt. Josiah, 515
Kittanning, PA, 211, 346; ladies of, flag presented to 78th Infantry, 212
Kittochtinny Historical Society, 402
Kleckner, Col. Charles, 559
Kleinz, LtCol. Christopher, 182
Kline, Sgt. Edward S., 382
Knap, Capt. James M., 523
Knapp, Cpl. Ira, 156
Knight, Sgt. Joshua W., 520
Knipe, Col. Joseph F., 123
Knox, Sgt. Robert H., 61, 62
Knoxville, TN, 24, 71, 120, 129, 137, 140, 203, 210, 336, 465
Koch, Cpl. John V., 332
Kohler, Cpl. William, 96
Koons, Sgt. Charles M., 487
Koontz, Robert H., 12
Kuhn, Sgt. Albert A., 158
Kuhns, Cpl. John V., 62
LaFaver, Karen, 36
Lancaster, PA, 214, 395; ladies of, flags presented to 30th Infantry, 86; to 79th Infantry, 215
Lancaster County Historical Society, 8
Lancaster Fencibles, flag of, 8
Lancaster Guards, flag of, 86
Lane, Gen. James H., 137, 141, 143
Lane, Major William B., 42, 311, 314, 373, 377, 394, 487, 498, 506, 562
Lang, Cpl. George, 177
Langdon, Col. Loomis L., 471
Lantz, C. R., 34
Laughlin, Sgt. John M., 350

Laughlin, Sgt. William M., 391
Lavergne, TN, 211
Lawson, Sgt. Thomas C., 459
Leary, Sgt. Michael, 534
Lebanon, PA, 318, 355; ladies of, flag presented to 4th Cavalry, 181
Lebanon, TN, 217, 316
Lebanon County Historical Society, 320
Lee, Charles E., 12
Lee, Sgt. John, 506
Lee, Gen. Robert E., 20, 45, 49, 61, 63, 70, 71, 76, 82, 85, 88, 93, 94, 96, 97, 100, 106, 110, 117, 118, 122, 127, 128, 133, 135, 137, 138, 140, 141, 148, 154, 156, 157, 160, 163, 166, 169, 175, 180, 181, 184, 185, 186, 193, 201, 205, 220, 221, 227, 228, 238, 307, 308, 310, 311, 314, 319, 322, 332, 337, 342, 344, 346, 349, 357, 360, 367, 375, 377, 382, 384, 386, 387, 390, 402, 411, 421, 425, 427, 429, 430, 432, 434, 439, 448, 454, 457, 460, 463, 467, 469, 471, 480, 482, 484, 490, 492, 508, 511, 513, 515, 517, 524
Lee, Gen. W. H. F., 360
Lee's Mills, VA, 118
Leesburg, VA, 72
Lehman, Cpl. Franklin, 446, 447, 448
Lehman, Cpl. Jacob J., 62
Leidy, Col. Asher S., 334
Leightley, Cpl. Isaiah P., 443, 444
Lemaistre, Capt. George A., 328
Lemmon, Pvt. Robert, 105
Levan, Sgt. James H., 137
Lewis, Lieut. Elijah, 48
Lewis, Norman, 156
Lewis, Col. William D., Jr., 12
Lewisburg, VA, 463
Lexington, KY, 129, 336
Libby Prison, VA, 198
Liberty, TN, 214
Liberty Gap, TN, 209
Lillibridge, Cpl. John, 227
Lincoln, President Abraham, 8, 15, 28, 50, 56, 68, 80, 82, 387, 452, 473, 488, 494; mourning period for, 61, 63, 131, 135, 199, 319, 430, 505, 507, 561
Lincoln, Cpl. Richard S., 234, 538
Lincoln, Tad, 452
Link, Sgt. Charles, 373
Linn, Capt. James M., 560
Livingston, TN, 316
Lock Haven, PA, 112
Logan, Gen. John A., 533
Logan Guards, 123; flag of, 9, 532-33
Logue, Sgt. Hugh, 157
Lohr, Pvt. Michael, 535
Long, Cpl. Jeremiah, 511

Longley & Brother, 555, 556, 557
Longaker, Mrs. Mae L., 196
Longstreet, Gen. James, 61, 76, 82, 85, 88, 104, 120, 137, 140, 336, 360, 377, 454
Lookout Mountain, TN, 73, 76-77, 78, 211, 369, 441
Loomis, A. W., flag presented to 13th Infantry, 12
Loomis, Capt. Orlando M., 343
Looney, Cpl. John, 113
Loudoun Valley, VA, 485
Louisiana troops, 115-16; 2nd Infantry, 184
Louisville, KY, 208, 214, 217, 218, 316
Lovejoy Station, GA, 209, 218
Lovett, Sgt. George G., 391
Lovett, Sgt. Henry S., 405
Lower Merion, PA, ladies of, flag presented to 1st Cavalry, 535
Lower Merion Troop, flag of, 535
Lownes, Caleb, 7-8
Lumpkin, Pvt. John, 448
Luray, VA, 198
Lycoming County Historical Society, 8
Lyle, Col. Peter, 12, 311, 562
Lynch, Major Charles M., 439
Lynch, Capt. John W., 355
Lynchburg, VA, 181, 310, 361, 463, 467, 479, 480, 490, 509
Lyon, Gen. Hylan B., 466
Lyons, Sgt. William, 53

McAfee's Cross Roads, GA, 218
McAlisterville Academy, PA, 453
McBride, Sgt. Samuel M., 328
McCabe, Major G. L., 164
McCall, Gen. George A., 80, 81, 82, 85, 88, 91, 93, 95, 97, 104, 108, 110
McCall, LtCol. W. H. H., 501
McCalla, Major Theodore H., 322
McCandless, Col. William, 83, 88, 89, 100
McCarty, Sgt. William, 329
McClellan, Gen. George B., 62, 64, 65, 68, 72, 80, 81, 93, 95, 97, 106, 110, 128, 133, 136, 145, 148, 169, 331, 386
McClure, Alexander K., 480
McConnelly, Cpl. George A., 358
McCook, Gen. Edward M., 71
McCormick, J. C., 555
McCrea, Cassius E., 353
McCreary, Col. David B., 439, 440
McCrellish, Mrs. Frederick, flag presented to 26th Infantry, 69
McCrone Research Institute, 549
McCush, Cpl. Thomas, 460
McDougall, Lieut. Charles M., 411

McDowell, Gen. Irvin, 15, 61, 82, 117, 155, 180, 357, 366
McDowell, Pvt. William, 180
McFaren, Sgt. James, 537
McFarland, LtCol. George F., 561
McFarland, James E., 535
McFarland, Sgt. James E., 361
McFarland, Cpl. Theodore H., 135
McFeeters, Capt. James L., 337
Macferron, D., 103, 105
McGregor, Major James, 425
McHale, Sgt. James, 220
McKalip, Cpl. John H., 62
McKean County Rifles, flag of, 112-13
McKibbin, Col. David B., 519, 520
McKinley, Sgt. J. C., 227
McKinney's Ford, TN, 465
McKnight, Cpl. Charles, 308
McKnight, Rep. Robert, flags presented by, 70, 198, 201, 203
McLane, Mrs. John W., flag presented to 83rd Infantry, 228
McLarnon, Cpl. James, 186
McLaughlin, Sgt. Henry H., 410
McLaughlin, Sgt. John M., 350
McLean, Col. George P., 308
McLean, Sgt. Isaac, 221
McLeod, Sophia, flag presented to 34th Infantry, 96
McMichael, Mayor William, 28
McMillan, Rev. John W., flag presented to 109th Infantry, 365
McMinnville, TN, 214, 217, 465
McMinzie, Sgt. Solomon, 327
McMurray, Capt. John, 45
McNally, Sgt. William, 363
McNamee, Pvt. Thomas, 85
Macon, GA, 218
McPherson, Edward, 402
McPherson, Cpl. Lemuel E., 459
MacPherson, Pvt. Milton, 526
McQuillan, Sgt. James, 123
Madaus, Howard M., 192, 555, 557
Madge, Cpl. Robert G., 536
Madill, Col. Henry J., 429, 430
Mahone, Gen. William, 137, 143
Malvern Hill, VA, battle of (1862), 118, 166, 169, 175, 180, 188, 220, 223, 227, 325, 331, 342, 536; (1864) 310
Manassas, VA, 148, 166, 174, 191, 203, 220, 223, 325, 381, 423, 518
Manassas, VA, first battle of (1861), 11, 15, 70, 72, 85, 193
Manassas, VA, second battle of (1862), 41, 61-62, 64, 65, 68, 70, 72, 82, 85, 88, 91, 93, 95, 97, 100, 102, 104, 106, 108, 110, 113, 128-29, 136, 140, 148, 155, 159, 169, 175, 177, 186, 193, 195, 198, 200, 201, 203, 204, 220, 223, 227, 230, 307, 311, 321, 325, 331, 333, 336, 342, 351, 357, 363, 366, 369, 375, 379, 386, 390, 406, 408, 415, 458, 534
Manassas Junction, VA, 374, 434
Manchester, MD, 325
Mannes, Sgt. Frederick, 196, 197 n5
Mansfield, PA, ladies of, flag presented to 101st Infantry, 340
March to the Sea, 73, 77-78, 124, 199, 209, 215, 316-17, 364, 370, 442
Marchant, Lieut. Henry A., 533
Markoe, Capt. Abraham, 3
Marlin, Sgt. Thomas I., 459-60
Marquette, Sgt. Charles, 320
Martin, Cpl. Charles H., 78
Martin, Sgt. Davidson, 366
Martin, Sen. Franklin, 34
Martin, Capt. William J., 238
Martinsburg, WV, 91, 94, 151, 463, 485, 495; ladies of, flag presented to 11th Infantry, 12, 63-64
Marye's Heights, VA, 66, 148, 170, 175, 223, 318, 354, 381, 390, 396, 402, 406, 409, 410, 414, 415, 424, 439, 459
Maryland troops, 3rd Infantry, 373
Mason, Mrs. John, 112
Mason, Cpl. Theodore, 312
Massachusetts troops, 28th Infantry, 381
Mathews, Pvt. Daniel, 62
Mathews, Col. Joseph A., 405, 508
Mathews, Cpl. William, 62-63
Matthews, Cpl. Joseph C., 171-72
Matzdorf, LtCol. Alvin V., 203
Mauch Chunk, PA, ladies of, flag presented to 42nd Infantry, 114
Maurer, Sgt. Charles, 382
Mead, Col. L. G., 466
Meade, Gen. George G., 20, 24-25, 28-30, 45, 62, 82, 85, 88, 91, 95, 110, 167, 180, 224, 357, 467, 392, 417, 432, 561
Meadville, PA, ladies of, flag presented to 38th Infantry, 535
Meadville Volunteers, flag of, 535
Mechanicsville, VA, 82, 85, 88, 91, 93, 95, 99, 102, 104, 106, 108, 110, 112, 180, 191; mentioned, 331
Medal of Honor, presentations of, 20, 46, 68, 121, 154, 171-72, 223, 226, 237, 312, 320, 330, 334, 348, 373, 382, 407, 418, 452 n3, 460, 489, 490, 510, 564, 565
Megraw, Capt. David W., 382
Meigs, Gen. Montgomery C., 561
Mellin, Pvt. Gideon, 320
Melsom, Sgt. Thomas, 378
Meredith, Col. Sullivan A., 155, 158

Meridian, MS, 479
Meridian Hill, DC, 450
Methodist Episcopal Church, Liberty Street, Pittsburg, ladies of, flag presented to 62nd Inantry, 175
Mexican War, Pennsylvania flags of, 5-7
Meyer, Lieut. Frederick, 45
Michigan troops, 7th Infantry, 20; 6th Cavalry, 448
Middleburg, KY, 336
Middleburg, VA, 117, 180, 467
Middleton, TN, 316
Miles, Col. David, 537
Military Order of the Loyal Legion of the United States, 34
Military Service Institution of the United States, 471
Militia laws, Pennsylvania, (1777) 4, (1799) 4-5, (1824) 5
Mill Creek, GA, 199
Miller, Sgt. James, 153
Miller, Lieut. James H., 154
Miller, Sgt. Peter M., 407
Miller, Sgt. Solomon C., 206
Miller, Capt. William E., 167
Milledgeville, GA, 451
Milligan, Cpl. James, 172
Milroy, Gen. Robert H., 184, 236, 375
Mine Run, VA, 69, 83, 110, 117, 134, 149, 156, 159, 164, 166, 170, 175, 178, 184, 188, 191, 193, 195, 220, 223, 227, 231, 236, 307, 309, 311, 313, 318, 321, 325, 331, 334, 351, 354, 357, 367, 380, 382, 384, 386, 390, 420, 424, 427, 429, 434, 439, 443, 459, 467, 469, 537
Minersville, PA, 153
Minium, Sgt. Lewis, 371
Mintzer, Col. William M., 149, 150
Missionary Ridge, GA, 34, 198, 200
Mississippi River, 127
Mississippi troops, 42nd Infantry, 447
Mitchell, Capt. James H., 220
Mitchell, William G., 9
Mitchellville, TN, 214
Monocacy, MD, 237, 420
Monocacy Junction, MD, 495
Monongahela, PA, citizens of, flag presented to 140th Infantry, 428
Moody, Cpl. Joseph, 427
Moore, Sgt. John, 234, 538
Moore, Col. John W., 505
Moore, Oliver K., 437
Moore, Lieut. William E., 524
Moore, Sgt. William R., 517
Moorhead, Rep. James K., flags presented by, 177, 351
Morgan, Col. John H., 316
Morris Island, SC, 205
Mosby, Col. John S., 507

Mossy Creek, TN, 316, 465
Mott, Sgt. Henry A., 145, 147 n2
Mott, Lucretia, 40
Motts Military Museum, OH, 470
Mount Jackson, PA, ladies of, guidon presented to Battery B, 1st Artillery, 115
Mount Jackson Guards, flag of, 115
Mud March, 313, 321, 325
Muddy Creek Township. SEE Portersville
Mudey, James, 131
Mufty, Pvt. Jack, 536, 537
Mulholland, Col. St. Clair A., 382
Munfordville, KY, 211, 214
Munroe, Major Robert, 425
Munsell, Sgt. Harvey M., 333-34
Munyan, Sgt. John B., 220
Murfreesboro, TN. SEE Stones' River, TN
Murphy, Col. John K., 76
Murphy, Sgt. Patrick, 190
Murphy, Sgt. Thomas, 196
Murray, Sgt. James B., 220
Murray, Sgt. Michael, 153
Murray, Col. William G., 230, 231
Myerstown, PA, 446

Naber, Pvt. Henry, 508
Nagle, Capt. Daniel, 6
Nashville, TN, 18, 23, 73, 203-4, 208, 210, 211, 212, 214, 215, 217, 218, 465, 466, 479
National Guards, flag of, 11
Neely's Bend, TN, 211
Negley, Gen. James S., 28, 30, 214
Neil, Cpl. Hugh S., 444
Nevin, Capt. John I., 522
New Bern, NC, 11, 128, 139, 142, 147, 162, 233, 240, 340, 346, 474
New Bethlehem, PA, 211
New Castle, PA, 336
New Creek, WV, 91, 236, 463, 485
New Galilee, ladies of, flag presented to 39th Infantry, 107
New Hampshire troops, 4th Infantry, 489
New Hope Church, GA, 77, 124, 212, 441
New Jersey troops, 4th Infantry, 82, 108
New Market, VA, 152, 479
New Market Cross Roads, VA. SEE Glendale, VA
New Market Heights, VA, 45-46, 49, 50, 56, 206, 234, 566
New Orleans, LA, 6, 52, 127
New York City, 193
New York troops, 13th Battery, 364; 8th Heavy Artillery, 20; 34th Infantry, 412, 413; 44th Infantry, 227; 51st Infantry, 140; 60th Infantry, 370; 63rd Infantry, 381; 65th Infantry, 170, 223; 67th Infantry,

65; 69th Infantry, 381; 88th Infantry, 381; 124th Infantry, 431; 164th Infantry, 20
Newhall, Col. F. C., 192
Newhall, Capt. Walter S., 167
Newport News, VA, 120, 140, 336
Newtown, VA, 469
Nicholson, James B., 74
Niles, Capt. Alanson E., 112
1914 ceremonies, 33-35, 200; list of flag-bearers, 38-39
Nimmo, Sgt. Archibald, 314
Norfolk, VA, 162, 182, 349, 473, 474
Norristown, PA, 11, 94; citizens of, flags presented to 4th Infantry, 19; to 51st Infantry, 139, 141-43; to 138th Infantry, 421
North Anna River, VA, 62, 69, 83, 89, 96, 98, 101, 107, 109, 111, 113, 121, 129, 134, 149, 157, 160, 175, 178, 188, 191, 220, 224, 227, 231, 236, 308, 311, 314, 318, 334, 351, 354, 357, 367, 387, 390, 393, 420, 424, 427, 429, 432, 435-36, 439, 443, 448, 451, 459, 469
North Carolina troops, 6th Infantry, 156; 12th Infantry, 124; 14th Infantry, 451; 37th Infantry, 141
North Mountain, WV, 151
North Point, battle of (1814), 5
Northumberland, PA, 526
Norton, Lieut. Oliver W., 48
Norton, Sgt. William A., 366
Nottoway Court House, VA, 501
Ny River, VA, 137

Occoquan, VA, 469
Occoquan River, VA, 164
O'Donnell, Sgt. Benjamin F., 34, 200
O'Donnell, Cpl. Francis, 196
Ohio troops, 5th Infantry, 364; 19th Infantry, 212; 29th Infantry, 364; 195th Infantry, 143
Oil City, PA, 452, 534, 537
Olive Branch Church, VA, 182
Oliver, Sgt. Charles, 337
Oliver, Cpl. John M., 103
Oliver, Robert S., 33
Oliver, Cpl. Thomas, 327
Olmstead, Sgt. Francis A., 462
Olustee, FL, 48-49
103rd Engineer Battalion, museum of, 387, 391
O'Neill, Sgt. Henry, 190
Opequon Creek, VA, 171
Orbin, Pvt. George, 234, 538
Ord, Gen. Edward O. C., 45, 81, 97, 110, 112
Orr, Col. Robert L., 169, 170, 171-72, 561
Orth, Sgt. Jacob G., 75
Ortner, Cpl. William, 327

Osman, Lemuel, 444
Owen, Gen. Joshua T., 31
Oyster, Capt. Daniel, 127

Page, Alfred, 310
Page, Col. James, 224
Paine's Cross Roads, VA, 480
Palmer, Col. William J., 465
Pardee, LtCol. Ario, Jr., 441
Pardee Guards, flag of, 75
Paris, KY, 120
Parker, Mrs., flag presented to 4th Cavalry, 537
Parker, Cpl. William L., 505
Parkersburg, WV, 463
Parkhill, Sgt. William D., 221
Parks, Cpl. William, 412
Parkton, MD, 426
Patchell, Col. James, 343, 344
Patterson, Gen. Robert, 28, 63
Paul, Sgt. William H., 312
Peach Tree Creek, GA, 73, 77, 363-64, 365, 370, 441
Pearson, Col. Alfred L., 459, 460
Peck, Capt. Benjamin M., 431
Peebles' Farm, VA, 459
Pemberton, Gen. John C., 8
Pennsylvania, Civil War flags, 550
　altered, 124-25, 152, 169, 227, 501, 535, 553-54
　artillery colors and standards, 553
　artist signatures on, 550-51
　bill discrepancies, 554
　cavalry standards, designs of, 553
　canton widths of, 550
　conservation of, 543-49
　　chiffon sleeves over, 544
　　cleaning of, 545, 546
　　documentation of, 546
　　fringe, 547
　　humidification of, 546-47, 548
　　photographing of, 545
　　removal of, from capitol, 36, 543, 544
　　removal of, from staffs, 544-45
　　storage of, 545, 548; of staffs, 545
　　testing of, 549
　　textile lab, development of, 36, 543
　　unrolling of, 544-45
　contracts for, 14-16
　cord & tassels of, 553
　destroyed during war, 211, 354-55, 439
　finial designs of, 553, 556
　flag rooms, 31-33, 103, 182, 513, 561-62; flag stolen from, 462; labels of flags in, 561-62; misidentified flags in, 561-62
　fringe of, 553

Index 599

lettering on, 17, 552, 553
loans of, 561, 562
missing flags (unknown disposition), 192, 220, 221, 310, 335, 343, 360, 375, 377, 425, 464, 466, 476, 505
number furnished, 16-17
painting on, 550-52
presentations of, 17-18
price of, 16
prison, flags in, 198, 347, 440 n3
procurement of, 13-18
replacement of, 17
return of, 27-28
sponsorship program of, 36, 570-1
staffs of, 553, 561
star patterns on, 552-53
state coat-of-arms differences, 7-8, 550-51
units not issued flags, 554

Pennsylvania militia, flags of, 5, 7-9
Pennsylvania Reserve Volunteer Corps, 14, 15, 16, 62, 80-119, 159, 180, 188, 333, 357, 392, 432, 492
Pennsylvania state agencies
Adjutant General, 14, 15, 16, 17, 24, 28, 31, 32, 33, 109, 157, 383, 398, 437, 466, 498, 515, 560, 561
Capitol Preservation Committee, 36, 218, 327, 532, 543
Department of Public Grounds, 373
Department of Property and Supplies, 35, 515
General Services, 36
Historical and Museum Commission, 6, 8, 9, 35, 36, 47, 157, 158, 176, 225, 322, 499
Inspector General, 15
Quartermaster General, 28
State Agency (Nashville), 18, 203-4, 215, 218
State Agency (Washington), 17-18, 27, 127, 141, 147, 154, 157, 166, 167, 171, 178, 181, 182, 193, 195, 206, 220, 221, 228, 307, 309, 310, 321, 333, 340, 342, 374, 375, 380, 382, 384, 390, 416, 419, 424, 425, 457, 462, 463, 467, 469, 471, 475, 484, 488, 501, 503, 505, 507, 509, 511, 513, 515, 517, 518, 519, 536, 554, 559

Pennsylvania state buildings
Arsenal, 31, 32, 35, 151, 369, 398, 466, 561
Capitol, 31, 32, 33, 34, 35, 36, 123, 153, 205, 217, 221, 230, 340, 346, 366, 561; flag cases, 33, 35, 36, 74, 151, 183, 373, 515
Governor's mansion, 316
Library and Museum Building, 32, 33, 131, 561
Pennsylvania state legislature, 13-14, 17, 27, 31, 33, 35, 80, 151, 486; Acts of, (#60, 1899), 486; Joint Resolutions of, (#6, 1861), 13-14, 27; (#6, 1863), 17, 151; (#11, 1863), 17, 212, 218, 227, 370; (1866), 27; (#291, 1913), 33

Pennsylvania troops (mentioned other than regular section)
Artillery, 1st Regiment, 91, 102, 104; 3rd Regiment, 489
Cavalry, 1st Regiment, 22, 535; 2nd Regiment, 28, 480; 3rd Regiment, 22, 28; 4th Regiment, 537; 5th Regiment, 167; 6th Regiment, 28, 118, 162, 184, 310; 8th Regiment, 343; 17th Regiment, 118; 18th Regiment, 485; 1st Provisional Regiment, 165, 480; 2nd Provisional Regiment, 118, 164; 3rd Provisional Regiment, 485
Infantry, 1st Regiment, 11; 2nd Regiment, 11; 4th Regiment, 11-12, 139; 5th Regiment, 12, 533; 7th Regiment, 12; 8th Regiment, 12, 317; 9th Regiment, 12; 11th Regiment, 11, 12; 12th Regiment, 12; 13th Regiment, 12, 342, 345 n4; 14th Regiment, 12; 15th Regiment, 12; 16th Regiment, 12; 18th Regiment, 12; 19th Regiment, 12, 311; 20th Regiment, 533; 21st Regiment, 331; 22nd Regiment, 12-13; 23rd Regiment, 13, 27, 169, 533; 25th Regiment, 13, 326;
26th Regiment, 44; 27th Regiment, 198, 533; 28th Regiment, 441, 533; 29th Regiment, 34, 533-34; 30th Regiment, 534; 31st Regiment, 100, 534; 32nd Regiment, 94, 534, 568; 33rd Regiment, 27, 91, 534; 34th Regiment, 112, 426, 534; 36th Regiment, 108, 567; 37th Regiment, 534; 38th Regiment, 535; 39th Regiment, 95, 535; 40th Regiment, 100; 41st Regiment, 42nd Regiment, 446, 492; 41, 418, 535; 46th Regiment, 533; 48th Regiment, 121, 535;
51st Regiment, 11-12, 32, 145, 148; 52nd Regiment, 139, 148, 535; 53rd Regiment, 139, 145, 535; 54th Regiment, 340, 346, 535; 55th Regiment, 205; 56th Regiment, 32, 151, 340, 343, 346, 536; 57th Regiment, 231, 536; 58th regiment, 184, 490, 536; 61st Regiment, 65, 536, 563; 62nd Regiment, 536-37; 63rd Regiment, 537, 567; 67th Regiment, 162; 68th Regiment, 537; 69th Regiment, 193, 354, 355, 537
71st Regiment, 354, 568; 72nd Regiment, 354; 73rd Regiment, 34; 74th Regiment, 198; 75th Regiment, 198; 76th Regiment, 153; 77th Regiment, 214, 465; 78th Regiment, 208, 214, 218, 537; 79th Regiment, 208, 537; 81st Regiment, 27, 526; 82nd Regiment, 29, 66, 537; 83rd Regiment, 48, 218; 84th Regiment, 48, 160; 85th Regiment, 537-38; 87th Regiment, 35; 88th Regiment, 40;
90th Regiment, 162, 184; 91st Regiment, 162, 184; 95th Regiment, 326, 563; 96th Regiment, 13; 97th Regiment, 505; 98th Regiment, 566; 99th Regiment, 69; 101st Regiment, 151, 346; 103rd

Regiment, 151, 340; 104th Regiment, 522; 105th Regiment, 179; 107th Regiment, 564; 109th Regiment, 34, 370, 532, 565; 110th Regiment, 380; 111th Regiment, 76, 218, 364; 116th Regiment, 568;

125th Regiment, 566; 126th Regiment, 415; 129th Regiment, 565; 132nd Regiment, 566; 134th Regiment, 402; 137th Regiment, 50; 138th Regiment, 19; 142nd Regiment, 563; 143rd Regiment, 450, 564; 147th Regiment, 72; 149th Regiment, 113, 434, 450, 451, 492, 568, flag presented to 42nd Infantry, 113-14; 150th Regiment, 434, 446; 151st Regiment, 432;

174th Regiment, 526; 183rd Regiment, 466; 188th Regiment, 234, 566; 190th-191st Regiments, 84, 113-14, 462, 526, 568; 201st Regiment, 34, 524; 205th Regiment, 501; 207th Regiment, 501; 208th Regiment, 501; 209th Regiment, 501; 211th Regiment, 501; 214th Regiment, 393, 568

Militia, 20th Regiment, 565; 27th Regiment, 565

Pennypacker, Col. Galusha, 329-30, 505
Pennypacker, Nathan A., 81
Pensacola, FL, 52, 53
Perryville, KY, 208, 214, 215, 217, 316
Petersburg, PA, ladies of, flag presented to 9th Cavalry, 317
Petersburg, VA, 45, 47, 49, 50, 54, 56, 57, 62, 63, 66, 114, 118, 121-22, 129, 134, 135, 138, 141, 149, 152, 153-54, 157, 160, 162, 164, 165, 167, 170, 171-72, 175, 178-79, 181, 182, 185, 188-89, 191, 192, 195, 205-6, 220, 224, 227-28, 231, 233-34, 236, 237, 238, 308, 310, 311, 314, 318, 319, 320, 321, 322, 323, 325-26, 328, 331, 332, 334, 337, 343, 349, 351, 354, 357, 360, 367, 372, 373, 377, 380, 382, 384, 387, 390, 393, 420, 424, 425, 427, 429, 432, 436, 439, 443, 444, 448, 451, 454, 459, 462, 467, 480, 482, 484, 488, 489, 492, 499, 501, 505, 508, 509, 510, 511, 513, 517, 563, 564
Petersburg, WV, 198
Petty, Cpl. Philip, 417-18
Petzinger, Pvt. Conrad, 347
Phifer, Sgt. Samuel, 450, 452 n3
Philadelphia camp, Sons of Union Veterans. SEE Grand Army of the Republic, Museum of
Philadelphia Coal Exchange, 495, 524
Philadelphia Commercial Exchange, 499
Philadelphia Corn Exchange, 386, 387; flags presented to 118th Infantry, 388
Philadelphia "friends," flags presented to 23rd Infantry, 66, 533; to 26th Infantry, 69; to 27th Infantry, 71; to 28th Infantry, 74, 533; to 29th Infantry, 78; to 61st Infantry, 172, 536; to 69th Infantry, 189-90, 537; to 72nd Infantry, 196; to 73rd Infantry, 199; to 82nd Infantry, 224-25, 537; to 91st Infantry, 314; to 95th Infantry, 322; to 114th Infantry, 377-78; to 115th Infantry, 380; to 5th Cavalry, 182; to 20th Militia, 533; to 32nd Militia, 524
Philadelphia High School, ladies of, flag presented to 19th Infantry, 12, 311
Philadelphia ladies, flags presented to 18th Infantry, 12; to 19th Infantry, 12, 311; 23rd Infantry, 13, 66; to 29th Infantry, 78, 534; to 31st Infantry, 89, 534; to 68th Infantry, 187; to 75th Infantry, 204; to 15th Cavalry, 466; to 21st Cavalry, 480; to 34th Militia, 524; to 59th Militia; to 3rd USCT, 44
Philadelphia Merchant Troop, guidon of, 167
Phillips, Sgt. Owen, 434, 435, 437, 438 n3
Pickett, Gen. George, 188, 193, 196
Piedmont, VA, 152
Pike, Sgt. 358
Pikeville, TN, 217
Pine Knob Mountain, GA, 73, 77, 363, 365, 370, 441
Pitts, Rep. Joseph R., 36
Pittsburgh "friends," flags presented to 123rd Infantry, 397
Pittsburgh ladies, flags presented to 13th Infantry, 12; to 37th Infantry, 103; to 38th Infantry, 105; to 61st Infantry, 172; to 102nd Infantry, 345; to 155th Infantry, 460; to Sanitary Fair, 125
Pittsburgh Rifles, flag of, 105
Pittston, PA, ladies of, flag presented to Battery M, 2nd Artillery, 373
Pleasant Hill, LA, 126-27
Pleasant Valley, MD, 76, 192, 485
Pleasants, LtCol. Henry, 129
Plymouth, NC, 340, 346, 347
Pocotaligo, SC, 126, 153, 205
Point of Rocks, MD, 384
Poland, Major John, 345
Pollak, Nancy, 549
Pollock, Gov. James, 199, 314, 363, 533
Pomeroy, Steven, 550
Poolesville, MD, 186, 188, 195, 354, 429
Pope, Gen. John, 61, 68, 70, 72, 76, 82, 85, 88, 91, 95, 100, 102, 104, 113, 133, 159, 201, 227, 331, 333, 342, 357, 379, 406
Poplar Spring Church, VA, 121, 129, 138, 160, 181, 228, 231, 310, 314, 335, 337, 351-52, 367, 384, 387, 393, 429, 462, 467, 480, 492, 497
Port Clinton, PA, ladies of, flag presented to 48th Infantry, 131
Port Clinton Artillery, flag of, 131
Port Republic, VA, 230, 366
Port Royal, SC, 146, 153, 328, 336, 349
Port Royal, VA, 488
Port Royal Ferry, SC, 136
Porter, Gen. Fitz-John, 82, 226
Porter, Cpl. Richard, 336

Portersville, PA, citizens of, flag presented to 100th Infantry, 338
Portsmouth, VA, 349, 360
Potomac River, 72, 80, 88, 123, 166, 193, 195, 309, 372, 384, 386, 410, 457, 463, 507, 518
Potts, Sgt. Joseph, 505
Pottstown, PA, 148
Pottsville, PA, 129, 325, 382; ladies of, flags presented to Washington Artillery, 6; 48th Infantry, 130; 7th Cavalry, 218; residents of, flag presented to 96th Infantry, 326-27
Powell, Cpl. William, 537
Power, Sgt. Jesse T., 427
Prevost, Col. Charles M., 28, 386
Price, Sgt. Frank, 447
Price, Major Isaiah, 328
Price, Gen. Sterling, 479
Proctor, Col. John, 4
Pryor, Sgt. Jesse K., 442
Pulaski, TN, 212, 217
Puleston, Col. J. H., 18, 169, 195, 342, 372
Pumpkin Vine Creek, GA, 73, 363
Purcell, Sgt. Hiram W., 348, 349, 350
Pyer, Sgt. William, 127

Quaker Road, VA, 352, 387, 459, 492, 497
Quay, Col. M. S., 18, 182
Quinlan, Lieut. Francis T., 381

Raccoon Ford, VA, 336
Radcliff, Cpl. Joseph N., 355
Raftsmen Rangers, flag of, 113
Rager, Sgt. William A., 185
Railroads:
    Baltimore & Ohio, 151, 202, 230, 236, 366, 375, 420, 463, 495
    Charleston & Savannah, 54
    Danville, 360
    Green River & Nashville, 211
    Manassas Gap, 61, 502, 503, 507
    Nashville & Decatur, 214
    Nashville & Northwestern, 204
    Northern Central, 236, 426, 443
    Orange & Alexandria, 61, 105, 180, 357, 375, 384, 392, 503, 518
    Petersburg & Weldon, 205
    Southside, 360
    Virginia & Tennessee, 463, 466
    Virginia Central, 118, 360
    SEE ALSO Weldon Railroad, VA
Raleigh, NC, 32, 46, 156, 206, 317, 330, 384, 506
Rambo, S. B., 373
Ramseur, Gen. Stephen D., 451
Ramsey, Sgt. Nathan H., 141

Rankin, Pvt. Joseph P., 537, 567
Rapidan River, VA, 136, 367, 471
Rappahannock River, VA, 117, 136, 156, 167, 170, 188, 193, 223, 325, 336, 343, 412, 416
Rappahannock Station, VA, 61, 134, 155, 390
Rausch, Major L. V., 33
Rawle, William B., 166
Reading, PA, 12, 13, 405, 473, 476; citizens of, flag presented to Battery D, 522
Reager, Sgt. Joseph G., 234, 538
Reams' Station, VA, 20, 118, 149, 160, 189, 220, 310, 360, 382, 384, 427, 439, 443, 467, 482, 484, 568
Red Hill, AL, 466
Red River Campaign, LA, 126-27
Redmond, Capt. Robert C., 163
Reed, Sgt. Henry, 537
Reed, J. R., 459
Reeder, Lieut. Frank, 475
Reeves, Lieut. Lemuel C., 78
Regan, Pvt. Cornelius, 358
Reichard, John, 437
Reigle, Sgt. Daniel P., 237, 238
Reigle, Sgt. Joseph, 120-21
Reisinger, Cpl. J. M., 452 n3
Relay House, MD, 420
Renkenberger, Cpl. Jacob, 319
Reno, James, flag presented to 123rd Infantry, 397
Reno, Col. Marcus A., 375
Resaca, GA, 73, 77, 124, 209, 212, 363, 365, 370
Revolutionary War, Pennsylvania flags of, 3-4
Reynolds, Gen. James L., 28
Reynolds, Gen. John F., 82, 97
Reynolds, Sgt. William, 57
Rhode Island troops, 3rd Heavy Artillery, 147
Rice's Station, VA, 499
Richards, Philip, 130
Richardson, Sgt. Thomas F., 352
Richardson, William, 483
Richmond, KY, 316
Richmond, VA, 45, 46, 49, 50, 51, 55, 56, 57, 68, 70, 82, 95, 99, 102, 104, 106, 108, 110, 112, 117, 133, 145, 148, 153, 154, 164, 167, 169, 171, 183, 185, 309, 325, 331, 346, 348, 360, 361, 425, 451, 467, 471, 499, 508, 509
Rickards, George, 534
Rickards, Col. William, Jr., 76, 77, 533-34
Ricketts, Gen. James B., 61, 358
Ricketts, Capt. R. Bruce, 115
Riddle, Sgt. Robert, 426-27
Riggin, James H., 116
Ringgold, GA, 73, 77, 369, 441
Ringgold Light Artillery, flags of, 8-9
Ripley, Col. Oliver H., 172
Risser, Sgt. William, 320

Roanoke Island, NC, 139, 340, 346
Roarty, Sgt. John, 130
Robb, Pvt. James, 172 n4
Roberts, Col. Joseph, 455
Roberts, Col. R. B., 12, 18, 85, 390, 419
Roberts, Sgt. William F., 534
Robinson, Gen. John C., 62
Rock Island, IL, 495
Rocky Face Ridge, GA, 71, 73, 212
Rodes, Gen. Robert E., 451
Rodgers, Col. Chauncey P., 228
Rodgers, Pvt. James A., 208
Rodgersville, AL, 214
Rogers, Sgt. Alexander, 226, 227
Roney, Sgt. Johnson, 311
Ronntree, Sgt. William H., 172
Roosevelt, Sgt. George W., 68, 69
Rose, Col. Thomas E., 208, 209
Rosecrans, Gen. William S., 24, 209, 211, 214, 316, 465
Rosengarten, Sgt. Henry E., 70
Rosengarten, Lieut. Joseph G., 392
Ross, Cpl. Alexander, 234, 538
Rost, Sgt. Zachariah, 34, 200
Rothermel, Peter F., 32
Rothwarf, Marta, 36
Rover, TN, 217, 316, 465
Row, Sgt. Charles A., 123
Rowe, LtCol. David W., 402
Rowland, Roger V., 35
Roxborough, PA, ladies of, flag presented to 58th Infantry, 163
Rudisill, Cpl. Abraham W., 537
Rush, Col. Richard H., 191
Russell, Gen. A. L., 17, 24, 28, 31, 74, 83, 105, 107, 112, 122, 141, 150, 156, 165, 167, 212, 233, 344, 351, 373, 375, 419, 462, 470, 474-75, 489, 495, 498, 554, 559
Russell, Sgt. John A., 328
Rutledge, Sgt. Henry F., 373
Ryan, James F., 177
Ryan, Cpl. James P., 535
Ryan, Rep. Matthew J., 36

Sabine Cross Roads, LA, 126
Saint John's Bluff, FL, 49
Saint John's River, FL, 126
Saint Mary's Church, VA, 118, 181, 310, 384, 467, 471
Salem Church, VA, 133, 170, 223, 318, 321, 331, 342, 390, 424
Salisbury, NC, 147, 466
San Francisco, CA, 72; ladies of, flags presented to 26th Infantry, 69
Sanders, Cpl. Albert, 206
Sanders, Dallas, 165

Sanders, Col. William W., 165
Sandy Ridge, NC, 162
Savage's Station, VA, 193, 195, 348, 354
Savannah, GA, 54, 73, 78, 124, 126, 127, 209, 215, 370, 442
Savannah River, 205
Sawyer's Lane, NC, 139-40
Saylor's Creek, VA, 135, 221, 224, 238, 319, 322, 323, 332, 344, 352, 377, 390, 421, 425, 430, 469, 480
Schaeffer, Sgt. 404
Schall, Lieut. Absalom, 62
Scheible, William F., 444, 555, 556, 557
Schell, Sgt. Reuben, 100-1, 567-68
Schenck, Gen. Robert C., 454
Scheurman, Sgt. J. C., 63
Schilleto Company, 555
Schlacter, Cpl. Henry, 332 n5
Schmid, Sgt. Jacob A., 332
Schofield, Gen. John M., 24
Schooley, Capt. David, 373
Schoonmaker, Col. John M., 464
Schultz's Mill, TN, 465
Schultzville, PA, citizens of, flag presented to 143rd Infantry, 438
Schuylkill Haven, PA, ladies of, flag presented to 50th Infantry, 138
Scott, Sgt. Charles, 431
Scott, Gen. Winfield, 6, 186
Scott Guards, flag of, 11
Scranton, PA, 532
Scroggs, Col. G. A., 52
Seabrook Island, SC, 202
Seagraves, Sgt. John, 431
Secessionville, SC, 205, 336
Sedgwick, Cpl. E. V., 371
Sedgwick, Gen. John, 325, 342, 343
Seesholtz, Capt. Isaac H., 388
Seitzinger, Pvt. James M., 382, 568
Selfridge, LtCol. Joseph L., 123
Selma, AL, 218, 219
Semple, William, flags presented to 139th Infantry, 423-24
Seven Days' Battles, VA, 65, 133, 145-46, 148, 159, 166, 169, 191, 195, 220, 223, 318, 321, 325, 331, 340, 342, 346, 348, 351, 354, 534
Seven Oaks, VA, 177
Seymour, Gen. Truman, 48-49
Shaler, Col. Alexander, 170, 223
Shaw, Sgt. Lewis, 363
Sheafer, Capt. Henry J., 358, 359 n4
Shelbyville, TN, 214, 217, 316
Shelheimer, John B., 9
Shenandoah Valley, VA, 66, 112, 113, 117, 127, 135, 152, 170-71, 185, 188, 191, 195, 198, 201, 203, 224,

230, 237, 318, 322, 332, 343, 349, 366, 369, 375, 377, 390, 420, 425, 463, 469, 471, 479, 485, 494, 495, 519

Shepherdstown, WV, 386, 387, 388, 467

Sheridan, Gen. Philip H., 24, 117, 118, 127, 164, 191, 192, 310, 318, 331, 332, 375, 384, 390, 467, 469, 471, 480, 485

Sherman, Gen. Thomas W., 120, 136, 336

Sherman, Gen. William T., 24, 46, 54, 71, 73, 77, 120, 124, 136, 140, 147, 156, 198, 199, 209, 212, 215, 218, 316, 363, 370, 384, 479

Shields, Gen. James, 230, 366

Shiloh, TN, 208

Shiner, Sgt. Andrew J., 221

Shippensburg, PA, ladies of, flag presented to 130th Infantry, 409

Shotstall, Cpl. Joseph J., 443

Shroad, Lieut. John C., 208

Shyrode, J. K., 12

Sickel, Col. H. G., 91, 498, 561

Sides, Col. Peter, 159

Sigel, Gen. Franz, 203

Simmons, Col. Seneca G., 95

Simpson, Sgt. George A., 400

Sipes, Sgt. William, 489

Sipes, Col. William B., 217, 218

Sirwell, Col. William, 212

Slack, Sgt. James L., 348

Slaven, Sgt. Cyrus P., 159, 160

Sloan, Sgt. Timothy A., 382

Slocum, Gen. Henry W., 123

Slonaker, Sgt. Benjamin F., 355

Slott, Sgt. Bertoless, 85

Small, Capt. William F., 6

Small, Mrs. William F., flag presented to 26th Infantry, 69

Small, Sgt. William S., 69

Smith, Sgt. Alder, 471

Smith, Sgt. Charles A., 409

Smith, Col. George F., 170, 171

Smith, Sgt. Hugh, 230

Smith, John L., 387

Smith, Pvt. Levi A., 501

Smith, Norman M., 479

Smith, Capt. P. J., 89, 90 n3

Smith, Cpl. S. Macey, 355

Smith, Sgt. William H., 319

Smithfield, VA, 192

Smithsonian Institution, 112, 549

Smyrna, GA, 209

Smyser, Daniel G., flags presented to 4th Infantry, 11, 141-42

Smyser, Cpl. Henry W., 358

Society of the Cincinnati, 14, 80, 81

Soldiers and Sailors Memorial Hall, Pittsburgh, PA, 5, 343, 344, 345, 347, 424

Soldiers' Home, DC, 452

Somerset, KY, 136

Sons of Union Veterans, Ezra S. Griffin Camp 8, Scranton, PA, 526, 532

Sornberger, Capt. Joseph H., 438

South Anna River, VA, 360

South Carolina troops, 17th Infantry, 103

South Mountain, MD, 62, 82, 85, 88, 91, 93, 95, 97, 100, 102-3, 104, 106, 109, 110, 113, 120, 129, 136, 140, 156, 321, 323, 325, 326, 327, 336, 357, 419

Spangler, Sgt. Anthony, 346

Spanish-American War, Pennsylvania flags of, 33-35

Sparta, TN, 218

Spaulding, Major Israel P., 429

Spayd, Sgt. Henry, 447, 448, 568

Spear, Col. George C., 170

Spear, Henry, 28

Spencer, Sgt. George W., 466

Spotsylvania, VA, 62, 69, 83, 86, 89, 96, 98, 101, 103, 107, 109, 110-11, 113, 121, 129, 134, 137-38, 140-41, 143, 149, 157, 159, 160, 170, 175, 178, 188, 193, 195, 220, 221, 227, 231, 236, 307, 311, 314, 318, 321, 323, 325, 327, 331, 334, 336, 343, 351, 354, 355, 367, 373, 380, 382, 384, 387, 390, 392-93, 420, 424, 427, 429, 431, 432, 435, 439, 443, 444, 448, 451, 459, 469, 471, 482

Springfield, IL, 495

Stafford Court House, VA, 76, 201, 203, 398, 401

Stainrook, Col. Henry J., 363, 370

Stanford, KY, 136, 140

Stanton, Secretary of War Edwin, 27, 41, 63, 334

Stanton, Cpl. Nathan, 50

State Capital Guards, flag of, 11

State Fencibles, flag of, 7-8

Staunton River, VA, 360

Stearns, George L., 40

Stephens, Sgt. George, 310

Stephenson's Depot, VA, 184

Stevens, Gen. Isaac I., 336

Stevens, Sgt. John G., 234

Stevens, Lieut. Thomas E., 380

Stevensburg, VA, 149, 188, 193, 195, 443

Stewart, Capt. Franklin B., 367

Stewart, Capt. James T., 135

Stewart, Gen. Thomas J., 33, 64, 114, 326, 486, 533, 557

Stewart, Sgt. Valentine, 367

Stockholm, Pvt. John J., 429, 430, 431 n4

Stiles, Sgt. Elbridge, 513

Stokes, Sgt. Edward, 230

Stone, Col. Roy, 112, 434, 446, 447, 450

Stonebach, Capt. John, 406-7

Stoneman, Gen. George, 466
Stones' River, TN, 24, 208, 211, 212, 214, 215, 217, 465
Stony Creek, VA, 360, 480
Storey, Sgt. John, 365
Stoud, Pvt. George K., 320
Strait, Cpl. Justus D., 121
Strasbaugh, Bernard, 373
Stratford, Sgt. Richard, 116
Strong, Theodore, 373
Stuart, Gen. James E. B., 81, 113, 191, 471
Stumbaugh, Col. Frederick S., 208
Suffolk, VA, 163, 233, 340, 346, 360, 454, 473
Suiter, Col. James A., 412
Sulphur Springs, VA, 201, 384
Sunbury, PA, 96, 127
Sunniver, Cpl. Henry, 358
Supervisory Committee for Recruiting Colored Regiments, 40, 41, 42, 44, 46, 52, 54, 56, 57
Susquehanna River, 524
Sutherland's Station, VA, 382, 427, 444, 482
Swart, Capt. Abram J., 429
Sweden's Cove, GA, 217
Sweeney, Pvt. James C., 314
Sweeton, Sgt. Joseph F., 89
Swope, Cpl. George K., 85-86
Swoyer, Sgt. Francis J., 358
Swyers, Cpl. David H., 444

Taft, President William H., 19
Taggart, Cpl. David, 427
Taggart, Col. John H., 41
Taggart, Lieut. Robert, 105
Tallahassee, FL, 44
Tapper, Col. Thomas F. B., 27, 93, 94
Tate, Sgt. George G., 367
Taylor, Sgt. John, 129
Taylor, Col. John P., 117
Taylor, Gen. Nelson, 62
Taylor, Cpl. William, 172 n4
Telford, Col. William H., 137
Temple, Cpl. Henry B., 64
Ten Mile Infantry, flag of, 428
Tenallytown, MD, 80, 85, 88, 91, 93, 97, 99, 108
Tener, Gov. John K., 33, 34
Tennessee River, 73
Terry, Gen. Alfred H., 329
Terry, LtCol. Ira C., 50
Texas Campaign (1865-66), 49, 50, 54, 55, 56, 57, 210, 479
Texas troops, 24th Cavalry, 215
Thomas, Gen. George H., 209, 210
Thomas, Cpl. John W., 62
Thomas, Col. Samuel B., 17, 186, 328, 377, 381, 386, 392, 395, 396, 398, 401, 402, 404, 405, 406, 409, 410, 413, 414, 415, 417, 420, 426, 429, 432, 439, 443, 446, 450, 458
Thompson, Sgt. Daniel, 53
Thompson, Sgt. John M., 133
Thompson, Cpl. Robert J., 346
Thompson's Station, TN, 316
Thoroughfare Gap, VA, 61, 117
Three-month militia (1861), flags of, 11-13, 533
Tidioute, PA, ladies of, flag presented to 145th Infantry, 440
Tiers, Major Edmund T., 462
Tilghman, Col. Benjamin C., 44
Todd, Sgt. Gabriel L., 520, 521, 568
Todd, Lieut. William A., 193
Todd's Tavern, VA, 164
Toft, James, 555
Tomkinsville, TN, 316
Toomey, Sgt. James, 89
Totopotomoy Creek, VA, 160, 382, 482, 484
Town, LtCol. Gustavus W., 323
Transue, Sgt. Stephen, 135 n4
Trevilian Station, VA, 164, 181, 191, 311, 384, 467, 469
Triune, TN, 316
Truitt, Sgt. Jefferson, 536
Tullahoma Campaign, 124, 209, 211, 316, 465
Tunstall's Station, VA, 97
Tyrrell, Sgt. William H., 381

Ulmer, Sgt. George W., 323
Union armies, departments, and corps
  Army of Georgia, 73
  Army of the James, 42, 45, 49, 50, 56, 57, 112, 115, 153, 182, 205, 233, 328, 349, 360, 372, 454, 489, 499, 501, 505, 508, 509, 510, 511, 513, 517
    Tenth Army Corps, 44, 49, 56, 57, 153, 205, 328, 505
    Eighteenth Army Corps, 42, 45, 50, 153, 162, 372, 489
    Twenty-fourth Army Corps, 43, 154, 206, 329, 489, 499, 505, 509
    Twenty-fifth Army Corps, 43, 49, 50, 54, 55, 56, 57
  Army of the Potomac, 20, 24, 45, 55, 61, 65, 67, 72, 76, 91, 97, 99, 100, 102, 104, 105, 108, 112, 115, 117, 123, 129, 140, 146, 148, 149, 153, 156, 164, 166, 170, 171, 174, 177, 180, 181, 182, 184, 186, 188, 191, 193, 195, 201, 203, 220, 223, 224, 226, 227, 230, 233, 307, 309, 311, 313, 318, 321, 331, 333, 334, 336, 340, 342, 346, 348, 351, 354, 357, 360, 363, 366, 369, 375, 377, 379, 381, 384, 386, 387, 390, 392, 396, 398, 400, 401, 402, 404, 408, 410, 411, 413, 414, 415, 416, 417, 419, 420, 423, 426, 429, 432, 434, 439, 441, 443, 446, 450, 453, 454, 456, 458, 462, 463, 467, 469, 471, 474,

480, 482, 484, 488, 489, 497, 501, 508, 510, 511, 513, 515, 517, 558
- First Army Corps, 62, 70, 82, 156, 166, 307, 311, 357, 358, 392, 416, 417, 419, 432, 434, 446, 450, 453
- Second Army Corps, 20, 69, 148, 149, 160, 178, 186, 193, 195, 220, 231, 334, 351, 354, 367, 380, 381, 404, 408, 411, 412, 426, 427, 439, 443, 482, 484
- Third Army Corps, 68, 83, 159, 177, 184, 186, 220, 230, 231, 333, 351, 366, 377, 379, 395, 420, 429
- Fourth Army Corps, 65, 133, 145, 169, 209, 223, 233, 309, 318, 331, 340, 342, 346, 348
- Fifth Army Corps, 24, 62, 82, 83, 96, 100, 107, 149, 157, 174, 175, 226, 227, 313, 357, 386, 392, 393, 396, 402, 406, 410, 414, 415, 432, 434, 436, 451, 458, 462, 470, 480, 488, 497, 515, 526
- Sixth Army Corps, 65, 133, 169, 170, 171, 184, 185, 193, 195, 223, 318, 321, 322, 325, 331, 342, 343, 344, 390, 419, 420, 423, 425
- Ninth Army Corps, 55, 120, 121, 122, 128, 129, 136, 137, 138, 140, 336, 373, 501, 508, 510, 511, 513, 517, 522
- Eleventh Army Corps, 70, 71, 123, 124, 177, 198, 201, 203, 395, 441, 456, 469
- Twelfth Army Corps, 72, 73, 76, 123, 124, 363, 369, 398, 400, 405, 441
- Cavalry Corps, 117, 164, 166, 180, 181, 191, 309, 384, 467, 469, 471, 480

Army of Virginia, 61, 64, 70, 72, 77, 82, 85, 91, 95, 102, 104, 117, 123, 133, 155, 159, 164, 198, 201, 203, 227, 230, 307, 311, 331, 357, 363, 366, 369, 379
- First Corps, 70, 203, 366
- Second Corps, 72, 123, 363, 369
- Third Corps, 61, 64, 155, 357

Middle Military Division, 24
Army of the Shenandoah, 464
- Eighth Army Corps, 184, 236

Department of North Carolina, 146
Department of the Cumberland, 24
Army of the Cumberland, 209, 211, 214, 217, 317, 363, 441, 465
- Fourteenth Army Corps, 211, 212, 214
- Twentieth Army Corps, 73, 77, 124, 203, 363, 370
- Wilson's Cavalry Corps, 71, 218

Department of the Gulf, 126, 127
- Nineteenth Army Corps, 126, 127

Department of the Ohio, 24, 120, 129, 136, 140, 336
- Twenty-third Army Corps, 147

Department of the South, 54, 146
Department of West Virginia, 83
Union Guards, flag of, 86
Union League of Philadelphia, 47, 53, 157, 158, 196, 225, 322, 498, 499, 519; flags presented to 88th Infantry, 307; to 183rd Infantry, 482; to 196th Infantry, 494, 495; to 198th Infantry, 497; to 213th Infantry, 520; to 45th Militia, 524; to 59th Militia, 524
Union Light Infantry, flag of, 12
Uniontown, PA, 233; ladies of, flag presented to 85th Infantry, 234, 537-38
Unionville, TN, 217
United States Colored Troops, 4th Infantry, 45; 6th Infantry, 566; 43rd Infantry, 566
United States Military Academy, 42, 54
United States Regular Army, 3rd Artillery, 48; 4th Artillery, 8; Office of Clothing and Equipage, 551-52, 554; Cincinnati Depot, 555, 556; New York Depot, 554, 555, 556; Philadelphia Depot, 552, 554, 555, 556
United States Sanitary Commission, 27, 125, 198
United States War Department, 20, 22, 23, 24, 27, 40, 41, 42, 54, 71, 108, 114, 115, 118, 124, 141, 155, 179, 183, 192, 209, 220, 337, 352, 373, 441, 451, 465, 532, 559, 561
Upper St. Clair Guards, flag of, 175
Upperville, VA, 72, 180, 469
Upton, Col. Emory, 134, 325, 390
Upton's Hill, VA, 106

Vale, E. M., 34
Valentine, W. W., 12
Valleau, Cpl. John M., 364
Vance, Gov. Zebulon, 451
Vansant, Sgt. Thomas, 193, 568-69
Vanscoten, Cpl. M. H., 93
Vaughn, Col. Alfred J., Jr., 209
Veale, Major Moses, 34
Veit, Sgt. J. C., 440 n3
Venango Museum of Art, Science and Industry, 452
Verbeke, Mrs. Marion, flag presented to 2nd Infantry, 11
Veterans of Foreign Wars, Post 255, 317
Vicksburg, MS, 120, 136, 140, 336
Vincent, Col. Strong, 227
Virginia troops, 10th Cavalry, 121; 12th Infantry, 143, 352; 16th Infantry, 337; 17th Infantry, 64; 55th Infantry, 448
Vogus, Cpl. M. Francis, 227, 228
von Schimmelfennig, Col. Alexander, 201
Vondersmith, Cpl. H. B., 537
Voris, Cpl. James C., 96

Wadsworth, Gen. James S., 83
Wagner, Sgt. Lewis, 373
Wagner, LtCol. Louis, 40-41, 44, 46, 307
Wagner, Sgt. William C., 355
Walbridge, Sgt. Henry, 495
Wallace, Capt. William W., 400
Walls, Sgt. Benjamin F., 126-27
Walter, Cpl. James X., 433
Walters, Samuel, 156
Waltman, Capt. Jacob K., 317
Waltz, Lieut. Lewis B., 534
Wapping heights, VA, 186, 420
War Library and Museum. SEE Civil War Library and Museum.
War of 1812, Pennsylvania flags of, 5
Ward, Sgt. William, 444
Ware, Sgt. David L., 388
Ware, Sgt. John S., 488
Ware Bottom Church, VA, 233
Waream, Sgt. J., 212
Wareing, Sgt. John D., 373
Warren, Gen. Gouverneur K., 24-25, 62
Warrenton, VA, 117, 180, 164, 166, 167, 175, 180, 459
Washington, George, 4
Washington, NC, 52, 162, 474
Washington, PA, 428, 485-86; ladies of, flags presented to 12th Infantry, 12; to 37th Infantry, 103
Washington Artillery, flag of, 6-7, 8
Washington Cadets, flag of, 96
Washington Grays, flag of, 11
Washington Invincibles, flag of, 12
Waterhouse, Sgt. George, 224, 225
Waterloo Bridge, VA, 201
Waters, Sgt. Samuel, 49
Wattson, Sgt. Lewis F., 400
Wauhatchie, TN, 76, 203, 363, 369; mentioned, 441
Waynesboro, PA, ladies of, flag presented to 126th Infantry, 402
Waynesborough, GA, 317
Waynesborough, VA, 471
Weaver, Capt. James F., 443
Weaver, Sgt. William H., 111
Webb, Gen. Alexander S., 196
Webber, Pvt. J. S., 124
Weber, William, 9
Webster, Thomas, 40, 42, 52
Weeks, Sgt. William W., 177
Weldon Railroad, VA, 55, 62, 114, 141, 157, 160, 164, 189, 195, 228, 236, 308, 311, 314, 337, 354-55, 360, 373, 384, 387, 393, 432, 436, 439, 443, 448, 451, 459, 462, 480, 488, 492, 515
Welty, Cpl. Frederick, 62
Welty, Pvt. William, 62
Wendler, Sgt. Charles, 198

Wentz, Franklin H., 9
Werner, John T., flag presented to 48th Infantry, 129
Wertz, Cpl. William, 382
West, Sgt. John D., 47
West, Pvt. William H., 64
West Chester, PA, 80, 85, 99, 328; ladies of, flag presented to Guss's Battery, 524
West Fairfield, PA, ladies of, flag presented to 11th Infantry, 64
West Point, GA, 71
West Point, VA, 321, 325
Westmoreland-Fayette Historical Society, 64, 234
Weston, WV, 494
Wetherel, Dr., flag presented to 138th Infantry, 421
Weygant, Capt. Charles H., 431
Wheeler, Sgt. Jacob, 534
Wheeler, Gen. Joseph, 218, 316
Whipple, Gen. Amiel W., 395
White, Sgt. Charles, 231
White, Harry, 28, 34
White, Cpl. Joseph, 367
White, Sgt. Lewis C., 343
White, Col. P. S., 466
White, Col. Richard, 153
White House, VA, 97, 118, 360
White Oak Church, VA, 321, 325
White Oak Road, VA, 382, 387, 443, 444, 467, 469, 480, 497, 515
White Oak Swamp, VA, 82, 166, 492
White Sulphur Spring, WV, 463
Whiteman, Sgt. C. W., 94
Whiteside, TN, 209
Wiggins, Lieut. O. A., 141
Wilcox, Gen. Cadmus M., 343
Wilcox, LtCol. Vincent M., 411
Wild, Cpl. William H., 388
Wilderness, VA, 55, 62, 69, 83, 86, 89, 96, 98, 100-1, 103, 107, 109, 110, 113, 121, 129, 134, 137, 149, 157, 160, 164, 170, 175, 178, 181, 188, 191, 193, 195, 220, 222, 227, 231, 236, 307, 310, 311, 314, 318, 321, 325, 331, 334, 336, 343, 351, 354, 355, 367, 373, 380, 382, 384, 387, 390, 392, 394, 420, 424, 425, 427, 429, 430, 432, 435, 439, 443, 448, 451, 459, 467, 469, 471, 482, 564, 567
Wilkinsburg, PA, 495
Wilkes-Barre, PA, 434, 437; ladies of, flag presented to 9th Cavalry, 317; to 143rd Infantry, 437-38
Williams, Sgt. Benjamin, 380
Williams, Sgt. Edgar, 159
Williams, Isaac, 215
Williams, Col. J. M., 184
Williams, Sgt. John W., 507
Williamsburg, VA, 65, 68, 133, 166, 182, 183, 318, 320, 331, 340, 342, 346, 351, 360

Williamson, Sgt. John H., 388
Williamsport, MD, 76
Williamsport, PA, ladies of, flag presented to 84th Infantry, 230
Wilmington, DE, 495
Wilmington, NC, 46, 206, 329-30, 384, 505
Wilson, Prof., 397
Wilson, Capt. Harry, 220, 222
Wilson, Gen. James H., 182, 218, 360
Wilson, Col. William, 27, 221
Wilson Rifles, flag of, 107
Wilson's Creek, MO, 24
Winchester, VA, 76, 123, 127, 135, 152, 184, 185, 189, 191-92, 201, 203, 224, 230, 236, 237, 319, 326, 332, 343, 366, 375, 384, 390, 420, 425, 463, 469, 471, 479, 485
Wisconsin troops, 36th Infantry, 20
Wise, Capt. William W., 12
Wiseman, Sgt. Thomas, 458, 459
Witt, Sgt. Stephen H., 373
Wolf, Sgt. Antoine, 535
Wolfley, Sgt. Jacob, 317
Wolfong, Sgt. Franklin C., 314
Wood, Sgt. Randall C., 194 n2
Woodbury, TN, 465
Woodside, John A., 8
Woodward Guards, flag of, 8
Woolslair, Cpl. W. H. H., 209
Workman, Sgt. George W., 342

Worth, Sgt. Francis M., 66
Wray, Pvt. Adam, 99
Wren, Capt. James, 8
Wright, Rep. Hendrick B., 333
Wright, Gen. Horatio G., 425
Wynkoop, Col. George E., 217
Wyoming Historical and Geological Society, 115-16
Yellow House, Va, 471
Yerger, Mrs. A. E., flag presented to 71st Infantry, 193
Yohe, Sgt. Josiah, 155, 156
York, PA, 236, 473; ladies of, flag presented to 16th Infantry, 12
York Volunteers, flag of, 5
Yorktown, VA, 45, 50, 65, 68, 133, 145, 146, 148, 149, 153, 159, 166, 169, 174, 177, 188, 193, 195, 220, 223, 226, 233, 318, 321, 325, 331, 340, 342, 346, 348, 351, 354, 360, 473
Young, Sgt. Daniel, 433
Young, Sgt. David W., 424, 425

Zane, A. V., flag presented to 12th Cavalry, 376
Zentmyer, Capt. Frank, 95
Ziegler, Sgt. Charles B., 327
Ziegler, Edward E., 9
Ziegler, George K., guidons presented to 75th Infantry, 204
Zinn, Col. Henry I., 409
Zuni, VA, 162

Photograph Credits

Unless otherwise noted, all color photographs of the flags and closeups of damage are courtesy of the Capitol Preservation Committee and are not to be reproduced without the express written consent of the Committee.

309: Steven Rogers
312: Beyer-Keydel
313: Ted Twardowski
317: (right) VFW Post 255, Duncannon
319: (right, both) Robert T. Lyon
321: (right) Robert Diem
322: (lower right) Russ Wunker
323: Russ Wunker
327: Ronn Palm
329: (lower left) USAMHI, Dickinson College Library Collection; (right) Chester County Historical Society
333: Ronn Palm
334: Ronn Palm
337: Michael Kraus
338: Michael Kraus
342: Ronn Palm
344: (upper right) Soldiers & Sailors, courtesy Al Richardson; (lower right) Ken Turner
347: Soldiers & Sailors, courtesy Al Richardson
349: Beyer-Keydel
352: Gettysburg National Military Park, courtesy Mike Winey, USAMHI
355: (left) Canton High School, photographed by Mildred G. Van Dyke; (right) Ward, *History of the 106th*
361: (right) Ken Turner
364: (left) USAMHI, Jim Elliott Collection; (right) J. Craig Nannos
368: USAMHI, Cliff Breidinger Collection
370: (lower) G. Craig Caba
371: Nicholas Graver
379: Ted Twardowski
380: Private Collection
381: (right) GAR Museum, Philadelphia
385: Cliff Breidinger
386: Civil War Library & Museum, courtesy Marlin Troutman
388: (lower) Mark Schaefer
393: (all) Strong, *History of the 121st*
398: (right) Green, *History of the 124th*
400: *Pennsylvania at Antietam*
407: USAMHI, Mass-MOLLUS Collection
408: (right) Ted Twardowski
412: USAMHI, William Gladstone Collection
417: Beyer-Keydel

421: (both) Civil War Library & Museum
423: Library of Congress
424: (lower) Soldiers & Sailors, courtesy Al Richardson
426: (right, both) Ronn Palm
427: (left, both) Stewart, *History of the 140th*
430: (lower right) Ronn Palm
435: (to) Rossiter Johnston, *Campfires and Battlefields;* (bottom) Susquehanna County Historical Society
436: (top) Robert Diem; (bottom) Garry Roche
437: (top right) Joseph Long
446: Richard Matthews, courtesy *Military Images*
447: (all) Whitmoyer Public Library, courtesy Richard Matthews
450: George & Ethel Ruhl
451: (top) Mitch McGlynn
456: (right) Kiefer, *History of the 153rd*
458: (bottom) *Under the Maltese Cross*
459: *Under the Maltese Cross*
460: *Under the Maltese Cross*
468: Library of Congress
470: (right) Warren Motts
485: Marshall Brighenti
490: Robert Diem
496: Fonda Thomsen
499: (bottom right) State Museum of Pennsylvania, PHMC
521: Dr. George Oldenbourg
522: (left) Paul Loane; (right) Cuffel, *Durell's Battery*
524: Howard M. Madaus
533: (left) Wayne Huss; (right) Oil City Armory
534: (left) Wendell Lang; (right) Noel Clemmer
535: Henry Deeks
536: (left) Ronn Palm; (right) Hollidaysburg High School
537: Robert Diem
544-548: (all) Capitol Preservation Committee
551: (all) Capitol Preservation Committee
552: RG 25, Pennsylvania State Archives
553: Capitol Preservation Committee
556: Capitol Preservation Committee
559: (above left) Joseph Fulginiti
560: USAMHI, Mass-MOLLUS Collection
564: (left) USAMHI, Joseph Long Collection; (right) Rodearmel, *Twentieth Century Pennsylvania State Government in Picture and Story*
566: Beyer-Keydel
567: (left) *Pittsburgh Press,* photographed by Thomas Ondrey; (right) Robert Ulrich